Remembering Childhood in the Middle East

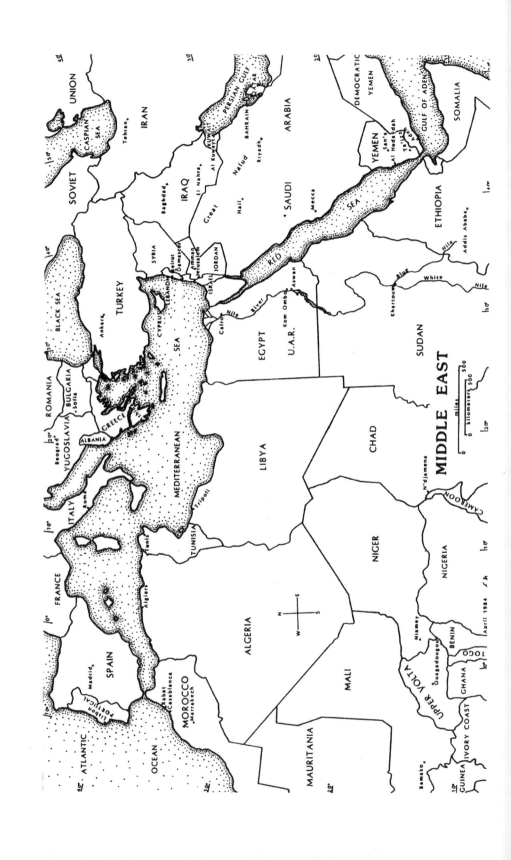

MIDDLE EAST

Remembering Childhood in the Middle East

MEMOIRS FROM A CENTURY OF CHANGE

Collected and edited by
ELIZABETH WARNOCK FERNEA

Introduction by
ROBERT A. FERNEA

University of Texas Press, *Austin*

Requests for permission to reproduce material from this work should
be sent to Permissions, University of Texas Press, P.O. Box 7819,
Austin, TX 78713-7819.

Portions of three of the essays have appeared elsewhere in different
form. Mohamed Fadel Jamali wrote about his background in *Asia*,
Vol. 35, 1935. Hassan Hassan's account formed part of a chapter in his
recent book, *In the House of Muhammad Ali, A Family Album, 1805–1952*,
published by the American University in Cairo Press in 2000. Leila
Abouzeid wrote an essay for this volume and then altered and
expanded it into her second book, *Return to Childhood*, published in
Arabic in Rabat in 1993 and in English in 1998 by the University
of Texas Center for Middle Eastern Studies.

⊗ The paper used in this book meets the minimum requirements of
ANSI/NISO Z39.48-1992 (R1997) (Permanence of Paper).

LIBRARY OF CONGRESS CATALOGING-IN-PUBLICATION DATA

Remembering childhood in the Middle East : memoirs from a century
of change / collected and edited by Elizabeth Warnock Fernea ;
introduction by Robert A. Fernea. — 1st ed.
    p.   cm.
Some essays translated from Arabic or French, and previously published.
    ISBN 0-292-72546-9 — ISBN 0-292-72547-7 (pbk.)
    1. Middle East—Biography. 2. Middle East—Social life
and customs—20th century. 3. Middle East—Ethnic relations.
I. Fernea, Elizabeth Warnock.
  DS61.5 .R46   2002

  920.056—dc21

  2002004651

CONTENTS

PREFACE

Elizabeth Fernea

 This book began unexpectedly about ten years ago with the arrival of a childhood narrative in my husband Bob's mailbox in the anthropology department at the University of Texas. "I heard that your wife was doing a book about children in the Middle East," said the accompanying letter. "Maybe she would be interested in my story." I read the account and was both moved and interested. Unfortunately, the book I was working on at the time, *Childhood in the Muslim Middle East,* was an anthology of social science and historical pieces from scholars in the area. The kind of personal narrative I had received did not fit into such a volume. But I mentioned the piece to several other Middle Eastern friends, and within a month, I had four childhood narratives, all unsolicited, and all very different from each other. I was intrigued enough to start a new project, the book which follows.

Life histories have in recent years been set down and published by anthropologists and folklorists, but these works, though valuable, tend to reflect the scholars' own interests and research rather than that of their subjects. The accounts which follow are different. They were written by the contributors themselves with no guidance from me except as to length, and the events, persons, and landscapes depicted are their choice, not mine.

The thirty-six men and women, recounting their childhood memories here, come from fourteen different countries. My husband, the social/cultural anthropologist Robert Fernea, and I have come to know almost all of them personally during our forty-two years of research and residence in the area. They have trusted me to present the accounts, and

I feel honored to do so. As teachers, poets, translators, and musicians, they may be seen as "unrepresentative" of the culture as a whole. Yet they are "representers," and like the wandering bards, minstrels, scholars, dervishes, and storytellers of past ages are carrying messages from one world to another, communicating ideas and feelings to us, a new audience in a strange land. And in the tradition of their own illustrious literary past they are such wonderful storytellers!

The transliteration of terms in Arabic, Persian, and Turkish may surprise some readers. In general, foreign words are defined at their first usage, and then not italicized afterward. Some words, titles, and names in common use throughout the Middle East are standardized. But spelling of given names of the authors is left as they themselves wished, as, for example, Leila Abouzeid.

Some of the pieces were originally written in Arabic and French; I thank the translators: Amal Chagumoum, Bassam Frangieh, Randa Jarrer, and Aziz Abbassi. Thanks also to Sharon Doerre and Persis Karim, who helped with the editing, and to Virginia Howell, who efficiently and patiently typed and retyped the different versions of the chronicles provided by the authors. Robert Fernea read every word, and, as my severest and most constructive critic, helped shape the accounts and tales into their present form. Thank you once more, Bob.

Remembering Childhood in the Middle East

INTRODUCTION

Robert A. Fernea

 The narratives of Middle Eastern childhood presented here are personal histories written by individuals. In contrast, histories of nations are chronicles of groups, constructions of the past by historians. Such historical writing is a shared effort, part of an ongoing discourse in which scholars build upon each other's versions of the past, agreeing and disagreeing in a process of revision and reinterpretation which will continue until the last history department shuts its doors. But people also have their private histories, narratives about the past which are tailored to differing personal needs and satisfactions. Whether written as autobiographies or simply recounted after dinner, personal histories become more and more well-attuned to self-perceptions and identities as individuals grow older. Indeed, such stories are often used to celebrate those momentous turns in people's lives when they perceive themselves as having moved from the dependency of childhood into the relative freedom of adult life.

For childhood is when things happen to us; adulthood is when we make things happen. Even if we share stories of our childhood with those with whom we grew up, each of us has our own version of what happened. Can anything be more amazing or more irritating than discovering from our friends and relatives how different their versions of the past are from our own? Yet often no "final authority" is present to mediate the differences. Our childhoods remain for us to construe as we will, as histories of ourselves.

Rarely do children represent their own lives—how many books like *The Diary of Anne Frank* can one recall? Rather, adults speak for the children they were. Children never do have control of their lives. Each person has her or his own imaginary childhood homeland, and therefore to write the autobiography of one's childhood is to share adult conceptions of a very personal and unique past. Nevertheless, it is impossible to hear of someone else's childhood without comparing it to one's own.

The paradox is the singularity of each childhood against the universality of childhood itself. This takes on a new significance when one moves out of one's own cultural environment and into the less familiar territory of foreign lands, such as those represented in this volume. Readers may expect to find that children's lives in other countries are not only unfamiliar but perhaps even exotic in comparison with their own. But the experience of losing a parent, of entering school for the first time, of emigrating to another city or another country, growing up rich or poor, male or female as told here, may seem quite familiar. Other experiences are far from familiar. How, for example, would you get through the long days when you and your family are under house arrest? How would you feel when freshly arrived colonial administrators requisition your home to billet their troops? Or upon discovering that the savory feast which is being cooked is to celebrate your own unanticipated circumcision? Someone has said that reading an autobiography, especially of childhood, is like looking over Narcissus's shoulder into the pool—and seeing oneself. But there may also remain unfamiliar reflections.

Moreover, in the narratives which follow, Narcissus is also looking back at us. With only a few exceptions, these autobiographical sketches of childhood were written for readers in English and also for a Western public which the contributors know quite well through travel, study, and work in Europe and America and through experiences at Western educational institutions in the Middle East. Would these narratives have been different if written in a Middle Eastern language for a local audience? One author, Leila Abouzeid, states that knowing that her story was intended for an American reader "helped me produce a more honest and critical text" than would have been the case if she had first considered writing it in Arabic for a local Moroccan audience. Is it always liberating to write for a foreign audience, as Abouzeid has said? Does it not also place a special obligation on both parties, the writer and the reader?

As with any autobiography, the reality of having authors speaking about themselves gives a special authority to what they say. At the same time, these authors know the Western reader may not be familiar with the events and circumstances which have affected their personal lives. They can relate themselves to us through the landmarks in the human life cycle we all share, but the human consequences of the momentous events of Middle Eastern history may be foreign to the Westerner. In this respect, the contributors to this volume have been able to draw upon their acquired knowledge of the Western reader and to tell us stories in a way we can understand. Indeed, we should recognize that this is what they *want* us to understand about themselves and their homelands, something distinct and particular and unique for a change, something personal in contrast to the scholarly generalizations and popular pontifications by which their homelands and their histories are commonly understood.

Reading these adult constructions of childhood experience, one is privileged to share mature, private recollections of the time when the writers were "formed and molded" into adulthood. In a sense, they are accounting for themselves. Is this done by Middle Easterners in the same way that we do? Do they share the Western "big oaks from little acorns grow" view of human life? The accounts suggest that this view may be part of a Middle Eastern understanding of childhood but is not necessarily based on the same set of assumptions. We "explain" ourselves, justify ourselves, find reasons for our strengths and weaknesses, in our childhood experiences. We read with fascination all the evidence about the early lives of the famously talented and fabulously wealthy, looking for a logical progression from infancy to celebrity. *Post hoc ergo propter hoc* is the common result. But many other assumptions about human development are found in these stories, involving the importance of "blood," or fate, of free will or of determinisms of various kinds. In the essays which follow, Westerners with faith in the possibilities of upward mobility will be gratified to discover the great leaps some of these authors have made from very humble origins to various heights of personal success and public recognition. Even so, these are not "American success stories," as we might write them. The implicit tension between family origins and personal achievement is played out here in a variety of ways often very different from the Western experience. Also, the importance of families over the importance of peers in these stories seems to be a characteristic which distinguishes all the accounts from the tales we might tell.

However, is this a collection where a reader will be able to identify and define the "typical" Middle Eastern childhood? Not likely. In the mid-twentieth century, social scientists looked long and hard at children's lives in many places in order to find the productive core of cultural distinctiveness, the relationship between personality and culture. Psychologist Erik Erikson looked at child rearing practices as an index of a society's values. Abram Kardiner, Margaret Mead, Ruth Benedict, and many other cultural anthropologists were proponents of culture and personality theories. The idea was that each culture produced a distinctive core of shared personality characteristics, with individual differences a minor or secondary variation on the shared central theme. Common child rearing practices were seen as the key factor in producing this core of shared personality traits which, in turn, produced a common culture.

But cultural anthropologists are not so likely to study cultural patterns of child rearing any longer. Is this because we believe that childhood has no effect on adulthood? Not at all. It is rather because, as these accounts so well reveal, the experience of childhood in the same culture can be so different from one family to another, from one class to the next, between males and females, and within and between religious and ethnic groups. The imagined homelands of a Middle Eastern childhood vary as much among Middle Easterners as they do among ourselves. Furthermore, in our time, it has become more and more impossible to talk about "distinctive cultures," bounded and untouched by outside influences. Attitudes toward and practices of child rearing now travel around the world, both as products of global capitalism and as the practices of migrating human populations. To attempt to see a single, distinctive way of raising children is now as misleading as talking about a homogeneous population.

But this collection of different Middle Eastern childhood memories offers a reader more than simply a discovery of how diverse Middle Easterners may be. Chronologically, these accounts span the entire twentieth century: Mohammed Fadhel Jamali of Iraq was born in 1902, while Randa Abou Bakr of Egypt was born in 1966. The men and women are Berber, Persian, Arab, Turkish, Circassian, Muslim, Kurdish, Jewish, and Christian. Their families vary in social status from aristocracy to peasantry, from obscure poverty to wealth and power. The tales are set in town and country, in palaces and mud brick houses. Among the narrators' families of origin are merchants, clerics, farmers, bankers, teachers, politicians, soldiers, princes, and servants. The reader is given the opportunity to look at the same period of history in the same region of the world from a variety of very different remembered experiences, experiences affected by the drama of rapid, even catastrophic, change.

Change, whether political, social, or economic, is relative. Humans have no absolute measurement for the speed of change, but we are more or less aware of changing circumstances in our own lifetimes. One thing that makes most of our lives different from those in this collection is the implicit assumptions these writers have of how much more their personal worlds have changed than those of most Western readers. Some of the childhoods recalled here begin while the last vestiges of the Ottoman Empire were still struggling to maintain control in the Arab world; the childhoods of the younger writers involve memories following independence from colonial rule in the 1950s. Many writers look back and see their childhood as marked by these radical changes in the circumstances of their own lives and the lives of the people around them. Embedded in all these stories are the emotional outcomes of these rapid changes: the end of the Ottoman Empire, the dawn of Middle Eastern nationalism and the struggle against Western rule, the establishment of Israel, the Israeli-Arab wars, the rise of oil-rich countries, the beginnings of the Palestinian state, the modern renaissance of Islamic thought. The writers are telling us, the Others, what it has been like to live in and through their tumultuous times. The private accounts which are the crux of these childhood autobiographies are therefore set within circumstances which most of us know about only from a distance. Thus, if many of the events of these lives remind us of our own pasts, this background of political, economic, and social differences also cannot be ignored.

In these accounts, the child is part of a family in ways which continue on into adult life. Growing up and leaving home does not mean the end of playing an active part in a network of family and kin. Families of origin remain a point of reference, a part of each person's past which continues into the present and remains included in the way these people think about themselves. Thus, extended families in the Middle East, so often discussed and compared in academic studies with Western nuclear families, are eloquently represented here, not as a static backdrop to personal life but rather as a complex set of needs and responsibilities which always require individual attention and effort. Indeed, this may be one of the greatest differences between their childhood memories and our own. Westerners and Middle Easterners may both grow up into styles of life very different than those of their families, but, in a sense more profound than our own, Middle Easterners never leave home.

The narratives which follow are about childhood, but, of course, they are far from childish. Rather, they are sophisticated and humorous descriptive excursions into personal pasts, journeys to childhood homelands in the Middle East. They help explain what these individuals have become and how they have developed these identities within familial, national, and international circumstances very different from those of the West. Following the great tradition of Shaharazade, the stories are told to both inform and intrigue the reader. They remind one of the similarities of the human experience, of birth and death, of joys and sadness. They also remind us of how different human lives can be. But most of all, these authors are giving us their own personal understanding of who they are, of what they have become, seen through the prism of childhoods remembered. For this we are much in their debt.

The End of the Ottoman Empire (1923)

 The Ottoman Empire dominated much of the world for
more than five hundred years, including not only Turkey,
but most of what is today known as the Middle East, North
Africa, and Eastern Europe. But at the end of World War I,
in 1918, the Ottoman Sultanate ceased to exist, and the
vast territory was carved up by the winning Allied powers.
Thus, the Middle East, as a concept and a descriptive term,
is relatively new in world history. Over the centuries, the
area has been known not only as part of the Ottoman
Empire, but also as the Muslim world, the lands of Barba-
ray, the countries of Southwest Asia, or simply the Orient.
Some would argue that the term came into use during the
European colonial period of the eighteenth and nineteenth
centuries. Middle Eastern peoples themselves had always
used the term *Mashriq* to refer to the eastern section of
the area, and called the west the *Maghreb*. Britain began to
call its area of control the Middle East, for of course it was
the middle of the British Empire, but most of that Empire
lay east of Suez. The *Maghreb*, largely under French domination, began to be called the "near East and North Africa."
It was, after all, near the French port of Marseilles.

But from the fifteenth until the early twentieth century,
the majority of the Middle East and North Africa lay in
the territory of the Ottoman Empire. Thus, the parents of
Mohammed Fadhel Jamali, Charles Issawi, Nazik Ali Jawdat,
Salma Khadra Jayyusi, and Janset Shami did not think of
themselves as citizens of separate nations but rather as subjects of the Ottoman rulers in Istanbul.

Charles Issawi's father was a local official of the Empire,

first in Cairo and then in Khartoum. Salma Khadra Jayyusi's parents were from 'Akka, then in Palestine; Mohammed Fadhel Jamali's father was a religious official in the Ottoman province of Iraq. The Empire had welcomed Muslim immigrants from Soviet Central Asia, like the parents of Janset Shami, who felt threatened by the Russian government. Only Mansour al-Hazimi was outside Ottoman boundaries in the Arabian Peninsula, where his home was soon to be folded into a new kingdom, Saudi Arabia.

Historians document the growing influence of Europe in the Middle East in the eighteenth and nineteenth centuries. Napoleon invaded Egypt in 1798 but withdrew soon afterward; the Suez Canal was completed in 1869 with financial backing and control from Europeans; France established colonies in Algeria in 1830; Italy launched an attack against Libya in the late nineteenth century; Britain occupied the port of Aden, on the Persian/Arabian Gulf, in 1839, as a crucial connection in its East India trade. And in fact, if not in name, Britain ruled Egypt from 1882.

The decline of the Turkish pashas or overlords, who ruled through local elites, is also noted by historians who describe growing corruption in the Empire, and growing demands for Arab-based rule. Even as the Empire was declining, however, Ottoman officials set up secular schools to teach young people Western technology and provide them with knowledge to deal with growing Western influence. Nazik Jawdat attended such a school, as did Janset Shami and Salma Jayyusi. Mohammed Fadhel Jamali was a product of traditional religious education in Baghdad but received a scholarship to the American University of Beirut, which was founded by Christian missionaries. Charles Issawi was sent to Victoria College, a British-inspired private school in Cairo. Again, Mansour al-Hazimi was the exception, in that all of his early schooling took place in the traditional schools of Arabia at the time.

Europe was moving in almost everywhere, and the old system was crumbling. New forces, both Western and Eastern, were emerging, which were to change the countryside, the names of the areas, and the lives of its people.

Mohammed Fadhel Jamali

IRAQ *Mohammed Fadhel Jamali was born in 1902 in the holy
city of Kadhimain, near Baghdad. He was given a traditional religious education in Iraq, then went to the American University in Beirut, and on to Columbia University
Teachers College, where he received his Ph.D. After working
for many years in the Iraqi Ministry of Education, he was
transferred to the Ministry of Foreign Affairs in 1943.
He served briefly as prime minister in the 1950s. After the*

*Iraqi revolution of 1958,
he was condemned to
death but was pardoned
by the government pro-
vided that he left the
country. In exile, he
worked with educational
institutions in Switzer-
land and taught in
Tunisia. He died in
Tunis in 1997.*

AN ARAB FACES THE

MODERN WORLD

Mohammed Fadhel Jamali

 My life history is a typical example of a complete transition from one civilization into another, and from an old culture into a new one.

I was born in the holy town of Kadhimain (near Baghdad) in the year 1902. My community belongs to the Shiite sect of Islam, and its members are known to be upholders of the Shiite tenets and are usually pious people. My father was Sheikh Abbas al Jamali, one of the religious men of the aforementioned sect. My mother was a descendant of the Prophet Mohammad, and was regarded by the people of the community as a saintly lady whose prayers for the people were rewarded by God. She conducted special rituals for the ladies and gave threads to be hung round patients' necks, inspiring the hope of gaining recovery. Thus in my childhood I grew up in a home rich with superstitions, quite rigid in its religious tenets, and strict in regular performance of religious duties. The following are among the habits and attitudes which I had cultivated in me early in my life and which I had to overcome later with a great effort, overcoming something in myself in the first place, and overcoming something in the community in the second place:

I cherished a negative attitude against the Sunnite Muslims, and thought that they would be sent to hell by God.

I was taught that all non-Muslims, although I had rare occasion to see any of them, were unclean and untouchable. Eating and drinking with them was sacrilegious.

I was taught that I should go daily to the holy shrine for prayer and to perform my religious duties regularly.

I was taught that as a man I should not look at ladies'

faces, other than those of the members of my own family, or listen to their voices.

I was taught to salute the great religious men most respectfully and to kiss their right hands on meeting them.

A negative attitude was inculcated in me against the government and its officials; for they all belonged to the Sunnite sect and consequently they were not honest people.

I used to watch and sympathize greatly with the bands of people who tortured themselves once a year on the anniversary of the martyrdom of the grandson of the Prophet.

As a tiny child I used to play in the street with the children of the neighborhood, and there I learned all the filthy words and dirty habits which a child usually acquires in the streets, although I never practiced those words before my father for fear he would beat me. Still, I cherished the gang membership and used to join the children of the neighborhood in attacking and stoning the children of a different quarter.

My father and mother were rarely in harmony with each other, and, perhaps on economic grounds, my father rarely satisfied my mother. Quarreling and dispute between the two were not rare. I was always on my father's side. I used to fear my father and like him at the same time. He was one of the most unselfish and watchful fathers I have ever known. My relations with my mother, however, were not always favorable. My mother was a selfish lady who used to buy nice food and sweets but give me very little. I frequently had quarrels with my mother. I wanted her to divide what she got justly among us as my father did, but she never did. In spite of this apparent continual skirmishing between us, I loved her at heart and she loved me, too. She used to caress me whenever I was cross or angry.

My father, a religious leader, was mainly supported by the community, and was to a great extent economically dependent upon my uncle. When I was four years old, my father left Kadhimain to go to the holy town of Najaf to continue his study of theology. During his absence I was entrusted to my uncle for support, whose home was well-conducted; I had a much more peaceful life there, for my uncle and his wife inculcated in me better social and personal habits. I was deprived of street contacts altogether and had as examples my older cousins, who were well brought up according to the old ideals.

My behavior was directed, all the way, by fear. Serious punishment by either my father or my uncle awaited me if I infringed any order or rule of behavior; in their absence the "doves" would inform them of what I had done. Thus I had to behave myself in their presence or absence.

The neighborhood at home included the houses in the surrounding streets, which were narrow and winding. Relatives usually clustered to-gether in neighboring houses. This was especially true of my uncle's house. Families still had the patriarchal relationship; the married sons with their families lived together in their father's home, and many such homes were connected by passages. Free exchange of visits and cooperation in house-hold affairs went on among these homes. When a special dish was cooked in one home, neighboring homes usually got their share. The children met together and played. It must be made clear, however, that cleanliness or tidi-ness was often absent from these homes. Many unhealthy practices were per-formed and given religious sanction.

In short, I can say that I opened my eyes in an old and traditional so-ciety, with its rigid religious practices and superstitious practices on the one hand and its good-hearted, cooperative, and patriarchal kinship on the other. And until I went to school I did not question the *status quo.*

My first schooling began when I was seven years old. My father took me to a mosque school where reading the Quran was taught first, and later on some writing and arithmetic. The pupils used to sit on mats on the ground with legs folded. The Sheikh, the one teacher, sat on a high bench with a bundle of sticks before him and a *falakah,* a rope attached to the two ends of a stick for binding a guilty pupil after making him lie down in order to strike his bare feet with as many strokes as the Sheikh deemed worthy. A dungeon room with ankle shackles was ready for pupils guilty of a great misdemeanor. To begin with, I used to go to the mosque not for instruction in the Quran but simply to get habituated to regularity and punctuality. I sat idle with hands and legs folded all the day. Once it occurred to me that I should dis-charge the contents of my heavily loaded nostrils on a Persian pupil who sat opposite me. The Persian pupil told the Sheikh, who came to me with the stick in his hands and applied it to my bare feet and legs quite mercilessly until my feet began bleeding. That event was quite significant in my life, for it left a permanent negative attitude toward the old mosque school. I ran away from the mosque school and refused to go back for a few months. Then my father took me back to the same Sheikh and we came to good terms. This time I began learning the Arabic alphabet and the first chapter of the Quran, this being our "first reader."

In 1910 a school on the Western model was for the first time inaugurated in the town of Kadhimain. It belonged to the Society of Union and Prog-ress, which was conducted by the Young Turks. As a member of this soci-ety, my father had many personal friends among the military and civil offi-cials of the state who were running the school. Having been induced by these friends to send me to the school, he did so enthusiastically. At that time I began to dream of being a general, or *pasha.* I was put in the first grade and had a grand time enjoying the relatively great liberty in this school as compared with the old mosque school. I took matters quite easily there. My father used to visit the school often and to attend my class. One day he advised me to pin my eyes to the book while the teacher was reading before us. I told him that I did not need to, since reading was quite easy for me. But when I was called by the teacher to read the same passage, I stopped at several places and could not read fluently. As a punishment my father slapped me hard across the face, which knocked my face against the desk and made my mouth bleed. This was a very significant incident in my life, for I have tried ever since to concentrate in my classes and to be attentive to what the teacher says. My father showed a great interest in my development from the very beginning. The method of harsh punishment was soon changed to one of arousing and rewarding my desire to excel and to surpass others. The school of Union and Progress, for economic reasons, did not survive long; after a year or so, it closed its doors.

Along with that school, however, two other schools had appeared in the town: one a state school, which was called the Ottoman School, and the other a private Persian school. After long hesitation my father decided to put me in the Persian school; for, although the Persians were of a different nationality, still they were Shiites and belonged to the same sect, while the state school was run by Sunnites. I was put in the first grade in the Persian school, and I soon picked up the Persian language. After three months of constant effort to learn the language I became quite fluent. My progress in this school was regular and continual. The motive of racial supremacy strengthened my desire to excel, for, as an Arab, I felt I should not let any Persian be superior to me in class. I fought my way to the top even at the cost of overtaxing my health. Competition was greatly overdone in this school. A weekly changing of seats put the more advanced students in front. I got into the habit of preserving the head seat for myself. On rare occasions I lost my post but only for a short time.

This school, where I spent five years, had a far-reaching effect upon reshaping my ideas and ideals. It was conducted by the late Hajji Ali Akbar Arabi, a Persian Turk, one of the great exponents of the Pan-Islamic movement under the leadership of the Sultan, the Caliph of Islam. He was an inspiring personality. He pointed out very clearly to us, his pupils, how retarded we were and how Western imperialism was taking advantage of our ignorance, superstition, and internal dissension. Some of us felt very deeply the responsibility which we would bear as future leaders in awaking the nation and saving it from the Western danger. My old idea of dissension between Shiites and Sunnites gave way to thoughts of a larger Pan-Islamic union. Meanwhile World War I had begun; songs and dramas raised our sentiments against the Allies to the highest pitch. In a drama performed one day in the open air, I took the part of the first Muslim martyr. In school I was trained to memorize and deliver speeches before distinguished personages on various occasions. Also, I had a critical attitude toward the clergy inculcated in me for the first time in this school. I completed the fifth grade there, though this school was forced for economic reasons to have poorer teachers toward the end of the war.

For the sixth grade I moved to "The Model School," a state school in Baghdad where instruction was in Turkish, although Arabic and French were also taught. During this period, which was toward the end of the war, my uncle was under great economic pressure, and his two sons were taken to the army by the Turks. Thus I had to be content with very simple food, usually bread and dates alone for luncheon, but I continued going to school. My uncle died a few days before the occupation of Baghdad. His death was an important event in my life, for it made me conscious of my economic future.

Baghdad was occupied by the British before I had finished the sixth grade. I was only fourteen years old then. The fall of Baghdad into the hands of the British was a great catastrophe for me, for I thought the world of Islam was overcome and that at last we had fallen as victims into the hands of a non-Muslim power. I used to watch the march of the British troops into Kadhimain with tears flowing down my cheeks. For a few months after the occupation of Baghdad, there was no school in the city. The new British administration soon opened a few elementary schools and a short session for training teachers.

My father, a religious man and head of the Jamali clan after the death of my uncle, would not support me unless I followed him and became a religious Sheikh. My elder cousins, even after the death of their father, kept supporting me, but that could not go on for long. Thus my first thought was to enter the teacher training session and support myself as a teacher, even though I looked down on the profession of teaching. This, however, was no easy thing to achieve, for at fifteen I was too young to be admitted to the Teacher Training College. I was finally admitted to the six-month teacher training session with the understanding that I would not be employed immediately after graduation. Much beyond my expectations, I ranked second in the class, and the principal regretted that I could not be employed. After a long effort I was made assistant to the teacher in physical education in the elementary school of Kadhimain, with half the regular salary. This, however, did not last long; for no need for such a post existed and I had to remain jobless with no school to attend.

Later, my father advised me to give up teaching and study Arabic and religion at the Theological Institute. I accepted that suggestion and joined the Khalisi Institute of Kadhimain, where I had the tutorship of their most competent man, Sheikh Mohammed al Khalisi. I spent a whole year as a student of divinity and made good progress, especially in mixing with the public and showing them a pious mode of life. I figured that in five or six years I might become a *mujtahid*, which is the highest clerical position one can attain in the Shiite sect, after which I might play the role of a reformer. At the same time my desire to continue the study of modern learning had never ceased, and I came to discover more and more that honesty and straightforwardness among the clergy do not work very well. I found that young men of lower standing in the knowledge of religion and classics but with a better knowledge of how to act politically and hypocritically would surpass me.

At last I decided to go back to the Ministry of Education and ask for a teaching job again. The principal of the Teacher Training College, Mohammed Abdul Aziz, an Egyptian, took a great interest in my placement on account of my high standing in the class of teachers. Failing to secure an appointment for me, he advised me to reenter the Teacher Training College, the standard of which was now raised to two years. After six months I graduated again, first in the college. This time, at the age of seventeen, I gained a decent appointment as an elementary school teacher. I taught for two years and entered a new era of self-support and independence.

Having succeeded on my own, I was dissatisfied with my lot in life and aimed at higher study. In Baghdad there was at that time no higher institution than the one from which I had been graduated. The government of Iraq was invited to send six students to the American University of Beirut. I was chosen and thus, in the year 1921–1922, was part of the first education mission to be sent out by the Iraq government.

I kept the news of my departure secret until I had signed the contract with my government. When I announced the news to my father, he was shocked, not only because he hated to have me leave him for several years, but also because his social prestige would be undermined if it became publicly known that I had gone to a Christian institution. All his efforts to prevent me from leaving home and to make the government refrain from sending me abroad failed. His last plea was that I should save his position by winning the consent of the great *mujtahid*, the last Sheikh Mahdi al Khalisi, whose word was taken as an absolute sanction. Sheikh Mahdi refused at first; for he argued that I would imbibe Christian ways and learn to accept Christian authority over me. I had a very hard time convincing him that my departure would be of service to the world of Islam. At last he signed a paper which I took to my father and which stated that there seemed to be no danger in my going to a Christian institution with the aim of serving Islam in the future. Leaving this valuable document with my father, I left for Beirut via India. On the first day of the journey, I put on Western dress and shaved my beard for the first time in my life.

It is to be remembered that I left home as a vigorous orthodox Muslim. My prayers were performed on time, and my attitude towards non-Muslims was one of abhorrence. This attitude continued for the first two years of my stay at the University. I attended chapel, as was then required, with a tense feeling. Whenever the Christian hymns were sung, I would refrain from joining the group or substitute the name of Mohammed or Allah for Jesus or the Lord.

Two big factors were active in gradually changing and ultimately revolutionizing my attitudes toward life. The first was the Brotherhood Society, an interreligious organization, and the second was the study of science and especially zoology with its emphasis on the theory of evolution. Gradually and imperceptibly, I developed a spirit of tolerance, open-mindedness, and critical-mindedness. I began to look at our life at home in a critical way and to reevaluate our sacred social institutions. After the study of the history of modern Europe and after the recent political development at home, the political bond of Pan-Islamism, which I used to cherish so much, gave way completely to the more modern bond of nationalism. Thus I, Fadhel, the relatively fanatic Muslim, the Pan-Islamist and the warrior, gave way to a new Fadhel who cherished the brotherhood of man, who was a pacifist and at the same time a nationalist. Great aspirations for developing Iraq in particular and the Arabic world in general began to dominate my whole life.

In my junior year in the college, with the cooperation of the students from Kadhimain, I printed one thousand copies each of two publications, which I carried home with me as a gift after my absence of nearly five years. I had these publications distributed by the school children in the markets of Kadhimain. They contained a challenge to the public to take up modern education, change their traditional mode of living, and educate the girls, since these measures are the basis of improving our lives. After two days these pamphlets were carried to the clerical circles. The opinion was that I had grown into a heretic, and I was cautioned to leave the country soon in order to avoid the possibility of danger. I ran back to my college, and through a long series of letters the matter was straightened out.

In the summer of 1927, the season of my graduation, I was delegated to represent the students of the University of Beirut at the International Student Service Conference in Switzerland. This trip, which was my first experience in an international situation, contributed much to confirming my ideals of human brotherhood, nationalism, and internationalism. As time went on, I traveled east and west and began to appreciate and to tolerate people of all classes, all nations, all races, and all religions.

After graduation, I was appointed as a teacher of education at the Teacher Training College at Baghdad, and at the same time I worked on the curriculum and textbook committees. I was known to represent always the left wing, but as a matter of fact, I was not dogmatic. Opposed to blind tradition, I desired to undermine any stereotyped institution and to reconstruct it. My social ideas were not fixed; they were in the making. I firmly believed that the human mind, especially in the Orient, needed to be freed from the bondage of the past. Wherever the past could be of use, it should be used as a tool, but it should not be made an end in itself.

Another clash with the clergy came after I went back home. This clash was on Christmas Day, when I addressed the students of the Teacher Training College. Differentiating between religion and the clergy, I called on the students not to give way to clerical influences and to cease dissensions in our national life. I was called to a meeting of a body of clergy at the holy shrine of Kadhimain. I explained my stand there, convincing some, while others remained unconvinced. Letters began to spread rumors that I was an apostate from Islam, but when the matter became serious, a word of warning to the propagandists quieted things down.

I must not leave out two incidents in my personal life which had a great effect on my personality. In my sophomore year, as a result of hard work, my health broke down. I was forced to spend a whole year at a sanatorium in Mount Lebanon, a most beautiful spot. I spent the idle hours in enjoying books and nature and composing love poetry. In this hospital I cherished a friendship with the head nurse, a bright Muslim girl, who later returned my love for her. But her people objected to having their daughter marry a man with whom she had fallen in love, which was contrary to Muslim custom. It was a tragic moment for both of us when we had to yield to the blind force of tradition.

As time went on, however, I overcame the sadness of that experience and fell in love with a charming young Christian girl whom I came to know in one of the villages of Mount Lebanon. I knew from the beginning that the affair was hopeless, for the walls of sectarianism which separated the Muslims from the Christians were too high to be surmounted in that part of the world. Her marriage to a rich relative ended my second experience.

In 1929, through the help of the Ministry of Education and a fellowship from the International Institute, Teachers College, Columbia University, I had the great opportunity of going for postgraduate study to America, visiting on the way several European countries and attending two educational conferences, one at Geneva, Switzerland, and the other at Elsinore, Denmark. From the time I left the Near East until I returned as an Iraqi government attaché to the Monroe Commission of Educational Inquiry and later became Supervisor-General and then Director-General of Education in Iraq, my ideas changed. These changes comprise another chapter in my autobiography which I hope to write at some future time.

Nazik Jawdat

SYRIA   *Nazik Ali Jawdat was born near Aleppo in 1903, her*

   *father a Circassian and her mother from the Sbhai family.*

IRAQ   *She married Ali Jawdat al Ayoubi, military governor of*

Aleppo, in 1919 and went on with him to other postings

in Syria and eventually to Iraq, which he served at various

times as ambassador, cabinet minister, and prime minister.

She died in Abu Dhabi in 1997, survived by three children,

nine grandchildren, and eleven great-grandchildren.

PICTURES FROM THE PAST

Nazik Ali Jawdat

Mumbuj is a Circassian village in the Province of Aleppo. My memories of it are disconnected and vague; horses, fields, and a house with a garden. One of the images: a man sitting up in bed holding me on his knee. From a cup he puts a spoonful into my mouth and then another into the mouth of the child sitting on his other knee. Again and again. He is ill; I feel his rough chin—hot and unshaven—against my face. That was my father and I never saw him again. Another picture; outside the house, hubbub and confusion, weeping and strange noises. On a bed with its mosquito net down, my younger sister, Amina, and I bounce up and down. This was the day of my father's death, I now know.

After my father died, my mother took me, Amina, and my five-month-old sister, Madiha, to live at her father's house in the city of Aleppo itself. I was five years old. The next two years were the happiest of my childhood and the memory of them remains bright and clear.

As was the custom in Aleppo, my grandfather's house was really two houses, one within the other, a *salamlik* and a *harem*. Life in this big house with all my aunts, uncles, and nannies was like a fairy tale. Being the first child of the favorite daughter, having lost my father, and being naughty and lively, I became everyone's cherished plaything.

The house contained two spacious courtyards with *liwans*, numerous staircases, terraces, and roofs. In the center of the larger courtyard was an oval pool with a fountain and goldfish swimming in it. Next to it was an orchard—with oranges, lemons, and pomegranates and a large grapevine arbor in whose shade straw mats would be laid down. On these the ladies and servants of the family would sit to make *kibbe* and prepare the winter's provisions. On the other side of the pool was a rainwater cistern topped by a very large stone cylinder with a wooden cover; we children were forbidden to play there, but whenever the opportunity arose, I would remove the wooden cover, look at my reflection, and listen to the echo of my voice.

In the *salamlik* was a suite where my grandfather received his guests, and above that was his bedroom, which opened onto a big terrace and his library. The courtyard of this house, though small, still had a little garden of its own. For us children to grow up among so many people and in such a vast place in which to run around and play hide-and-seek, was a blessing not to be forgotten.

Across from the fountain, were three rooms; the middle was the drawing room, only opened up for visitors, with Persian carpets and a crystal chandelier. The divans were upholstered in lilac-colored Aleppo silk, which was embroidered in geometric shapes with gold thread.

On the right was my great-aunt's "domed room"; the dome was inset with round thick pieces of colored glass, and two little windows opened onto the courtyard for ventilation. This large, dim room was my favorite.

My grandfather, Sipahizade Haji Said Effendi, being his father's only son, was sent at the age of nineteen on a pilgrimage to Mecca and on his return was married. My grandmother, one of Aleppo's loveliest girls, gave birth five times in less than twenty years, and died in deliberately attempting to lose the sixth child. Thus on the shoulders of my sixteen-year-old Aunt Fattoum fell the responsibility for the younger children: my mother, Bahia, and my uncles, Jamil and Kamil.

After losing his beloved wife, my grandfather fell into a deep sadness. Relatives soon decided that he should marry again and began looking for a wife. On the wedding night he removed the bridal veil of the first girl chosen for him and found that her nose was too long for his taste. He promptly sent the poor girl home to her father with the bridal portion due to her.

After one or two similar fiascos, he married Hadije, a young widow from a newly arrived Circassian family. Her beautiful coloring and features met with my grandfather's approval. Speaking no Arabic and little Turkish, she came to join our crowded household with her frail, blond daughter, Samia.

Hadije bore my grandfather two children: a girl, Emet, and a boy, Ahmad. A few years later Grandfather married off his second daughter, my mother, to the younger brother of his Circassian wife; from this marriage, I and my younger sisters were born. In this way, my grandfather's wife, Hadije Hanum, was my paternal aunt but also my step-grandmother; likewise, her children were my cousins but also my aunt and uncle.

When I think of those days in my grandfather's house, I can never picture my mother, perhaps because it was my Aunt Fattoum who really raised me; my mother was busy bringing up my two younger sisters with the help of my nanny, Iqbal.

Aunt Fattoum's room was large and majestic and furnished from her mother's trousseau with Persian rugs, sofas in bright-colored Aleppo upholstery, and big chandeliers. A huge cupboard by the door was crammed full of mattresses, pillows, and many-colored quilts of Aleppo silk. Every night the servants would bring out the furnishings from that cupboard and make my aunt's bed. Since I was my aunt's favorite, I would sleep beside her most nights.

Close family friends or relatives would often come to visit. These were occasions of great excitement and activity. Special food was prepared, and the children would run all over the courtyards, and up and down the stairs to the roof. At night the women would tell jokes, play riddle games, make music on the *oud* and *darbouka*, and dance.

Life in that house was like being in Paradise. In summer I splashed in the big pool, ran around the gardens and the roofs, climbed the trees, and teased the grown-ups. In winter I sat by the charcoal brazier watching the rain or snow falling outside my windows. Snuggled up to my nanny Iqbal or my Aunt Fattoum, I listened to their tales of fairies and witchcraft. The person I was most attached to was my Aunt Emet; not only was she like an older sister to me, but she also bore all my pranks and mischief with an amused tolerance.

My mother, however, seems to have led an altogether different kind of life in that house. Later, when I had grown up, she told me how deprived of love and happiness she had felt. Having lost her mother very young, she was very attached to her father. But when he married Aunt Hadije and their children Emet and Ahmad were born, he devoted all his love and attention to them. Naturally, my mother felt this loss very deeply and developed a hatred for her half-sister and brother. On top of that, she was made to marry her Circassian stepmother's brother, a man much older than herself, and nobody had asked her consent. Thus the woman who had taken her father away from her also became a sister-in-law who used to visit their room and keep her husband talking for hours in Circassian, which my mother did not understand. In her heart she found no place for the marital love which might have compensated for the loss of parental affection. She felt disillusioned and embittered about life and people.

One day the wonderful life in my grandfather's house came to an abrupt end. I was six or seven when Aunt Fattoum died. The large courtyard filled with people in black, weeping and wailing—at the time I did not know why.

Someone pulled me out of the crowd and took me to Havva Hanum's house. As she and her husband had no children of their own, they occasionally asked me over to stay with them. Havva Hanum taught me how to embroider bead lace, and sew clothes for my dolls in all kinds of colorful materials, and I owe her the high marks I got in handicrafts when I went to primary school.

This particular visit lasted rather a long time—for weeks. The day I was taken back to my grandfather's, there was a crowd in the men's quarter and a sacrificed sheep lying on the ground. A turbaned man was reciting the Quran, and in the women's quarters people dressed in black were weeping. These are my last memories of that house; it must have been the fortieth day of mourning for my Aunt Fattoum. My mother later told me that I had taken very ill, and no one thought I would survive.

His beloved daughter's absence was so intolerable to my grandfather that he sold the house and we all moved to a smaller one in the more modest neighborhood of Akebe. My nannies said the house was inhabited by fairies and other supernatural beings. The previous owners had once seen a white cow walk out of the dark basement loaded with gold. The mistress of the house had screamed in fright, whereupon the cow walked back into the basement and never came out again, thus depriving the family of her treasure. If the woman had had the courage to stroke the cow's head, the animal would have left the gold and gone away. My older nanny used to tell this story in a regretful tone of voice and then wait hopefully for something to happen. As for me, I found it difficult not to look in the direction of the basement after dark or go past it without holding my nanny's hand. Would it really be possible *not* to scream if the cow suddenly appeared so big and white out of the darkness?

I was now of an age when I could not keep entirely aloof from the troubles and worries of the grown-ups. I was beginning to understand their difficulties, all of which had their roots in the old house.

A year or two before we moved to the new house, my aunt Hadije had given herself over to prayers and piety and had begun neglecting my grandfather. As a result, because he was a lively and cheerful man, he became fascinated with a singer renowned in Aleppo for her beautiful voice. He was so infatuated that all attempts to cure his condition were in vain: his own prayers and those of the family, offerings to the saints, and even the talismans he wore that were inscribed by great spiritual sheikhs. All useless. Although my poor grandfather prayed five times a day and was extremely conservative in his views of social conduct, he gradually drifted away from Hadije and finally deserted her to live with the singer, who had by that time given up her career. Aunt Hadije then devoted herself entirely to praying and fasting and never spoke to her husband again. I remember her on her rug, praying and telling her beads or reading the Quran on her cushion by the window.

I finished my Quran classes and started primary school. In the mornings I had breakfast in my grandfather's room with its wood-burning stove and yellow tray with a samovar and teapot on it. He would beckon me to his side and help me snuggle under his fur cloak to keep warm until he finished telling his beads and reciting his prayers. Then we sat around the copper tray and ate our breakfast; special Aleppo cheese, bread toasted on the stove, and tea taken in small glasses with plenty of honey for me, as I was a child. Once breakfast was over, I put on my boots and wrapped a red scarf around my head. My nanny would be waiting for me with my lunch box and we would rush off to school.

The usher, Fatima, used to walk up and down the stone-paved courtyard of the school waiting for the children to arrive. I will never forget her cold, accusing "late-as-usual" look as she took the lunch box from my nanny's hand. I was generally late to class and was continually punished not only for not being punctual but also because I was naughty and would not learn my lessons. Our teacher, Zekiye Hanum, was tall and thin and used to wear layers and layers of long, wide woolen skirts. Only the tips of her black-booted feet showed as she turned round to face me when I walked into the classroom late. We were all terrified of her because she could be exceptionally fierce when she was angry. But in spite of her ugly appearance she had a very kind heart.

Life in the new house gradually took on a regular pattern. Grandfather spent more and more time with the woman he loved. My eldest uncle, Kassim, finished medical school and settled in Istanbul as a military doctor. Uncle Kamil was still at a military academy in Aleppo. And Uncle Jamil had set up his pharmacy in one of Aleppo's best quarters; he was making a lot of money and had assumed a position of responsibility in the family.

A handsome young man with money and freedom, Uncle Jamil was drawn to the world of entertainment and pleasure. Courageous and of a generous disposition, he was much loved by everyone, but occasionally came home drunk, which caused a great commotion in the house. This happened once during the winter of our second year in the new house. There was an exceptional snowfall which lasted for forty days. Everything froze. Workmen came with shovels to open up a path in our courtyard so that we could get from one room to another; mountains of snow were piled up on both sides. Late one night Uncle Jamil came home drunk. My nanny, Iqbal, heard him banging on the door and scurried to let him in, but the wooden door was frozen shut. Uncle Jamil shouted insistently to let him in. We all tried to force the door open and no one could convince him that he had not been deliberately locked out. I remember how my teeth chattered from cold and fright that night, and how I prayed that the door would not open.

On another terrifying night when I was about eight or nine, the silence of the dark, narrow street on which we lived was shattered by a woman's cries followed by my uncle's shouts. Everyone rushed to the windows. In the weak light of the street lamp, I could see my uncle running after a woman and hear him threatening to kill her. I clung to Aunt Emet and wept while she tried to soothe me: "No, Nazik, no, he won't kill her, he's just trying to scare her." When I got a bit older, I understood that Uncle Jamil had a relationship with a young woman called Marie whom he kept in a house in our neighborhood. He was very much in love with her, and, suspicious of other relationships she might have, he would threaten to kill her, as he had done that night, when he had had too much to drink and felt jealous.

On feast days we used to dress up in the new clothes my mother made especially for such occasions and were taken to visit my paternal aunt, Aysha Hanum. After we kissed her hand, she gave us each a colored silk handkerchief and a little gold coin. Then she unlocked her cupboard and took out all sorts of sweets and dried fruits and put them in our handkerchiefs. Although she didn't consider that girls were real offspring like boys and she had wept that my father had had no sons, she loved me because I was her dear brother's firstborn and was named after her mother.

During one of my stays at Aunt Aysha's, I woke up one morning shivering with fever. My aunt consulted with a number of wise women and decided to follow their advice on a course of treatment for my condition. The next morning before sunrise, I was woken up, dressed, and taken on a very long walk to a spring where mules and camels were watered. Once the animals had finished drinking and had been driven away, I was undressed and, despite my shivering and protestations, my aunt held me fast and began pouring ice cold water all over me with a bowl that she'd brought along, all the while reciting prayers from the Quran. After seven bowls of water down my back, I was quickly dried, dressed, and taken home. I don't remember how effective this treatment with holy water was.

Like other houses in Aleppo, ours had no bath that could be heated in winter, but each neighborhood had its own public baths. The bath attendant, who knew each family's bath day, would come early in the morning to collect the underwear, the towels wrapped in elegant covers, and all the other necessary things like soap, wash basins, and a bathmat to sit on. All this she used to carry to the baths on her head; the women of the family, the children, and the nannies would follow later.

The wooden door of the baths, up a few steps from the street, opened onto a wide, domed courtyard with a fountain in the middle. This was the antechamber of the baths and all around it were cubicles, separated by wooden lattices, where the mats were spread and the underwear laid out for each family. We would undress and then be ushered into the main bathing hall in our cotton wraps, each carrying our own bar of soap and washing bowl. The main hall consisted of three adjoining courtyards, each hotter than the other, and each full of naked women and children: some women on steaming stone slabs, scrubbing themselves with loofahs, others washing their hair under hot water flowing into carved stone basins from taps on the wall. The whole place was permeated by the fragrance of oranges and lavender and the acrid smell of human sweat, all mixed in a dense cloud of steam which made everything hazy. My sisters and I were handed over to the bathwoman who took us captive between her knees and washed our hair, drowning us in soap suds and boiling water. Despite all our yelling and struggling, she never let go till she was finished with us. Everything looked rosy after that ordeal. We ate oranges, blew bubbles and, once we were out of the hall and had dried ourselves with fragrant towels and put on our clothes, we were rewarded with *heytaliye,* an iced sherbet which was a specialty of Aleppo and was served in china bowls with china spoons. In the evening the family went home exhausted and we children were usually fed lentil soup and put to bed.

My mother had assumed absolute authority in the household when my Aunt Fattoum died, for Aunt Hatije had broken away completely from my grandfather, keeping to her own room and devoting herself entirely to religion and her two children, Emet and Ahmad. When my grandfather was in she wouldn't even come out of her room. Their separation had reunited my grandfather and my mother, who was now determined to keep him for herself. In those years I was increasingly saddened by the way in which my mother discriminated against Aunt Hatije and her children. Their inferior position became very apparent: during meals, in the furnishing and heating of rooms in winter, in the provision of clothes, and in the way they were served by our nannies who took it for granted that such discrimination was natural. I was very upset about my mother's unfairness. But they submitted to this unjust treatment patiently, without complaint or resentment, and their gentle resignation was a great moral lesson for me.

Aunt Emet and I would lie down side by side on summer nights, gazing at the stars and talking about the new things I was learning; I felt as if I was discovering the universe. We were brought even closer together by our love of books. My mother didn't approve of novels but I used to read secretly and swiftly many of the books that Aunt Emet borrowed from her friends. By the time I was thirteen, I'd read translations of Dumas, Rousseau, and

Victor Hugo as well as works by Abdulhaq Hamid, Cenap Shehabettin, and Halide Edip.

The family decided to arrange a marriage for Uncle Jamil so that he would stop wasting his money and settle down and have children. Having got his consent, friends and relatives began looking for a wise, sensible girl who would make a good wife. After considerable searching my mother announced that she'd met someone to her liking, but wanted the approval of others in the family. A second visit was arranged and Uncle Jamil instructed the elders to take Aunt Emet and me with them. I was delighted; I was now thirteen and this would be the first time I would wear a *sharshaf*, or all-enveloping cloak, and go on a formal visit. My mother and Aunt Aysha spent days sewing clothes for this occasion; they made my sharshaf out of the very wide skirt of my mother's canary yellow brocade wedding dress. On the day of the visit Aunt Emet and I had a hard time not laughing as I tried to walk in the new garment.

We were met at the door by the bride-to-be's grandmother. Aunt Emet and I sat on the chairs nearest the door. Finally the bride-to-be, Shifa, came in with the coffee tray, as was the custom, and the visiting ladies sitting in a row began their scrutiny of her physique—eyes roaming over her arms, legs, neck, waist. Once we had our coffee, the girl went out of the room and we all stood up and left. I heaved a sigh of relief, quickly joined the others in the street, took a few steps, and then the dreaded thing happened. Wearing my veil and overcome by the excitement of the visit, I tripped and fell as I was trying to walk in the long narrow garment; the yellow silk, which had frayed in the trunk over the years, was torn from top to bottom. Aunt Emet and I were hysterical with laughter, paying no attention to the reprimands of the grown-ups. Hidden from the view of men who sat about in the coffeehouses, I was taken home in the middle of our group.

Uncle Jamil did finally marry Shifa, and a grand wedding was held in our house. Aunt Shifa was pretty but not attractive or intelligent enough to make her husband forget his days of uncontrolled debauchery. Besides, she couldn't have children. So, Uncle Jamil eventually went back to his old ways. But Aunt Shifa and her grandmother continued to live with us as part of the family.

Leading up to and during the First World War, the fervor of Turkish nationalism reached Aleppo in the form of new reforms. Orders were received to set up a Teacher's Training College for girls, which, as we found out later, was intended to promote Turkish patriotism and suppress the awakening of Arab nationalism in the region.

Fifth form girls were to be admitted provided they passed the test. My

grandfather had my age altered from thirteen to fourteen on my birth certificate so that I could qualify to apply. I passed the test and was admitted
with twelve other girls. For the first time in Aleppo, girls were going to be
taught by men, some of whom had come from the University of Istanbul
to teach important subjects like mathematics.

During my first year I felt somewhat lost among the older and more
knowledgeable girls, for I was one of the youngest to be admitted. Teaching was entirely in Turkish and we were forbidden to speak Arabic—even
during the breaks. I was too young to understand fully the general zeal for
Turkification in the final years of the Ottoman Empire, but it was obvious
that our school had a share in it. During the war, Enver Pasha, the Minister of Defense, came to visit the college. We knew him from pictures in
magazines and on postcards and were very excited about the prospect of
seeing him in person. We welcomed our visitor wearing red ribbons in our
hair and new uniforms and red shoes. We gave displays of games and acro-
batics, recited poems, and sang songs ringing with patriotic feeling. Enver
Pasha thanked us "Turkish" girls for doing him proud.

On Thursday evenings we went home for the weekend. Home was becoming less and less attractive to me. There was no one much left there.
Aunt Hadije had died, Aunt Emet was in Istanbul pursuing her education,
and all my uncles were fighting at the front. My elder nanny had been taken
ill and was in hospital. As for my younger nanny, Iqbal, she'd taken her
bundle of clothes and the bottle of Mikado perfume, which she'd kept in
her trunk for years, and run off with the private that my uncle had left to
guard the house. Thus, she had put an end to her years of slavery. And my
mother, always severe with us, had grown even more fierce and irritable. I
have never forgotten how I envied my friend Bedirye when I saw how her
mother greeted her—affectionately with a kiss. How I longed to have a
mother like that.

After much preparation, our oral examinations were held by a joint committee of staff and examiners from the Ministry of Education. One by one
we girls were taken into the examination room and asked questions. For the
first time I became aware that I was in competition with girls who were older
and more knowledgeable than I was, and I stood anxiously waiting for the
results. The headmistress read out the names and numbers, finally naming
me as the top girl in my class. I was stunned and thrilled as she pinned on
my badge of honor.

During the school year, literary figures would visit the college in an effort to boost our patriotism with nationalistic speeches and poetry readings.
But the change from Ottoman patriotism to strong Turkish nationalism gave
rise to an opposite reaction in my case; instead of reinforcing my "Turk-

ishness," it awakened a consciousness of my Circassian identity which had been dormant for years. The Great Jemal Pasha, as he was known, while visiting our art class, stopped to look at my drawing. After complimenting me, he said, "You're Turkish, aren't you, young lady?" "No, Sir, I'm Circassian," I answered. "Well, Circassian means Turkish," he replied.

In the third year of the war, conditions in Aleppo deteriorated badly; hardly any food or medical supplies were left. I remember how a private who guarded our house once brought back the gold coin my mother had given him to buy bread because he could not find a loaf in any marketplace in town. Grandfather asked my mother to visit one of the mosques in the city that were beginning to fill with refugees from the war. Everyone in Aleppo tried to help the refugees, offering food and hospitality.

My mother and my sister Madiha and I—Amina had become very ill and died six years before—joined my eldest Uncle's wife, Aunt Nimet, in the country in Kilis. Over the summer I became very close to Aunt Nimet's sister, Nuzhet. No longer little girls who shared their lunch at school, we'd become young women of fifteen, aware of our youth and beauty. We also felt old enough to discuss the laws of nature regarding love and affection as we read our books, observed the lives of adults, and watched the stars and moon in the bright Kilis night sky. Nuzhet's brother had studied political science and economics in Germany and sometimes joined in our discussions on literary topics. One day Nuzhet secretly tried to hand me a bundle of letters saying they were written by her brother. I promptly rejected them, for I considered his interest in me an act of disloyalty to my friend, his sister. No matter how hard Nuzhet tried to persuade me, I refused to read the letters. Her brother, on the other hand, tried to ingratiate himself with my mother, who, it seemed, was willing to promise him my hand in marriage. When I found out, I was very distressed; if my mother insisted on the marriage, I decided, I would commit suicide by throwing myself into the well in the courtyard.

In the meantime, there was worse news from the front as the number of Ottoman defeats rose. In those years, news traveled by word of mouth and was unreliable. But we began to hear rumors about the Arab uprising in Syria, which Jemal Pasha, despite all his efforts, had failed to crush, and about how he had had Syrian youths hanged without trial. Many officers had deserted the Ottoman army to join forces with Sharif Hussein, who was leading the Arab rebellion in the Hijaz. "Treacherous Arabs," they were called and we were all frightened of these barbarous men who were said to regard women as their inferiors. I had been brought up as an Ottoman patriot, and I was one, but now things had changed; the Ottomans were divided and killing each other. The war had forced us—Turks, Arabs, Kurds,

Circassians—to question our identity. On which side did I belong and what was I expected to do?

My uncle wrote saying he'd been appointed Health Minister in the Arab government newly set up in Aleppo. I convinced my mother to let me go stay with him in his temporary residence. The spare room in my uncle's house was tiny, just big enough for a bed, but I was happy there, reading, painting, and going out with my Aunt Nimet when my uncle was at work. The sudden arrival of my aunt's younger brother from Kilis brought this arrangement to an end. I realized that he'd come to persuade me to marry him, and I decided to escape to my Uncle Jamil's house, where I wouldn't have to think about drowning myself in the well.

The war had changed the economic situation of most families in Aleppo. Grandfather had retired and was living in a small house with his new wife.

People talked about the new Arab government that had just been set up. I wouldn't have noticed any change if I hadn't come across a few Arab officers in strange headgear on the streets or occasional British officers instead of the Germans we were used to seeing. I was very anxious to continue my education, but the college had been closed, so I begged my mother to promise that I would be allowed to go to Istanbul to study as soon as the chance arose. I lived in the hope of such promises and made plans. My driving ambition was to study literature and become a journalist.

In the meanwhile, I decided to make use of my time and take French lessons with Saadet, a lady from a well-known Christian family. She was only a few years my senior and became a very good friend. I went to her house four times a week, and we soon forgot about the lessons and found other topics to discuss. Often there was a young man, said to be Saadet's cousin, in the hall with her father and brothers. Had I known that he was later to play such an important role in my life, I might have paid a bit more attention to this young man, but I was too shy and proper to linger longer than for a quick greeting.

Several times I heard footsteps following me back to my uncle's house, but I dared not look back. Once, as I walked up to the door, I looked from behind my veil and saw two Arab officers. When in my next lesson I told Saadet about this outrageous conduct, she pretended to be surprised and equally annoyed.

At about this time, Aunt Emet came back from Istanbul, having graduated from the university. One day she announced that an Arab officer had asked for my hand in marriage and that this was the very person who had followed me home and was said to be Saadet's "cousin." I was astounded. Aunt Emet also made it clear that my elders wanted me to agree to this marriage, having already made enquiries and given their approval. The young man, called Ali Jawdat, was not only a friend of my older uncle's but also a brave and honorable officer who had fought with Emir Faisal in the Arab revolt.

As it was the custom for the elders to decide such matters among themselves without caring much about the opinion of the girls involved, my objections on the grounds that I wanted to pursue my education were all in vain. Aunt Emet acted as an intermediary; if I agreed to marry, we would be engaged immediately, but my conditions regarding school would be taken into consideration. Eventually, I was persuaded to agree. I felt I had no choice; I couldn't refuse and cause my mother further grief. Besides, for a sixteen-year-old girl, promises of freedom, independence, and the possibility of further education held much attraction. A few days later, my fiancé sent a diamond medallion and gold ring for the engagement.

The marriage ceremony took place shortly afterwards. I came down with a fever the day before and announced my defeat by consenting to have my cousin represent me at the ceremony. Jawdat sent a carefully taken photograph of himself which he'd signed for me. It was hung on the wall in the reception room, and I could only steal furtive glances at it as I tried to form an opinion of the man who was going to share my life.

Ours was the first grand wedding celebrated in Aleppo after the war. All the prominent families were invited, and entertainment was provided by famous musicians and dancers. I sat through the jubilation passively, shy and thin in my white gown amid a huge crowd of people to whom I had been introduced only a short while before. That day I came face to face with my husband for the first time, and that evening I remember talking to him about nothing but my school and friends. I didn't know what else to say.

In the days that followed I wanted to stop the game, put on my short dress again, and get on with my life as before. Everybody was grown-up in my new life and far too serious. A few days after the wedding, we set out to visit Saadet and her family in Intab, a few kilometers from Aleppo. We traveled there in Jawdat's war-weary Ford with its makeshift roof composed of four planks and an awning. Because of the stony roads and the ancient car, it took us much longer to drive the distance than we expected. The sun had set, and Jawdat was getting more and more nervous; he kept warning the driver to keep away from the slope. Soon, with a terrible screech of tires, the car overturned, and we found ourselves at the bottom of the slope. One of the wooden planks had kept us from being crushed under the car. We regained consciousness in complete darkness and started walking toward Intab. It was past midnight and I kept falling asleep. I leaned on Jawdat's left arm while he dragged me along holding a pistol in his right hand. Armed gangs and robbers had begun roaming the countryside after the war and were a real danger to travelers. We finally arrived in Intab at dawn and found an inn—the room was small and filthy, but it was enough that we had a bed. As I took off my silk sharshaf, which had torn on the brambles during our long walk, Jawdat took off his jacket, and I saw that he was trying to hide something from me. A large piece of his left sleeve was torn and hanging loose and covered in blood. Poor Jawdat had offered me his affectionate protection and let me hang on to his wounded arm without a word about his pain. This incident helped rid me of my childish, romantic notions about marriage and formed the basis of my love for Jawdat, who, until then, had been a stranger to me. I felt that nothing could frighten me again as long as he was alive.

Charles Issawi

EGYPT *Charles Issawi was born in Cairo, where his father served as an official in the Anglo-Egyptian Sudan Government Service. The family was transferred to the Sudan, but Charles was sent back to Egypt at the age of eleven and enrolled in Victoria College, an English boarding school in Alexandria. With a degree from the American University in Beirut, he went on to take a Ph.D. in economics at Columbia University and was for several years resident*

at the Institute for Advanced Studies, Princeton University. Among his many books are **The Economic History of the Fertile Crescent** *and* **The Economic History of Turkey.** *He died in 2000.*

CHARLES
ISSAWI,
RIGHT

GROWING UP DIFFERENT

Charles Issawi

Most people grow up sharing a language, religion, and culture with their neighbors. Some societies, however, include foreign enclaves; in Cairo, when I was born in 1916, they were very conspicuous and included the British, French, Italians, Greeks, Jews, Armenians, and others. The Syrians were a group that included the Lebanese, Jordanians, and Palestinians as well; such distinctions were unknown and all were *Shawam*, that is, from greater Syria and the Levant. This enclave differed from others in one important respect: we more or less shared a language with the Egyptians and indeed made notable contributions to Egyptian letters and journalism. Still, in our religion and, to some extent, our culture, we were different from the Egyptians. Moreover, a large proportion of the middle class knew French or, occasionally, English better than classical Arabic and hence were more at home in European culture.

My parents moved to Egypt in the early years of the 20th century. My paternal grandfather was a customs official in Jaffa. His family had migrated to Palestine from Hauran, in the nineteenth century; his wife came from the Damascene family of Sarruf; her uncle, Fadlallah Sarruf, taught Arabic at St. Petersburg University and has a paragraph attributed to him in both Kratchkovsky's and Krimsky's books. My maternal grandfather, Nuʿman Abouchar (Abu Shaʿr) was educated at ʿAntura, a French boarding school in Lebanon. He served as a judge in Damascus and as an Ottoman consul in Liége, where he was in charge of purchases for the Hijaz railway; but, alas, he was honest and we never made any money.

He did not get on well with the Young Turks, was one of the founders of the Arab nationalist *La-markaziya*, and settled in Egypt because he could not return to Damascus. His wife came from the Arabized Ionian family of Avierinos, which claimed Genoese descent; I believe one of her brothers did some gunrunning, a welcome spot of color in my not-too-exciting family. All of my grandparents were Greek Orthodox; people normally married within their sect.

My father was educated at Bishop Gobat's school in Jerusalem and the American University in Beirut. He joined the Anglo-Egyptian Sudan Government service and worked in its Cairo office as Director of Budget and Personnel until 1923, when he moved to Khartoum. In Cairo, he also moonlighted as a correspondent for the *Egyptian Gazette*, covering scholarly lectures and meetings. In recognition of his services, he was made an Officer of the British Empire and received the title of bey. My mother grew up in Constantinople, where she was sent to a French convent school.

I was an only child, adored and protected by my parents, but I was not pampered. For one thing, I had constant intestinal trouble, so I seldom ate my fill, much less indulged. Secondly, I was taught that self-denial was good for a person; encouraged to practice it, I have never shaken off this belief. Thirdly, I was properly disciplined in certain things, though not in others. While I had to mind my manners and eat whatever was on my plate, I never had to put away my clothes or brush my shoes or make my bed—that was for servants to do. The results of my upbringing have stayed with me and have aroused much comment from my wife, who has often said that military service would have done me a lot of good. Lastly, my parents did their best to prevent my becoming a sissy. "Mummy, he hit me." "Hit him back." "But he is bigger than me"—most boys were. "Hit him back all the same." I should add that, like most Middle Eastern boys, I was never taught to do anything with my hands.

When necessary I was properly punished. One day, at age four or five, I came home with a beautiful apple. My mother asked me where I had gotten it. When I indicated that it was from the Greek grocer below our apartment, she said: "Did he give it to you?" "No," I answered. "So you stole it." "Hum." "Then you must return it and apologize." I did so. This lesson in the sanctity of private property no doubt explains my deep bourgeois propensities. My lies, too, were always soon discovered by my mother. Rarely, and only for really serious offenses, I was belted by my father and locked up in the bathroom. I am told I took my revenge by drawing, on the walls, a cartoon of my father with a big belly and my mother in a large hat with long ostrich feathers.

I was brought up to say my prayers, which were in French. When I accompanied my mother to church, my memory is one of interminable Orthodox services, in Greek, and stifling heat.

My earliest recollection is of a thorough fright. My mother had taken me to the park. When we got back home, we saw a large crowd waving their arms and shouting. This was in 1919 during the Egyptian Nationalist Independence Movement; a demonstration was taking place outside the Italian consulate, which was located one floor below us in the same apartment building. We made our way through the crowd, which was very friendly and repeatedly said to my mother, "Don't be afraid." But she obviously was and so was I. To make matters worse, my mother had forgotten to take the apartment keys. I remember her ringing frantically and banging at the door. The demonstrators kept on repeating, "Don't be afraid."

Otherwise, my childhood memories are almost all happy ones, especially after we moved to Heliopolis when I was about four. A small and brand-new satellite suburb of Cairo that had been built in the desert by a Belgian company, Heliopolis was clean, quiet, and healthy.

I had lots of friends, but the closest were four Egyptian Muslim brothers who were about my own age and were neighbors of my grandmother. Their father, a high government official, had studied law and spoke good French. Their mother was typically *baladi:* a plump, good-looking, simple woman with hardly any education but a very warm and affectionate heart and a vast and commanding array of colorful expressions. Through the eyes of my friends, I began to see Egypt as a rich, generous country to which many foreigners (Syrians, Greeks, Maltese, and others) came in search of bread. At that time, Mustafa Kemal (Ataturk) was a great hero in Egypt and I remember hearing from my friends how, on the quarterdeck, he had fought off the whole British fleet with his sword.

I also had two American friends, and I remember the elder one telling me: "Muslims don't believe in God; they say, 'there is no God and Muhammad is His Prophet.'" It took me many years to figure out that the American was hearing "no God" rather that "one God."

Thus far, I had grown up on French and Arabic, which was basically Syrian Arabic sprinkled with some Egyptian. With my mother I spoke only French, and continued to do so, most of the time, for the rest of my life; with others, though, I used either language. However, when I was about five, I was sent to a kindergarten run by two English women who taught in English. That moment began my long love affair with the English language.

First of all, it gave me something with which to challenge parental authority. Secondly, and more importantly, the English language was the key to the world's greatest treasure house of boys' literature. No one had even thought of adapting the *Arabian Nights* for children—admittedly, they need a lot of adapting—and it was in English that I first read these wonderful tales. It was only much later that I read them in Arabic.

I do not remember any Egyptians among the children at school, though there probably were some. I do remember English, Syrian, Armenian, Jewish, and other boys and girls. We were taught English history (I still remember a picture of dark, hook-nosed Phoenicians offering purple cloth to fair Britons, clad in skins); geography (Germany, capital Berlin, on the Spree, etc.), arithmetic, English songs, etc. I was thoroughly happy and remember falling in love with a pink-cheeked English girl called Joan.

This cultural Anglophilia did not lead to political Anglophilia. By the time I had reached the age of discretion, say eighteen, I was steadily and firmly, though not passionately, opposed to the British presence in Egypt and Palestine. Of course, this feeling did not apply to the period of the Second World War, when there were more important issues at stake and I was a staunch supporter of Britain.

In 1923 or so, we moved to Khartoum, of which I have very pleasant memories. For a short while, I was sent to an Italian Catholic school, but it was judged unsuitable, so I was soon taken out. After that, I was tutored at home until age eleven. My mother taught me an hour of French each day, and a Copt tried without much success to teach me classical Arabic. But my real luck was that, just then, Edward Atiyah came down from Oxford and for three or four years tutored me in everything else.

Edward was a very warm person indeed, drawn to people, happy in their company, and profoundly convinced that they could be persuaded by rational argument. Having a lively mind, which was well-stocked with literary and historical allusions and quotations, he expressed himself fluently and vividly in speech and writing. He opened a whole new world to me. Naturally, he gave me the British view of history, but he tells me that I always checked his version by looking words up in the Larousse dictionary and presenting the French version—which, in his opinion, did not show a very critical sense on my part. He was a convinced liberal socialist, and I imbibed his secular, progressive view of history and his political values. He familiarized me with English literature, and I still remember some poems he made me learn by heart: Shelley's "The Cloud," Byron's "The Isles of Greece," and others. To this day, one of my great pleasures is reciting aloud poems to myself when walking. (I have also noticed that it keeps muggers off in New York since, like everyone else, they assumed I must be crazy.)

Most of the time I was alone and developed a self-sufficiency that was to be broken down only by marriage. We had a large garden and I built myself a house in a tree, which I would climb and then pull up my rope ladder after me. We had a dog, a gazelle, a monkey, and a horse to pull our cart until we got a car. I had a small vegetable garden and sold the produce to my parents at exorbitant prices. Above all I read whatever there was: Shakespeare, Darwin, Kipling, and two beautifully illustrated books, *The Wonder Book of Ships* and *The Wonder Book of Wonders*.

I had some friends, all Syrian, but since they were very few, to play football I would gather a bunch of Egyptian street boys. "Charles, don't play with the little street boys." "Well, find me nice white boys and I will play with them." I have never had much use for racism or social—as distinct from intellectual—snobbery. But most of the time I was alone and, in a sense, have remained alone. Although I have always found it very easy to work with others in an organization—Ministry of Finance and National Bank in Cairo, United Nations, Arab Office—or in committees, I have never shown the least entrepreneurial or managerial ability, was uncomfortable even directing a thesis, and have never been able to use a research assistant.

We all enjoyed our years in Khartoum. The town had some amenities—piped water, electricity, and a cinema, but no telephones or sewers—and each evening camel carts took away the pails from the lavatories, accompanied by a fearful stench. My father's salary enabled us to live very well; we had two servants, a gardener, and a car. In April or May, my mother and I would leave for Cairo; my father would join us in June, and we would all go on to Lebanon. He would return to Khartoum early in September, and we followed in October.

The journey to Cairo took four and a half days, two of which were glorious ones on the Nile steamer between Aswan and Wadi Halfa that stopped at Abu Simbel and other sights. I remember only two or three of the devastating sandstorms—*hubub*—which were so prevalent in summer. For three days, we stayed indoors; when the storm was over, the floors, beds, and furniture had a thick coat of dust. The approach of the storm, in the form of a huge black and red cloud, was truly awesome. But the winters were lovely. Occasionally, we would drive along the Nile, and I was told to watch out for crocodiles. To my disappointment, we never saw any, but a friend of ours saw a parked car on the road that suddenly walked off and turned out to be a hippopotamus.

Like everyone else, my parents lived in their "colony," but they visited and entertained some of my father's Sudanese, Egyptian, and British colleagues. But most of their friends were drawn from the rather large group of Syro-Lebanese businessmen and civil servants who formed the link between the ruling British and the Sudanese masses—a role that had its counterpart in many Third World countries. My father enjoyed much respect both as the second most senior non-British civil servant (Edward Atiyah's uncle, Samuel, was number one) and because of his straightforwardness and integrity. Over the years, many people have told me how much they enjoyed working with him.

Like the other foreign "colonies," the Syrians had their club; the British, of course, had two, for senior and junior staff. The Syrian Club included a couple of tennis courts and billiard and card tables. My parents and their friends would also organize dances, fancy-dress balls, bridge parties, and, while the craze lasted, games of mah-jongg.

In 1924, I witnessed a historical event. The Governor-General, Sir Lee Stack, was assassinated by some Egyptian nationalists; in response, Britain sent an ultimatum that demanded, among other things, the withdrawal of Egyptian troops from Sudan. Some Sudanese units mutinied; for three days, I believe, there was fighting in Khartoum. Our house shook with the sound of artillery, and we found much shrapnel in the garden. I rather enjoyed the noise, but my parents were not amused. Now, it so happened that our next-door neighbor was "The Pasha," the stout and elderly commander in chief of the Egyptian forces in the Sudan. We saw a good deal of each other, and I had a crush on his young and very beautiful wife. He had received evacuation orders and had no inclination to disobey them. But a group of younger Egyptian officers wanted to join the Sudanese revolt, which would have given the British a great deal of trouble. To put an end to their importuning, the Pasha came over to our house, but they followed him and pleaded with him. Some of them wept with indignation. But he refused to give way and eventually they all left. I do not know whether this incident has found its way into the history books.

In Cairo, each spring, my mother and I stayed at my grandmother's, and I had much fun with my uncles. Then we would visit my grandfather in Damascus and from there go to Lebanon, where my father would join us. Our usual route was by train from Cairo to Haifa, crossing the Canal by ferry, then by taxi to Beirut, spending the night at one of its dingy hotels, and the next day taking another taxi to Damascus; these taxis were, as they still are, shared cars in which one paid for one's seat. Occasionally, we took a French or Italian ship directly to Beirut, and that was fun.

In the early 1920s, Damascus was a rather gloomy and boring place, except during the nationalist revolt of 1925–1926, when the streets were full of French patrols and soldiers behind sandbags saying: "*Halte-là—qui vive,*" a game my cousins and I quickly adopted.

Lebanon, however, was wonderful. Romping up and down the slopes with a group of boys my age or slightly older, scaling rocks and climbing trees, falling all the time—that was real joy. But there was more to it than that. Even at that age I could sense that in Lebanon we were in a much more relaxed atmosphere than in Syria. We were all freer and less guarded in our behavior, especially the women. My grandfather, who as a boy of eleven had to flee Damascus during the 1860 massacres while carrying his younger brother on his back, was singularly free from bigotry, and I never heard a word of anti-Muslim prejudice from him. But on one point he stood firm: if Muslim men kept their women in seclusion, they should not be allowed to see his women-folk in his house. Whenever Muslim visitors came, my mother and aunt were ordered off to their rooms.

In the early 1920s, both Lebanon and Syria were still very much what they had been before the First World War. All the roads were dirt roads, and we arrived at our destination covered with the dust raised by the cars that were trying to move ahead of each other. The taxis were usually seven-seater Buicks, Hudsons, Reos, Delages—I knew all the makes and could distinguish them at a distance.

Electricity, which I had always taken for granted, had reached Damascus and Beirut before the First World War but not the villages or summer resorts; in these places, the hotels used kerosene "Primus" lamps, which gave a bright light. Since piped water also came later, jugs and basins were used for washing.

At that time, hotels consisted of two or three traditional houses, which lodged a dozen tourist families in all. Our favorite was the "Grand Hotel" in the village of Suq-al-Gharb, which was described by the press during the Lebanese civil war as "a strategic point!" The hotel was owned and managed by René Sursock, a member of one of Beirut's most distinguished Christian families. The atmosphere was very pleasant and enduring friendships were made. Some of the most enjoyable events were jousts or contests between village poets (*qawwal*). Having been plied with *'araq*, a local liquor, the poets improvised verse in which they usually attacked each other.

Alas, that activity has passed away. We came back year after year and saw the hotel grow and acquire one amenity after another—including fancy-dress balls, jazz bands, and other horrors—under Sursock's careful management. Eventually, the hotel developed into a huge establishment.

When I was eleven, my parents sent me to boarding school. My mother's preference would have been for a French education, and the Jesuit school in Cairo had a well-deserved reputation for providing intellectual training. Two considerations, however, favored an English school. First, I would play more games and get the physical toughening my parents judged I needed. Secondly, my mother was concerned that if I went to a Jesuit school I would undergo some kind of religious conversion and end up as a Jesuit, a prospect that did not in the least appeal to her. Victoria College, in Alexandria,

was chosen instead, and I am sure that Edward Atiyah, who was an enthusiastic old Victorian, had much to do with that choice.

My parents thought that being put in a boarding school that was four
and a half days away from home would be a terrible shock for their little
darling. My mother, therefore, accompanied me to Alexandria and, a few
hours later, came back to cheer and console me. When she asked for me,
the janitor pointed to a group of sweating, disheveled boys who were thoroughly enjoying the horseplay boys love. I was called for and, after assuring
her that I was all right, said, "Please don't stay too long, I want to go back
and play with my friends." Slightly hurt but deeply relieved, she left, and I
settled down to six very happy years at Victoria College.

Victoria was founded in 1901 as the one British effort to counter France's
overwhelming cultural influence in Egypt. Its large, airy buildings, surrounded by ample, green playgrounds, still stand—they can be seen in Yusuf Shahine's film, *Iskandariya lay*—but it has been converted into an Egyptian school. E. M. Forster, in his *Alexandria*, describes its purpose well: "It
offers an education on English Public School lines to residents of Egypt,
whatever their creed or race." The public school pattern was meticulously—
and, in retrospect, rather absurdly—followed. We wore blazers and caps
with the initials V. C. on them, and we had captains and prefects with a good
deal of authority over the other boys. Bullying, however, was only sponta-
neous, not organized. When necessary, we were caned by the headmaster, and
no one else. Soccer, cricket, and swimming were compulsory. I worked hard
at games but was not much good; the high point of my life was playing for
the second cricket eleven. Also, we had Speech Day, when prizes were distributed by the British High Commissioner or some other dignitary.

All instruction was in English and—since parents were paying what was
then the large sum of 100 Egyptian pounds a year mainly in order that we
learn the language—only English was, in principle, allowed on the grounds.
But, of course, such a rule was impossible to enforce, and one heard much
French, Arabic, Italian, and Greek. For if the seed was English, the soil was
Levantine Alexandria in its heyday. Alexandria had an active cultural life,
and we were often taken to see Shakespearean plays, which were performed
by distinguished British actors such as Sybil Thorndyke, and to recitals given
by Heifetz, von Sauer, Huberman, or Borovsky.

The school motto was "Cuncti gens una sumus," and every effort was
made to live up to it. Ethnic slurs were frowned upon, but there was much
good-humored abuse, centered as usual on national food, e.g. for Syrians,
"you fat *kubaiba*," or for Armenians, "you smelly *pasturma*." But religious abuse
was taboo and no one, after he had been warned of the awful consequences,

would have dreamed of saying, "you something Muslim/Christian/Jew" —and of course we all knew who was Muslim, Christian, or Jewish, if only by our names. Nor was it just fear of punishment—we really learned to live together, work together, and play together. Like other boys in similar circumstances, we soon came to believe that the fact that X was a good fast bowler or center-forward was far more important than his nationality or religion. Our friendships and enmities had nothing to do with race or creed but originated in the mysterious chemistry that operates in people. My closest friends included Egyptians, Jews, Armenians, and only one Syrian.

The school was secular, but every boy got one hour's religious instruction a week from a Catholic priest, Protestant pastor, sheikh, or rabbi— Greek Orthodox boys being lumped with Protestants.

There were about one hundred boarders and twice as many day boys. The high fees meant that only upper- and middle-class families could afford to send their children to Victoria, and we were rather snobbish and thought of ourselves as a social elite. Our parents included cabinet ministers, landowners, financiers, merchants, civil servants, and professional people. But we had more exotic schoolmates as well, including, for example, two Malayan princes, one of whom was a splendid runner and high jumper. The younger son of Emir ʿAbdullah of Jordan, Nayif, was another contemporary. Nayif was a husky boy; once, when I had to box with him, he made mincemeat of me. Long after he left, his nephew, who became King Hussein of Jordan, attended school. Their cousin, ʿAbdel Ilah, son of the former King of Hijaz and future regent of Iraq, who was killed in the 1958 Revolution, was also a contemporary. We were good—though not close— friends, and I respected his dignity and calm sense of assurance. However, I was put off by a vindictive strain in him, whether directed at the Saudis, who had overthrown and exiled his father, or at his current school enemies. His closest friend was a ruddy-cheeked, pleasant-looking Kurd, Baba ʿAli (his real name was ʿAli Baba but that would have been an irresistible provocation to the boys). He was the son of Sheikh Mahmud of Sulaymaniya, who had given the British so much trouble, and I believe the boy was a sort of hostage to insure his father's good behavior. Once he showed us a picture of a very tough man, loaded with bandoliers, who was holding a machine gun in his right hand and a rifle in his left, and was surrounded by equally tough men: "My father," he said, "dispensing justice." We were impressed. He took a degree from Columbia and served in several cabinets. There also were other Iraqis from the ʿAskari and Saʿdun families.

Another exotic element was a contingent of Ethiopians, the first to be sent abroad for education. One of them, Yilma Deressa, was a particular hero of mine, since he was an all-round splendid athlete. He later became

Minister of Foreign Affairs and of Finance, and we were to meet again at the United Nations in the 1950s. The company of these Ethiopians helped to further reduce my racial prejudice.

Graduates of Victoria College have done well in business, the professions, and the civil service, but, as far as I know, there have been only two outstanding scholars, both of whom are sons of my former tutor: the great mathematician Sir Michael Atiyah and his brother, Patrick, a law professor at Oxford.

The trouble lay not in the curriculum but in the insufficient stress on intellect and, in a few classes, the failure of some of the younger teachers to control the boys. One man who had no problems with discipline was our French teacher, whose method was in sharp contrast to prevalent practice at English schools. Georges Dumont, a Swiss Protestant, was a martinet who drilled us in irregular verbs, gave us lots of poetry and prose to memorize, made us write compositions almost every day, and greatly improved our French. He was the most bourgeois of men and, it seemed to me, wrong on every issue. When he was young, he once told us, bringing a distant look to our eyes, and doing military service in the Alps, blankets were passed out and there was one extra one. "Give it to Dumont," said the corporal. "He is always chilly." "And besides," he added, "he's a socialist." What that had to do with anything was beyond me.

Victoria was good for me because it toughened me and taught me to live with others. Since I was passionately fond of reading and devoured books, I did not suffer from the school's insufficient emphasis on intellect. I got on well with my schoolmates and was liked by them. My reputation was helped by a fortunate accident that occurred in my first week at school. I was passing by the prefect's study when one of them, who must have been preparing for a history test, leaned out of the window and, seeing me, a new boy, said, "What do you know about the Partitions of Poland?" Quite unfazed, I answered, "Which of the three did you have in mind?" I believe the story made the rounds of the school, but, as far as I know, surprisingly, no one said I was an obnoxious brat. I also engaged in many extracurricular activities. I scraped the violin, producing dreadful sounds but acquiring a taste for music in the process, performed in school plays, and edited the school magazine, often writing much of it. I was a scout for several years, ending as a patrol leader.

Still, in one subject, Arabic, I made little progress in spite of my parents' exhortations. That was hardly my teachers' fault, since I spent most of the class reading Edgar Wallace or Sherlock Holmes or something of the kind. My interest in Arabic began only when I was about fifteen or sixteen. The only one of our English teachers who had learned classical Arabic, R. J.

Highwood, taught us Arab history, which I found interesting, and it was from him I first heard of Ibn Khaldun. Then I acquired a copy of S. Lane-Poole's *The Story of Cairo* and began exploring the magnificent mosques in that city. Shortly after, it occurred to me that Arabic was a great language and, helped by a tutor, I began to learn it. As a result, I was later able to carry on in Arabic with no difficulty; work at the Ministry of Finance; edit the journal *Al-Abhath* in Beirut; write numerous articles, the first appearing in *al-Muqtataf* in 1935; and translate selections from Ibn Khaldun under the title *An Arab Philosophy of History*. But all that belongs to my grown-up years.

Mansour al-Hazimi

SAUDI ARABIA *Born in the holy city of Mecca in 1935, Mansour al-Hazimi was educated in his birthplace, in Egypt, and in London, where he received his Ph.D. in Arabic literature. He has published poetry and short stories as well as literary criticism and served most recently as Chairman of the Arabic Department at King Saud University in Riyadh.*

AL-DAHLAH

Mansour al-Hazimi

 Professor Atiq bin Ghayth al-Bilady's book, *Popular Literature in Hijaz,* aroused old memories in my mind and no doubt in the minds of others who experienced their childhood in the Hijaz. In spite of the fact that this book describes an era long past, it still retains value, and we cannot help but regard that era with nostalgia.

Professor al-Bilady raises many issues that were almost forgotten before he recorded them. The younger generation does not perhaps understand the value of his effort to reclaim the past, nor are they interested in the images brought to them by the local popular literature of today. Those who have grown up in the modern era reading American stories about Mickey Mouse and Superman and watching Hollywood horror movies may have difficulty understanding the legends of Al-Zir Salim and Abu Zayd al-Hilaly, the legends of our own history which Professor al-Bilady narrates.

But those of us who grew up in the difficult days during World War II and the Palestinian War of 1948 are familiar with al-Bilady's description of the old popular culture. For those games, traditions, and beliefs are part of our own minds and personalities even today.

I grew up in the district of al-Dahlah, west of Mecca, in the midst of that old popular culture. Al-Dahlah owes its name to its placement in the Hijaz landscape. In classical Arabic, al-Dahlah means a kind of well, which is what the place is, a hollow surrounded by mountains. It is difficult to think of something special about al-Dahlah. Like many other small districts and villages near Mecca at that time, al-Dahlah was often cited as an example of not only poverty, but ignorance.

True, in those days al-Dahlah was very proud of the two residents who had finished primary school and held public jobs. It was also proud of a scholar who came originally from Morocco; he was a nice man who used to wash the dead ceremonially and was also a good cook; another was the driver for the post office, the man in charge of the mail. Because of his job, this man had to travel a lot, so he was the source of all kinds of stories and news.

The people of al-Dahlah were proud of another resident, too, a woman named Um Ali, the mother of Ali, who had not changed her way of life in many years, even though she had lived for some time in Mecca. She used to go out in public, covering her face, but wearing men's clothes. Her opinion was so important that no one in al-Dahlah made any decision without first consulting her and asking for her approval. Why this was so I do not know, but perhaps it was because she had been so long in the holy city of Mecca.

Al-Dahlah was in a good position geographically, slightly west of Mecca, which meant that many pilgrims passed through the district. This was good for business, and thus benefited everyone, including all of us children. The children in those days had specific songs that they made up and sang to ask the pilgrims for alms.

But at night, the district and the town were dark, very dark, and thus a frightening place for children. The darkness meant that jinns and ghosts might be present, wandering through the streets. There were many children's stories about the jinns.

All people in al-Dahlah were accustomed to thinking about jinns and other spirits. The jinns were said to be particularly fond of women and children, though I never knew why; maybe it was because the spirits preferred the meek, who were more sensitive and open to the visitation of spirits. The children, of course, had not yet achieved their full intellectual faculties, and woman, by nature, it was usually claimed, lacks reason. The belief existed that if a woman was visited by a jinn, she might lose her mind, and her family was obligated to help her out of her difficulty. For these kinds of problems, the best remedy was considered to be the *zar*, which was a ceremony involving music and dance to chase away the jinn. The family of the woman in need of help would hire a group of women to play and sing certain songs and rhythms; the woman was encouraged to get up and dance with the group until she went into a kind of trance and lost consciousness. After the woman awoke, she was supposedly better. The jinn had been frightened away, or exorcised. And the zar did seem to help many women.

But the jinns who frightened women and children were supposed to make men courageous. It was considered a sin of weakness for a man to carry a light if he walked out during the night. In fact, men used to compete with each other to walk in the most scary places after dark.

Tawfiq al-Hakim argues in the introduction of his play *Ya Talia al-shajarah* that the drama of the absurd has its origin in Arabic popular literature. He gives the example of the traditional Egyptian song:

> *You, who climb the tree—*
> *Bring me a cow*
> *That will give milk*
> *Which will feed me*
> *With a Chinese spoon.*

Here the cow is a metaphor for a woman, a lover. The poet is asking the woman to be generous in her love, like a cow with her milk, and feed him with an exotic "Chinese spoon." The popular poets of the Hijaz were similar. They used many different images to convey their feelings and needs. If what the poet felt was either forbidden or intolerable to describe within the society, he spoke indirectly, as in the Egyptian song.

Toward the end of the Second World War, a very important event took place in al-Dahlah. The man who was in charge of the mail brought in a radio, the first in the district. People were fascinated by this strange box and started spending all their time listening to it. They waited for the news of the war, although they knew nothing about it except that the Germans were fighting against the British. So they wanted the German Hitler to win the war over his British enemies just like the mythical Arab heroes Antar and Sayf ibn di Yazan had won over their enemies in the past.

The songs of the radio cut into the audience for the popular poets. But not all people turned away from the old poets. Why? Because the radio personnel did not know how to tell the old stories of love and life and death as the poets did so well.

After the Palestinian war, when the Arabs lost everything, life in al-Dahlah changed. Many families left when the district lost its advantageous position on the pilgrimage route to Mecca. Roads were built that did not pass through Dahlah, so business declined. Um Ali stayed, however. She refused to leave because she said she hated life in the cities and especially the food!

But on the morning of the new year 1957, the people of al-Dahlah lost their friend and neighbor, Um Ali. Even in her last hours she wanted freedom. She asked to die under the sky. "Take me outside," she said. "I want to see my God." And the people did so. After her death, the old al-Dahlah no longer existed.

Translated from the Arabic by Amal Chagumoum and Aziz Abbassi

JORDAN *Janset Berkok Shami*

Janset Berkok Shami was born in Turkey, studied at Ankara University and Queen Mary College, London, before marrying and moving to Jordan, where she lives. Her first novel, **Cages on Opposite Shores,** *was published in 1995 by Interlink, New York, and has since been translated into Turkish. She has published numerous short stories in literary magazines in the United States; one,* **Waiting,** *has been translated into Arabic, Swedish, and Turkish. She has also been a participant in the International Writing Program at the University of Iowa.*

JANSET SHAMI, LOWER RIGHT

CIRCASSIAN MEMORIES

Janset Berkok Shami

 My grandparents were among those Circassians who left the Caucasus when Czar Nicholas II made it clear that the Circassian people had two choices: they could either submit to the rule of Czarist Russia or be massacred—men, women, and children. Most settled within the borders of the Ottoman Empire because of the affinity Circassians felt toward its mostly Muslim population. The reasons were obviously more complicated, but this particular religious reason was hammered into me by my father, my mother, and their contemporaries.

My mother's parents found themselves in West Anatolia, on the shores of the Aegean Sea, while the Ottoman authorities settled my father's parents in the arid lands of Middle Anatolia. My mother's father had had the chance to study and become a judge; my father's family became farmers.

My maternal grandfather had an advantage in that one of his aunts had already settled in Istanbul. By the time he and his family arrived on the shores of the Aegean, that aunt already was the wife of an influential Turkish pasha in Istanbul. She not only provided an education for my grandfather, but being childless, she also made him a wealthy man when she died. In addition to several other properties, my grandfather also inherited a twenty-room house on the Bosporus strait, together with its furniture. In 1939 my grandfather sold that property to a rich toothpaste manufacturer called Radyolin Cemil. The furniture was passed on to my mother and then to me. When I was married and came to live in Jordan, a fourteen-piece ebony and mother-of-pearl set of furniture came with me. This set still embellishes my modest villa in Amman.

My mother lost her own mother when she was only a baby, and so grew up under the care of a nanny and several servants until her father remarried and brought a new wife to the household. Fortunately, my mother liked her stepmother, and her stepmother liked her. My mother was an easygoing girl and was such a good student that after high school her father encouraged her to continue with her studies at the *Dar-ul-Funun.* The degree my mother obtained from Dar-ul-Funun was the highest a female could hold in Ottoman Turkey. It was somewhat equivalent to a college degree.

My father also studied in Istanbul, but his circumstances were quite different. Yağlipinar village of Kayseri province, where he was born, did not have even a primary school during his early years. But it did have a mosque and the Imam took upon himself the duty of educating the children. My father's attentiveness and sharpness impressed the Imam. "It's a pity to keep Ismail in this village," the Imam said to my grandfather. "He must have a proper education. You must send him to Istanbul." My grandfather had a daughter who was married to the son of a wealthy merchant in Istanbul. He wrote her asking if she would take her brother to live with her. My aunt agreed to look after her brother and to educate him. So my father took off to Istanbul, travelling many days in an ox cart. When he arrived, he learned that his sister had passed away. His sister's husband did register my father in a nearby school, but they did not treat him as one of the family. They let him sleep in a storage room under the stairs and kept him busy with household chores. Although my father realized that the treatment he received was not what a relative expects, he kept his spirits up and concentrated on his studies. His patience and his perseverance paid off; after a year, he was admitted to the military school at Pasabahçe as a boarder.

My father adjusted to the life at the military school quite easily and surpassed his classmates in most subjects. The one subject he could not grasp, however, was the most important of all: the Turkish language. Having spoken his native language in the village, he was barely able to express himself in Turkish.

One day when the teacher asked my father to take dictation and read it back to him, the results shocked him. My father had written the commas, periods, and the question marks as words.

"What is this?" the teacher shouted angrily. "What kind of a dictation is that? Aren't you ashamed of being so ignorant?"

After that incident, my father set up a schedule for himself. Every afternoon after classes, he took a notebook and pencil and climbed up to the hill behind the sprawling school building. Sitting down on a rock, he wrote in Turkish about everything within his visual scope. He wrote about the ferryboats carrying passengers through the narrow Bosporus strait. He described the windows on the upper and lower decks of the ferry; their thick pipes through which they sent a wavy column of smoke into the air; and their wheels, which left trails of foamy waves behind them. He described the intricate walls of the Dolmabahçe Palace, which embellished the opposite shore, and the seagulls taking short rests on its majestic garden gate. These efforts must have improved his Turkish, for he later became a writer.

My father married my mother in 1919 when he was still a captain. The First World War had just ended in Europe, but the Turkish War of Independence was in its early stages. A few months after his marriage, my father was sent to the southern borders of the Empire. My mother did not hear from him for a long time.

In 1921, the Greeks were attempting to capture towns on the Aegean coast and many families were evacuating the west coast as well as Istanbul. My mother and her five-month-old son were among those who fled Istanbul in the company of several other families. They traveled to central Anatolia in a long convoy of oxcarts. Due to her desire for privacy, my mother told me, she had not been able to breast-feed her baby properly and the accumulated milk had caused an abscess in one of her breasts. She continued breast-feeding my brother, although the abscess made it excruciatingly painful.

When my father was promoted to the rank of major, he became one of the instructors at the military academy. He taught military strategy, and began to write textbooks on the subject. Until that time, the books the academy used had been translated from other languages. Eventually my father's long years of teaching, as well as the books he had written, earned him an unofficial title: the teacher of the army. Whenever his name was mentioned, people said, "Oh, you mean that general? The teacher of the army?" The books my father wrote, however, were not always military. He also wrote a book on the life of Atatürk, a comprehensive history of Circassians, and some other books.

I was lucky to have been born quite a few years after the Ottoman Empire had given birth to the Turkish Republic. During the first ten years of my life, enormous changes took place in the country. The Arabic letters were replaced by the Latin alphabet, and the red fez with the black tassel that people had been wearing for generations had been abandoned. What replaced the fez was called a "melon hat." A select group of women began to dress like European women. Their dresses and suits were copies of Parisian fashions; their shoes had pointed tips and spiked heels. My mother was one of these fashionable women. Having grown up in a mansion on the Bosporus and having attended the Dar-ul-Funun, the transition was not hard for her. She told me that she hardly ever wore a *sharshaf* before or after her marriage. And she never covered her face.

My mother eventually revolted against my father's expectations that she would continue to roam with him from "one primitive town to the other." She told him that she understood that he had to obey orders, and accept any post he was asked to take, but she was a free citizen. She decided to settle in Istanbul. My younger brother was then four, I was eight, and my elder brother was fifteen.

My mother rented a four-storied house in the district of Moda on the Anatolian coast of Istanbul. *Moda*, which means fashion, was a suitable name for that neighborhood with its big mansions and well-kept gardens. It was also fashionable to promenade on its curving coastline, which offered a different view with each of its twists and turns. One curve spread the city's majestic mosques and their numerous minarets before one's eyes, while another showed the protrusion of a slim, peaceful strip of land with a lighthouse at its tip. The islands of Burgaz, Kinaliada, Heybeliada, and Büyükada were behind the lighthouse. On summer afternoons, when the sea was absolutely smooth, one imagined that the islands were shifting slightly.

On the day I received my report card from elementary school showing that I was promoted to the fifth grade, my mother announced to her three children that she had plans for our holiday. "In a few days' time, we'll go to Suadiye hotel, to spend a week," she said. "You can swim as much as you want, and have ice cream after every meal. Then we'll take a boat and cross Karadeniz, leave the boat in Zanguldauk, and go to Karaköse."

"Where is Karaköse? Why are we going there?" my younger brother asked. He was the most curious of us three children.

"Because," replied my mother, "your father is there. He has been promoted to the rank of general. Wouldn't you like to congratulate him?"

My elder brother, who was already six-foot-two at the age of seventeen, shifted his weight from one long leg to the other. "Don't you think this is a dangerous journey?" he asked. This was his way of expressing his objection. We were raised to be cautious with our parents. We did our best not to aggravate them, and they did their best not to punish us in any way.

I don't remember my mother's answer to my brother's guarded objection, or even my own reaction. What I remember is the luxurious Suadiye Hotel and its sandy beach, the long swims, the games we played with other children, the fragrance of jasmine coming from the same corners in which I hid during our games of hide-and-seek, the music of the band sneaking out of the glassed-in ballroom, and the sailboat trip we took.

My clearest memory is of the big, big boat, *Tari,* which carried us to Zonduldak. I remember its departure from the Galata bridge. I remember the numerous handkerchiefs waving in the air and my mother, wrapped in her black silk dress printed with yellow flowers, moving from one section of the railing to the other as she looked at the people down on the landing.

The boat stopped only in Sinop on its way to Zonguldak. Then we continued with our long journey by land.

I remember the bus ride and the hotel where we stayed in Sarikamis. It was next to a vigorous waterfall. Leaning down from the balcony of the room I could see the joyful surrender of the river to the fall. I remember darkness, imagining that it was not the water that was falling, but myself. Falling, falling, falling. I felt that the waterfall was carrying me off to the future, to maturity.

The next day we traveled through a monotonous, barren landscape to Kagizman, our last destination before Karaköse. We were doing this last leg of the journey in an ancient taxi. To me, the time we spent going from Kagizman to Karaköse was the most memorable part of the trip.

We stopped in the shade of some frail trees to have a picnic lunch and suddenly were aware of eyes watching us. They were children, and they were naked. I knew these solemn-eyed children were not prepared to have a bath, so I wondered why they were stripped of their clothes. We were in the highlands, and the weather was quite cool even though noontime was the warmest hour of the day. Not only were the children naked, but they all had bulging stomachs. My mother had heard that the Kurdish children suffered from malaria, so she had come prepared. She distributed quinine to their mothers, who also appeared out of nowhere. My mother did not stop at that. She wanted to give them some of our clothes. But the driver stopped us. "*Hanimefendi*," he said, "please don't. What will they do when the clothes you give them wear out? How will they replace them?" The middle-aged driver's logic seemed to convince my mother. So, instead of giving the children clothes, she gave them some food.

I was still thinking about the bulging stomachs of the children when our taxi broke down.

"This happens quite often. It's a minor problem. I'll fix it in a few minutes," the driver said, opening the hood and beginning to fiddle with the motor. But the minor problem turned into a major one. He kept working on the car while the minutes turned into hours, while the night descended on us. When it became pitch dark, he continued working using his lighter, which he cursed from time to time for burning his fingers.

His efforts were futile. He could not fix the car. I felt the man's disappointment when he sat on a nearby rock and lit a cigarette.

My mother ignored my elder brother who whispered that he could hear the howls of wolves. She walked toward the man sitting on the rock. "We better use our legs. Let's march on," she said to him in a calm voice.

The driver was taken aback. "Hanimefendi, I'll walk with you, I have no objection to walking. I know of an inn a mile or so from here. But I don't take the responsibility for the dangers on our way. There may be wild animals, there may be highwaymen. It is not uncommon to meet them in these areas, you know. We may face the danger of. . . ."

My mother made a sharp decisive gesture with her hand and cut him short. "Do you take responsibility if we stay here?" she asked with a brave smile.

We walked. I don't remember how long we walked. My younger brother was lucky. My elder brother and the driver carried him in their arms most of the way. But I had to do it on my own. I don't know how with my weak ankles, which used to twist on uneven roads, I managed to walk such a long distance on that unpaved road. I wondered how the driver knew his way in that pitch darkness, in that nothingness. But suddenly the whitewashed face of a mud-brick wall appeared. When we crossed the narrow yard behind that wall, we saw the inn.

The innkeeper must have been in a very deep sleep. The driver had to knock for several minutes before the face of an unshaven man filled the crack of a cautiously opened door. He began to rub his eyes when he saw a beautiful young woman and three well-dressed children. After the driver explained our situation, the innkeeper let us in.

Several oil lamps were placed in the corners of the large hall; in their light, we could see bodies lying on the floor. They were all men. They had kicked off their shoes but had kept their clothes on. Some of the sleepers had mattresses beneath their huddled shapes. The rest lay directly on the mud-packed floor and had no covers.

"We're tired," my mother said to the innkeeper. "Do you have a place for us to rest?"

I noticed the bedstead standing like a throne in the middle of the hall. Obviously, that bed with its thin mattress and crumpled cover was the innkeeper's. He offered it to us with a gesture of his hand. Almost before he completed the gesture, my younger brother and I were under the crumpled cover. My mother followed suit. The driver disappeared somewhere, and my elder brother remained standing at the foot of the bed, asserting in his manner that he was neither cold nor tired. He might not have been as exhausted as the rest of us were, but how could he not be cold in that below-zero temperature?

Then I heard my mother's clear voice. "Beyefendi," she said, endowing the scruffy innkeeper with the extravagant title which was reserved for a certain class of people in my childhood. I knew that the correct title for the Innkeeper was "efendi." An extra-polite person might call him "bey," but the unsuitable title, "beyefendi," might easily be heard as sarcasm by the man himself. The danger of people of one class being misunderstood by those of another class lingered in Turkey long after Ataturk made it clear that we, the Turkish citizens of the new Republic, were stripped of "class and privileges." So I was surprised at my mother's use of the title "Beyefendi."

"Beyefendi," she said again. "Are there lice in this cover?"

The innkeeper shrugged his shoulders. "There might be," he said, approaching the bed. He pulled the cover off and turned it upside down over us.

The last thing I heard that evening in that candle-lit, smelly hall was my elder brother. "Do you think we'll really find our father and be able to congratulate him?" my brother asked my mother.

"Of course we will. Of course!" she replied.

Much later, after I had married and come to live in a country where people lived under the teachings of a different culture than my people, and having met various pitfalls on my way, I was able to pursue my aims by creating a motto: "Failure? It is impossible!" That motto carried and still carries the echoes of the unshakable conviction I had heard in my mother's voice that day.

Eventually, we returned to Istanbul. I went into the fifth grade at the Eighth School of Moda, and our teacher assigned us a composition on any subject.

I wrote about the inn where we had spent those few hours on our way to Kagizman and my mother's inquiry about the lice in the cover of the innkeeper's bed. I also wrote about the poor children suffering from malaria, their naked bodies, and bulging stomachs. To my great surprise, I received an "A" for that composition. Since my achievement so far had not been great, the "A" came as a surprise. I didn't think that I had done anything more than simply reporting what I saw and heard. Had the teacher favored me because of the gifts she received from my mother every now and then? I desperately hoped that this wasn't the case. Both my younger and older brother were not only studious, but brilliant. Why couldn't I be like them? Perhaps this was the beginning, perhaps I was going to become a better student.

Thus I promised myself that I would open a new page at the secondary school where the teachers wouldn't know of my old records.

I studied only two years in that secondary school. We moved to Ankara, where my father headed the General Directorate of Mobilization in the Ministry of Defense. Those were the years of the Second World War. And eventually—yes, I became a writer.

Salma Khadra Jayyusi

PALESTINE *Palestinian poet, critic, scholar, and anthologist, Salma Jayyusi was born in 'Akka, then in Palestine, and educated in Beirut and London. In 1980, she founded PROTA (Project of Translation from Arabic Literature) which she continues to direct, a project which has produced some thirty volumes so far. The novels, short stories, and collections of essays published by PROTA include* **Modern Arabaic Poetry;** **The Literature of Modern Arabia,** *and*

The Legacy of Muslim Spain. *She divides her time between the Arab world and Cambridge, Massachusetts.*

ON THE ELUSIVE CHORDS OF MEMORY: REMEMBERING 'AKKA

Salma Khadra Jayyusi

 When I think of my childhood, it is 'Akka, or Acre, that first comes to mind. 'Akka has indeed taken on the aspect of a paradise in my memory, although I am not sure I was completely happy then, even as a child. I do not recall any sense of complacency or full acceptance in my heart of things as they were. In fact, I did all the things girls were not supposed to do. But 'Akka's own original lifestyle, based, in many ways, on a sense of harmony in its people, on a kind of innocent, almost primordial love of merriment and festivity, fascinated me. Beliefs as old as humankind still lived on in that region, side-by-side with newly adopted ones which only people like the "'Akakweh" could have embraced. For example, they still believed that the first Wednesday in Safar, the second month of the Islamic calendar, should not find them beneath the roofs of their homes but under the open sky. On that day, they went at dawn to the seashore, even on bleak winter days, with food and music, and there they washed themselves in sea water, perhaps cleansing themselves of the devil, or protecting against disease, as Job had done.

At the same time, the people of 'Akka, during the pre-1948 decades of the twentieth century, made a habit of picnicking and feasting in al-Bahjeh and al-Shahuta gardens, which were owned by the Baha'is. They were planted with lovely trees, bushes, and flowers and tended by Iranian gardeners. Al-Bahjeh was one of the two Baha'i centers established in Palestine. Here it was, to the outskirts of 'Akka, that Baha' Ullah, the father and founder of Baha'ism had come to flee persecution in Iran and to establish his headquarters. (What better place on earth?) His followers built him a mansion there on the outskirts of the new 'Akka, the modern city built outside the massive walls encircling the ancient town. This mansion in al-Bahjeh where Baha' Ullah had lived and died was extremely simple, reflecting, in fact, the simplicity advocated by the Baha'is — quite unlike the more sumptuous Baha'i mansion in Haifa, built on the lovely slopes of Mount Carmel overlooking the Mediterranean, where Baha' Ullah's son, 'Abbas, is buried and which is the site of the world's main Baha'i center even until now.

Every time we went to al-Bahjeh, I made a point of visiting the holy man's sunny and spacious room (such is the image I keep from my childhood memory), with its very sparse furnishings, with Baha' Ullah's own bed, a simple mattress laid reverently on a small carpet on the floor, with his slippers still set neatly alongside. There it was, we were told, that he had died, on that very same mattress. But to my child's sensibility, (which otherwise had the tremulous apprehension of the death that took loved ones away), the mattress was surrounded by no aura of death; it rather conveyed, in its utter ascetic simplicity, a kind of vague spiritual message that spoke to my heart. It was there, and in the Zawiya in the old town, the home of the Shadhili sufi sect, that I first knew those strange sensations I could not understand, the sudden surging zest and elevation of the spirit, the incomprehensible yearning for something beyond my reach. Reflecting on this in later years, I could see that what I then experienced was a sense of personal communion with an idealized spiritual world, but what I remember clearly from that time is the total loathing I felt, during those moments of secret flight, for everything that was humdrum and habitual.

Just as I was fascinated by the utter simplicity and aloneness of the older Baha', I was equally fascinated by the rituals of the nearby Shadhili Zawiya. Nothing could have stopped me going there on the Mawled evenings when the Prophet's birthday was celebrated with a sacred dervish dance. I stood at the outer window of the Zawiya hall of prayer, gazing with wonder at the men and women dancing inside, arm entangled with arm, in a delirious circle. Each dancer whirled and rolled and swayed dizzily, repeating incessantly a thousand times over the two words, "Allah Hayy" (God is alive):

> *They dance and dance!*[1]
> *finding as they drink together*
> *the taste of ecstasy:*
> *eager feet stepping in*

[1] From "Birth," by M. M. al-Majdhoub, translated into English by S. K. Jayyusi and Charles Doria. Published in my *Modern Arabic Poetry, an Anthology* (New York, Columbia University Press, 1987, 1990).

treading out the dance!
so swift they move like birds,
kicking up [their robes]
dervishes turning,
never stopping, spinning!
feet jerking, swaying
in the nets of their robes
like fires of flame!

The Zawiya was the center of the Shadhiliyya Sufi sect, and was controlled by the Yashurti family whose pious and, as I remember them now, angellike women were friends of my mother. It stood in an old building, one of a line of major buildings in old 'Akka, just inside the walls. First came the great Jazzar Mosque, built by Ahmad Pasha al-Jazzar, probably at the end of the eighteenth century; then to the left, just a two-minute walk away, our school. Then, we were confronted almost immediately by the little miniature hell of the *ammim*—the frightening furnace room filled·with black dust and raging fire, which fed the famous Basha baths with constant hot water. Whenever we went by, we would see men endlessly feeding this huge furnace, with blackened faces and tattered blackened clothes that looked quite frightening. They would raise their faces to look at us little girls with braids and ribbons flying in the air, running to the Basha baths to buy *turmus* (lupines soaked in salt water) and pickled lemons from Jillou, the caretaker. Past the *ammim* on our way to Jillou, we would go through a short, narrow, covered pathway flanked on the right by part of the massive wall of 'Akka's notorious prison. It was with this prison that the names of many illustrious Palestinian revolutionaries were linked, and there it was that many martyrs were executed. Then the walls of the prison curved round, giving way to the Zawiya, with the Basha Baths perched majestically on the left.

Cities have their own characters. Since those enchanting years of my childhood in 'Akka, I have lived, as a Palestinian exile, in very many cities of the world: Arab, African, European, and American, but never have I seen another city with the liberal, merry, outgoing, festive, and compassionate spirit of 'Akka.

The "'Akakweh" feasted on every possible occasion. Where, in any other town, would you have heard of Muslims feasting on Easter Sunday and even more on the Saturday night before it? The "'Akakweh" called it "*Sabt al-Nur*" (Saturday of light), and we'd go to the big square in the old town where the Great Church was, and watch our Christian friends and neighbors celebrate the imminent resurrection of Jesus. They carried lighted candles, we carried lighted candles. They dressed up, we dressed up. They made

Ma'mul cakes, and cakes filled with dates, and we did the same. No one had an oven at home in those days, so everything had to be baked in the public ovens scattered throughout the city. There would be fierce competition during the pre-Easter days, with Christian neighbors protesting at the encroachment, "It's *our* feast!" But we looked forward to it just as we looked forward to the Muslim feasts. The "'Akakweh" had their own philosophy of life, and, being only eight when I went to live there, I embraced all the habits and customs of a true citizen.

And it was in 'Akka that I first discovered my adventurist spirit. I used, for example, to take the short-cut to school along the city walls—a path strictly forbidden to us girls. The massive walls of 'Akka were surrounded by two moats separated from each other by what seemed like an artificial hill but which must, in fact, have been the original terrain before the moats were dug. In the old fighting days, the two deep grooves would be flooded with sea water, making it extremely difficult for an enemy to cross. Our house was about thirty yards away from the outer moat, which was planted with quinine trees to discourage mosquitoes from breeding in the damp trench. In the middle of the groove was a pebble path to the "hill" which separated the two moats. Then, on top of this barren, dusty, extremely rugged elevation was a narrow pathway twisting and winding all the way around various smaller elevations that popped up here and there, hiding whatever was behind them. This pathway eventually led to the main street of 'Akka. Because I was always late leaving home for school in the morning, I almost always took this road and was probably the only girl who ever did so on her own.

"Are you mad?" Amm Muhammad, our cook, would say, "It's used by the workers and the *fellaheen* (peasants). What if some rough fellow attacked you?" I'd shrug my shoulders. "They never do," I'd say. "I like the fellaheen. They'd never hurt me." And they never did. I cannot describe the secret joy I felt as I walked along that dusty road, and the dreams I spun in my head in that state of total aloneness: an aloneness emphasized a million times over by the fact that I was walking in a domain where no girl ever walked on her own. I felt utterly free. My sister Aida never joined me in these adventures. She was always respectful of the rules and conditions of a life which, even in our relatively liberal home, was a difficult one for girls. Our cook never told on me. But my mother heard of it from the neighbors.

My mother tried to channel my wayward streak in what she saw as the right direction. A great storyteller, she would tell me tales (some she had read and some she had invented) which she thought would foster an idealistic attitude in me. She idealized love; after all, she enjoyed my father's love, fortunate woman, until death parted them in 1954. She also idealized nationalism, poetry, selfless endeavor, and the capacity to strive for a good cause. She detested, however, the quest for wealth and material goods; fortunately, she never lived to see the mad pursuit of wealth which infected the Arabs after the advent of oil. Just before her death in 1955, she told me how much she had worried about me when I was a child: "You seemed so fearless, so strong-headed, always going your own way." She also always emphasized the need for perfectionism: "Either do a thing properly, or don't do it at all." I loved this principle and took full advantage of it too, using it as a pretext not to do things I was not inclined to do. I think she knew this— I would see the realization flash in her eyes—but she'd let me off the hook. Later on, under the guidance of Sister Guida, the German nun at Schmidt's Boarding School whom I idealized, I came under the same kind of insistence on perfectionism.

The Jazzar Mosque was the very heart of 'Akka. Situated just inside the walls, which had been partly demolished in modern times to make way for the asphalt road, it was big and majestic, with two gates, a main gate and another opening onto the blacksmith's *suq*. It had many rooms in which male students lodged, two to a room, and was elevated so that one had to climb a wide rounded stairway of seven or eight steps into the large open courtyard with the ablution fountain in its midst. At the side of the stairs was the *sabeel al-tasat* ("the vessel fountain"), a once beautiful fountain with a frieze and about fifteen small basins with an equal number of metal vessels, each attached to the basin by a long chain; those passing would drink the cool, constantly refreshed water. Drinking from these vessels was forbidden by Mother. A doctor's daughter, she had a keen sense of microbiology. This was perhaps the only prohibition I faithfully obeyed.

It was in the courtyard of the Great Mosque that the first anti-Mandate, anti-Zionist demonstration convened. Men and veiled women met there, delivering many enthusiastic speeches (some of them by the women), then going on in a huge procession to the Three Martyrs' Graves at the main cemetery near the public gardens; in fact, all demonstrations came to include a march to this spot, which was treated almost as holy ground. And it was in the offices of the mosque that my father's office was located. He had been appointed director general of the Islamic Waqf, the religious endowment of Galilee, whose headquarters was the Jazzar Mosque. He loved being there, as the mosque had, in its lower cells, extensive archives. He was then completing his exams for the bar as a mature student; he felt it was important to be able to combat the Zionist aggressions on Palestinian land in a formal, legal way. Although he fought, with all his strength, against British policy and the British presence in Palestine, he had the highest respect for the British legal system, believing it to be independent of the political arm and to be characterized by integrity and justice. He felt that legal struggle was a sure way of regaining land acquired by the Zionists in illegal ways; and he was highly successful in this effort later—only to lose everything again in the upheaval of 1948! While still working as director general of the Galilee Waqf, he familiarized himself with firsthand information about the lands in Galilee and their rightful owners, information contained in those old archives.

We sometimes visited Father at his offices in the mosque. But there was a special trip I often took to the mosque which remained a secret.

In the mid-eighties, my two daughters visited me in 'Akka, where I was staying briefly. They both spoke at once: "We stood on the very spot, Mother, where you must have stood in fear so many times, holding back your tears. We went to the Jazzar Mosque, and a very old man with a hoarse voice showed us where Grandfather's office was and where his desk had stood. He said he used to serve coffee to Grandfather there." Was the man *Shaikh Sa'do*, I wondered? To my child's imagination in the mid-thirties, Shaikh Sa'do already seemed old, one of the legends of 'Akka. He was caretaker at the Great Mosque, but also served as a factotum for my father. Shaikh Sa'do had liked me at first, always laughing when I sang the song written about him by a worshipper who had lost the new shoes he left at the gate, as Muslims must do before entering a mosque:

> *Shaikh Sa'do, listen to me.*
> *My shoes were stolen from me.*
> *My shoes were black and shining,*
> *among the shoes of the crowd;*
> *were it not for shame and cleanliness,*
> *I'd have put them in my breast.*

The song had bouncy rhythms and rhymes, and the young girls used to sing it at our school and giggle. But I dared to sing it straight to Shaikh Sa'do himself. Soon afterwards, though, our friendship came to an end when a funny little story was circulated by Baghbaghan (which means "parrot" in Palestinian colloquial). This Baghbaghan was the town's gossip. If you wanted the whole town to know something, you let her hear about it. She had been widowed, and it was said that the missing half of her middle finger had been bitten off by her own son in anger at her spiteful tongue. It was supposed she was happy with her constant daily round of all the prominent families, who welcomed her, though half in terror of her tongue. Great was the surprise when it was rumored that she coveted Shaikh Sa'do. I wondered if anyone could covet that rugged, unceremonious fellow with the hoarse voice? My father used to send him to her with a monthly stipend from the Waqf money, and the story had it that on one of those occasions she said, "Shaikh Sa'do, let me put my cheese on your bread and let's make a life for ourselves together!" He was horrified. "Shame on you, woman!" he barked, then ran away. But she, true gossip that she was, told the story to some other women and, when I heard it being told to my mother, I couldn't stop giggling. Whenever I saw Shaikh Sa'do after that, I would murmur cruelly, "Why don't I put my cheese on your bread, Shaikh Sa'do?" and burst out into uncontrollable giggles. And from that time on he avoided me.

"We tried to work out the very spot where you must have stood," my daughters continued, "just opposite the corner of Grandfather's office where his desk was. And we saw the minaret, too. Then we went to the school building and walked along the same road you must have taken that day you told us about." "You tried to live that experience, then?" I asked them.

But no one can. It was one of those utterly terrifying experiences that take over a child's whole being, and even now the memory of it can still shake me.

It started one day at school, when I was almost nine. We heard the *adhan* call from the nearby Jazzar Mosque at ten-thirty in the morning. But that was no time for adhan. What did it mean? The teacher explained that this was not adhan but *tadhkir,* an announcement that some dignitary had died. In the recess, I went to the teacher. "If you please," I asked, my voice breaking, "Would they say tadhkir if someone who had helped found a party died?" "A *political* party, you mean?" she said. "Of course. Every minaret in the whole of Palestine would announce it." From that moment on, the tadhkir was the repetition of a constantly renewed nightmare. My father was a political activist, and one of the founders of the Istiqlal political party. If he should die, I reasoned, tadhkir would certainly be said; and so whenever I heard tadhkir, I would go tremulously to the teacher and say in a tone so decisive as to leave no doubt in her mind, "*Tridi,* if you please, I need to go out." She always let me, and down the stairs I would tumble. Then I stood behind a wall until Amm Ahmad, the school porter, had turned partially away, which is when I would run to the huge gate, open the small door in the left half of the gate, and dash to the mosque. I would run up the few wide stairs near the *sabeel* fountain and stand in a place where I could see my father when his door opened; then, the moment I saw him busy at work, I'd run back to my class again like lightning, often hearing Amm Ahmad's scolding remarks about "those who come so late to school."

Once, as I had begun crossing the large middle room at home (the *liwan,* we called it), I heard Father tell Mother, "It's as if, every now and then, I see Salma a long way off, while I'm at my desk. Then, when I go out to look for her, I find that she's disappeared without a trace, like a little genie." I looked at him, feigning complete innocence, but still he persisted, "Yes, I'd see her, red ribbon always loose on one braid." "That's Salma all right," Mother laughed. "You must be thinking of her all the time, and so you see her phantom everywhere, with the red ribbon loose on her braid!"

But he caught me at the end. I was standing in the usual place, but when the office door opened, there was no trace of my father. Had he perhaps gone to fetch a book from the opposite wall? I waited. Was he perhaps sitting with some guests in the opposite corner? I waited, Was he . . .? Time passed, but wild horses couldn't have moved me. I fought back the tears welling up in my breast and stood there, mesmerized, for probably fifteen minutes. Then, all of a sudden, two hands were laid on my shoulders and a most welcome voice called my name, "Salma, what are you doing here?"

My mind worked frantically to invent a quick excuse. "Baba," I wailed, tears of relief and embarrassment gushing out like torrents, "Baba, I am huuuungry!"

"That was very clever of you," my mother told me many years later. "You knew his preoccupation with feeding his family properly." I'd realized it, of course, instinctively. He'd often been hungry himself when he was a boy.

My grandfather had died when Father was very young, and he'd been left in the care of his older brother, Uncle Fayyad. A very handsome man of great piety and patience, Uncle Fayyad had married a girl from a poor background, and everyone around her suffered from this lady's memory of her impoverished early life. The marriage had been my grandmother's deliberate choice. During the First World War young Arab men were conscripted into the Ottoman army, but the Ottomans had also made a law that any young man married to a woman who was poor, orphaned, and had no adult male relative would not be required to join the army. Three of my grandmother's four unmarried sons were old enough to be conscripted, and so she searched far and wide to find "suitable" wives, coming finally to Sidon (or was it Tyre?) to select the wife for her oldest son. Having been poor all her life, the lady continued a tradition of penury, and my father suffered at her hands. Later, as a boarder at the Sultaniyya School in Beirut, enjoying the freedom of his own actions for the first time, he had, on his weekly outings from school, to choose between buying a book, or some delicious *fateereh* pastry or a piece of *kubbeh* in the bustling, colorful Beirut market. He often told us how he would stand pondering for a while, his stomach screaming for some delicacy, but how he would invariably buy a book instead. He was never going to let us suffer hunger, or long for something to eat, if he could help it.

So I, instinctively, exploited his preoccupation. He immediately called Shaikh Sa'do who came warily toward us, and, not realizing the broken state I was in, avoided looking at me. "Ahmad," Father asked, turning to his companion, "How would you like to have an early lunch with Salma?" It was already past eleven o'clock. "Shaikh Saʻdo can bring us some nice grilled *kabab* and *hummus,* with some *turshi* [pickles] and olives." His friend very readily agreed. He was Ahmad Shuqairy, who, in the sixties, became the first leader of the PLO, but at that time was a young, aspiring lawyer at the beginning of his political career. By a happy chance, my father's companion was bent on talking politics during that miserable lunch, and two Palestinian men talking politics had no time to notice a still petrified little girl choking on her food. I couldn't swallow a thing, but the two men were happily absorbed, eating in an absentminded way, enjoying the discussion. At last the ordeal was over. "Have you finished, sweetheart?" Father asked. I nodded in the affirmative. "Shaikh Saʻdo," he said, "take her back to school." Then, turning to me, he produced a shilling and said, "Here, buy some sweets."

Shaikh Saʻdo walked miserably on at my side till he realized, from my sullen silence, that he was in no danger. "What is a little girl like this brooding about, O God? What could have upset her so?" he kept murmuring as if to himself. I, for my part, was thinking hard. Jolted and thoroughly demoralized by my experience, I now felt ashamed of all the trouble I'd caused, of the meal I'd forced my father to buy, of having left my mathematics class when I needed to concentrate on it. Suddenly, a kind of a deep-rooted rationality took hold of me: "I'll never humiliate myself like this again! Never again will I listen to the devil. My father wasn't going to die. Of course he wasn't!" I decided then and there, as I walked alongside a sympathetic Shaikh Saʻdo, never to give in to this kind of fear again. And at that I felt the surge of freedom rise once more in my breast. My old mischievous spirit took hold of me again, and I looked at Shaikh Saʻdo, my eyes twinkling, "Let me put my cheese on your bread, Shaikh Saʻdo," I hummed in a low voice, and burst out into uncontrollable giggles.

Note: I checked these memories with Muyassar Abu 'l-Naja (Imm Riyad), who lives now in Boston but who was originally from ʻAkka and went to the same school as I did. I owe her many thanks for refreshing my memory.

European Colonial Rule and the Rise of Arab Nationalism (1830–1971) Establishment of the State of Israel (1948)

 Europe emerged as a collective superpower at the end of World War I (1918), when the official end of the Ottoman Empire was marked by the post-war treaties of Paris (1919), Versailles (1919), and finally Sèvres (1923). Turkey, the loser in the First World War, ceded control to parts of Europe and most of the Middle East, was granted Anatolia and Thrace, and declared itself a republic under the reformist general Mustafa Kamel Ataturk. Iraq and the territory known as Palestine/Jordan became British mandates; Syria became a French mandate. In addition, France continued its rule in Algeria, which it had colonized in 1830; Morocco, which was conquered in 1912; and Tunisia, which had been a French protectorate since 1881. Libya was subdued by Italy in a series of campaigns from 1911–1913. Britain kept its hold on Egypt and the Sudan as well as the crucial port of Aden.

Movements for independence from Europe had begun long before 1918 with the establishment of small groups in areas such as Syria, Lebanon, and Egypt, where they called themselves Arab nationalists. These early activists were products of the new Western schools and had learned their lessons well; they, too, wanted representative government and civil liberties, as well as control of their own natural resources of oil, phosphates, and cotton. Britain and France had actually promised the Arabs independence in exchange for their support against the old Ottoman Empire in World War I. But the 1919 Treaty of Versailles did not honor those promises. The division of the area into French, Brit-ish, and Italian protectorates not only created boundaries for countries that still exist today—Kuwait, Iraq, Jordan, and Tunisia—but fueled a wave of protests and uprisings that continued, with greater or lesser violence, until after World War II, when Europe began to withdraw from the Middle East. Coupled with protests in the Middle East were protests in Europe by the growing Zionist movement, which had won earlier support for its challenge to the Dreyfus case in France and its criticism of the anti-Semitic pogroms and persecutions of Jews all over Europe. Before World War II, many young Jews had emigrated to Palestine, then under British mandate, and calls for European support of this movement led to the famous Balfour Declaration, which stated that "His Majesty's government view with favor the establishment in Palestine of a national home for the Jewish people, and will use their best endeavors to facilitate the achievement of this object, it being clearly understood that nothing shall be done which may prejudice the civil and religious rights of existing non-Jewish communities in Palestine, or the rights and political status enjoyed by Jews in any other country."

How did these complex struggles translate into the everyday lives of the children of the time? Hoda al-Naamani still remembers the angry students who stoned her French secondary school in Damascus in the 1930s. Basima Bezirgan's family house in Baghdad was taken over for the use of British troops. In Egypt, Afaf Marsot faced the painful contradictions between local values and the lessons assigned by British teachers. Yildiray Erdener writes about his own father's decision to name his son not after Ataturk or the Prophet Mohammad, but in honor of the first republican Turkish submarine! Güneli Gün's father was a casualty of political differences in the new Turkey and hence was exiled to "Quarantine Island." Mahnaz Afkhami and Mohammed Ghanoonparvar document children's recognitions that old ways of life were disappearing. And Prince Hassan Aziz Hassan witnessed the end of the monarchy in Egypt, the withdrawal of Britain, and the rise of General Gamal Abdel Nasser's new Arab socialism.

World War II was a turning point for millions of people all over the world. To escape the dreadful genocide of the Holocaust, many European Jews fled to Palestine, then still under British mandate. In addition, many Jews who had lived for centuries in Arab lands, like Avraham Zilkha's family, settled in Israel. In 1947, after United Nations emissaries had been unable to resolve the conflict between resident Arabs and Jews emigrating into Palestine, the British began to withdraw. Jews successfully fought Arab armies for control of the land, and Israel was declared a state in 1948. Thousands of Palestinians fled; they became stateless refugees in camps set up by the United Nations in Lebanon and Jordan, camps which still exist.

Rural people suffered from the turmoil; this is clear, not from specific references to the struggles in the childhood memories of Halim Barakat and Zbida Shetlan, but from their realization that local economies could no longer provide a decent living for their families.

The final European withdrawal from the Middle East came in 1971. Aden ceased being a British crown colony in 1967 and declared itself an independent nation; by 1971, Britain had withdrawn completely from the Gulf.

SYRIA   *Hoda al-Naamani*

LEBANON   *Hoda al-Naamani is a distinguished poet and painter who lives in Beirut. She was born in Damascus, attended French schools there, and graduated from the law school of the Syrian University. After her marriage to her cousin, Abdul Kader al-Naamani, she moved to Cairo, where Dr. Naamani was dean of the American University in Cairo. Hoda Naamani considers herself a Sufi, and much of her poetry has been termed that. She writes regularly for Arabic newspapers and journals. Among her many books are* **I Remember I Was a Point I Was a Circle,** *which appeared in 1978 during the Lebanese Civil War and has been translated into English. Her paintings have been exhibited in London and Washington as well as in Lebanon.*

DAMASCUS THE GOLDEN

Hoda al-Naamani

 What I have been asked to remember I hope constantly to forget. A great nostalgia for my birthplace, Damascus, haunts me in my dreams, fills me with sadness, questions, and answers that make me sometimes fear that a source of beauty and respect is gone forever. A page from the history of our country, a page rich in dignity, honor, tradition, and magic has been dramatically turned.

During the thirties, Damascus was the spiritual wealth that meant to me, as to others, happiness, values, stability, and contentment. It summarized the East for us in its privacy, prejudice, and seclusion. Syria with its castles and palaces. Lebanon with its mountains, rivers, beaches, and meadows. Iraq with its mosques, deserts, and palm trees. Egypt with its Nile, pyramids, temples, its warmth of spices, cotton, and wool. The Arabian peninsula with its pearls, rubies, and the power of its holy places. Like one large, whirling circle, the windows, doors, and rocks of all these countries carry a hundred stories about dervishes, traders, caravans, conquests, knights, silk, velvet, perfumes, incense, merchants, and pilgrims. Here in this land is the trace of Adam's fall and of the blood of Abel, who was murdered by Cain. Here is the water which was transformed into wine by Jesus Christ. Here the head of John, still gazing at the world, was presented on a silver platter. Here is where Mohammad stopped and said, "I won't enter paradise twice."

Yes, Damascus, to me, is the beginning and the end of Creation, the throne of God. When I close my eyes, I see old Damascus as a flower from which life sparkles. Every dawn the windows and doors were opened. The streets were crowded with men going to their jobs, children going to school, women bustling to shop for what they needed. Sounds of carts and horses, drifts of scents and perfumes. Singing by the vendors.

A beautiful beginning. A general agreement among people about appropriate habits. For every job its clothes. For every village its summits. For each place and state its accents. Then, the same language, dreams, and memories did unify everybody.

I close my eyes and see Damascus wearing the confining garb of the night illuminated by the light of the minarets; I hear the murmur from the mosque's readings. For each month its ethics, motives, congratulations, and cakes. For each time its invocations. For everything, its fixed time—its claim— for meetings, for fasting, for prayers, for parties, for marriages; even for burial there was a specific hour. In those days, Wednesday was not the time to see a sick person, and Monday was the day to clean the house. And by 10 P.M. women were driven away from the roofs of their houses because that time had been set for men to sell doves.

I believed then that these routines demonstrated love, universal beliefs, justice, truth, and stability. How could I have been so naive and so idealistic? Why did I not see in the cultural, political, and economic opening to the west a new age that blew away the life and nature of Damascus? Travel, new languages, technologies, factories, electricity, offices, schools—all of these things were the beginning of separations and differences between social classes. How was it possible for the success of the Arab Revolt to lead to the division of the Arab countries (after the Sykes-Picot Agreement), to result in a convulsion that changed everything? How could the Mandate not be a shame, horrifying all those who are today so proud of the past? How could Damascus defend itself after these transformations which caused many other changes, changes in which stronger countries had a hand?

Why did I not notice these dangers when I was living in the midst of them? Did I not understand in my happy childhood that I was living not on a mountain rooted to the ground but on the back of an animal which was being pushed to move? For me, then, the Mandate was a toy, a distraction, a passing shame. I was proud of my French school because it was a temple of learning. Every day we were told that French culture was an example of orderliness that should be followed. France was the most beautiful country in the world; its history and literature the greatest. I still remember Victor Hugo's poems that we had to memorize.

Am I wrong to wish to forget this dilemma? My own family was governing the country at this time, so I was part of this conflict and irregularity. The conflict was dangerous, like playing with fire. Who is with whom and who is against whom? Where is strength? Who is capable of staying strong?

Who could save the country? Who knew the past? Who knows the future? Where was hope and safety, good and evil? I did not understand that the period of my childhood was the beginning of another era, of another danger, of another war. I did not see that all the world was beginning to change.

As a child, I believed it was normal for my house to be the biggest one in the district, to be open day and night, full of people, for political meetings and parties. I never judged my family's life. I believed that there was a logical reason for our wealth and social separation. Since Mohammad until now. Since the Ummayids until now. Since the Abbasids until now.

The families of Damascus were like a forest. Each family had its tree. The past was very important for the present. Only those who could trace their descent from Mohammad and his family were nobles (*ashraf*) and held titles and positions. And those who had noble lineages plus politics, land, and knowledge were the most lucky. By chance—only chance—we were one of those families. With this lineage, I thought we were invincible. Is not this a reason to try to forget?

In those days, pride about origins made all life choices very fixed, very direct, very easy. This was true for every relationship, especially marriage. Couples should come from the same class. Jobs should be suitable to social position. Such traditions and beliefs controlled everything. How could I not have noticed in other children's eyes other dreams, other hopes of better and different lives? At the time of political demonstrations, students from other schools would come into my school, throw stones at the windows (aiming for our hearts), run on our stairs, and knock at our doors. They asked us to come out, to share the revolt with them and cry, "Injustice!" Afraid of their anger, we would leave when school closed to go home rather than to join the protests. We did not understand that these sounds were not an expression of despair or weakness but the beginning of a conflagration that would destroy all the old principles and traditions and establish a new Damascus.

I did not understand the students who were protesting. I considered Damascus a paradise—my paradise—which was eternal and able to remain strong against any wind. Political differences, I felt, would be solved at the right time. And we were sheltered from these problems.

What did we feel when the streets were closed, when officers were pelted with stones, when nobody was allowed to go out? What was the government to do, we wondered, meet the protesters and ask what they wanted? We had been taught that every demand had a right to be realized if possible. But I thought that what was happening then was only a cloud which would eventually pass away.

Damascus was paradise for wealthy people. Differences in religion did not imply enmity to me or my family then. I looked at it as a way of knowledge, of richness. Most of the people who visited my house were Christians: the teachers of piano and language, the dressmaker, close friends who were artists, judges, doctors, and lawyers. Religious difference did not exist in front of food or laughter or poetry. Difference of religion—what was that? I never thought about it.

The difference in Muslim religious principles did not seem to be a problem either. Because the Sunni Muslims were the majority, we had no reason to question differences between Muslims.

For me, then, life was peace, perfection, and blessing. I thought that with the smells of coffee and the sounds of money came love, friendship, respect, and understanding.

As a child I lived behind a mask. I never tried to understand what is frightening and hurtful in life or to worry about what I did not know. Our house was heaven! What made me angry was if the servants did not answer when I rang the bell or if one of my dresses was not ready to wear for a joyful party. I took for granted my good fortune and even my good grades in school.

Oh God. In my memory, life was beautiful, perfect, innocent, and peaceful. There was no place for fear and danger in our house. The twenty rooms could hold hundreds of people. Tree-lined gardens had fountains fed by majestic stone lions. Tall pillars decorated the walls. There were pools of water, rooms of inlaid tiles, and doors made of carved wooden stars. Blue opaline lights hung from the painted arabesque ceilings. As they played with the water, the trees, and the colorful marble floors, the sun's rays illuminated the lemon trees, the thick grape vines, and the tall pots of flowers.

I remember all that. I remember also that I was an object of love, for I was the youngest, the child who had finally come after seven long years of waiting. All the love that used to be given to my mother—who was everyone's favorite—was given to me. This love protected me like the walls of a strong castle. I thought nothing could penetrate this earthly paradise, even death. However, I was wrong.

The sound of water only suggested nature's continuity. The sound of doves suggested a relationship between the earth and the sky. The playfulness and laziness of my cat Fulla created continual moments of tenderness. My grandfather's cloak was a symbol of the strength and greatness of the big house. The sound of my mother's slippers, decorated with feathers, signaled seduction and warmth. And stories! What stories were told in my house. Stories of pilgrims that my grandfather Gazzi led to Mecca nine times successively. About the caravans headed by the Naamanis which came from Beirut to Damascus on their way to Palestine and Egypt or to Iraq and Arabia. The tale of my parents' wedding in Beirut that lasted for seven days and continued in Damascus, where all the city's population was invited and many people took the train back and forth to our house. Stories about King Faisal or about Said Basha El Yousef (my grandfather's cousin who was the governor of Damascus). Jokes about this old, rich, and authoritarian age. Summer and winter provisions came on camels filling the streets, bringing food from my grandfather's estates: onions, potatoes, lentils, burghul, wheat. Horses carrying pots of honey and butter, tomato sauce, olive oil, baskets of eggs, milk and cream, sacks of bread, and watermelon.

Because of the nature of the era, work seemed a fantasy, not an obligation for everyone. The big door of our house stood open to welcome and help people. My Uncle Said, who was a minister and first deputy in the Parliament, used our street to deliver speeches and meet people during his election campaign.

I was seven years old when I shared these events and spoke at a political meeting my Uncle Said had set up at our house for Shukry Kouatly. I memorized a poem to recite, a poem written by Wadi Talhouna, my private teacher of Arabic literature. On the day of the party, the servants put on their best clothes. They set up chairs in the big garden, and a big table on top of which I was to stand. My mother worked with two dressmakers, preparing my dress. I was shaking. But I knew I must not fail. For I was supposed to be the star of the evening.

My father saved me.

"Do you see those chairs?" he asked.

I nodded.

"There are seven hundred of them. Nobody's sitting on them now, right?"

I nodded again.

"When people are here tonight I want you to imagine them empty."

And it worked! I was fine.

But I did know that war might come and take me away from these wonderful moments. Nothing stopped disillusion. Not even the stories of *A Thousand and One Nights*. Ends would come slowly in the darkness. Reality might grab you, take you by the shoulders, or strangle you and thus tell you the party is over. This is how the years fall away, or jump like a cat in the darkness, or disappear and reappear, like the voices that I still remember.

It was my aunt, speaking to my mother.

"Salwa, Salwa, what happened? I saw your light on and heard noises, so I came," she said, coming from her apartment to ours.

I jumped out of my bed and opened my door. My mother was taking a pan of hot water from Amina, the youngest servant; my father was smiling, although the traces of pain were clear on his face.

"Go back to sleep," he said to me.

My mother said to my father, "Fouad, you sat near the lake holding Hoda's hand. Why don't you care about your health? The cold and the humidity were bad for your kidney. You're just like the children."

"Salwa, don't exaggerate, I'm fine," he said, and added to my aunt, "Did you finish your makeup?"

To lighten the mood, my mother said, "Ihassan needs two hours to dress and two others for the makeup. There's a strong friendship between her and her mirror."

I did not laugh as the others did.

My grandfather came out of his room wearing his black cloak. "Maybe he's just exhausted," he suggested. "This month was very hard for him. Why does he make himself mad, trying to set up a new law for the farmers? They always rob us."

"He asked me to go with him to Beirut. I said no. Maybe he's mad because of that," whispered my mother.

"Stop analyzing. It's just the cold," said my father.

"It's not only the cold," said my mother. "You've lost fourteen pounds on this diet. We should try another way. I will call Dr. Roshdy immediately."

I went close to my father. I put a hand on his chest and told him, "Do not feel sick," and I went on to add, "Do not leave us." I was afraid. I did not sleep that night because I dreamed a woman in black was trying to get in my house through the windows. In the morning, my father did not watch me eating my breakfast and taking the big bus to school as he usually did.

When I came back from school he was still in bed. Around his eyes were big black circles. "Did the doctor come? What did he say?" I asked.

"Nothing, he is fine," said my mother.

But he was not fine. After a few days he felt better, but after that he became worse week by week. His handsome face paled because of the medicine. Even Arabic formulas did not make him feel better. After months without any improvement, the doctor decided to take him to the American hospital in Beirut. When my mother told me this, I cried very hard. I asked to go along but they would not let me go because of school. They came and went more than once. To me, my father seemed to be traveling far away.

During the holiday of the new year, we had a tree and my father decorated it with numbers and colored balls. However, the dark circles around his eyes were bigger and bigger. He became the central subject of interest for all the people in the house. Silence for Fouad. Special food for Fouad.

New pajamas for Fouad. A new clock for Fouad. Nothing else was interesting. The political problems, the loss of a crop because of rain, the fighting between my uncle and his wife, and the threat of their divorce became less important. My father's sickness and suffering were the most important events for everybody. Everyone was especially nice to me—as if a catastrophe was about to happen.

The catastrophe took place on February the fifteenth. They took my father to Beirut for the operation. That night I saw in my dream a black owl making horrible sounds up on one of the trees in my house. And in my dream suddenly the owl left the tree to sit on my chest and started screaming in my face. I shouted, of course, and cried so hard that the bird left. More than one person came into my room to see what was the matter. But what could I say? Could I say that a bird came from my dream to sit on my chest? That his eyes, his mouth . . . I started crying. Suddenly the electricity went out. They brought candles and tried to calm me down. However, the bird's smell did not leave me and I sometimes still hear the sound of those wings near my face.

I got up in the morning. It was clear to me that I was not the first child to have this dream. The stories of my childhood contained many similar examples in which walls crouched and objects spoke. These were nights, the magicians used to say, of battles between evil and good, innocence and injustice, peace and war. Was the bird a messenger of bad news? Was it singing of the possibility that the sky could be opened? I remember worrying about what I could say and whom I could tell about what happened.

I was getting ready for school. I was combing my hair and looking in the mirror when the blue ashtray I had given my father months before fell and broke. I became frightened. No one had touched it. It broke by itself, but who would believe me? A few minutes later I heard noises. Someone was running upstairs. I heard my uncle saying, "In the night at 2 A.M., Fouad left us." I was eight years old. He was forty-two. He left by himself. And the old Damascus left with him.

Yıldıray Erdener

TURKEY   *Yıldıray Erdener was born and received his early education in Turkey. He studied music and the art of the cello in Germany and received a diploma from the Staatliche Hochschule für Musik in Freiburg. His Ph.D. is in folklore and ethnomusicology from Indiana University, and he is the author of many articles and books; notable among them is* **The Song Contest of Turkish Minstrels.** *He teaches at The University of Texas at Austin.*

TOO HEAVY A NAME

Yıldıray Erdener

 In Turkey, those who feel connected to Islamic culture give their babies Islamic names. Others argue that we should use old Turkic names because we originally came from Central Asia. Another group either makes up their babies' names or uses already made-up ones. My parents made up names for all four of their children. I am named after a submarine. After the Second World War, Turkey purchased three submarines from Germany, a former ally in the First World War. The Turkish government named the submarines *Batıray, Saldıray,* and *Yıldıray.* In Turkish *ay* means moon or month, and the verb roots preceding *ay* (*batır, saldır, yıldır*) mean to sink, to attack, and to scare, respectively. My father, a customs clerk who had an interest in military things, must have liked the made-up names of the submarines, for he chose to call me Yıldıray. My three sisters are named Ilkay (first month or first moon), Birgül (a rose), and Esen (the one who breezes or creates a breeze).

I was born in Trabzon but spent my first five years in a village called Iskefiye, which is located on the eastern Black Sea. At the center of downtown Iskefiye, there was a small mosque and a huge mulberry tree. That tree seemed to be the center of my early childhood. During the season when the mulberries were ripe, villagers shook the branches of the tree early in the morning while people held a big net underneath to collect the mulberries. Since the tree belonged to the village, whoever was present got some mulberries. Neighbors who heard the sound of the shaking tree rushed there to get their share. The whole village was always on the alert, listening for the particular sound of the branches at dawn. My mother, who arose early to pray, always heard the sound of the tree. She would quickly awaken us and, with sleepy eyes, we would grab a container and rush to the tree as fast as we could.

Early one morning, instead of the pleasant sound of the mulberry tree, we heard gunshots coming from the center of the village. We later learned that a man had been killed when he was leaving the mosque near the mulberry tree. There was an ancient blood feud between two families from Tonya, a place well-known for blood feuds. One son, only a small boy when his father was killed, had followed his father's murderer for years. He finally carried out his revenge early that morning in front of the mosque.

As a four-year-old, I could not understand how one person could take another person's life, because my maternal grandmother used to tell us that the angel Azrail would take the souls of people to end their lives in this world. I remember asking my grandmother if Azrail had lots of guns. After that incident, I did not want to go near the mosque or the mulberry tree. Because of this shocking experience, I came to dislike guns and, later, the military.

The downtown area of Iskefiye was about a kilometer away from the seashore, but we never went swimming because our parents told us scary stories about people who were taken away by the Black Sea's big, powerful waves. The sand contained puddles full of mosquitoes that transmitted malaria and I remember once having a high fever and in the next second getting terrible chills. My mother covered me with all of our quilts, although it didn't help my terrible shivers at all. During the first five years of my life I was sick most of the time and my maternal grandmother (Fikriye), who gave unsolicited advice to everyone, told my mother to change my name, because Yıldıray was "too heavy" a name for me. She insisted that I should have a Quranic or a religious name such as "Osman," the name of the third Caliph after the Prophet Mohammed; this was also my paternal grandfather's name.

My grandfather Osman came from Caucasia in the 1850s. After the Russian forces invaded Circassia, about one hundred and fifty boys were sent to the Ottoman Empire. My paternal grandfather was among them. He was adopted by a big landowner near Trabzon and was given the name of Osman. For some reason, he got married late in his life. When he died at the age of fifty-one my father (Ömer) was only one year old. By a strange coincidence, my father also died at the age of fifty-one and I thought that there was an undiscovered gene which determined people's life-spans, and I must have inherited it from my father. I was prepared to die at the age of fifty-one, but fortunately there was no such gene.

My maternal grandfather, Sahbaz, who was Georgian, used to live in Batumi, an area controlled by the Ottoman Empire from the sixteenth century until after the Russian-Turkish War of 1877–1878, when it was ceded to Russia. His parents arranged his marriage and my grandmother moved from Trabzon to Batumi. When the 1917 Bolshevik revolution took place, my grandparents left everything, including their "beautiful home" with the stove still lit, and hopped on a tiny boat bound for Trabzon. Although my grandmother was happy to come back to her family, her husband was restless. During the Stalinist era, people inside Russia were not permitted to correspond with people outside. My grandfather never saw or corresponded with any of his family again. After 1948, he lived in Istanbul; whenever Russian tourists came to Istanbul, he followed them around, trying to get information about his family, especially about his brothers who were supposedly exiled to Siberia and later died there.

When my name was changed from Yıldıray to Osman, I did not respond to the new name for a long time until I got used to it. Although I was rid of the "heavy name," those terrible malaria attacks stayed with me. One day I asked my mother if I could take back my old name because I didn't like the new one. She said that the name of Yıldıray had never been changed on my official birth certificate, and that if I wanted to I could use it later. All my relatives and friends called me Osman until I graduated from elementary school.

When I was a small boy, we did not have any money to buy toys. But one day we got a big toy without paying any money at all. A Russian plane, low on fuel, made an emergency landing in the sand on our playground. It was such exciting news for a small, sleepy village with a population of several hundred people. As no one in the village had ever seen a plane before, the entire population of Iskefiye came to see the plane in our playground. My father and other town officials arrested the pilot and sent him to Trabzon, but his plane stayed in that sand forever. After the grownups lost interest in the plane, it became the children's favorite toy. We used to jump down from the wings onto the sand, sit on the pilot's seat, and pretend that, unlike the Russian pilot, we were the best pilots in the world.

Besides this big toy, the only other toy I had was a small red car. I used to wind it up and watch with admiration and excitement as it went around in circles. I had such a burning desire to open the car and see what made it move like that. One day I did. I was, of course, unable to put it back together again. I remember crying bitterly for a long time because it was my only toy. Today my children have many toys and every Christmas we buy them many more, although Santa Claus gets the credit, and they think that they don't have enough and want more. Because I didn't have any toys, I started making my own toys with clay. My two sisters and I made little animals such as donkeys, cows, and lambs. The exciting part was to put a bunch of green grass in their mouths. For some reason that was my favorite thing to do; I liked it very much.

We had neither electricity nor running water in our house in Iskefiye. My father used to bring home a whole leg or shoulder of lamb and, using a butcher knife, my mother spent hours chopping the meat to make burgers. Because we had no electricity, we did not have a refrigerator or an icebox, and I do not remember how we preserved our food.

I was five years old when I entered the first grade. Although the required age to start elementary school was seven, I was permitted to come into the class because my father knew the principal of the school, who was also the only teacher for all five grades. All the students sat in the same room and our teacher used to move from one grade to the next giving his lessons. Parents and students did not complain about the poor conditions of the school because there was no other way of getting an education.

During the first school year, my father was appointed clerk to another small town (Viçe), which was located east of Trabzon. While my parents were packing to move, I fell down on the grass and dislocated my left elbow. Years later, when my mother talked about the incident, she said that my dislocated lower arm was hanging down and was held only by the skin. My father immediately found an old woman who was a specialist in broken and dislocated arms and legs. Using egg yolks, she prepared an ointment and applied it to my elbow. After we moved to the new village, another accident happened. I stepped on my untied shoelaces and fell down, dislocating my elbow again. This time, there was no village doctor to take care of my arm; when we finally did find one, it was already too late. She said that it would be too painful to re-dislocate the arm and therefore decided to do nothing. Since then, I get nervous when I see a child with loose shoelaces.

Our house in Viçe was very close to the ocean with only a road between the pebble beach and our house. My sister Birgül and I used to walk on the beach for hours, collecting interesting pebbles and sea shells. When there were big storms, beautiful white waves came all the way up to the door of our house. I can vividly remember our dining room, which was an extension of the kitchen. At the dinner table, only my father and my mother used to talk and we children were prohibited from laughing, talking, or expressing any opinion. I still don't say much at the dinner table because my children have lots of stories to tell, and they, of course, giggle. I often ask them if we can take turns so that I can tell them about my day.

Since we were not permitted to laugh at the dinner table, there was always something to giggle about. This, of course, made my father angry. All of us were afraid of him. I was thirteen years old when he died. I have no memories of my father and me spending quality time together. He never kissed or hugged us or showed any real affection. We knew from my mother that he loved us because he kissed us when we were asleep, and told her that he didn't want us to be spoiled. I don't remember my father showing any affection towards my mother either. In the Middle East, married couples do not display affection in public, in front of their parents, or their children; even holding hands is often considered inappropriate behavior.

My father was not a religious person. He did not go to the mosque, fast during Ramadan, or perform the daily prayers. My mother, on the other hand, was a pious Muslim. She felt sorry for my father, and felt responsible for teaching us the religion of Islam. She said that she would go to hell if we did not memorize some chapters from the Quran. Since Turkish is not related to Arabic, we memorized a few chapters to make her happy, but we did not understand a single word, except for the word Allah. In my teenage years, she used to ask me to go to the mosque on Fridays, but I usually took a walk instead.

We grew up hearing all kinds of stories about the jinn who were everywhere. Some of the jinn were good (Muslims), and some were bad (infidels); the bad ones caused sickness by entering a person's body. As small boys, we used to seek the permission of the jinn when we urinated outside. There was a young man in our town who had epileptic seizures and everyone was convinced that he must have made the jinn angry. At night, we were extremely nervous and afraid of the dark. Since our bathroom was at the end of the porch, we usually went there as a team; while one was inside, the other one waited outside. One night I took the kerosene lamp and decided to go alone. As soon as I entered the bathroom, I heard a strange noise which did not resemble any noise I had heard before. I was absolutely certain that it was the Jinn. I quickly ran back to the house, leaving the lamp in front of the bathroom, not even having time to pull my pants up. Reciting something from the Quran, my mother, sisters, and I came back to get the lamp and found a baby bird that had probably been attracted to the light and fell from a nest.

Perhaps it was fear of the jinn that made me always carefully collect the cuttings of my fingernails. I made sure that no one could get them. It was only later that I realized hair and nails contain soul-stuff and could be used by enemies. After reading James Frazer, I understood exactly why I had collected my nail clippings; he suggests that any object that was once in close physical proximity to a person retains an essential connection with that person even after physical separation has taken place. These beliefs about the power of hair and nails and jinns is prevalent throughout the Middle East.

When I observe my behavior, I realize how much I have been influenced and shaped by my childhood and my culture. Although I do not believe that nail pairings contain soul-stuff, I still collect and dispose of my nails carefully. Stories about the jinn, the change of my name to a Quranic one, and other events of my childhood shook my belief in religion. The death of the man in front of the mosque made me an anti-gun, anti-military person. Like everyone else, I am the product of my childhood.

Hassan Aziz Hassan

EGYPT *Hassan Aziz Hassan was born in Cairo in 1923, the second son of Prince Aziz, brother of King Fouad, who was succeeded on his death by King Farouk. Prince Hassan was educated at home with his brother and sisters, and then sent abroad to school in England and in Turkey. In 1952, when the Free Officers under Gamal Abdul Nasser took power and King Farouk was deposed, Prince Hassan stayed in Egypt. A well-known painter whose works are in many private collections in Europe and the United States as well as in Egypt, Prince Hassan died in 2000.*

HASSAN
AZIZ
HASSAN,
RIGHT

SAN REMO AND MARG

Hassan Aziz Hassan

The First World War was the cause of my father's exile from Egypt and his meeting my mother in Spain. An ardent nationalist, he was informed by the British authorities in Egypt in 1913 that he was to choose a foreign land as his home. He decided on Spain and there he fell in love with my mother, a beautiful Spanish girl with black hair, big reddish-brown eyes, a splendid complexion, and a wonderfully easygoing disposition who could be equally delighted with the most trivial or beautiful things that life would offer her.

To marry Prince Aziz, my father, she had to become a Muslim, and this she did, choosing to be known henceforth by the name of Ikbal. Despite the considerable difference in their age, I believe that theirs was a truly carefree and happy union. Their two elder children, my brother Ismail and my sister Hadidja, were born in Madrid, followed by my sister Aicha at the palace of Shubra in Cairo and myself in San Remo, Italy.

In summer we used to move to our Italian home at San Remo. The departure was quite an expedition, as each child had his or her own nurse, apart from the maids, chauffeurs, Berberine servants, and dogs; one year we had eleven Alsatians and two Pekinese with us.

My father built our house just outside San Remo. All the rooms faced the sea, and the main Riviera road ran behind the house, between us and the hills. The garden, which was extremely long, was surrounded on the road side by a high wall and on the sea side by a low parapet that overhung, much further down, a small strip of farmed land, and, even further down, the pebbly beach where we used to swim.

Life was completely informal for us children, as we picknicked in the hills, swam in the sea, and played with our friends, the children of the farmer below us. At night I remember running out in the garden to try and catch the fireflies so luminous in the gentle Mediterranean air.

My father always had guests. The Sultan of Turkey would pass by or his cousin the Khedive Abbas Helmi II of Egypt, then both in exile. Many other friends came, also, who were relatives or people of interest.

This was our European headquarters from where we used to travel to France or Spain, usually in two cars. I have vague memories of crossing the Pyrenees and getting lost in the dark with a heavy mist around us. I remember the scent of carnations as we crossed the frontier at Ventimilia. While formalities were being completed, a young man strummed a guitar and sang. Monte-Carlo, Fontainebleau, is where we spent a winter while my brother Ismail attended school at nearby Melun. Fakhri Pacha, our ambassador to France, came to see us and entertained us in Paris, where my mother considered driving too dangerous to one not born in that city. Thus we abandoned cars for local taxis!

This happy-go-lucky existence was to last only during my father's lifetime and a few years more while my mother was left in charge of us. For unexpected powers were to disrupt our quiet little world.

My father died at the age of fifty-six from the aftereffects of an overstrenuous slimming diet. Sixteen days of official mourning were proclaimed and the state funeral was suitable to my father's position. As children, we were not allowed to attend.

But what impressed spectators most, according to observers, was not the pomp and ceremony of the occasion but the enormous crowds along the way that were held back by cordons of police under the command of Russell Pacha on his white horse. The whole country seemed to have collected together in those streets to bid him a final farewell.

For us, nothing would ever be the same again. In our father's name, my mother gave the yacht, the Cavala, to the nation as a gift, and Egypt used it as a training ship for naval cadets until the Second World War, when it was sunk bringing supplies to Tobrouk.

My father's affairs had been grossly mishandled during his exile, and, just as things were straightening out, he died, leaving his widow in what for her was a foreign land, in a confused situation, and with a group of more or less hostile in-laws.

So my mother left Shubra to take a convenient flat in town, where she managed as well as she could with lawyers and tutors as well as in-laws, not all hostile but mostly so. But there was one refuge left—San Remo, and as time went by, we stayed there more and more in idyllic bliss, until the disadvantages of royal birth suddenly loomed up between us and normal family life.

King Fouad, Grandfather's brother, had been invested by my father with the supreme authority over our upbringing. And the course of that upbringing became, quite soon after my father's death, a matter of discussion within the larger family. My mother, after all, was a foreigner and not expected to know much about the family's traditions and ways. Thus the idea got started that the childless Princess Ziba, the youngest of my father's four sisters, might be a more suitable person to bring us up. The suggestion was raised in a grand family council composed of King Fouad himself; my aunts; my grandfather's sister, Aunt Nimet; and her husband, Mahmoud Moukhtar Pasha, who was also our great-uncle.

The idea did not begin with Princess Ziba, who would have been terrified at the thought. But everything was pointing to our landing in her lap when the unexpected occurred. Moukhtar Pacha, addressing himself to his wife, my great-aunt Nimet, asked her if she would not consider looking after us; all their children had grown up and the house was empty without them. King Fouad was delighted at the suggestion, as he was very fond of his sister, and joined his wishes to Moukhtar Pacha's proposal. That settled the matter; after all, the King was the King, the head of our family, and his wishes were law among us. Aunt Nimet readily adapted, being utterly devoted to her husband and always willing to accede to his wishes. So Aunt Ziba returned to her solitary five prayers a day and we were to join Aunt Nimet and Mahmoud Moukhtar Pacha in due time at Marg, their estate near Cairo.

Let it be said here that this arrangement was strictly against my father's wishes, as in his remarkable will he demanded that we be brought up away from the rest of the family, that my brother and I should become an engineer and a doctor respectively, and my sisters should become trained medical nurses, for people of these professions would always be needed come what may. He also specified that we should not touch a piastre of our inheritance before the four of us were able to earn our own living by the stated professions. The day would come, he continued prophetically, when we would be reduced to these means as our only source of livelihood. But there was no one to heed the stern words of the dead, for the sky was without a cloud and the sun shed a glorious light on the generous valley of the Nile, which seemed to us our indestructible home.

The first to leave for Marg were my sisters, followed after a few months by my brother, and then myself, when I was about nine years old. I remember well arriving with my mother at Marg one beautiful afternoon and meeting Aunt Nimet for the first time. She was seated in the main drawing room wearing a pale blue gown reaching to the ground with a sprinkling of diamonds on her chest. Hair carefully set, she was very composed and very regal with extremely expressive dark eyes and a firm, wide mouth. I was shy, hardly managing a mumble when talked to but consoled by the presence of a most beautiful painting hanging behind my aunt. It was a Claude Gelée Le Lorrain landscape I grew to love dearly and which has influenced my taste in art all my life.

My mother seemed to be her usual self, talking mainly about me, my habits, and health, and all seemed very normal until the moment for parting arrived, and then she could no longer restrain her tears. I did not completely realize that I was leaving her forever and, although I was rather bewildered, it was not till later that I understood the irreplaceable loss. In the meantime, I was looking forward to meeting my sisters whom I had not seen for some time; but for my mother it was the handing over of her last child, her last born, and the solitude of a home without her children.

Looking back, I find surprising how easily I adapted myself to my new life despite the fact that I was passionately attached to my mother and, being the youngest, had been something of a favorite child, pampered, spoiled, and capricious. True, she could come and see us once a month, and Marg was only twenty minutes by car from Cairo, but surely nothing can replace the atmosphere of one's home under the natural guidance of one's parents.

When my aunt decided to live at Marg, the Palace of Marg was a simple hunting lodge set in grounds that were partly desert and marsh. In front of the house were four date trees. From this wilderness my aunt was to create a home of great charm. The marshes for miles around were drained, the desert pushed back, and beautiful formal gardens laid out. Lawns, a golf course, tennis courts, a small forest, long alleys bordered by tall eucalyptus trees, and fruit groves surrounded by hedges all sprang up under careful supervision and design. Fifty gardeners under the control of an old Italian kept this lovely creation in impeccable form. Not a leaf out of place, not a grain of red sand in disorder. No detail was too small to escape my aunt's notice, and it was this careful supervision that gave the place the air of a royal residence, for the "palace" itself remained a roomy, unpretentious, one-storied house which my aunt would refer to as her bungalow.

Our day was carefully organized, starting with a morning visit to our aunt and uncle, followed immediately by a series of teachers and tutors for French, Turkish, Arabic, history, mathematics, and geography, and, of course, a sheikh for the Quran; then we had a luncheon break, which was followed by more classes and homework. At sunset we used to walk around the garden with Miss Machray. She was a wonderful Englishwoman who had been in the family since her early youth as a companion to Princess Eminé, Aunt

Nimet's sister, to whom she was utterly devoted. At Princess Eminé's death, Miss Machray came to Marg; when we arrived, she was set to look after my sisters and myself. Tall, straight, and vigorous, she had a plain face, great character, a charming smile, and a very musical voice. She spoke Turkish like a Turk and knew all the intricacies and ways of our family. At times she would accompany Aunt Nimet on visits and could not be distinguished from any other Oriental lady of her position.

We would walk with her around the ground until we reached the part of the garden where the fields started. There we would wait for the sun to set beyond the estate of Marg and its cluster of mud-brick huts around the little mosque that was outlined against an orange and green sky. The muezzin in a distant voice would call the faithful to prayer. Slowly the light would change and peasants with water buffaloes, sheep led by a donkey, would make their way home through a soft haze of dust, while birds flew low over the darkening fields.

Aunt Nimet was the last surviving daughter of the Khedive Ismail and as such the last of King Fouad's sisters. This gave her a unique position in the family, and both her royal brother and her other relatives often accepted her opinions on subjects as law. She was the most remarkable woman I have as yet met: regal without the least pompousness or any mannerisms; a sense of humor; an education combining old traditions with the most up-to-date scientific views; an intellect abreast with the latest literary or philosophical thoughts in English, French, or German (languages she spoke equally well); a devoted wife; and an impeccable public figure who commanded undisputed respect. She was born to rule, and the miniature example one had of her capacities in her household and family life proved that she would have done well in wider fields of action. However much I disagreed with some of her attitudes or autocratic decisions, she always left me with the uncomfortable feeling that in a mysterious way she was invariably in the right. I can only think of her with a feeling of the utmost affection and respect.

Life at Marg was very different from San Remo or Shubra. Life with our parents might have been compared to the music of Schubert or Schumann. But Marg had more of the classical rigor of Handel.

After the novelty of our new environment had worn off, we felt keenly the absence of our mother. With me at one time it must have shown quite visibly, as I recall Miss Machray saying, "My dear, your aunt is quite ready to love you if you do exactly as she wants," and my answering naively, "I did not know one had to prepare oneself to love." Yet I cannot think of a better substitute for genuine affection than well-organized discipline, though to us it seemed a bit far-fetched at times and a little artificial. The morning ceremony of greeting our aunt was a fairly good example: we would leave Uncle Ala'adin's house (my sisters dressed in their dreary no-nonsense dresses), cross the grounds, stop in the rose garden to pick one flower each to offer our aunt, proceed to the main house and up the steps into the hall, turn to the right into a small drawing room or anteroom, and then enter our aunt's boudoir, which was separated from her bedroom by a lofty archway. This room was very pleasant with comfortable furniture and armchairs covered in a pastel cretonne.

Our aunt would be sitting in an armchair facing the door at a slight angle; on each side of her stood small tables covered with books or paper, pens, and pencils. She would be perfectly groomed (I never saw her otherwise) in a dressing gown reaching the floor, with perhaps a servant on a footstool near her or another servant behind her chair massaging the back of her neck.

We would enter just inside the room and plunge into a deep témménah, or obeisance, advance according to age, the eldest first, kiss our aunt's hand, and raise it to our forehead, while simultaneously she would kiss us on both cheeks. Then we would present her with our flowers, which would be handed to a waiting servant to be put in water; then we would plunge into another témménah, take a few steps backwards, and wait for permission to be seated. Out of respect, we would sit on the edge of the chair rather than leaning back; our hands were to be folded in our laps and our ankles crossed slightly to one side.

There were of course variations of this theme. If one had done something to displease, there would be only one kiss on one cheek; something worse—no kiss at all, just the hand; something even worse, not even the hand, just a severe look of recognition; or worse than this, just a glance while proceeding with whatever she was doing.

But in normal circumstances, she would talk to us very pleasantly, and we would answer but not start a conversation. Then she might carry on with whatever she was doing or have the telephone brought to her while we would wait in silence. If there was some question we had to ask, we would consult Miss Machray, who would inform our aunt beforehand; if the subject was approved, Miss Machray would tell us to go ahead and broach the subject with our aunt. After a time she would dismiss us; we would do a témménah and, walking backwards to the door, leave.

All this seemed rather formal to begin with, but soon it was the only natural thing to do, especially as it was the same procedure in all branches of the family between the younger and older generations of both sexes. When I, just under ten, was introduced to my little cousin Faizi, who was about two years younger than myself, he of course kissed my hand; but not being used to the custom from children, I also kissed his, thinking that the least I could do was to be as polite as he was!

My brother Ismail was the only one who could get around Aunt Nimet's forbidding manner when in trouble. He could be extremely comical. One day after lunch we were all sitting in the small drawing room next to the dining room. There was always a moment of silence after meals while Aunt Nimet made a silent prayer of thanks for the food received that day; after that the conversation became general, except that day Ismail, who for some reason was in disgrace, was sitting rather apart from the rest of us and was supposedly being ignored by our aunt. However, she could not help glancing in his direction from time to time. There he was in penitence but with such a funny expression on his face that finally she could not refrain from laughing and all was forgiven, if not entirely forgotten.

But things changed for me rather quickly. I was sent to Turkey in 1933, at the age of nine, to live with an American family at the International College in Izmir. When I was eleven, my family sent me on to England, where I received a good classical education at Leighton Park, Reading. In 1940, after the outbreak of World War II, when I was sixteen, I was brought back to Egypt. I have lived there ever since.

Basima Qattan Bezirgan

IRAQ *Basima Qattan Bezirgan was born in Baghdad, educated in Iraq (B.A.) and in England (graduate study in English) before coming to the United States in 1967. She is co-editor and translator of* **Middle Eastern Muslim Women Speak** *and has published many translations from Arabic poetry and prose with Elizabeth Fernea. She earned an MLS degree in Texas and now serves as the Arabic bibliographer at the Regenstein Library, University of Chicago.*

BASIMA
QATTAN
BEZIRGAN,
THIRD
FROM LEFT

AN IRAQI CHILDHOOD

Basima Qattan Bezirgan

 My earliest memory is from the year King Ghazi died. That was in 1939, and I must have been very small. Our house in Karradat Marriam in Baghdad was on the route of the funeral procession. People stood on the street to pay their last respects to the king. So we could see better, we went up on the balcony of our neighbor's house; he was a professor in the Higher Teachers Training College, named Taha Rawi.

Soon after that, we moved from Baghdad to Diwaniyah, for my father's business. He was really a scholar and poet and did not care much for business, but he had twelve children. So my grandfather, my mother's father, a well-to-do businessman, set him up in Diwaniyah and gave him a house to live in. Grandfather had come from Bahrain with money earned from the pearl industry and used his capital to buy up real estate. My father was responsible for collecting the rents and taking care of the property, which included a *seef* or granary and a *musafarkhan* or small hotel. After the harvest, farmers would bring their grain on camels and store it in the seef, which also had space for the animals. The farmers themselves stayed next door in the musafarkhan.

Our house in Diwaniyah was built around a big courtyard with a small garden and lots of oleander trees, pink and white. In my memory, it was a wonderful house. We had a cow, too, somewhere nearby. My father hired a woman to milk the cow twice a day, so we had fresh, clean milk. That was a healthy cow, who calved regularly; as children, we would go to visit the cow and her new calves.

I was the last of the twelve children. One died at birth, so my mother had twelve pregnancies. Being the youngest was both a blessing and a curse—a blessing because my parents spoiled me and a curse because my siblings were always working on me to do their errands. I feared and respected my older sister Bahija and my older brothers as much as I did my parents. If we were naughty, Mother would say, "Wait till your older sister comes home and I'll tell her what you've done." Bahija was a schoolteacher in Diwaniyah, and she eventually became headmistress of Diwaniyah's main school for girls. My mother gave her a lot of power and responsibility. If Bahija gave us permission to do something, my mother would go along with it, saying, "Okay, go ahead. Bahija knows what's out there in the world, not me."

My mother was illiterate but very intelligent. She was very young when she married, and her first child was born when she was still in her teens. My father was fifteen or even twenty years older than she was. He was a learned man, a grammarian, largely self-educated, who in his younger years taught in a private school. Mustafa Jawad, a well-known linguist and scholar in Baghdad, was a student of his, and my father encouraged him to go to France and study. The Shi'as had their own private schools then, and educated Shi'as felt it was a duty to support those schools and often volunteered their time to teach. My father taught languages, which included German and French as well as Arabic. He was part of the Iraqi nationalist movement against the Ottoman Turks.

What I admired and still think of with admiration about my parents' relationship is that my father raised my illiterate mother to his own intellectual level by reading to her. Early in the marriage, my sisters and brothers told me, Mother complained that my father always had a book in his hand, and so he began reading to her. After we were grown up, they used to sit together in the garden; he would read, she would ask questions, he would explain—they were almost like love birds in their old age. When he died in January 1954, she said, "I can't survive without your father." Five months later she died.

Those years in Diwaniyah were great for us as children. What we didn't realize was that we were lucky to have a place in Diwaniyah, for during the war, from 1940 on, the British appropriated all the houses in Karradat Marriam for Allied troops. Our house was one they took, and they didn't give it back until the end of 1947. They paid rent, but didn't ask whether people wanted them or not—they just took the houses.

Our house in Diwaniyah was next door to the seef, the granary where the farmers brought the wheat and barley to store and sell. The *wazzan*, an employee of my father, was the official weigher; he weighed the grain when it was brought in on camel caravans, before storage, and he weighed it again after it was taken out of storage to sell. The farmers paid my father a small fee to store the grain and stable the camels in the seef and to sleep in the musafarkhan. In addition to the wazzan, there were maybe a hundred men who worked in the seef and musafarkhan. My father paid them all; what was left was his. My father had a little office in the musafarkhan. Fawzia, Kamel, Mohammed Ali, and I, who were the four youngest kids, used to love to go in and see him and then go next door to the seef and ride the camels. That is, until one day when I fell in the mud, and a camel stepped on my back; after that I was afraid of camels.

As a little girl, I liked rice very much, and my father said he would have to marry me to a rice merchant! We ate dolma and *kubbeh,* and *marga,* a kind of stew, and rice with *bagella,* or broad beans, just like people do today.

I have good memories of the food preparation that went on in our house. As children, we all took part in the tasks of drying food and preparing it for the winter. That way we learned about the seasons and what each season produced. My mother instructed Zahra, our maid, to make the yogurt and cheese and ghee from butter, but we all helped in drying the vegetables—okra and lima beans. We had big needles and cotton upholstery thread. We'd string the okra and hang it between the pillars of our courtyard like necklaces. For the beans, we'd tear off the tops of each bean, then split them in half. We'd lay these bean halves on clean straw mats on the roof to dry. Sometimes we did eggplant and even tomatoes.

But what we looked forward to the most was making *ma'jun,* or tomato paste. No one does it much anymore, but in those days, there were no food factories and each house made its own, which we used for all kinds of things, especially the sauce for marga and also for dolma and many other dishes.

We made ma'jun in late summer when the tomatoes were cheap and ripe. Preparations started at least two weeks before. My father would ask one of his workers to come and collect the *tishts,* or big tubs, and the trays, and take them to the market to be re-zinced. When they were ready, Father would go to the wholesale vegetable merchants and buy crates full of tomatoes. He would go early in the morning, so when we woke up, the courtyard was full of tomatoes—eight or ten crates of them. Bahija and Mother would put the tomatoes into big strainers and wash them well with the hose before dumping them into the newly-zinced tishts. All the little kids put on old clothes; we washed our hands and everyone helped, boys as well as girls.

The littlest kids would sit around the tishts and pull the green stems out of the tomatoes. When one tisht was done, we got to squeeze the tomatoes and squeeze and squeeze—that was the fun time. Then the older, stronger children would squeeze some more until the peel began to separate from the tomatoes. The next stage was to scoop the tomatoes into strainers and press them through till every drop of juice was out. The leftover skins and seeds were put aside and given to Zahra, who dried them and used them for fuel.

The big boys first carried the trays up to the roof and then carried up buckets of the tomato pulp and juice, filling the trays. Mother would put salt in each one, and then cover each tray with cheesecloth to keep out flies and other insects. The tomatoes were left to dry for three or four days. Every morning Mother would uncover the juice and pulp and stir it up in the hot sun before covering it again with cheesecloth. By the end of the fourth day, the mixture had turned to paste, and the delicious ma'jun was ladled into *bastoogas,* which were big earthenware jars — I remember they had a beautiful turquoise glaze.

Each bastooga was covered with unbleached muslin to keep the air out; the covered bastooga was tied with string and then sealed with gypsum and put in the storeroom for winter. By the time we were finished each summer, we had two or even three enormous bastoogas full of ma'jun.

I went to primary school in Diwaniyah, and my sister Bahija was my second grade teacher. She was one of the few Iraqi women trained as teachers then; we had three Lebanese teachers. At the end of each school year, the teachers organized an exhibit of handwork, sewing, and embroidery. It went on for four days — two days for men and two days for women; the proceeds helped poorer girls pay for books and shoes and uniforms. We also sold cakes during the exhibit. Hundreds of people came. The cakes were the most popular; we sold all we had, because at that time not every person in Diwaniyah had an oven to bake a cake. (The *tanoor* ovens only worked for bread.) Bahija's handwork was highly prized — she was a master at embroidery, and she taught me, but I was never as good as she was. I exhibited for the first time in the sixth grade, a bedsheet with a border embroidered in blue thread. I worked so hard on that sheet that I decided not to sell it but to keep it myself. Needless to say, Bahija was not pleased with me!

On the big feasts, an amusement park was set up in the fields south of town. The children all got new clothes for the three days of the Iid al Fitr and the four days of Iid al Adha; my sisters and I had a dress for each day. We were lucky; and our father gave us spending money so we could ride the ferris wheel or the swings. At home, lots of guests came and offered the greetings of the feast.

Those years in Diwaniyah were good for us children but bad years for most of the people in the town. We didn't feel World War II very much, though there was some rationing, particularly of cloth. The shops would be allotted 5 or 6 bolts of cloth, all the same. People presented their ration stamps in exchange for cloth, which they used to make whatever they needed at the time. I remember wearing a new dress cut from that rationed cloth and then noticing that the neighbor had made curtains of the same pattern! We listened to the news every night from Turkey, which was considered a neutral country. After the news from Radio Ankara, we had dinner, and then it was family time—stories, poems, and games.

The worst thing about those years was the epidemic of tuberculosis. A majority of the people in the town were infected, and my parents were very afraid for us. In the house across the street from us, the whole family had TB and died one after the other. The last surviving member of the family, a daughter, often came to the *krayas*, the ritual prayers and sermons held during Ashura, the period of mourning for Hussein, the Prophet Muhammad's nephew who was killed in Kerbela. Mother took me sometimes, and I asked her why this girl cried so hard and beat her breast during the chanting. "She's mourning for her own family," my mother said, explaining that the girl identified with the survivors of Hussein. When that daughter died, my oldest brother, by this time a doctor, came to visit and told my mother how to protect us from the disease. We were told firmly that if we ate anything outside the house, we would die, and we believed him. We did have guests at the house, even then, but my doctor brother made my mother promise to boil the tea glasses after people left. And she did. None of us, fortunately, got TB. My illiterate mother listened to her son, followed his advice, and protected us all.

My brother Kamel died but not from TB. I was in the fourth grade then, and I didn't understand what was happening. No one told me what was going on.

"What happened? What's wrong with Bahija and Daddy?"

"Kamel died."

"What does that mean?"

"We won't see him anymore."

I remember going to Kamel's desk to get his pencil box, which I had always wanted. My mother yelled at me for one of the few times in my life, but my sister Bahija convinced her that it was okay for me to have that box.

Kamal's death was not easy for my mother. We had a tanoor oven on the roof, and we had a woman who made the bread for us. She'd come early to knead the bread and then again at noon to bake it. She'd lost a child, too, so she and my mother would sit and cry. I hated that woman because I thought she was making my mother cry. They didn't talk to children about death then.

My father lost his business when my grandfather died. My uncle Salim came and said everything belonged to him now. He was right, because my grandfather had put all the property in his son's name to avoid taxes. So Father worked as an accountant for a big merchant for two years, and in 1945, when the war ended, the whole family moved back to Baghdad. By that time, many of the children were grown and able to support the family so my father no longer needed to work. Abdul Rahman was a doctor, Abdul Wahab a pharmacist, Karim was working in a bank in Basra, Abdul Razzak was a civil servant, and Bahija was teaching.

I went to secondary school in Baghdad, a small-town girl going to the big city, and I was terrified. But it worked out. I was the only girl in the family who never wore the abbaya, the all-enveloping black cloak. Usually, girls were wearing it by the seventh grade. But we moved to Baghdad, and not everyone wore it there, so there was no need for me to put it on. Bahija had to wear the abbaya in Diwaniyah, though, and even the *pushi* or face veil. But eventually all the girls in our family living in Baghdad took it off.

We didn't get to move back into our Baghdadi house right away. The British took a long time to leave, and we had to rent a house for several months until the soldiers moved out at the end of 1947. We loved that house, too, which was the talk of the neighborhood, because my father had designed it as a "modern" house, that is, with no central courtyard. People said it was a European house. But my best memories are of Diwaniyah.

Afaf Lutfi al-Sayyid Marsot

EGYPT

*Afaf Lutfi al-Sayyid Marsot, born in Cairo, was educated in Egypt, the United States, and England. She was the first Egyptian woman to receive a D. Phil. from Oxford and to become a junior research fellow at St. Anthony's College, Oxford. Her many books include **Egypt's Liberal Experiment, Egypt in the Reign of Muhammad Ali,** and **Women and Men in 18th Century Egypt.** She is presently professor emeritus of history at the University of California at Los Angeles.*

AN EGYPTIAN CHILDHOOD

Afaf Lutfi Al-Sayyid Marsot

 My earliest childhood memory is being handed out of the kitchen window to my father on the back of a horse. Our house overlooked the desert in Heliopolis, an oasis and suburb of Cairo, and every morning my father went horseback riding in the desert. He often would put me up in front of him on the horse and send the horse galloping.

My father and I had a special relationship. I had two much older brothers, but I was the only daughter. A few years before I was born, my father found himself without a job. He had been a civil servant, and his last position had been as governor of the province of Giza. The civil service was no refuge against tyranny. King Fuad detested my uncle, Ahmad Lutfi al-Sayyid, because he was co-founder and ideologue of the opposition party in Egypt, but, because my uncle was not a civil servant, he could not be touched by the king. King Fuad decided to get to him through his brother, so he forcibly retired my father at the age of forty. This was also the year of Egypt's depression. The price of cotton fell drastically so that both my parents, who were landowners, found their incomes wiped out. They could no longer afford to live in the city and had to go and live in the village. There, my mother, a pampered lady of the high bourgeoisie and of Circassian/Greek descent had to learn to cook and clean and do all the things that previously a houseful of servants had done for her, all without the benefit of running water or electricity.

When she learned that she was pregnant with me, Mother thought it was the last straw, but suddenly my father was offered a wonderful new position. Marconi Broadcasting, which ran the Egyptian State Broadcasting station, offered him the position of director of the Arabic programs. The same year I was born, the price of cotton increased, and my parents were once again wealthy. Father thought I was an auspicious baby. I was his good luck charm who brought good things to him, he often told me. Where most Egyptian men are fondest of their sons, my father doted on me. Whenever we rode in the car, I would always sit in front with my father. Every Sunday, which was his day of rest, since the ESB was then affiliated with the BBC, he would take me for an outing; my brothers, who went to government schools that were closed on Fridays, were never included.

Our outings together taught me a great deal. At the zoo, Daddy would point out the different animals and tell me about their habits. When we traveled, he would ask me about the plants growing in the fields, teach me to identify the crops, and explain the process of agriculture. As a child, I was not really interested in crops and irrigation, but later on I realized the amount I had absorbed without even being aware of it.

At other times, he would take me to museums, and I am certain my love of history was nurtured through these visits. I was not aware that I was being taught history, but Daddy was a gifted raconteur.

Once, when I was about ten or twelve years old, we were visiting Saqqara and met with Etienne Drioton, the director of the Egyptian museum. That very morning they had just opened a tomb and discovered some delicate gold necklaces, which are now in the Cairo Museum. Drioton was literally jumping for joy at his discovery. His delight and enthusiasm made an indelible impression on me and helped foster an interest in Egyptology that grew over the years, especially when, in winter, we would spend a fortnight in Luxor and Aswan.

We also visited the mosques of Cairo, and Daddy would tell me tales from Maqrizi and other historians, so I learned Islamic history. Once in a while my parents would picnic with their friends near the caves of the Bektashi dervishes. We also went on picnics with my father's ESB colleague, the man who headed the foreign service, a Mr. Ferguson, who had three sons. Together the Fergusons and the Lutfis would picnic in the desert on the road to Suez at one of Abbas Pasha's ruined palaces. It was a sad day for us children when the Fergusons eventually moved back to England.

Once my parents' financial situation had improved, they went back to their old lifestyle. Soon after I was born, I was put in the hands of a most affectionate woman, Nonna Emma, a fat, jolly Italian woman who had lost her husband and her child and had no family in Egypt. My father told her that as she had lost her family, we were her new family, and I was her daughter, and that was how she treated me. She spoiled me and I adored her, every last gigantic inch of her, for she was a mountain of a woman. She spoke to me in Italian and that became my first language.

My mother was an aloof figure who only showed up to issue orders, so Nonna Emma and Daddy were the foundations of my life. Our house was filled with servants and young maids, and all of them, knowing how my father doted on me, spoiled me. I was a most biddable child and, compared to the naughty doings of my irrepressible brothers who were six and seven years older, less bothersome to the servants than they were. When they were younger, my brothers were given a French governess. But Mademoiselle did not last long when Mummy caught her hitting my younger brother Mohsen on the head with her sewing scissors. Both boys were then sent to school where they could work off their high spirits.

Nonna Emma encouraged my sweet tooth, for every day, after waking up from my afternoon nap, I would put my hand under my pillow and find a handful of sweets and chocolates. Nonna Emma was apparently planning on making me as fat as she was and gorged me on chocolate sandwiches and gateaux. But her diet did nothing except turn me into a chocoholic, for I remained a skinny little thing.

Nonna Emma died when I was barely five years old. I didn't know what happened to her, but one day she was gone, and nobody would tell me where she went. Then Mummy took me to church, which was a surprise, for though I went to church on Sundays with Nonna Emma, I had never been with my mother. My parents did not mind that I was taken to church. Daddy said there was only one God, and it didn't matter how He was worshipped, and the more one knew about other religions the better. This was a most liberal attitude for a Muslim family to take, but I suppose my parents thought I was too young to understand anything at that age, and they were absolutely right. All church meant to me was a pretty place with statues of a pretty lady and music. After the church service, Mummy took me to a strange place, and we put flowers on a marble stone. It was only later that I realized it was Nonna Emma's grave.

Nonna Emma was replaced by an English governess, Mrs. Queenland. She had been married to an Australian who ran out on her, and I didn't blame him. I would have done the same thing. She was a strict disciplinarian who taught me to read and write English and in the process inflicted the first corporal punishment on me. Every time I made a mistake between *am* and *an* she would twist my ear, which was painful and unexpected for someone who, up to then, had only received hugs and kisses from the entire household. I was so terrified of both my governess and my mother that I never dared complain of such treatment. The only time I complained was when, at the age of six, I went to a French convent school, Notre Dame des

Apôtres, where one of the nuns pinched me for some misdeed. I told my father who was so outraged he immediately took me out of school. From that point on, I was educated at home until I was old enough to attend an English school run by missionaries. A year later Mrs. Queenland died and, heartless child that I was, I delighted in her passing.

Mrs. Queenland and my mother believed that I should share my toys, of which I had more than my fair share. My bedroom looked like a toy shop, but I was only allowed to play with one toy at a time, which I thought grossly unfair. How could I give a tea party for my dolls with only one doll? This was very much like real life, for I was not allowed to mix with other children, not even cousins, because Mrs. Queenland decreed they had bad manners and would teach me naughtiness. Very rarely was a cousin allowed to come and play with me under the eagle eye of our warden. Occasionally my cousin Suad would come, but I hated her visits, because she always clung to my biggest doll and took it home with her. When I dared object to such acts of pillage, my mother and governess would scold me for being selfish since I had a roomful of toys. My favorite doll was Bella, who was not very big and didn't wear a gorgeous silk dress like the other dolls but had a lovely smile that captured my heart even when she lost her arms and legs in a battle with my brothers.

Husain and Muhsin were the bane of my life, especially Muhsin, who teased me unmercifully and always managed to make me cry. Then Mrs. Queenland would blame me for being a "silly child" who deserved punishment for playing with "naughty boys." I can't say this attitude did much for nursery harmony. My brothers and I waged wars against each other, which I constantly lost, for most of our preteen years. It was only when they reached their late teens that they came to tolerate me and even to spoil me in a careless fashion.

Our house was always filled with animals. One was a cat, an orange tabby called "Pussy," who had adopted my mother. She simply walked into the house one day, sat next to my mother, and refused to budge. Her owners finally gave her to Mummy. Pussy was a smart cat. When she wanted to be let into the house, she jumped and hit the doorbell with her paw so the servants could open the door for her. We had German shepherds in the garden, Shirley and Lucky, who had been trained by the police academy. My brother Husain also raised rabbits, doves, turtles, and a pet snake, which he kept in his violin case until one day when my mother opened the case. Her shriek could have been heard at the other end of town.

Heliopolis was then a small town and all the inhabitants knew one another. They all frequented the same sporting club, the same open-air cinemas, and the same tea shops. The only outings I was allowed to attend were at the Heliopolis Sporting Club with Mrs. Queenland. There, too, I played by myself, because I was too shy to play with the other children and would not have been allowed to do so anyway.

When Mrs. Queenland died, I had no other governess. By then, World War II had broken out. I remember Husain coming into the house one day with Daddy carrying paper bags of canned food, biscuits, and water and shouting, "Rommel is at our door." I hurried to the front door to see who this Rommel was and was most disappointed to find no one. A few nights later I was terrified by the first air raid. But great fun was in store for us. The boys and I were evacuated to our uncle's farm, where we had six cousins—five girls and one boy, who was just a year older than myself. My mother stayed on in Cairo with my father.

At the farm, we had a glorious summer. We rode donkeys all day long and visited other cousins. My father had thirteen brothers and sisters who were all prolific parents themselves and were scattered throughout the village. No one told us what to do so long as we showed up for meals. My aunt and uncle were loving people who gave us as much freedom as possible. We went fishing in the streams and when we caught a miniature fish and handed it to the cook with pride, he smiled and gave us fish for dinner. When cousin Ahmad and I doubted that the fish we had caught had supplied a whole meal for the family, the cook simply said that fish expanded when cooked.

One day one of the servants told my aunt that he had spotted a snake in the garden, so they sent for the snake charmer, the Rifaii. We watched in awe as his incantations drew an enormous snake from his hole and into his bag. My uncle laughingly claimed that the snake had come in the bag, but we always avoided that area of the garden.

Soon our parents felt that it was safe to bring us back to Cairo, and we left the farm with regret. That regret grew once classes had started at the English school. The missionaries' excellent education was tailored for a little English child. As an Egyptian, I did not relish the underlying theme, hammered into us daily, of the inferiority of my nation, my religion, and my culture. We were given scripture lessons, and I eventually won the scripture prize, but I remember standing in class one day and telling the teacher that what she told us about Christianity being the only path to salvation contradicted what we were told at home. "Who are we to believe?" I asked. "You or our parents?" The teacher grew red in the face and mumbled something about it being a personal decision. I didn't realize that my naive question was to turn me into a heroine in the eyes of the other Muslim girls in class who would remind me of this incident decades later.

Most of my classmates were either Christian or Jewish. The missionaries were trying to convert the Coptic girls and the Jewish girls to Protestantism. They had only one success among the Jewish girls, but many of the Coptic girls later became Protestants.

My dearest friends were two girls, one Jewish and one Christian. Religion didn't matter; what mattered was whether you liked or disliked each other. Most of the time I didn't know which religion the other girls belonged to. Many of the girls carried passports from different countries: Poland, Germany, Italy, and so on. Some had parents who were born and raised in Egypt but carried foreign passports to benefit from the Capitulations, which allowed foreigners rights of extraterritoriality. Other girls' parents were refugees who fled Nazi Europe.

School was a place where you were punished if you spoke any language other than English and where Anglophilia was the name of the game. There was a uniform, a most unattractive shade of brown that might have been lovely on British blondes but looked awful on darker Egyptians. All of our teachers were British except for Madame Chafiroff, an elegant Russian aristocrat who taught us excellent French, and Miss Bassily, an Egyptian, who taught us poor Arabic.

We were given the history of England for eight years running; the history of Egypt from the Pharoahs to the present day was taught in one trimester. I could recite the railway stations of the Canadian Pacific Railway but could not say whether Isna was in Upper or Lower Egypt. The school sought to turn us into little Britons who despised their country and culture and who knew little about either. It took many years for me to overcome that handicap.

It was at school that my talent for storytelling blossomed. Because I was a lonely child, I read voraciously. Before I could read, I would corner the maids and make them tell me stories. As I was also a sickly child, my mother would then sit on my bed and regale me with stories. That was the only time she paid attention to me other than to scold me for something. At school I would regurgitate some of these stories to my friends or invent new ones. Soon the circle listening to my stories grew, and invariably, I had an audience. When I was elected class captain, I could always make the class sit silently while I wove my stories. The teachers never understood how I kept such a rowdy lot quiet, and I did not see fit to tell them.

By and large, I enjoyed school, except for mathematics. We had a male math teacher who put the fear of God into all of us. He was sarcastic and nasty and hated us as much as we hated him. I never understood a word of his explanations and never dared ask for more. Eventually he left and was replaced by a kindly man who loved math and wanted us to understand it. I asked him for a few private lessons, and within a year, I jumped from being the worst in the class to being among the top students. Mr. Wissa encouraged me to spend three hours every Saturday morning at home doing one of the Oxford and Cambridge School Leaving Certificate Examinations, and I grew to enjoy them.

The love of my school life, however, was literature. There I shone and always got top grades. My love for poetry had been instilled in me by Daddy, who had learned thousands of lines of poetry by heart in three languages. He would assign *qasidas* or odes to my brothers and me for a pound each, which was a large sum of money in those days. Each mistake subtracted a piastre. After father's daily nap he would call me in and, while dressing, he would make me read some of his favorite poets, either Shawqi, who was a friend of his, or Mutanabbi, whom he adored.

I was reading *Masraʿ Cliopatra* when Daddy chanced to pick up the book and found every Arabic work accompanied by an English translation. That was when he decided to provide me with an Arabic tutor.

Shaikh Abd al-Basit was a gentle man who ate onions and chewed gum to cover up the odor. Throughout the lesson whiffs of onion were accompanied by long drawn out burps and mutterings of "al-Hamdu lillah." I can't say that he was an effective teacher, but he did tell wonderful stories. He was followed by a succession of more competent tutors, as I continued to have tutorials for the next several years.

Throughout my childhood, my father stressed the necessity of sports. Husain was a born sportsman who practised everything with ease, including falling off his horse, breaking his collar bone, and getting right on again. Muhsin took to fencing, and I took to nothing. Daddy made me play tennis, for which I had no natural affinity; the racket always flew out of my hand at the crucial moment. He also made me do calisthenics, which I despised. Horseback riding was fun, and every morning before school, he and I would go riding in the desert. One day my horse took off and I couldn't stop it. A few soldiers in a nearby camp managed to subdue the horse and in the process I fell off and cracked my ankle. My father was so proud that I had not done anything foolish like jumping off the horse that he bought me my first wrist watch, a Movado. My mother did not think much of this and stopped me from getting back on a horse again. Father protested that it would give me a fear of horses. My mother's answer was the equivalent of, "Big deal, next time she might break her neck." I did eventually acquire a complex about horses.

During the summers, we went to the seaside. Alexandria was out of the question then because Rommel was within a day's distance. So we went to Ras al-Bar, a resort across the Nile from Damietta. From there, we could see clouds of smoke rising from Alexandria as the British burned their documents prior to evacuating the city. In those days, all of Egypt's politicians were gathered at Ras al-Bar, a sandy peninsula which was submerged during the winter but in summer had glorious white sand. We could swim either in the river or in the sea, at least until the Nile waters rose and the river was no longer swimmable. The sign of a good swimmer in our family was when one of us was able to swim across the Nile.

After the scare of the German invasion had died down, we continued to go to Ras al-Bar in the summer. One year there was tremendous excitement because the prime minister, Nahhas Pasha, came to give a public speech. He dressed in silk pajamas, which was the favorite attire of some men, and carried a white umbrella like that of most *umdas*, or mayors, in the villages. In the middle of his speech, Nahhas would get carried away by his own rhetoric and irritated by the interruptions of shouted slogans. Forgetting that he had paid these men to shout slogans, he would yell ("Shut up you son of a b...h!") and hit them with his umbrella.

Some of the elites gathered round my uncle Lutfi at the Beau Rivage hotel, which was located on the other side of the Nile. He was popular with all the servants in the hotel and all the shoeshine boys would fight to shine his shoes because he gave them such generous tips. My uncle always had time to pay attention to me. He used to tease me and call me his Abyssinian princess. He'd point to my mother, who was fair skinned, and then to my dark skin and tell me that I was not really her daughter but an Abyssinian princess she had adopted. I didn't mind, since I was not close to my mother anyway, and being a princess sounded great.

Among the people in Ras al-Bar was the very beautiful singer, Asmahan. Once when I was sick, she came to visit and sat on the veranda with my mother and started singing. I was then eating toast, and I stopped eating so I could listen to her lovely voice. Umm Kulthum was also there, as she was a friend of the family. My mother knitted vests for her in a very fine white wool. My father had been instrumental in spreading Umm Kulthum's music, because he arranged for the BBC to broadcast her songs to the Arab world. Once a month, on Thursdays, Umm Kulthum gave a recorded concert which was the big event in the Middle East for the rest of her life. She was always a favorite with us children because she had time to play with us.

Once I became a little older, my mother started paying some attention to me. I was taken on visits to relatives, especially to her elderly aunts. These aunts, referred to as *Teyze Amina Hanim*, or *Teyze Zeinab Hanim*, always had their hands kissed by my mother, while I was kissed on the cheek. My father never allowed his children to kiss anyone's hands, and said, "The Ottoman period is over." I didn't know what that meant until much later, but I knew that I was not to kiss hands, not even that of my maternal grandmother, Sitti, a lovely woman of Circassian heritage whose family had emigrated to Turkey after fleeing the Russians. Her aunt was the only legal wife my grandfather, Rashwan Pasha, had married; the other women were concubines. Rashwan Pasha was one of the last Mamluks. He had been captured by Muhammad Ali's armies in Chios during the Greek War of Independence and brought to Egypt as a small child. He was brought up in the palace and rose in the administrative ranks to become inspector general of Upper Egypt. My grandmother was brought to Egypt at the age of sixteen to marry her cousin.

My paternal grandfather was a self-made man, an umda who had become rich and died a Pasha. He looked remarkably like Shaikh Muhammad Abduh, and that partly explained the bond that tied my uncle Lutfi to Shaikh Abduh. Uncle Lutfi was eighteen years older than my father and was really more like a father to him. The two men saw each other twice a day every day of their lives. Once I asked my uncle who his students were and he answered, "Taha Husain, Husain Haikal, and your father." Lutfi, as the eldest son, had great influence on his father and induced him to send all his sisters to school.

My mother met my father for the first time on their wedding day. He was eighteen years older, and they had little in common, except, of course, their three children who came later. My father was a disciplinarian, punctual to a fault, and hated sloppiness of thought or deed. The servants lived in terror of him, and the house was silent so long as he was in it. If a door banged, a hinge squeaked, or a fly entered the house, the servants were summoned. We were the only fly-less house in Egypt, and it always smelled of FLIT, an insecticide. Yet, we all knew the real power in the house was my mother, who deferred to her husband but blithely did things her own way. Father had great respect for her and admired her intelligence, even though, like all women of her age and station, she had had very little schooling. She had gone to the French convent school of La Mere de Dieu for a couple of years and then was made to stay at home until she married. In contrast, my father was a highly educated man with an Oxford degree in modern history. They were complete opposites in everything. My mother had the exquisite manners of the Turco-Circassian elite, my father was the son of an umda and often had rough manners. She was generous and supported a number of needy families; no one who ever appealed to her for aid was turned away. But then, she was rich in her own right, since she had inherited land from her father. My father, who was also wealthy, was tightfisted and begrudged every penny he spent. Both of them were extremely elegant. My father was whippet-thin, a sportsman who quit riding horses only when he reached the age of seventy. He always wore beautifully cut suits that were made for him by an Armenian tailor, Chaldjian, who sewed clothes for Egypt's elite. His shirts were custom-made by an Armenian woman named Madame Kirmiz, and his shoes were hand-sewn by a pair of Italians, the Gaeta brothers, in Alexandria.

Many years later, I went to their shop in Alexandria, and one of them asked me it I were "La fille de son Excellence." By then my father had been made a pasha by King Farouk. I asked which excellence and was told it was my father. I asked the man how he knew I was my father's daughter and he smiled and said that I looked exactly like him.

My mother was equally elegant, and when I turned sixteen, she bought me haute couture fashions and custom-made shoes. In fact, she bought me anything I asked for but was seldom around or attentive to me. She and Daddy left the house every day at around 5 P.M. to go to the club and returned only after the club closed at 10 P.M., by which time I had long been sent to bed. Mummy also woke up late, so I barely saw her except for half an hour when I came back from school.

During the war years I was left in the care of servants—two older maids and two younger ones who took us to the cinema every day one summer. They waited until my parents had left the house, and then at sundown, without telling anyone, they would take us to the open-air movies. We saw *King Kong* three days in a row but never saw the end because we had to rush home before my parents returned. Our maids were not afraid of being sacked because they were all family retainers whose mothers had been my grandmother's maids. Eventually, my mother found husbands for the younger maids, giving them a lovely wedding and a fitting trousseau.

My last year at school was sheer heaven. I was the head girl and the house captain as well as a prefect, and I gloried in the power and responsibilities it gave me. One of my responsibilities was to read the Bible lesson in the morning assembly. The irony of a Muslim girl reading the Bible in a missionary school did not strike any one of us. We all had to work hard that year, for I wanted to be admitted into pre-medicine, and to do that I had to get high grades in the Oxford and Cambridge School Leaving Certificate, with exemption from matriculation, which I eventually did.

Once I finished school, my mother decided it was time for me to get married and trotted out her candidates. Before I could even meet the first candidate, Daddy took me aside and said, "Don't listen to your mother, go to university, get a degree, and you will never need to have a man support you. Marry a man only because you want to marry him." These were heady words, especially since every one of my cousins had been married off before they'd even had a year of university. My uncle, who had been the first rector of the university and who had admitted women into the university, also encouraged me to get an education.

I entered pre-medicine, and my father and I lied to my mother and told her I was entering the Faculty of Science. She was against medicine, since it took many years of study, and she was afraid that no man would want to marry a female doctor. At a dinner party, she ran into the rector of the university, a famous surgeon, Dr. Morro, and the dean of the Faculty of Medicine, an internist. Both of them were family friends, and they berated her for allowing her delicate daughter to enter such a tough profession. That is how she learned I was studying medicine. I was allowed to finish the year but not to go any further.

That year, 1948, was a year of riots, so we seldom finished a day of lectures without being disrupted by the students of the Faculty of Law who barged into the lecture halls, gave political speeches, and forced the men in our class to go out in a demonstration against the government. I enjoyed pre-medicine and the only time I skipped a class was when we had to dissect cockroaches. I have always had a phobia of cockroaches; frogs, worms, and rabbits I didn't mind. The day my mother saw me coming out of the kitchen carrying a rabbit with its throat slit was the day the roof fell. My mother was very tenderhearted and collected strays, both human and animal, so she could not bear to see me dissecting such creatures.

Once I was forced to leave pre-med, Daddy and I looked around for an alternative, and we decided on the American University in Cairo. There I spent three of my happiest years and made friends who have lasted throughout my life.

Mohammed Ghanoonparvar

IRAN *Mohammed Ghanoonparvar was born in Esfahan and begin teaching at the University of Isfahan as an instructor in English. He studied English literature at Eastern Michigan University and received a Ph.D. in comparative literature from the University of Texas at Austin, where he currently teaches. He translates frequently from Persian and is the author of* **In a Persian Mirror: Images of the West and Westerners in Contemporary Iranian Fiction** *and* **Translating the Garden.** *He is also well*

known for his work on the culinary arts of his native land, particularly for the two books **Persian Cuisine I: Traditional Food;** *and* **Persian Cuisine II: Regional and Modern Food.**

MY EDUCATION IN HALF

THE WORLD

Mohammed Ghanoonparvar

 I often think back on my youth and my "informal" education in the city that has been known for centuries as "*Esfahan, Nesf-e Jahan,*" "Esfahan, Half the World." Now that I am
an educator and also a father, this experience means more to
me than it ever has; I understand and appreciate it as a loving memory of a world that, for all intents and purposes, no
longer exists.

According to the custom of my youth, mothers were responsible for their daughters' education and training, while
fathers were charged with seeing to the same tasks for their
sons. My father, therefore, following tradition, was the chief
architect of my education. I am not referring to his choice
of formal schooling, which also had its effect on the person
I have become, but more importantly, his approach in creating that person who was his eldest son. My father was a simple man, and as simple men so often do, he had a clear understanding of the right and wrong ways of doing things. He
was stubborn enough to see that things were done correctly
as far as he was in control of them. He was not by any means
egotistical, but he was practical, and I can only hope that I
have inherited some portion of those traits I have admired
in him. Among the things that he knew intuitively was that
there was a right way to rear a son who would make his
father proud and who would have what it takes to follow in
his footsteps and those of his grandfathers before him. I
don't believe he had the course of my education plotted out,
but he knew, instinctively, what I needed to know to survive
in a complicated world and what I needed to understand to
become a responsible adult, and he went about seeing that I
would get it.

My father was an *attar*, an herbalist or traditional apothecary, who prescribed remedies for all sorts of ailments. His clients included not only the townspeople but people from distant villages who had heard of his reputation as an experienced attar. As an attar in Iran, he was also a seller of spices, herbs, teas, and other essentials. Like his father before him, he was a respected man in our community, undoubtedly in part because his father had been a highly regarded member of the community; in fact, his father had been a political activist during the time of the 1906–1911 Constitutional Revolution, an event from which our family name was derived: *ghanoon*, or law, and *parvar*, nurturer. My father was also respected because he had a formal education. He could not only read and write, but he had completed the seventh grade, something of an accomplishment for his time, especially among working-class families such as ours.

As the eldest male child of my father, I was naturally expected to become an attar and continue the family tradition, which dated back at least to the Saffavid period in the sixteenth century, when Esfahan was at the peak of its glory as the city known as "Half the World." I was groomed for this vocation. From as far back as I can remember, I was taken by my father at dawn every day to his store and given small chores to perform such as fetching a certain box containing an herb that he was prescribing for a customer or preparing and cleaning roots and flowers that were delivered to the store. This was a normal routine during my school years, yet I always understood that I was expected to finish my formal education before taking over my father's business. My "medical" education under my father continued even after the age of five, when I began attending a parochial Islamic school, and later during high school and college, when I would spend most of my free time at the store, assisting in selling and even sometimes prescribing herbs. Summers were another story, and this is where the genius of my father's plan for me lay. I am certain that other male children of my class and era were inducted into a similar routine devised by their fathers.

My earliest recollection of summertime had to have been when I was about three years old. My father had taken me to a stone-carver's shop, where I was allowed to sit in my own spot surrounded by other workers and was given a "job" to do. I was given a scaled-down hammer and chisel and a stone, and I was assigned the task of chipping away at the middle of that stone to eventually make a mortar. Every day throughout the summer, I would walk from my father's store to the stone-carver's shop to work on my mortar. I remember liking the workshop very much. It was so different from other shops, mainly because the floor was full of loose chipped stone instead of dirt, and it felt good to sit on. I don't remember much about the mortar itself, but I do recall my pride and sense of power in making a dent in the stone. At the end of every day, I remember proudly inspecting my mortar, my head tilted sideways, and essentially convincing myself that I had actually made the "hole" a little deeper.

Undoubtedly, the idea of somehow shaping the hardest material I could imagine at the time, a stone, has served as a metaphor for making an effort at what may seem an impossible task and has instilled in me the idea that any task, no matter how difficult, can be accomplished with perseverance. This experience has also made me look at stonework in a completely different light. Every summer after that, my father would arrange for me to be sent to some neighborhood craftsman to work as an apprentice so as to become familiar with a wide variety of crafts. I learned much later that my father had arranged to pay these craftsmen whatever he thought I should earn as my "wage" so that there was no expense on their part in allowing me to work for them. So, in addition to my experience in stone carving, I worked as an apprentice to a carpenter, a tailor, a shoemaker, a shoe repairman, a plumber, a barber, an electrician, a green grocer, a butcher, the owner of a kabob shop, a clerk, a turner, and the operator of a bookstore. When I think back, I realize that, with the exception of the butcher shop, I enjoyed every one of these experiences and crafts. And I remember that each summer that I worked with a new craftsman, I was convinced that that job would be my life's calling, that it was the career for me.

Whether my father was conscious of the effect this smorgasbord training would have on my life, or whether he was merely following the example provided for him by his own father and the culture in which he was brought up, I will probably never know. But what I do know is that these summertime occupations provided not only a sort of insurance that I would never be without a skill with which to earn a living but also an understanding of and respect for other crafts and occupations. This, I believe, was an important part of the culture in which I grew up, the idea that, firstly, with few exceptions, everyone is capable of doing any job, and, secondly, no profession is above or beneath one's dignity.

For many children of my generation, this philosophy served to build in us a sense of self-confidence which has been lost in the decades of relative urban prosperity. This scheme, I am certain, was also devised to instill in us the necessity that one must work and "earn" a living, that work is a natural and gratifying part of human life. More importantly, however, the lesson that fathers like my own were imparting to my generation growing up in the Iran of the 1940s and 1950s was that the greatest vice in the world is idleness. Of course, the older generation often interpreted idleness as including anything that was not productive, such as participation in sports or spending time with one's peers. For example, my father became furious when I

spent my precious time at the age of ten or eleven making a model of a theater, which I had seen only once when attending a political play with my
mother. Undoubtedly, the sternness of this kind of upbringing was partially
the result of the sociopolitical and economic conditions in post–World
War II Iran. For many of the children of my generation, or at least those of
my socioeconomic background, our parents and teachers tried to expedite
the passage from childhood to adulthood, and this was accomplished by involving us very early not only in adult work but also in the turbulent and
highly charged political climate of those two decades in Iran both prior to
and after the premiership of Dr. Mohammad Mosaddeq in the early 1950s.

I came to realize later in life that the sort of education I had been exposed to had deep historical roots and was evident in many old Persian tales
and romances.

What I have called my "informal" education was obviously only a part
of the education my parents had planned for their children. As a member
of the first post–World War II generation, especially in the cities, I was also
required to receive a formal education in modern-style schools. In order to
become a valuable asset to my community and my family, I needed to learn
to read and write. I must have been three or four years old in the mid-1940s
when my parents arranged for my attendance at a *maktab*, a sort of neighborhood preschool. A handful of other children from the neighborhood also
attended the maktab. Every morning, we all went to *Mollabaji's* (a name for
an old-fashioned schoolmistress) with our school supplies and a small rug
rolled up under our arms. We sat in a row on the rugs that we spread on the
ground, and the mistress drilled us in the alphabet, verses from great poets,
or phrases from the Quran. We each had a flat tin slate, which was perhaps
fifteen inches square, and an ink pot, with which we practiced writing the
alphabet. Paper in post–World War II Iran, like everything else, was quite
precious; hence, the resourcefulness of such a device. After we wrote, or
rather copied, the letters to fill the slate, we would show our work to the
mistress, who would make corrections; we would then go to the courtyard
pool and wash the slate clean. I am not certain to what degree at this age I
was able to absorb the lessons that I was taught, but I was well aware that
the subject matter was important.

My formal education began with elementary school, which I attended at
the age of five and a half years. Many of the post–World War II generation
of parents who had come to appreciate the benefits of modern education
but, at the same time, resented Reza Shah's attempt at the secularization and
de-Islamization of the country helped establish a chain of private elementary and high schools in which Islamic learning was emphasized. Just such
a school was selected for me. The elementary school that I attended for the

first two years of my education was in a small, old house, but before the school year was over, a new, larger branch of the elementary school had opened and most of us were transferred to it. On the whole, I suppose what distinguished the Islamic schools from secular schools at that time was that every morning we would have to stand for ten or fifteen minutes, even on the coldest days of winter, in the school courtyard to listen to recitations from the Quran. We listened to one student or another who was thought to have a good voice, and then at noon, we marched to a nearby mosque for noon prayers. There was, of course, emphasis on Islamic subjects, such as Arabic lessons, to enable us to understand the Quran, and the memorization of Quranic passages. On certain occasions, such as the annual PTA meetings, we were supposed to impress our parents with our Arabic and Quranic recitation. The effect of the Islamic schools on those of us who attended them was that, initially, we became fanatic Muslims, who later on either became even more zealous, continuing at the religious seminaries in Qom and other places, or developed into adolescent atheists and agnostics by the time we had finished high school.

My high school years were secular and coincided with the politically turbulent Mosaddeq and post-Mosaddeq years. In that charged climate, like other students, I was exposed to the diverse political issues of the time. Of utmost significance, however, I think, was the intellectual, or perhaps pseudo-intellectual, climate of large cities like Esfahan, which was conducive to creating in us a sense of curiosity about "intellectual matters," almost at any price. We craved exposure to new concepts and experiences. In my own case, at the age of fourteen or fifteen, I would spend several hours a week in the municipal library reading whatever I could get my hands on: philosophy, art, history, even the texts of Western operas, translated and published in Persian. The impetus behind this compulsion might have been, to a large extent, merely the adolescent desire to "show off," to demonstrate that I was familiar with the persons and ideas being discussed.

When I think back on my childhood and my education, becoming a "literate" person was obviously important and has certainly affected my life. But what builds character has a great deal to do with that informal education which I have described.

Of course, my informal education was not all designed, prepared, and provided for me by my father. The city of Esfahan, or as it is sometimes spelled in English, Isphahan, with its bazaars, streets, historical monuments, and industrious people, all contributed to my "education." Growing up in an ancient city that is believed to date back to the Achaemenid (553–330 BC) and, perhaps, pre-Achaemenid period and which has consistently been an important center in Iranian history, especially during the time of the

Seljuks (eleventh–thirteenth centuries AD) and the Saffavids (sixteenth–seventeenth centuries AD), and the time when it was the capital, created a sense of tangible history. Every quarter of the city is known for and bears the marks of some distant event or notable person in the past. As children, we were constantly told these stories by our elders. More importantly, though, all this created in us a sense of belonging to a city, a country, and a culture, which is the main ingredient of collective and individual identity.

Avraham Zilkha

IRAQ   *Avraham Zilkha was born in Iraq but emigrated to Israel with his parents when he was a child. He was educated at the Hebrew University in Jerusalem and received a Ph.D. from the University of Texas at Austin, where he teaches Hebrew language and linguistics. His **Modern Hebrew-English Dictionary** (Yale, 1989) was nominated as one of the best books to be published in the United States during that year. He also writes about the Israeli-Arab conflict.*

BY THE RIVERS OF
BABYLON (PSALM 137)

Avraham Zilkha

 The old city of Baghdad in the forties did not bear any resemblance to the exotic town of Arabian Nights portrayed in Hollywood movies. There were no domed roofs, no flying horses, and no magic carpets. Beautiful women in silky belly-dance outfits were not seen in the streets. It was mostly crowded blocs of old brick houses built along winding, narrow alleys. They touched each other, and a passerby saw only one or two small windows facing the outside. It was said that the flat, adjacent roofs enabled the inhabitants over the centuries to flee from one house to the other during invasions and other calamities.

Going through a heavy wooden door, one entered a spacious, clay-tiled courtyard around which the large-window rooms were situated. Up to the time when modern, affluent neighborhoods were built along the Tigris River, the typical Baghdadi house consisted of two stories. The lower floor, lined with wooden pillars, was the living quarters during the summer, while in the winter residents moved to the warmer, upper floor. The living room, the *tarar*, was usually an open space furnished with rug-covered sofas. Often there was a dark room downstairs used mostly for storage. For children, however, it was the place where the jinn lived. Those evil creatures, that had the face of bats, would come out at night to terrorize you in your dreams.

In many houses there was a *kabishkan*, an enclosed loft upstairs, which served as an extra bedroom or a playroom where children could dig through piles of books, pictures, and other hidden treasures. During the dry, hot summer months, it was customary to sleep on the roof. It was fun for kids and good for adults, who were kept by the early sun from oversleeping and being late to work. Except, of course, when one woke up in the middle of the night suffocating from the heavy dust carried by a sudden desert storm.

The Jewish quarter, where I spent my early childhood, had a population of about 100,000. It occupied a large area of the old city east of the river, between two major streets, Ghazi and al-Rashid. The latter was the busiest in the city and was lined with shops, cinemas, and cafes. Since the buildings extended over the sidewalks, pedestrians found it comfortable to crowd the street, protected from the rain and the scorching summer sun. It was easy to tell when evening fell on the city, as the traffic chaos in the street and the constant, loud honking marked the beginning of Baghdad's nightlife. In the less crowded street, Ghazi, one still found wagons to be a convenient means of transportation. I know, because I took my first breath in one of those vehicles, when my mother decided that her seventh child should be born in a hospital. While the wagoner was whipping his horses, my father and aunt assisted in the delivery. Despite that rocky start, I discovered a few years later that it was rather fun to get a free ride on one of those wagons. All one needed was to find a wagon whose rear was not protected from stowaways by barbed wire. It was risky, though, if a nasty kid shouted "arabanchi warak!" ("Wagoner, look behind you!"), and a whip landed on your head. The last time I did it was quite costly, when a classmate of mine told my father, who gave me a physical lesson in street safety. From then on I was content riding a skateboard on the sidewalk.

There were no cars to be found in the alleys of our neighborhood, only pedestrians and donkeys. The latter did not actually live there but served as the moving vans of the time. Their competition were men carrying heavy loads of furniture on their backs. Other outsiders, who announced their presence with melodic cries, included peddlers, buyers of junk and old clothes, and those who did all kinds of repairs. One peddler in particular, who had a candy stand under our window, caught my attention one day by spitting on the chocolate bars and then buffing them with his sleeve for a nice shine. Interesting to watch was the man who repaired dishes by stapling the broken pieces together and then covering the cracks with grout. Conversely, the most repulsive sight was that of the *nazzah*, the sewer cleaner, who would take off his clothes and dip into the septic tank to empty it with a bucket and then come out covered head to toe with thick, black sewage. His only break was during the spring floods when water from the Tigris would seep into the ground and surface in homes and alleys. On the days of his appearance in the alley, homework preparation and school attendance would be perfect, because nothing motivated kids better than mothers saying, "If you don't get a good education, you will end up being a nazzah."

That river, the Tigris, was always active. As the snows in the north began melting in the spring, the water level would rise, threatening the areas along the riverbanks. Pedestrians were then picked up in the streets to fill sandbags, the extent of the Iraqi flood-control program at the time. Soon thereafter, as the hot season began, the water would recede and gradually create an island, the *jazra.* What was a raving stream of water disappeared and revealed a sandy ground. Eventually, the island connected with the shore in some places and enabled people to walk on the wet sand for a great distance across the river. Those were the summer beaches of Baghdad, where the city dwellers went to swim, stroll, and picnic. The biggest attraction, though, was the *samak mazgoof,* freshly caught fish grilled with a topping of curry. Well-equipped fishermen also provided *amba,* spicy, appetizing mango pickles pasted inside a loaf of bread. That hot stuff, next to which jalapeño tastes like candy, was popular among kids. On the way back from school, it was routine to stop at one of those amba stands, a single-item Wendy's or McDonald's of sorts. After verifying that the yellow delicacy was indeed from its original motherland India, it was time to stuff the *sammoon,* the Iraqi version of French bread. No one minded the lizards that were crawling on the barrels or the risk of gastrointestinal disorders that was high among amba eaters.

But the real food of Iraq was the dates. In no other country existed richer and more delicious varieties, differing in taste, color, consistency, and texture. Their different names would fill a dictionary, and they constituted a primary diet for the poor, rural population. Dates were consumed either in their natural form or mixed with walnuts, crushed and cut into cubes. Forget about sugar and honey. Nothing was sweeter than *silaan,* date syrup.

If you wanted to see plenty of dates hanging from trees, you traveled to the water-rich south, where hundreds of square kilometers were covered with palm trees. That is what I did when I traveled to Basra with my oldest sister, who had settled in the city as a schoolteacher. All the way down to Shatt-el-Arab, the extra-wide river that separates Iraq from Iran, there was nothing but dense forests of tall palm trees, separated by an elaborate network of narrow canals. The reflection of the trees in the water added to the thickness of the forest. Occasionally I spotted a waterwheel or a *guffa,* a round dinghy. But the highlight of that trip was a visit to the airport, where I saw an airplane on the ground for the first time. When we heard those things passing slowly over our house in Baghdad and rushed to the roof to watch them, I knew they had to be bigger than what they seemed from the ground so that they could carry people. But only at the Basra airport did I realize how big an airplane really was, and it grew bigger and bigger every time I repeated the story to kids back home. From a twin-engine Dakota it

became a four-engine Constellation. While at the airport, I rode an elevator for the first time. Forget that it was only a three-story terminal. For a
ten-year-old Baghdadi kid then, not even riding the elevator of New York's
Empire State Building today could have matched the thrill of that twenty-
second trip. At the time I thought it was one of the best things that the British brought to the country.

· Speaking of the British, I had heard about all the things they had built,
such as roads, railways, the port of Basra, and the power station. The latter
was the Big Ben of Baghdad, as it announced the time at noon with a long,
loud siren that was heard all over the city. We even went once to see an exhibit of prefabricated homes imported from England. An amazing place to
walk through, with modern amenities, but no one wanted to live there. It
was impossible to imagine living in a home made of wood with no courtyard in the middle. People were accustomed to living in the safety of brick
houses with meter-thick walls and no windows facing the outside. Never
mind the crevices where lizards, spiders, and scorpions had established their
habitat. Every house had a set of big forceps and someone who knew how
to catch those pests as they came out at night looking for food. As a precaution, we made sure to shake our clothes in the morning before putting
them on.

So, the British were supposed to be the good guys. We knew that there
were those bad Communists who, as we were told by the media, were even
worse than the Zionists in Palestine. But the Ingleez were friends. That is
why one day I was surprised to hear that there were people who were willing to die in denunciation of the British. It happened suddenly when we were
sent home from school early and warned to stay away from main streets.
On the way home, we were accompanied by the constant sound of machine
guns. That was the first time I heard real firearms. It was quite different
from shots fired in movies, louder and more frightening. The radio told of
government forces firing at demonstrators who were protesting a treaty
with Britain. The incidents continued for a number of days, during which
no one left the house. While the whole family was listening to radio reports
about the crisis, I spent my time reading books that I had fortunately checked
out from the school library. That was my first lesson in Iraqi politics.

In the heart of the Jewish quarter was the Alliance school, named after
the Sassoons, a well-known family of Iraqi merchants, travelers, and philan-
thropists. It was established in the nineteenth century by the French organization Alliance Francaise as part of a network of schools designed to promote modern education in the Middle East. Since then thousands of pupils
had passed through its doors, including my father. The school contained
two enclosed courtyards used as playgrounds as well as outdoor gyms. Like

many structures in old Baghdad, there were the typical rows of wooden pillars holding the upper-floor balconies overlooking the yards.

I came to that respectable institution from a crummy, traditional preschool, in which boys and girls did nothing but learn the alphabet, sing Arabic rhymes, and listen to the *ustadh* (teacher) tell stories. To keep him cool and comfortable, we had to take turns pulling ropes that operated the heavy-fabric ceiling fan. Thus, going to the all-boys Alliance school was a new, wondrous experience, despite the separation from girls and the requirement to learn French as early as the first grade. Alliance students were distinguishable from the ordinary crowd by whether or not they knew by heart the chapter *René va a l'ecole* in the French textbook. Once you memorized that chapter, you were in.

Six days a week, students would gather in the morning in the large courtyard to salute the flag and sing the national anthem in honor of His Majesty, King Faisal the 2nd. It resembled a military review except that the lines of children were rarely straight. No one liked it, particularly on a freezing wintry morning, but it was an obligation to display loyalty to the throne. If an inspector from the Ministry of Education happened to visit early that day, the school administrators would be in serious trouble if the routine was not followed.

As soon as the ceremony ended, everyone was screaming and running in all directions, making it difficult to find one's way to the classroom. As the mayhem went out of control, Monsieur Bonfisse would suddenly appear. He was a big man, carrying a sizable belly, well-dressed in a gray suit and bow tie. I never heard his voice, but I was told that he came to the school from Turkey as a French teacher. Supposedly, his Arabic was not very good and he had a foreign accent. Perhaps that was the reason why he spoke only French. But it did not matter, because just seeing him standing there in silence was enough to instill fear. What made it even more unnerving was that we could not tell exactly at whom he was looking. I was particularly concerned at the possibility that one of my older brothers who attended that school may have done some mischief and I would be the one to take the punishment. Although there was no evidence that Monsieur Bonfisse had ever physically punished one of the pupils, his presence was enough to take that possibility into consideration.

In addition to the French principal, Monsieur Laredo, there was another foreigner in the school, a British teacher who taught, of course, English. Contrary to the dreaded Monsieur Bonfisse, he was the type that children like to make fun of. Not only was he a wimpy person who did not know any Arabic, but his name was Dick. To be called *deek* (rooster) was not something that brought respect to a teacher.

The children in the school came from all parts of town. There were those who dressed nicely and arrived by car and others who came from poor neighborhoods and needed to borrow textbooks to do their homework. In fifth grade, which was my last, the son of a deputy minister shared my desk. He came to school in a luxury car, and the chauffeur waited for him outside until classes were over. He was always well-groomed, wearing a shiny golden watch on his wrist, but did not speak much except to ask me occasionally to explain some French words.

Events in Palestine were beginning to cause concern. The state-controlled radio kept blasting the *yahood* (Jews), promising a quick victory. The Jewish community contributed to the war effort and the Chief Rabbi denounced Zionism, but it was not certain if the man in the street would distinguish between Jews fighting Arabs in Palestine and Iraqi Jews who had been in the country since the Babylonian era. When a Jewish state was declared, there was fear that the pogrom of 1941 during the pro-Nazi coup would be repeated, but nothing happened. Slowly a feeling of safety returned, although we were cautioned to stay home during funeral processions of fallen soldiers.

It was clear thereafter that life in Iraq would no longer be the same. A rising wave of nationalism created an atmosphere of intolerance toward minorities. The newspaper *al-Istiqlal* published anti-Jewish propaganda daily. There were arrests of young men accused of being Communists or Zionists, amidst stories of harsh interrogation and torture. The show trial and public execution of a Jewish businessman in Basra was seen as a warning sign, resembling the Dreyfus trial in France in 1894. It became difficult not to notice that more and more children at school were absent, presumably fleeing the country with their families. One day the radio announced that Jews were allowed to leave Iraq, provided they renounced their citizenship. Not many people were interested at first, but gradually the numbers grew. In my family, there was a great deal of uncertainty. There was not much interest in Palestine and a lot of attachment to Iraq. The prospect of becoming stateless refugees just as the young generation was graduating from school and ready to look for employment was not something to look forward to. Yet as the slow wave of emigration became a mass exodus and the community began to disintegrate, I found myself standing in line with my parents to be fingerprinted. My two brothers and a married sister, as well as most of my larger, extended family, did not want to leave.

That was at the time when *id al-sikka* (the Feast of Tabernacle) was approaching. For children it was a favorite holiday, because spending seven days in the booth was like camping in the middle of the house. It was constructed of a wooden frame draped with white sheets. The roof was made of fresh palm branches, cut for the holiday and sold by peasants as Christmas trees are sold in the United States. Several fruits, such as oranges and pomegranates, were hung from the ceiling. Inside, sofas and small tables were arranged to resemble a living room. Since there was no school during that week, children could spend their time playing and eating the holiday food inside the sikka. The hanging fruit was left to dry and saved for Passover, which came about six months later. That holiday was less exciting, but the meal of the seder, the home-baked matzo, and the gallons of raisin juice made it worth looking forward to, not to mention a week without school. On the last evening of the holiday, there was a rush to the bakeries to buy bread, which one was forbidden to eat or have in the house during Passover.

Waiting for the papers to be processed, which took several months, was a period of adjusting to the idea of the impending one-way trip. While we did not know what lay ahead, it was clear what we were leaving behind: everything. It was a separation from home, people, and a way of life, which included basic cultural components such as age-old traditions, customs, and even our own Arabic dialect. The community was the oldest Jewish diaspora, which had lived under the reign of Nebuchadnezzar, Cyrus, and Haroon al-Rashid. It witnessed the rise of Islam, the Mongol invasion, and the modernization of Iraq.

At school, friends were looking for ways to establish future contact but no one had an idea how to do it. One day, on the way home from the *shorja*, the busiest marketplace at the time, I bumped into my geography teacher, a self-declared Muslim nationalist. He was one of my favorite instructors, primarily because he gave me high grades. To avoid telling him the real reason, I was thinking of an excuse for being absent from school for two weeks. But before I could say anything he went straight to the point: "So, you are going to Falastin, huh?" I felt some embarrassment and guilt.

The highlight of my last night in Baghdad was a trip to the cinema with my brother and his fiancée to see *Gone with the Wind.* The movie was too intense for me at that age, and the scene of Atlanta burning was too frightening to watch. I spent much of the time admiring the phosphorous dial of my new Omega watch. In late afternoon the next day I was on the way to the airport with my parents. My father objected at first to leaving on the holy Sabbath, but that was not the kind of flight that could be arranged at a travel agency.

While going through the body search at the inspection counter, the policeman noticed small crystal plates that I was carrying in my coat pockets so they would not break in the trunk. He checked them against the light for clarity and, while he was putting them in his bag, I ran before he could see my watch. We stood on the steps of the airplane to wave goodbye to the family, not knowing whom we would see again. After we took off, the pilot flew over Baghdad for a while, giving me a chance to watch the city lights from the air for the first and last time.

Halim Barakat

SYRIA

LEBANON

*Born in Syria, Halim Barakat was educated at the American University in Beirut and received a Ph.D. in social psychology from the University of Michigan. A novelist as well as a social psychologist, Dr. Barakat writes regularly for Arabic as well as English journals. His novel, **Days of Dust,** which chronicled events during the 1967 Israeli-Palestinian war, was translated into English.*

CHILDHOOD MEMORIES

Halim Barakat

 I have a vision from my childhood of quickly descending through thick black clouds lit up by flashes of lightning. It is my father's death that comes into my mind. He died suddenly when he was in his thirties without leaving us much of a legacy except for a stone house with a dirt roof and a mule which he had used for transporting goods.

He died during the days of harvest at the end of spring and the beginning of summer. The men were working hard throughout the days to reap the golden stalks of wheat that swayed harmoniously on the rolling hills.

That particular hot day changed into a rainy night. The trees, roads, and houses were cleansed of their dust and covered with cold air. My father washed away his daily fatigue and climbed up to a sleeping hut which he had built in the summer between two trees in front of our house. But his friends Najeeb and Mighal came and talked to him for a long time about a dispute which had taken place that day on who should have been first to irrigate his land.

When I got up the following morning, I didn't see my father. My mother explained that he had gone to Marmarita and that he would spend a day or two there as well as in Hab Namra, where he would order a new saddle for his mule.

Two days later, my father came back, but he was ill, doubled over in pain. That night his condition worsened and he was unable to sleep. Mother called my grandfather Salim, and my uncles Jamil and Yousef. The neighbors also came to spend the night with my father. Before dawn they sent my uncle Jamil to Al-Mashta to bring the doctor. I don't remember where I was, but I think I was asleep. My mother says that my uncle returned an hour later and told them that the doctor had refused to come with him unless he gave him three lira in advance. My mother gave him the money and he went back to Al-Mashta. Suddenly my father felt better. He got up, washed his face, and talked with my grandfather and my uncle Yousef about several matters.

The doctor came and examined my father and joked with him. He concluded that he had pneumonia and gave him an injection. He told my mother how to care for him and then left to visit one of our distinguished neighbors. The visitors also left and my father returned to his bed. My mother went to prepare the compress for him according to the doctor's instruction, while I remained alone with him. This is all I remember, but my mother told me that my father must have lost consciousness as soon as the doctor gave him that accursed injection. She later counted the names of the doctor's other victims in our village and the neighboring areas.

I remember that my father motioned to me to come sit next to him. I approached him in fear. I saw a bronzed face become increasingly pale. The clouds outside returned to encircle the earth and to smother its breath. Their dark shadows entered the house and sat with me next to my father. The air didn't move, and it seemed to me as though crouched on my father's chest were many thick clouds but no rain. I alone sat next to him while my mother was outside preparing the compress for him. He didn't talk to me, nor did I know what to say to him.

He stretched out his hand to hold mine. It was hot and shaking. He tried to smile. His smile was unusually cold, pale, and emaciated. I was afraid and didn't know what to say, drowning in deep silence. The dark shadows of the clouds lay in waiting on the walls and almost concealed the corners.

My father's hand reached out and took mine. He took it to his lips and kissed it. He pulled me to him and leaned his face against mine. He laughed when he felt me trying to wiggle my face away from him.

His hands rose suddenly toward the ceiling and descended slowly. He gnashed his teeth, and I stared at him, terrified. In his eyes I saw a big change. He must have seen death face to face. I couldn't move. I called my mother in a strangled voice. My father gnashed his teeth again. Then he died.

It seems to me that there is a thin, invisible thread connecting extreme sadness with extreme joy. Sometimes I think that death was both sadness and joy for the children in our village. It happened so often to every family. Four of my brothers and sisters had already died. Death was one of our games.

When a man died in the village, we children dropped everything and went to the cemetery. We watched all the faces and expressions and listened to the hymns and climbed the trees or stared in between people's legs to the casket as it was lowered into the grave and showered with dirt and rocks.

After the mourners dispersed, we would pick the acorns from the huge oak trees. We used to take those special acorns and play with them, making up games of chance.

So that fearful day after my father died, I went to play with my friends Munif and Salim. Their mothers passed by our game on their way to our house to console my mother. My eyes met the eyes of Munif's mother, and she stared at me strangely. She said to Salim's mother, "Is this the son of the deceased? The boy is playing. He doesn't know the meaning of death."

Salim's mother disagreed. "He is only a child, the poor thing," she said.

I lowered my head, embarrassed and ashamed, and rushed toward our house. I got lost in the crowd of mourners once again. They had laid my father in a wooden casket and made the necessary arrangements to take him to the cemetery. They decided to bury him on the same day, only a few hours after his death. Out of mercy for my mother and us children, his friends carried him to the cemetery, where he would forever lie beneath the large oak trees.

Burying him only a few hours after his death did not ease my mother's grieving. Her sadness deepened, and her grief stayed with her until the end of her long life. On the day that he died, she shouted while women held onto her, "They took you away from me, my beloved. They took you away from me. Return him to me. His body is still warm. You buried him while his body was still warm." Quietly she sang to him, "You vanished beneath the earth like a grain of wheat. Who will give me rivers of tears so I can cry?"

The next day, it was said that a man from the neighboring Al-Mahairey village passed through the cemetery the evening that my father had been buried. He heard moaning from inside my father's grave and ran away in fear. One of the neighbors told my mother about this rumor and she fainted. Since then, using what little I know of scientific principles, I have been trying to convince her that the rumor could not have been true. I have tried in vain. She still thinks that my father passed away because of the shot that the physician gave him and that the people who buried him only a few hours after his death were brutes.

After my father's death, my mother struggled in vain to make a living in the village and was finally forced to go to Beirut. She found work as a baker and also worked as a seasonal harvester in a distant area which the people of the village called the East. When she had established herself and found a place to live, she sent for us. I was about ten years old, my sister was eight, and my brother was six when my uncle Jamil loaded some of our things on his best mule and we walked behind him on rough, narrow roads toward the town of Safita. Umm Yousef, also a widow working in Beirut, accompanied us. We climbed mountains and hills and descended into valleys near and through villages and landmarks which we had often heard of. Every time we crossed a river or a brook, I took off my clothes and dipped into the water. I would put my clothes back on without even drying myself and continue walking. We rested on hilltops in the shadows of the trees of the ancient shrines, especially when it was necessary to pull out the thorns from our bare feet. We slept in the shadow of Safita's tower, and the following morning we took the bus from Safifa to Tripoli. There were more chickens on the bus than there were passengers; they were tied together by the dozen.

In Tripoli, I remember being amazed at the crowds of people, carts, horses, donkeys, dogs, sweets, vegetables, fruits, trash, and dust. Was this the city I had heard so much about? We rode a horse car up a hill and took a larger, newer, and cleaner bus into Beirut. I don't remember anything else except for the hills rising out of the sea, the waves breaking on the rocks, and the Ra's al-Shaq'a Tunnel. That's because I remember the Senegalese soldiers who stopped the bus at the entrance of the tunnel. It was the first time I had ever seen a black man. They took us out of the bus and asked for our identification cards, something which I hadn't heard of before. Umm Yousef explained that we were too young to have I.D. cards. They insisted, threatening to send us back to where we had come from.

Umm Yousef managed to convince the Senegalese soldiers to allow us to continue our trip to Beirut. We arrived there late in the evening in the autumn of 1942, and this city was to become my second home. World War II was in progress; the hidden struggle had already begun between the darkness and the dim lamps that were painted dark blue to deter air strikes. For Beirut was involved in the war, whether it wanted to be or not. The bus driver set us down in a small alley which branched off Al-Burj Square towards the east. I heard whisperings that we were in the middle of the red light district, but I did not exactly understand what that meant. I found it strange, however, to see women shamelessly showing their legs.

We had to go to Al-Hamra Street in Ras Beirut, so we walked behind Umm Yousef toward the train station. My sister wore wooden clogs, which made a lot of noise on those silent, dark, tiled streets. Jokingly, I told her to take off her clogs so she wouldn't wake up the city and get us taken to prison by the guards. She quickly took them off, putting the clogs in a small bundle she was carrying on her head. We still remind her of this and laugh together. We were surprised to see the train approach, since it was not what we expected. We rushed at it like the others did, climbing in without hesitation. We entered its belly like Jonah entered the belly of the whale. But this whale had windows. I contemplated its glass windows, which were painted dark blue, and I thought about how colorful the city was.

To this day, my mother insists that my father was the sacrifice for her life, that he died instead of her so that we would not be orphans. My mother used to say, "The orphan who loses his father is no orphan." She meant that the mother would not remarry after the death of her husband, but instead, would devote her life completely to her children and then to her grandchildren. And my mother has done exactly that.

Translated from the Arabic by Bassam Frangieh

Güneli Gün

TURKEY   *Güneli Gün grew up in Izmir, where she attended the*
American Girls College. She graduated from Hollins Col-
lege and attended the Iowa International Writers Work-
shop. Her first work, **Book of Trances,** *was published*
in 1979. **On the Road to Baghdad,** *her second novel,*
is the basis for a multi-media production, directed by Fergus
Early, which was selected in 1999 for the newly refurbished
Sadlers Wells Theater in London. She translates regularly
from Turkish and won the 1997 National Prize of the
American Literary Translators Association for her work
on **A New Life,** *by Turkish novelist Orhan Pamuk.*

ON QUARANTINE ISLAND

Güneli Gün

 That spring the island folk caught scabies. At first, each family scratched in secret, but soon everybody was itching so irresistibly that they couldn't help scratching even those parts you don't touch when someone is looking. The men did their best to keep out of my father's sight, terrified he'd notice the taint, and they worked harder than usual, which was still not quite hard enough to suit him. They called him "Doctor Nimrod" behind his back, and they didn't mind saying it in my presence, as if I were hard of hearing, or else, some sort of foreigner who couldn't understand who "Doctor Nimrod" was. But I caught on. For one thing, my father was the only doctor on the island, and he ruled the place, by his own admission, with an iron hand. Things that were not meant for my ears were often spoken in my presence, perhaps because I was so quiet, or because people think children don't understand. I had already noticed a lot of things, but I didn't say much. When I did, someone got into trouble.

The island folk burgeoned with scabs and scurfs as miraculously as the island burst forth with anemones. In early spring, the ground was covered with anemones in shades so fragile that Mother said there weren't simple colors to assign them. I spent most of my time sitting on top of an ancient pine which the west wind had bent into a natural tree house. The pine grew in the back of the villa where we lived, which had been stylishly built by the Turkish Republic as the residence for the doctor-in-chief. The villa stood on top of one of two hills that formed the island, softly swelling out of the Aegean Sea, as my father put it, "like the buttocks of a marine Venus."

On top of the other hill was the directorate building where my father worked. The rest of the housing for the staff had been built along the shore, facing west toward the daily sunset. But I was the only one who had full command on all sides of the open sea which Homer had called "wine-dark." Only someone sitting on top of a tree could see the earth itching into flowers and the folks flowering into scabies. The islanders didn't seem to notice the beauty of their island or their own beauty. My mother did notice things but didn't want to get involved; my father was always deeply involved in changing things and putting an end to what he said was "the agony of the East," by which he meant the scientific backwardness he believed Islam had "brought upon" us.

"What's scabies?" I asked at the dinner table that fine spring evening. "All the kids have the scabies, except me."

"Scabies!" Father cried out. "So! That's what all the scratching is about! Filthy savages! They've got the scabies and they're trying to keep it a secret from me."

He stormed out without touching his dessert. I wished I'd remembered what the cook, Aunt Baklava, had told me. "The throat has nine knots," she said, "so swallow nine times before you speak." Aunt Baklava was the only black person ever seen on the island; the inhabitants used to spit into the air and say "thirteen-and-a-half" behind her back while pinching themselves so they, too, wouldn't turn black.

The denizens must have wondered how Doctor Nimrod got wind of their affliction. But he was right there at the crack of dawn, battering at their doors with his riding crop, taking stock of the situation family by family.

"You mangy curs!" he insulted the men who were his long-suffering staff. "Scabies yet! In this day and age! I haven't seen a case since the last war! Scabies! Spreads among dogs, cows, and those humans who don't keep themselves clean!"

Father had been assigned to the directorship of Quarantine Island as a means of punishing and insulting him with exile to an Aegean island which Ankara considered out of the way. He had done something mysterious, something that had to do with "defying authority." It had taken Father only a few days to acquire the name of Doctor Nimrod after his arrival on the island. The island folk liked giving everyone nicknames rather than calling them by their given names, especially if there was something exceptional about the person: a deformity, sickness, color, madness, beauty, intelligence, power. These nicknames kept them safe from the person and the person safe from them. Aunt Baklava, for example, wasn't the cook's real name.

The men on the island were all minor officials of the ministry, the staff that would have been necessary to run a quarantine installation in case a ship ar-

rived from some foreign port where an outbreak of the black plague, cholera, typhus, or typhoid occurred. In the days of the Ottoman Empire, the
island had been established to quarantine shipfuls of pilgrims who might
arrive from Mecca, for example, carrying deadly epidemics. Pilgrims had
even been exiled to die on this beautiful island, and their bodies were eventually placed in mass graves and covered with lime so their germs wouldn't
escape.

The crew on the island had become used to taking it easy ever since the
wonder drugs had put an end to dreadfully contagious epidemic diseases.
Not only did Father require them to tend to the rusting machinery and to
keep the buildings spic and span, as if in readiness for an impending contagious outbreak, but to work even after hours. He assigned them plots of
land to grow vegetables for their own families, to reforest the island, to
learn animal husbandry and newfangled methods of fishing. He even had
them excavating an ancient mosaic floor that was discovered when he was
having a formal garden put in around the directorate building. The men had
to painstakingly unearth it using spoons and brushes because Father had
read how this was done by real archaeologists.

The mosaic was a hunting scene: a rider on a horse, a long spear in his
hand, his brown hound running ahead. In response to Father's summons,
the director of the Museum of Antiquity in Izmir came with his aides; they
removed the mosaic scene layer by layer, numbered them, placed them in
crates. They took the whole thing back to their museum, but I have never
seen it displayed. Perhaps they forgot to open the crates, or else it ended up
in some museum abroad that was rich and powerful enough to acquire it.

Even in the old days, some Doctor Pasha who had fallen out of favor
with the Ottomans was sent here in disgrace to cool his heels in comfortable oblivion while waiting to be forgiven and recalled back to Istanbul. In
my father's day, most doctors-in-chief didn't stay too long. The former doctor had been a hermit, the one before him a gambler who had turned the
villa into a casino.

In time, the staff had forgotten how to operate the machinery, the sulfur
baths, the medicine showers, the colossal steam sterilizers, and the giant
dryers. Folks didn't even go near the installation building. They scared their
children, and themselves, with horror stories about pestilent ghosts who
frequented the quarantines. They forgot that they were employees of a distant centralized government until it came time to pick up their monthly
salaries. Until Father showed up, they had always penned their sheep and
goats in the isolation hospital, kept their fishing gear in the storerooms at
the docks, and used the dispensary for unloading their bowels.

Father must have known no ship would ever arrive at the island from some distant port of contagion. None had for at least twenty years. The older staff couldn't quite remember; the new staff didn't rightly know the full implication of a quarantine station. All they knew was that the government had named their island "Quarantine Island" and the gatehouse flew a dark yellow flag. Doctors came and doctors went, but the staff had been here for generations since before the time of King Klazomenaeus.

Seeing things from the eyes of the denizens, I imagined the men had been surprised and dismayed when the new chief, the day after his arrival, had ordered a full-dress rehearsal. Not only did they have to find and put on their uniforms, they had to stoke the furnaces, run the engines, and God knows what else. But nothing they did was ever good enough. Doctor Nimrod brought the installation down around their ears. "What an ugly cuss!" they said about him. Nimrod shouted so much that his face turned the color of liver as he accused them of laziness and gross incompetence. Not only had they defecated everywhere, not only were their uniforms filthy and little better than rags, but they looked like a convention of clowns! "Why do you think you're called orderlies and guardians?" he shouted. They wondered why. They were told they'd ravaged the place, the shiny instruments, the powerful sterilizers, the hospital which could accommodate more than a hundred infected persons. "Think of that!" he shouted. They thought about it. "Think of the taxpayer's money spent on a place like this!" he shouted. They thought about that, too. "Think about the labor!" he shouted. They didn't want to think about labor.

But they had to. God, how they had to! Day and night he kept them toiling. Not only did they have to clean up, put in new parts, polish the fixtures, wash the mildewed linen, and restore the beds, but they had to be given courses at night, suffering sermons from Doctor Nimrod on animals so small that the naked eye couldn't see the creatures. Sure, sure, they said to one another; how come Nimrod knows so much about animals he can't see? If some infectious vessel arrived on the island, they were supposed to sterilize the marrows out of these unseen animals. "But, the bugs too are God's creatures!" the men balked. "Do you want to catch the black plague?" Nimrod wanted to know. "Cholera? Small-pox? Typhus?"

The staff didn't know what the little animals had to do with some pestilence God sends to punish people. Nimrod, too, was a disaster sent upon them by God. "One thing's for sure," Pocks, the headman, said as soon as Nimrod was out of earshot, "the same disaster doesn't visit you twice." They watched Nimrod walk up to the villa, slapping his riding crop on his boots. They hoped he'd get his.

But instead here they were, caught scratching themselves to death with the itchy pestilence God sent as punishment. "Nimrod could sack us all for being dirty and disorderly," Pocks the headman said. "And where would we go then?"

"I may be itchy," Captain Forty-Lies said, "but I am proud." His wife, who cleaned at the villa, had been dismissed. "And the wife has only a slight case," he added, "just between the toes." Anyone could see the humid patch on top of the poor woman's head, but nobody wanted to contradict Forty-Lies who had more words in his mouth than God has fish in his ocean. "I tell you what I'll do if he fires us," he said, tugging at his big red mustache, "I'll spirit Nimrod's wife to Donkey Island and hold her for ransom." The men roared and slapped their thighs. They could listen to Forty-Lies all day.

I had heard them say that some folks are born and die without seeing a beauty such as my mother. She was a gift from God, a favor that must not be taxed with too much looking. Older women looked away when she passed, as if eyes could put the scabies on her pure skin. And often when she went by under her silk parasol, husky island girls burst into tears, possessed by an emotion I too sometimes felt but could not name. But pregnant women forced themselves to stare at Mother, their hands pressed against their hard bellies, just long enough to steal some of that grace for the features of their unborn babies.

Up at the villa, Father was quite distressed. "Scabies!" he exclaimed over and over. "On Quarantine Island yet! How ironic! How embarrassing! They are scratching like mangy dogs!"

"You could always resign," Mother said, resorting to her perpetual solution to Father's troubles with his career. "You could put up a shingle in the City."

"And who would pay the bills while I built up a practice?" he retorted. "And the boarding school tuition for You-Know-Who?"

You-Know-Who was me. The City was Izmir. We got to town occasionally to see friends and do some shopping but not enough to make me into a savvy little girl being groomed for private school. Still, I was expected to make it with flying colors through the entrance exams, winning a place as a boarding student at the private American School for Girls. Had my family lived in Izmir, I could have gone as a day student, which would have made it easier both on my brain and the family pocketbook. But I was expected to do the impossible. I was told, over and over, that the year I would be ready to begin, the year I was eleven, only six boarding students would be admitted, but the daughters of the high and mighty in the entire country would also be competing for the space. If I made it in, there was still the problem of paying for the privilege. My father could just manage it . . . if only he didn't lose his head getting mad at some idiots who were scratching their hearts out on this obscure Aegean island.

So it was all touch and go. Mother was worried sick that I was not getting properly educated at the village school where the first, second, and third grades sat in the same classroom being taught by a single teacher. It was the law of the land that every child, rich or poor, had to attend the nearest public elementary school so that we would all acquire a national identity that was "Turkish." That was why Mother thought that if I were forced to complete my fifth year at the village school, I would not test high enough to land one of those six coveted spaces at the American school. She regretted that while I was being formed into a proper little Turk, I wasn't learning the stuff that would launch me into the greater world.

My half-sister had done it just fine. She, my father's daughter from his previous marriage, was out in the world. Her voice was heard all over the country, coming to us every evening at 8:15 P.M. on Radio Ankara to teach the nation the *Essentials of English,* as her program was called. Father, who knew French, Arabic, and Persian, as well as a smattering of German, had not studied English in school; so he was one of his daughter's devoted students, repeating after her the English words she spoke so self-confidently, following amusedly the dialogues in which she pretended her name was Lucy Brown, and dutifully doing the exercises at the end of the lessons in his workbook. He was proud of her accomplishment as a linguist.

My glamorous sister was eighteen years older than I was, one of Atatürk's first-generation brave new bluestockings who had begun to do interesting things. Father had hoped she would do graduate work, but she had chosen to take a well-paying job with the British Council as well as moonlight as a radio personality. I realize now that she spoke English with the sort of Anglophile American diction so popular in Hollywood films of the forties, clipped and classy like Rosalind Russell's and Katherine Hepburn's. Father had sent her to Istanbul to study at Robert College, a secondary school, despite what the name implies, but still a hoity-toity tendril of the American Ivy League; it was a decision he regretted because he thought her identification with the idle rich had spoiled her for hard work and a true vocation. That's why I was to go to a humbler and more Spartan school where the emphasis was on "service."

My sister was making better money at twenty-six than Father did as a senior official of the Republic who had spent twenty-six grueling years battling for "this miserable country." He complained that her real interest was in chic clothes and diplomatic parties. He thought her aiding the ends of British colonialism was hardly the reason he had knocked himself out giving her a good education. He wanted his children to know firsthand what it meant to be "Western." France was not Western enough to suit him, he was disgusted with Germany, England no longer counted, but America was the magnet, the True West! If his children managed to get truly Western-ized, then they could truly be instrumental in Westernizing Turkey, some-thing he felt his generation fell short in accomplishing. He was a patriot who loved and hated his homeland.

But I admired my sister just the way she was. She was my hero. Her voice on the radio was so intelligent and, in person, she lit up a room. She was having the time of her life and could care less what Father thought.

Father thought he could coach me in math and science, as well as in history and literature; when I turned eight, he hired a tutor in English. He was convinced that I should hurry up and learn everything I could because after puberty set in, I would turn into a hopeless boob like all the other ado-lescent girls. But Father was a terrible coach. If I didn't get some math con-cept immediately, he taunted and insulted me. I got stomachaches just think-ing about another coaching session.

But the teacher at the village school recognized my predicament. A few weeks after I was placed with the kids in the second grade, she handed me a sketch book of her own. "I realize you already know the material," she said; "so, here, take my sketch book and draw me some pictures and write me stories instead of doing the classwork; and when you've filled up the book, I want it back." I thought I had died and gone to heaven. I was such a lucky girl, being given permission to ignore the routine lessons. But I was careful not to mention it at home because I knew my parents would con-sider writing and drawing a poor substitute for math and science. So that's how I began illustrating for my teacher my versions of the stories of the ancient myths that came from our part of the world, stories I had read in a wonderful book my mother had given me — an illustrated children's version of classical literature and mythology, which included the stories of the *Iliad* and the *Odyssey*, Gilgamesh and Scheherazade, and the troubles of the House of Atreus as stories of the gods and the goddesses who animated the land-scape, the heroes that our climate had bred, and the names of the earliest phi-losophers who were native to this place.

I loved the island. I loved it secretly, silently, passionately. I belonged to this place. I thought I would expire if I ever had to leave it. I sat on top of the pine tree, reading. I had secretly resorted to helping myself to the novels in my parents' library, some of which I understood, considering what I already knew about the sex lives of the gods and the heroes. But I did man-age to keep my mouth shut.

My mother looked like someone who came out of a novel. She smelled good and wore clothes that rustled and fluttered. My father still doted on her as he had when she had eloped to marry him. Theirs was a love marriage. And I was a love child. But Mother did not love the island; she would have preferred to be in the company of other people who ate with knives and forks. The island women's idea of afternoon tea was to go down to the shore with their bread and some lemons. There they would gorge themselves on sea urchins and other shellfish which they cracked open on the spot, squeezed a lemon on, and ate. They spoke in monotones and rough gestures, and they playfully shoved each other around. They could pull a writhing octopus out of the water and slap it on the rocks forty times to make the meat tender, they could turn over a mattress all by themselves, and they could take a running start and spring on a donkey at ten paces.

We often had house guests so that Mother could, as she said, "fool herself into thinking we lived civilized lives." Guests were good, Father also thought; guests made dinner taste better "if the number of the company exceeded the Three Graces and were somewhat less than the number of the Muses."

But I noticed he had invited more than nine women to the island on May Day when the students and teachers from the American School for Girls descended on the island to celebrate their annual spring picnic. A huge number arrived from Izmir on buses. The Yankee schoolmarms who ran the school also fell in love with the island almost as deeply as I had, but they were vocal about it. Of course, my parents were trying to score a favor with the school administrators; this was the reason why Father had given them permission to hold their traditional May Day outing on the island, which was normally closed to nonresidents. The guests had brought along their own food and kitchen staff and invited my parents and me to their American-style picnic.

This was the first time I set eyes on the Three Graces—or were they the Three Fates?—who were to shape my life, as well as the intellectual lives of an incredibly large segment of upper-class Turkish women: Olive Green, Lynda Blake, and Naomi Foster. Not only were all three New Englanders, as I understood later, but they were all products of women's colleges, called the Seven Sisters, where they had been inspired by a messianic zeal for women's education. The principal at the time was Olive Green, who had come with her easel and oils to do a quick landscape of the olive grove—a subject and the color of green she favored for obvious reasons. Each of the Fates was to take her turn being the school principal, but Father, cognizant of power that was real and formidable, was immediately drawn to Lynda Blake. Unlike the other two Fates, who were spinsters, Lynda Blake was married; she had a regal bearing, and she was the first person I ever met who was truly bilingual. The other two also spoke Turkish after a fashion, but the reason I didn't laugh was because I had good manners. Lynda Blake, whom I still think of as Mrs. Blake, was not only a head taller than my father, but her command of the language was swifter than his. I was plenty scared.

"Take a good look," Mother whispered to me. "One day you will be just like these girls."

They looked all right. They certainly seemed to be having more fun than the island girls; they were free and easy, bursting with good health, and they followed Mrs. Blake's example, making sure to pick up all the picnic trash. But I couldn't wait for them to leave my island. I didn't want to leave my mother and go to some boarding school. I wanted to always be with Mother.

The islanders had named me Little Yusuf, a kind of dragonfly that buzzes around limpid pools looking for sustenance. I suppose I appeared so transparent that they thought they could almost see my heart. I was not an unattractive child and yet, compared with my mother, folks must have thought that Nature had not felt any need to surpass Herself twice. They watched me bound around my mother on our walks to the tombs and gather for her the flowers of the season: tulips, daffodils, narcissi, daisies, violets, poppies, and, of course, lots of anemones.

Every afternoon Mother walked to the tombs of the dead wives of former chiefs. The cemetery was located above an escarpment on the north end of the island which drew violent winds like a magnet; the water there was darker than wine and full of sharp rocks and whirlpools. The island folk called this exclusive cemetery "The Tombs of Nine Women," but they never visited it. "What is there to see?" the island women asked. "Except what's going to happen to us all?" But Mother preferred the company of the dead women to theirs.

On the morning of the first day of the religious holidays, twice a year, the doors of the villa were opened to the island residents; this was the fitting time to go and kiss the chief's hand. But Father didn't allow it. "None of that now!" he said, explaining that we were a modern republic and no longer needed to observe those old feudal practices. So the island folk sat in the drawing room, saying nothing, smiling shyly, and cracking their knuckles for a quarter of an hour.

When the quarantine installation was ready to deal with contagious diseases, the island folk were the first to get treated. Their skins, Doctor Nimrod informed them, were crawling with unseen animals. The itch drove them wild.

"They get no sugar in their diet," Aunt Baklava told me in the kitchen. "You get scabies if you don't eat sugar."

The folks would have preferred combatting the mange with amulets. But they were ordered to take the full course of quarantine treatment. They were scrubbed, steamed, thrown into sulfur baths, showered three times a day by the machines they themselves serviced and feared. Their clothes, bed linen, hats, shawls, curtains, and mats came out of the giant dryers wrinkled like accordions. They always kept some cherished item back; what Doctor Nimrod didn't know couldn't hurt them. Their mattresses kept the furnaces stoked for days. Although they received government-issue bedding, they grumbled. It's blasphemy to be this clean, they said. Perfect cleanliness is reserved for God.

But no sooner did they begin to scratch less than they began to scratch more. "Continuous reinfection," Father explained to me. "You aren't to go anywhere near the other children, that is, unless you want to receive the full treatment for the scabies."

Mother always said Father went overboard with his "draconian measures." When she pointed out the error in his ways, he listened but still ran the island as his father had run his fiefdom north of Ankara. My grandfather had been an Aga, one of those traditional feudal lords whose local powers had been so absolute that they had constantly challenged the authority of the sultan and had to be put down by the full military might of the Ottoman army. The Aga's despotism had been the reason Father said he had walked away from his duties and privileges as the heir. Yet he couldn't overcome the lessons taught by his father anymore than I can forget the many lessons he taught me.

"I won't go anywhere near the other kids!" I promised, hoping I wasn't already contagious.

I knew I wasn't a real child like the other island children, but I wished the island children could be made to believe I was one of them. Yet it was written all over my face that I was a little miss who had to be treated differently. The children had no playthings, so the girls collected old shards of broken plates that surfaced out of the earth after it rained, which they swapped with each other for shards that showed more elaborate designs. Old broken dinnerware on which old contagious people might have eaten gave Mother the willies, so I was told I had better not be caught playing with any old trash. The others were experts at hopscotch and jump rope; I didn't even know the rules.

If the weather was inclement, the children were driven to school over the causeway, riding in the cart pulled by a great big draft horse called Gentle. When the weather was good, Captain Forty-Lies had been given strict orders that I had to be isolated from the others. "On account of the scabies, ma'am," he said to the teacher.

"I see," said the teacher in a cool voice. "Tell the doctor it will be no trouble. I give his daughter advanced work anyway."

"Smart, huh?" Forty-Lies said, looking as if he disliked cool women.

"Smart enough," she said, waving him away.

Captain Forty-Lies liked teasing me, getting back at me for being associated with uppity women like the teacher and my mother. But he soured if he didn't get the last word, so he taunted me from the helm on the way back in the afternoon, "What are you reading at school, Miss Advanced?"

"*Gulliver's Travels*," I said, knowing it would stymie him. My glamorous half-sister had just sent me the book for my birthday. Captain Forty-Lies soured immediately. So when he said, "What's cooking at the villa?" he probably hadn't expected an answer. He was probably only joking about the cook, who was black and huge and stirred more curiosity on the island than even my mother.

"A cake," I said, shouting back over the thud-thud of the motor. "A birthday cake." Then weighing each word seriously, I added, "Today is my birthday." I knew none of the other children's parents remembered their birthdays.

"How old will you be then?"

"Eight."

"Imagine!" he shouted back. "A cake! I wouldn't know a cake if a cake came and bit me."

Something odd went through me, something like an electric current, a feeling of sorrow and regret. But I had already said the word *cake* and all the children were looking up at me with bright faces from where they sat on the floor. I remembered what Aunt Baklava had said about how you got scabies because you didn't get any sugar. When we docked at the island, I said, "Everybody is invited to my birthday party this evening. There will be chocolate cake and other good things to eat." I was surprised at myself, but there I was, inviting everyone.

"Oh, go on!" Captain Forty-Lies said.

"I'm serious," I said.

"Just the children, right?" he said.

"Everybody," I said. "Everyone on the island."

He didn't quite believe me, I guess, but nonetheless he spread the word. No one believed him, either, but the children said he was telling the truth.

I went up the tree as soon as I got home to do some serious worrying. I knew I had invited too many people. There were over twenty families on the island, and some had a lot of children. What would we feed them all?

But I said nothing to my parents about the party I was throwing. I said nothing even when Father gave me a handful of mosaic pieces from King Klazomenaeus' fabled palace. Back then, you could still find bits of mosaic that the waves spat out on the shore.

"Imagine," Father said, "these pieces might have been in a scene showing wood nymphs and satyrs. Chariots. Bronzed men. The king himself. Or a mystery based on the queen of the underworld pining for her mother."

Then he told me one of the early philosophers, Anaxagoras, had been born on this island, a philosopher of science who postulated that everything contained a portion of everything. "On this island, you get an inkling why he came up with that notion," Father said. "I'm not a rhapsodist, but I feel Anaxogoras' presence when I stand on the shore." He put the stones in my palm and closed my fingers over the treasure. "Happy birthday, little one. You will get your other presents when you cut your cake, but the mosaic pieces are your true gift."

They knew nothing about the party until the electrician arrived to string light bulbs from tree to tree.

"Begging your pardon, sir," the electrician said, "but the lights are for the party tonight. For the little girl."

That's when the electrician revealed to them the whole story. I was back up the tree before they had a chance to question me. I intended never to come down; nor would I ever provide any answers. The electrician wondered if it would be all right for him to run the generators past midnight, in honor of the occasion.

"They're planning to stay the whole night!" Father gasped when the man had left. "What kind of people accept the invitation of a child?"

"Really!" Mother said. "They're worse than children."

"We must put a good face on it," Father said, "and rise to the occasion."

"All those people!" Mother said, shuddering. "With the scabies!"

"I'm going to bed," said Aunt Baklava, who had lumbered into the scene. She already had a bandanna tied tightly around her forehead. "My head is killing me."

"Oh no, you don't!" Mother said. "If you go to bed now, I will do something I've wanted to do for a long time. I'll fire you."

"I'm not used to being talked to like that!" Aunt Baklava said, "But I'll go see what's in the pantry."

"I'll be there to help you," Mother said.

"Count me in," Father said.

"Come on down," Mother said to me.

I didn't say anything, nor did I budge. Soon the gardener arrived to place huge bouquets of Shasta daisies in the stone urns on the patio and to hang the garlands the children had been weaving all afternoon.

Captain Forty-Lies arrived with two baskets of fish which were so fresh, Aunt Baklava exclaimed, they were still jumping! Red snappers, silver flounder, pink perch, and mirror-bright *chipura* with red cheeks. He'd brought only the best fish, he said; no eel, mackerel, or stupid-faced groupers.

Pocks arrived with the game he'd bagged: quail, partridge, squab. He'd brought some men along to help him dress the birds in the kitchen yard. They dug deep trenches which they filled with hot coals. They laid branches and aromatic leaves on the embers, then the naked birds, then more leaves and branches, and covered it all with earth until dinner time.

And later, the women began arriving with platters of vegetables from their gardens, dishes cooked in olive oil in the island manner, leeks, artichokes, purslane, peas, fresh fava beans. They arrived bringing plums, cherries, tart green apples. They arrived carrying baskets of lettuce, spring onions, radishes, cucumbers first in the season. They set to making great mounds of salad. They arrived with the last of the last year's homemade wine, with dark olives, with dried figs and raisins. They arrived with all the bounty they'd been saving for a mysterious occasion, delicacies they'd been hiding from their own children. They wished they could've brought more. It's nothing, they said, just a few poor things.

But I would not come down the pine tree. I watched my scabrous guests eat and dance, sing songs about the heroes of the past and lovers who never meet, songs about animals, songs about the sea. I watched Forty-Lies pull himself to his wonderful height and tell lies in verse, daring the listeners to top him. No one could. I watched Chick-Pea, the chauffeur, dance with a woman's face painted on his naked torso, a dance that embarrassed me because, I guess, it was a man doing a belly dance. His nipples were the eyes and his navel, the mouth. I knew this stuff had something to do with sex. I was relieved when Aunt Baklava played her drum, the *darbuka*. Little Ayshe and her brother Ahmet recited poems they'd learned in school.

I watched it all from a distance. I watched my mother's splendid form weave among my guests. I watched my father dressed in evening black, in honor of the occasion. I watched the two of them show the islanders a few steps of the Samba, all the rage back in places where Mother wished she were, which embarrassed the islanders because the dance from Brazil was, I guess, so sexy that it made them double up with laughter. But they clapped and clapped. I watched the cook allow the children to touch her black skin and, as the evening wore on, I watched four toddlers fall asleep on her black bosoms which were as large as two pillows. After I was admonished again and again to come down and wouldn't, I watched my cake being cut and eaten.

I wondered about the dangerous contagions stirring in the air. About the subtle light of a hundred lanterns and the patches of color that were people. And long after my parents went to bed, the island folk remained there with their children sleeping in their arms. It was a mellow night, the most perfect night of the year. I burst into tears, wishing I weren't stuck up the tree like someone's stupid cat. But I was. If only I could be down there too in the picture, melting into someone's arms! How can I ever give back to them the birthday party they gave to me? I asked the tree. I have nothing precious to give.

And I fell asleep, melting into another world where I saw everything through the gauze of forgetting. And I woke up shivering. From up here, I thought, anemones are just a field of color, but down there below, each flower knows the pain of its own color: vermilion, crimson, ruby, carmine, claret, damson, lavender, amethyst, royal. Each color was mixed, each had a part of another color. Everything is part of everything else, I thought with joy. Then my heart leapt up. The people down there were not scratching. Not a sound. They really were not scratching anymore.

"They aren't scratching anymore, Old Man," I said to the tree. "I'll have you know that I've cured everybody."

I wondered if I didn't love this tree better than anything in the world, this old and churlish tree whose bark tore my knees, whose needles pricked my arms and hands. A tree so old, it must have been planted a long time ago by the philosopher who discovered that everything is part of everything. I thought about the tree. The tree had it worse than I did. Only a philosopher's tree could bend and bend in the wind and still not topple over.

"Some day, when I know how, I'll fetch up this island and invite the whole world," I promised the tree. "You just wait and see if I don't." Then I began scratching my ankles, then my throat, then the base of my spine. "You just wait, Old Man."

TUNISIA   *Zbida Shetlan*

Zbida Shetlan is a pseudonym for a woman from Korba, a small town on the Cap Bon, or northeastern peninsula of Tunisia. The interview from which this narrative came was collected in 1986 by Zeineb Tmani, a native of Korba and then a university student, as part of a research project on language variation that became the basis of Keith Walters' 1989 dissertation. Walters is now associate professor in the linguistics department at The University of Texas at Austin and continues to write on issues of language, identity, and society in Tunisia. The translation was done by Naima Elarbi, Maître Assistant, the Université de Tunis I (The Bourguiba Institute of Modern Languages) and Keith Walters.

MY STORY

Zbida Shetlan

My name is Zbida Shetlan, and I'm about forty-five. Good Lord, I don't know how old I am for sure, maybe forty-five. I just get by. I don't own any gold jewelry. Everything about me belongs to the past. Well, let me tell you, we all used to be just poor farmers. Back then, when we were young, we used to take the cow and the bull out to the field, and then we'd go back home to have a nap. Then, we'd build a fire inside the tabouna (clay oven) and bake bread. We'd milk the cow and sleep for a while. Then, we'd wash the clothes and do whatever we had to do. If there wasn't anything to do, we'd rest a bit, and in the afternoon, we went back to work. At sunset, we'd come down the hillside and go back home. We'd light the tabouna or cook dinner or do whatever God gave us to do. It was always like that. The next day, if God gave us a next day, we did the same thing. We'd go to work in the fields, we'd draw water from the well to water the orchards, and things like that. We'd grow the peppers and harvest them, and grow the tomatoes and harvest them. Everything had its season.

When I was young, I worked with my uncle, my father's brother. I was raised by my grandfather. Sometimes I was beaten. Sometimes I cried. Sometimes I just let them do whatever they wanted. They made me work. Whatever. At least until women like me got older and got married. Then things got better for us.

Back then, Daddy Salah, my grandfather, and my father, he had—may God protect you [1]—a donkey. At night, we'd

---

[1] This phrase [ħašɛk], used by older Tunisians, especially older rural people and women in particular, is uttered before the mention of things that might offend the hearer. Items in this category include

ride it home or to the lake. He'd cover me up completely with a burnoose; I didn't go anywhere outside the house without being covered. He'd make me wear a big old burnoose, so heavy that I couldn't walk. I'd start crying and say, "To heck with the orchard. I won't wear that old wool cape," and he'd say, "You wanna go back home or go out without the burnoose—you might as well go out naked." So we'd go to the orchard and do whatever had to be done. Granny Fadhila, Daddy Salah's wife and my step-grandmother, would say to me, "No, let me do it. You go home and fix lunch. Heat up the tabouna and do the washing up." So I'd go and get the grinding stones and grind the barley, as much as I could—one or two or three pecks. I'd make porridge, heat the tabouna, leave the dough to rise, and go take them lunch. They'd eat, and I'd go back home to heat the tabouna. Then, I'd go back to grinding barley. That's what I did every day. Every day, the same thing.

In those days, there weren't any machines to do work, so we had to grind grain every day with stones. I'd haul a whole sheaf of grain on my back and grind away. When I'd done six pecks or so, I'd grill some up by putting a pan on top of the tabouna or the clay pot that held hot coals for steeping mint tea. Every day was the same: I'd grind and then make bread from the flour I'd ground. Things have changed now. Now they have machines to do all the work, and everything has changed. Before, we'd grind about two sacks of barley. We'd grind it, put it through the sieves of different sizes, and then send it to the mill to get ground some more. Since we had a grinding stone at home, Granny Fadhila would say, "Let's grind up some cornmeal. We can't get cornmeal from the mill." So we'd grind corn and make porridge with oil and sugar. We had honey. Those were the days.

One day, Daddy Salah said, "We're going to go to the Borj family orchard; it's a long way so wake up early; make bread and whatever we will have for lunch so you don't have to come back for that." Granny Fadhila woke up early. She tried and tried to get me up, and every time I'd say "I am tired," and I'd ask her to leave me in peace. Well, sir, I finally got up. I helped her a little bit, and we ground grain. God preserve you, while the fire was burning under the biggest copper pot we had, we were grinding away, getting the corn meal ready. We cooked a whole pot of porridge, poured it in a metal pail to keep it warm, and we took along the big, clay platter and left, hoping to have God's blessing. Before I left, I got the dough ready. Granny Fadhila stayed behind, baked the bread, and joined us later. We ate that por-

---

mules, fire, and toilets, among others. Like the use of the expressions 'Good Lord' and 'if God gave us a next day', this phrase is used in an effort to protect both the speaker and hearer from tempting fate or from jealousy associated with the evil eye.

ridge, then Granny brought the bread in the afternoon. It was a long way from home. While we were eating, Uncle Beshir came along. He asked what we were having for lunch. We told him cornmeal porridge, and he said he was tired of eating nothing but that or rice or sorghum. Back then, there wasn't anything else, none of the different kinds of macaroni and spaghetti or couscous folks buy at shops these days. Well, Daddy Salah told him, "My son, one day you will miss this kind of food because it's what has helped us stay alive. So, be quiet and thank God for what He's given you." Uncle Beshir sat down on the ground with us and ate porridge until he was full. Daddy Salah told him, "See, you've eaten a lot." Then, Uncle Beshir agreed and said, "I declare, in the name of God, it was mighty good. Yes, it was."

Well, I grew up and went back to live at my father's house. He was always a day laborer and was very poor. My momma was no different. There were seven of us, four other girls, two boys, and me. My momma earned money when she could by doing this and that for folks in town. She used to make money by grinding dried red peppers into powder with a mortar and pestle. Momma would grind six pecks or twelve pecks or so of peppers at a time. Heaven bless her. She'd start early in the morning and grind all day long. She'd try to get me up to help her, and I'd beg her to leave me alone. "For heaven's sake, let me sleep. You want me to help you grind every day, every single day, every single day."

But she'd just say, "Come on, my dear little daughter; let's work so we can buy some couscous." We'd buy couscous from Mr. Haddad's daughter, God rest her soul. She sold whole wheat couscous—not the kind we have now—by the twelve-peck sack. Momma would swap some of her ground peppers for couscous. Because we had couscous every blasted day, we were tired of it. There was no bread from the bakery, like now. Day in and day out, it was couscous or something like that, the same every day.

Daddy made a living working for Ali Ben Mabrouk. He didn't own any land, so he had to work for somebody else. He was a sharecropper. I remember one day he surprised us by coming home with a big load of corn and barley. Momma said, "God is merciful. Your father works hard all the time, and he's brought us something good to eat." You can imagine how happy we kids were then. There wasn't much to eat. We had a large family, God protect us, and we sometimes went hungry—not like now. So, we unloaded that barley and that corn; you can just imagine how proud Mr. Ben Mabrouk was at that time; it was as if he had given us something extraordinary, as if he had done a really good deed. That year, as I told you, God preserve us, the crops were bad. We unloaded that precious barley and that precious corn. Ah! My daddy, he worked so hard. Anyway, we gladly took that blessed corn and barley, what God was willing to give. Momma was still grinding pepper at that time. People brought her sacks and sacks of peppers to grind, two or three at a time.

Oh, I hate to think of how I treated her. "Leave me in peace, Momma, please." Sometimes I'd go and help her, but often I'd refuse and go to sleep. She, poor thing, would just grind away, singing the whole time. Unbelievable. She would grind until dawn. There wasn't any radio or television then, so when she got bored, she'd just start singing old songs. There were only two of us girls then and one of my younger brothers. My sister was older, so she did all of the chores, baking the bread and cooking the meals. She had to because as soon as the sun rose, Momma was putting peppers out in the sun to dry. She was always looking for sunny spots where she could dry peppers. I remember one day, Abdelkarim Naceur, who was well off, suddenly knocked at the door. He asked if he had found the Shetlans' house. When we told him he had, he offered us a sack of barley and corn. He was giving alms to the poor. Momma said, "God has blessed us with some corn and barley." She wanted me to put the barley on to soak so she could grind it, but I complained. "Stop it. You always want to see me working." Whenever she asked me to do something, I'd go out to play with the other kids. She'd come running after me, saying jokingly, "May mischief befall you." How I liked to hear her saying that to me. I'd be playing with my friends, and she'd come looking for me everywhere—even in the graveyard— until she finally found me. That day, I went back to take care of the barley. I soaked it and put it through the sieves.

One day, Daddy Salah came to our house and said he'd come to take me with him. Momma didn't want me to go because I'd grown up, and she didn't want me to be away from her. He said I had to go to the orchard to help out because Granny Fadhila was sick. I said I'd go with him. He took me to his house in town, where they had olive oil stored in big jars four or five feet high, not like where we lived. Like a lot of old people, they had olive trees and everything and kept the oil in jars. He sent me to get some oil for the kitchen. I went to get an empty can to get some oil in. But when I touched the jar, it tumbled over on me. I started screaming and crying and ran to hide in the toilet. Oil was running everywhere, all the way to the doorstep, and I was hiding in the toilet. Daddy Salah came back and saw the oil all over the place and began screaming, "I swear by the Prophet, you've done it now, girl." I was crying and felt sick. When I finally came out of the toilet, I told him. "I barely touched it and it turned over. I don't know what happened. It just fell down and rolled over on me."

He was really angry and said, "That jar has been there for I don't know how many years and now you've broken it, God protect us, and you've managed to get oil all over everything." He went to get our neighbor, Aziza—

they called her Aziza Khaladia. "Come and see, Aziza, she's flooded the place." Thank God, the oil did not flow out of the storage room. So we went out, she and I, together, and then we came back with pails and we started trying to put the oil back into another jar. What a terrible day! I had to sweep and mop and scrub and sponge that oil and I . . . that was it. He took me to the orchard and beat me till I thought he'd broken my bones. He told everybody, "She did it. She spilled the oil."

Granny Fadhila wasn't much consolation. She wanted to know why he'd let me get near the oil. She said I'd ruined the whole year, wasting all that oil. Daddy Salah told everyone what I did. He told Uncle Hamadi to take me out to the orchard the next morning, if God gave us another day, to help change the course of the water in the irrigation ditches. I promptly said I wouldn't go, so here comes Uncle Hamadi, chasing me with a whip, beating me. So the next morning, there I was, changing the course of the water in the ditches, crying to myself, changing the course of the water and crying. And I kept getting tangled up in the ropes they use. Uncle Hamadi would come back, beating me. Then he put me to watch the animals as they turned the waterwheel to bring the water up for the irrigation ditches.

Once, while I was turning the waterwheel, I saw a huge rabbit in the rows of wheat. Well, it was sleeping or in labor or had just delivered. I went over and caught it. It was there with its two little just-born bunnies. I was so happy I'd found that rabbit that I ran to Uncle Hamadi, screaming that I had a rabbit. I told him we should cut its throat and eat it. "May your own throat be cut," he said. "You want to kill a rabbit that has just given birth. May this and that happen to you." Instead, he put the rabbit in a box with its little ones. "Go turn that wheel," he said. "May you be turned upside down yourself just like you turned that rabbit upside down." I was crying and feeling miserable. I told him I was starving, and he said, "I swear, girl, I'd divorce my wife before you'd get a bite of anything." One of my aunts brought some food. I didn't eat anything, and I was left turning that waterwheel and crying, turning the wheel and crying. Well, when the day was half gone, he said, "Let's have lunch." I looked at him and told him I didn't want to eat because he'd sworn I wasn't going to have a bite of anything. He said, "We have, may God protect you, cantaloupe and watermelon." Well, sir, I just went on cutting and eating melon, cutting and eating whatever was there. All the while, he kept saying, "Please yourself. Eat or may your head be eaten. What goes around comes around," and stuff like that. When he fell asleep under the mulberry tree after lunch, I ran away. I went to the orchard where Daddy Salah was. He asked me to go back to work for Uncle Hamadi. I told him in no uncertain terms that I would not. "He beat me, he let me starve. He ate and I didn't." Well, Hamadi woke up, and I was nowhere to be seen. He was furious. "That bitch, she must have gone to the orchard." So he left the horses there and came to the orchard. He asked me why I had run away. I told him, "Because I was hungry and you didn't want to give me lunch. I won't go back there with you. I won't turn that waterwheel again. I'll go back home to my mother. I'm not staying here any longer."

Well, he made me walk in front of him and he beat me with his whip all the way back to the fields, and I was so miserable. I was crying. Finally, when we got there, he left me to change the course of the water in the ditches, and he turned the waterwheel.

So there I was, my feet in the mud, crying, while I messed with those irrigation ditches. The wheel would get stuck. The camel and the cow that were helping turn the wheel would stray, and I'd have to get them back in place. And he'd come back to check up on me and say, "What's the matter with you?" Well, I said that the camel didn't want to turn for me, the wheel got stuck, and the cow didn't want to turn for me, so I couldn't get any water. Of course, I didn't want to do anything for him, least of all work. My heart was stone cold after the way he treated me. Finally, he told me to finish up and we'd head home. Well, I said, I didn't care whether the work got finished or not, I was going home like I'd said I would, and tomorrow, if I was alive, he would not find me there. I don't remember what he said, but he rained curses down on my head. How I hated him. We put out the light over the well, undid the camel and cow from the water wheel, let the horses loose, and went home. That was it. When we got home, and he saw Daddy Salah, he said, pointing to me, "This one deserves a beating tonight. This one, if we live . . ." And I said, "You've already beat me. And you beat me hard. Why don't you look at my bruises?"

Then Granny Fadhila said, "Let her be, please, let her be. You're the one who's to blame. You spoiled her by letting her do as she pleased when she was a child. You spoiled her, and now she thinks she's too good for work."

And I said again, "If we live to see tomorrow, I'm going home."

And my uncle swore that he'd follow me if I left and bring me back.

Daddy Salah said: "OK, OK, you can go home! But only if I take you." But I said "Forget it. I won't come back here." I told Uncle Hamadi to give me the rabbit I'd found, but he refused.

Well, Uncle Hamadi got up to leave and said, "And if you go home, who is going to break the other jars of oil?"

"Well, there are a lot of jars, and I'm sure you can find someone," I told him. "You're not going to let me forget that, are you? You're always mocking me."

His parting shot was, "Go spill the oil in the other jar."

That was one of the worst weeks of my life.

But that week, while I was with Granny Fadhila, Daddy Salah had guests. You know, guests at that time were not like guests now. Back then, if you'd give them even a little barley bread, it was something. And if you as much as offered them four eggs, it was like a feast. It sure wasn't like now, when you have to give your guests meat and other things.

Well, Daddy Salah's friends arrived and then brought some of those yellow dates and lots of things, henna, and what have you. Daddy Salah said, "Go get dinner for our guests," so I went to the chicken coop to hunt for eggs, farm eggs, you know, not the kind you buy now. I fixed the four eggs and got a loaf of barley bread, and they acted liked we'd offered them something special. They spent the night, so Daddy Salah went to get some meat, and he got some, the kind that country folk still have, not meat all wrapped up in paper like you get at the butcher's, but meat stuck on a skewer made from a tree branch. Well, he went to the only place that had meat, from a place where some folks lived who'd been on the pilgrimage to Mecca. When he got back, we realized he'd brought camel meat. At that time, there were camels in this part of Tunisia and sometimes people ate them. So we got the fire ready and put a big copper pot on to boil the meat. Well, that meat boiled and boiled and boiled, and it was still so tough you couldn't begin to eat it. I kept checking on it, wondering if it'd ever get done. Daddy Salah came to check on it. I told him it might be ready the next day, if we lived that long. We added cumin to it and everything, but it still wasn't ready to eat. He came back again, asking when it would be ready, and I told him, "Let me alone. I'll let you know when it's ready. This is the lot God has assigned us." Well, the meat finally started to get done because I could pinch it a little, so we put the pot on the floor so the guests could have their dinner. They ate and were happy. In the old days, folks weren't picky about their food like they are now. They just ate and were happy. They stayed up late talking, but I remember I just collapsed as soon as the sun went down, wondering why I had to endure all this when I could have a better life with my mother.

You know, my own father worked on a farm with my mother. She held the family together. She was the one who'd carry barley in a basket on her back. She was the one who'd grind it. She was the one who'd light the clay oven. She was the one who made the bread in the old days until one day my father and Uncle Hamadi argued. Uncle Hamadi said he would work only if we'd get him a wife. Well, Momma asked him how he was going to support a wife. He said he'd get married right then to a cousin of ours. He said, "Work? Is that all you want me to do? Work? And never get married?" Momma told him to earn a living first, and then, she'd get him a wife. He kept saying he wanted a girl to marry. Well, Momma said, "OK, earn some money, and we'll get her for you." The girl was Mr. Jaafar's daughter. Anyway, he had been working hard all year long, and he was so happy, planting tomatoes and peppers, and Daddy Salah paid him for all that. In those days, every cent counted—every little penny had eyes. And you could buy a lot of things with a buck, not like these days. Anyway, at the end of the year, the family let him be engaged to the girl. We thought that he'd get married that year or the following year or the year after that, but every year, the crops were so bad that there was almost nothing. We harvested just a little, and we were such a big family. And Uncle Beshir, he was, as they say, a happily married man. He had two little daughters and a son. He worked, he lived in the town, and he wanted Daddy Salah, his father, who still lived in the country, to provide for him and give him everything while he lived in town. Well, Uncle Hamadi told Daddy Salah, "You cannot expect me to work and not get married while you provide Beshir with everything he needs for life in town, letting his children benefit from my work." And Daddy Salah promised to help him get married that year.

Well, Uncle Hamadi did his best to take advantage of us, treating us like plow animals. Me and my brothers and my mother and all of us, he took advantage of us. We worked hard, day and night. One day, Momma said, "What's the matter with this man? He's going to kill my children. Why? Should my kids and I be worked to death just so he can get married? I swear, I'll leave this place as soon as the year is over." Then, they quarreled. But in the end, we stayed there that year, counting the days.

Once Mamma had made up her mind to leave, she told us not to work hard and not to get up early. Well, Uncle Hamadi would come bother us. He'd beat us and insist we go to work. I'd just say, "I don't want to get up," and I didn't. She and he quarreled every day. Daddy Salah insulted my father, but it didn't change anything. My father, may Allah bless his soul, would just stand there and say nothing. He tried his best to keep quiet. Anyway, one day, we packed up and moved to another uncle's place, leaving Hamadi behind. For a while, things got better.

Mahnaz Afkhami

IRAN   *Mahnaz Afkhami was born in Iran. She was educated in both Iran and the United States and served as director of women's affairs in the pre-revolutionary Iranian government. She has served as the executive director of the cross-cultural Sisterhood Is Global Institute and currently is president and founder of Women's Learning Partnership in Bethesda, Maryland.*

MAHNAZ AFKHAMI, LEFT

DEATH OF THE PATRIARCH

Mahnaz Afkhami

 I was born in Kerman, a sleepy desert city in the south of Iran known for its carpets and pistachios. In those days, these native commodities also determined the position and attitude of those whose lives depended on the production and marketing of each. My nanny Fatima, who instilled in me my first notions of how the world is ordered, told me at a very early age that those who dealt with carpets dealt with money. They were merchants. They were called *aqa* or mister. A whole other category of people, among whom my family had a rather prominent position, dealt with land and its produce. They were called *khan*. The third category of people were workers, who were called *adama* or human beings. My nanny was a member of this last category. I later learned to appreciate the subtle value system implied by this categorization.

The house in which I was born was part of a complex where my grandparents, my uncle Moussa and his family, and my parents all lived. The buildings looked out on a pistachio orchard. Once a year, at the end of summer, the trees burst out into the grape-like pink clusters that contained the pistachio nuts. The rest of the year the leathery grayish-green leaves looked parched, dusty, and dry. The small pomegranate tree near the pool, however, had a profusion of shiny green leaves. Its flame-red flowers seemed to draw nourishment and moisture from some inner source.

Our rooms were part of the building that was called the *andaroon* or the inner house, where the private living quarters were located. To the left of this building was a larger compound with wide steps leading to a pillared terrace. This was the *birooni,* or the outer house, in which our grandfather entertained visitors, conducted business, and once a week mediated arguments and conflicts, or, in times of an epidemic, ministered to the sick.

He was a slight man with thin white hair. I remember him wearing a long gray coat over striped charcoal pants, a costume resembling the formal morning coats of the British. Every afternoon he walked about the terrace, his arms clasped behind his back, fingers moving swiftly around his string of prayer beads, with his head bent over, lost in thought. We were not to interrupt him during his walks, nor were we to approach him when he sat on a stool waiting on a line of men and women who came from the villages to ask for his help with problems. Sometimes the problem was medical. During an epidemic of trachoma, many families came from the villages to kneel before him while he lifted their heads and turned their eyelids outward, touching the inside of the lid with a medicated sugar cube intended to cure their trachoma. But silence was never so strictly observed as when *Sarkar Aqa,* the Honored One, the elder of the family and the religious leader of the Sheikhi clan, returned a visit. "Sarkar Aqa" walked in with slow, measured steps, his long black cloak and white turban giving him an air of great authority. He was always accompanied by one or two other members of the family who walked behind him at a respectful distance.

Grandfather was connected in my mind with situations of import and gravity. Once I saw him preside over the trial of a servant boy accused of stealing. A pot of boiling oil was placed in the middle of the terrace, and the entire household stood silently in a circle around the pot. The boy was brought forward, and Grandfather explained the rules to him in a calm, kind voice, as if he were the referee in some new sporting competition. If he had not stolen the object, he explained, Allah, who sees all and knows all, would protect him from harm, and his hand would not be hurt by the boiling oil. If he was guilty, then his hand would surely burn. Just as the boy was moved closer to the pot, he burst forth with his confession and asked for forgiveness. He was sentenced to ten lashes, and we all were told to forget the incident, for the boy had paid his dues, repented, and would now have a clean slate.

Another time I saw Grandfather punish a scorpion that had struck the gardener's son, nearly killing the boy. The scorpion was surrounded by a circle of red hot coals and it moved round and round inside the circle trying to escape, drawing back as it felt the heat from the burning coal on all sides. The scorpion's movements became quicker and more chaotic. I had never seen an angrier scorpion in my whole life. Then it did something amazing: it turned its poisonous sting upon itself, struck its own midsection, and died.

Powerful as my grandfather was, he was overshadowed by the status and authority of my grandmother, who was a Qajar princess. Grandmother never moved from her room, except at lunchtime, when she presided over the noon meal. She always sat in her usual place, leaning on cushions made of finely embroidered wool and receiving visitors the better part of the afternoon and evening. There was always a samovar steaming in the corner and a tray holding delicate tea glasses and many plates of carefully arranged sweets. Waterpipes, *nargileh,* were brought in at regular intervals for each new visitor. From this spot, Grandmother controlled the household, determined the power and prestige of various members of the extended family by giving or withholding special tokens of support and interest, and regulated the affairs of the staff.

At two in the afternoon the family gathered around a *sofreh,* a rectangular white tablecloth spread neatly across the long room. Dozens of cousins, children, grandchildren, and visiting relatives sat on the carpet around the edge of the cloth. Karbalai Songor, the wiry, dark-skinned cook, a stern and proud figure, was an important personage at these gatherings. Her title, *Karbalai,* which came from the privilege of having visited the tomb of Imam Hussein in Karbala, gave her an added air of authority. She insisted on carrying the first of a number of large round copper trays which were full of bowls of rice, *khoresht,* and yogurt across the cobblestoned courtyard, around the circular pool in front, up the stairs, and into the dining room. The serving dishes were placed on the sofreh near Grandmother, who would place special morsels of meat on the plates of her favorite guests. Grandfather, with much less deliberation, randomly took pieces of meat from plates nearby and fed them to his two cats.

At lunch we always had *abgoosht,* a thick soup or stew made with lamb, tomatoes, potatoes, and garbanzo beans, and spiced with herbs and lemon essence. It was a reliable dish, since with the arrival of unexpected guests of unpredictable numbers, at the last minute the cook could add extra hot water to the soup without much damage to its taste or quality.

The children were expected to be silent at lunch. Adults spoke as often as their age and status permitted or when asked a question by the elders. An occasional inquiry about the menu was answered by Karbalai Songor, who stood in the corner behind Grandfather during this meal. The children usually giggled quietly and carried on with their own private games unnoticed by the grown-ups.

Villagers came regularly. Usually, the front gates would swing open, and donkeys would saunter in carrying on their backs loads of fruits and vegetables from the farms—melons, cucumbers, and potatoes. They were followed by a villager wearing a long coat, a wide black sash, and a small felt cap perched on his head. Grandfather carefully listened to their reports and managed to figure out their various dialects.

The reports from the villages were seldom cheerful. The weather never seemed to behave as expected; it hailed when the orange blossoms were most vulnerable, a heat wave struck just when the fruit had ripened, and frost came when it could do the most harm. But the household managed these mishaps and went on with its usual routines, absorbing whatever news filtered in from the outside. Back then the world was solid. Everyone had his or her place in the hierarchy, and law and order presided over a peaceful household. There were very few surprises. Everyone knew what to expect and was trained to do what was right for him or her and to take the consequences for any transgression. The laws of nature, of God, and of the household were not questioned. No one went hungry or was without shelter or clothing. None of us questioned the rightness of the order of things. It was hard to predict how rapidly all that would change.

Late one afternoon, I was playing by the flower bed, where I was making a miniature garden with waterways and canals. I tried to plant the lentil I had gotten from the kitchen, but my heart wasn't in the project. I knew the gardener would eventually flood my garden when his own plants required watering.

A stillness had descended on the place. I knew that Grandfather was sick. Earlier, the doctor had come, and I had watched him walk up the steps to Grandfather's room, his black-suited figure moving hurriedly across the courtyard with Jalal, the head house servant, almost running after him, carrying his black leather bag. On other days, he would stop and ask, "How are you, little *khanom?*" He would leave an hour later, giving me a pat and a smile, and move on, leaving behind a whiff of alcohol. I felt lucky that I had not been the one given a shot. It was commonly understood that any doctor worthy of his name would give at least one injection a day to any patient considered to be ill. If he was a serious doctor, he would also give a combination of pills, powders, and ointments. One cure would never do; the more important the patient, the more varied and complicated the remedies.

But that particular afternoon, the doctor walked into the room and didn't come out for a long time. Then, suddenly, my mother rushed out, her long skirt sweeping around her legs. She came down the main staircase and bent over me. She took my hand and told me in a hushed voice that my grandfather wanted to see me. I bent down to pick up my shovel. She pulled my arm and rushed me toward the staircase. The room was dark and the doctor sat by Grandfather's bed. Uncle Moussa and my father stood by the window on the far side and two other men sat nearby and whispered.

Grandfather's bed was in the middle of the room. His head, buried among the small white pillows, seemed so small. He slowly turned his face toward me as Mother gently pushed me to his side. He looked at me with gray, watery eyes and patted my head and said something I couldn't understand. I looked at my mother and saw her smile. I stood shifting from leg to leg. My grandfather turned his face and stared at the ceiling. My mother gently took my hand and we walked out. She told me to be very quiet and then turned and went back inside.

That night Grandfather died and the whole household was flung into a new era.

From the forthcoming *Scenes from a Life*

New Nations (1956–1962)

Oil Wealth and OPEC (1973–)

Israeli-Palestinian Wars (1967, 1973)

Camp David Treaty (1979)

Iranian Revolution (1979)

 The new countries carved out of the old Ottoman Empire had fought hard to become independent nations. They came to power facing all the problems that accompanied the pride of independence. Young and idealistic new leaders promised everyone—men and women—free education, free health care, more rights for women, representative government. And an end to the kind of poverty represented in an earlier period by the lives of Zbeda Shetlan and Halim Barakat.

But those promises were not easy to fulfill. Economic dependence on former colonial powers would not simply end; the markets for Middle Eastern products lay in Europe; capital for industrial investment was scarce; unemployment soared, and millions of men from Turkey, Morocco, Tunisia, Algeria, Egypt, and Yemen traveled to Europe and to oil-rich countries like Kuwait and Saudi Arabia in search of work. The antagonism between Israel and the Arab states continued with two wars, in 1967 and 1973, which took a heavy toll of manpower and resources on both sides. The military coup of 1960 dealt a blow to Turkey's burgeoning democracy, as Akile Gürsoy remembers vividly. Stateless Palestinians continued to live in United Nations refugee camps, like the one where Rafiq Abdul Rahman grew up. In Iran, conflict over oil rights led to clashes in the streets and the deposition of elected leader Muhammad Mossadegh in favor of the Western-backed Shah. Those turbulent days, recorded by the teenager Ali Eftekhary, led eventually to the Iranian Revolution of 1979, which brought an Islamic-based government to power.

The Iran-Iraq war, which followed, dragged on for ten years, and produced a million casualties. The Camp David Treaty led to an uneasy peace between Israel and Egypt. Lebanon was devastated by religious conflict, as was Algeria.

Yet education did prosper, and millions of young people, like Salah-Dine Hammoud, Fedwa Malti-Douglas, and Abdelaziz Abbassi, benefited. Literacy rates shot up to 70 percent in Iraq, 50 percent in Egypt, and 80 percent in Israel. The isolation of small communities like those of Hamza el-Din and Awad Abdulgader literally came to an end with labor migration and increased travel opportunities. OPEC, the new organization of oil-producing nations that was formed to regulate fair prices for the area's great natural resource—oil—gained increased bargaining power in 1973, when Libya challenged Occidental Petroleum and gained a better price for its oil. The life of Saif Dehrab in Kuwait was transformed by the oil boom, a transformation that eventually affected the world and helped to shape future international politics.

Salah-Dine Hammoud

MOROCCO *Salah-Dine Hammoud is currently an associate professor of Arabic at the Air Force Academy in Colorado. He was born in Meknes, Morocco, hence the title of his essay. He attended Mohamed V University in Rabat and went on to receive both the M.A. and the Ph.D. in Foreign Language Education from The University of Texas at Austin. Before returning to Colorado, where he and his wife met in a Peace Corps summer training program, Salah had taught in Casablanca, Texas, California, Saudi Arabia, and England. His research interests include language and cul-*

ture learning and teaching, the sociolinguistics of Arabic, and contemporary issues in the Maghrib.

A MEKNASSI BOYHOOD

Salah-Dine Hammoud

 The city of Meknes of the 1950s and early 1960s provided my brothers and me with a great place to live and play. The area of the *medina* where I lived with my parents, brothers, and sister was not poor but it was not rich either. Our street (*zenqa*), *Zawiya Touhamiyya*, was a long, winding, unpaved alley where the houses, which were of different sizes, seemed to predate antiquity. The massive wood doors were adorned with huge embossed nails and heavy door knockers. Behind those doors, the houses teemed with activity.

Even from the street, one could hear the pounding and grinding of spices, babies crying, women ululating, and songs blaring from radios. The radios were the old German or Dutch kind encased in mahogany. The higher the price one paid for these wonders of the modern world, the better the reception. Their ability to receive broadcasts from far away places determined their quality. The more powerful ones, the kind one spent one's life savings to purchase, afforded the luxury of listening to Voice of Radio Tangier, the Voice of Arabs from Cairo, and Radio London, which carried the BBC Arabic programs. Although Radio Tangier was famous for its long variety and music shows, the outside stations were often preferred for their extensive news programs and the variety and talk shows that opened one's eyes to the wider world. News was authoritative if it came from London, Paris, or Cairo.

Neighborhoods, as they are everywhere in old cities, were often named after a patron saint (*siyyed*) who sought the area as a last resting place. Our neighborhood was no exception. We had three neighboring saints to keep watch over us. At one end of the street was Sidi Abdekrim Ben Radhi, at the other was Sidi Ahmed Ben Khaddhra. Between the two was Moulay Thami, whose shrine (zawiya) was in the center of the cemetery and the playground for many of us neighborhood children. The zawiya also provided a sanctuary for people who were down-and-out and a shelter for battered women.

Our street was, in fact, named after this zawiya, though we knew little about Moulay Thami Al-Wazzani except that he had lineage going back to the Prophet Muhammad and had come from Wazzan in northeastern Morocco. He was a favorite of many women who came to seek his counsel and *baraka*, or blessing, and recite ritual prayers every Friday morning at his tomb. The core group of regulars among these women used to chant their prayers by using a single long string of prayer beads. To us children, it seemed like the longest string of the largest wooden beads that were ever made, a wondrous affair, for the ladies of the zawiya had to have a giant basket to carry it in and out of the inner sanctuary housing the tomb of Moulay Thami himself. The *M'qadma*, or the ring leader of this group of women, worked the beads and her orders into the chants like an accomplished orchestra conductor. Often some of those who came to seek healing prayers brought a huge platter of couscous. Then the ladies of the zawiya, much like the members of a tight-knit club, would end their ritual chants to commune over lunch before they put away that giant basket of beads and disappeared to their mundane lives until the following Friday.

Not until my adult years did I understand that this zawiya was significant as a small circle of a women's sorority. The women respected Moulay Thami and his descendants for giving them a vision, certainly, and possible solutions to their problems, but perhaps also for giving them an excuse and a place to meet, pray together, and share a meal and conversation. This was their way to come together spiritually. As boys over the age of four or five, we were not allowed in the shrine, especially when the women's prayer circle was in session. Even when we just stood and watched the women from the low window grille, the M'qadma would indicate our unwelcome presence to a woman in the outer circle who would then chase us away. I still remember that M'qadma, a woman in her fifties or sixties who had a real aura about her. The zawiya building itself was the responsibility of the saint's descendants, who were the custodians of the zawiya and held its key. They chose a caretaker and paid him a small salary for keeping the grounds clean and undesirable persons away.

The patron saint of the entire city of Meknes was not very far away from our neighborhood, either. He was known as Sheikh el-Kamel El-Hadi Ben Aissa. He was an idol to a variety of city and country folk who celebrated him in a big *moussem* or festival around the same time as Muslims everywhere celebrated the *Mulid an-Nabawi*—the day of the Prophet Muhammad's birth. Sheikh El Kamel was also known as *Damen leblad*, "the guardian of the city." He was the spiritual leader of the Aisawa religious organization, which practiced self-mutilation much like some Shi'a communities in other parts of the Islamic world. We knew that several attempts had been made by the government to prevent the Aisawa from hurting themselves or other shrine visitors. During the moussem, we as children were always warned to avoid wearing anything red, the color of blood. For it was said that when the Aisawa dancers in trance saw anyone in red, they would go into a fit and tear their clothes.

Sheikh el Kamel's shrine was Madrasat Bab Siba, my elementary school in Bab Jdid. It was in a marginal small business neighborhood near the flea market, and every day I walked past the small shops along the streets between my house and the school. First I passed a stretch of fruit and vegetable sellers, then a blacksmith alley complete with constant pounding and red hot fire bellowing out of the ovens. After that, I crossed a dry goods area with heaps of olives, raisins, walnuts, almonds, sun-dried prunes, and spices of every color. Finally, before I emerged on the square of Bab Jdid where the school was located, there was an alley where barbers plied their trade. In its heyday, this square was a smaller version of the famed Jaama' El Fna in the city of Marrakech, the town square where people congregated to entertain and be entertained, to have teeth pulled, to buy medication for any ailment, to get a haircut or a shave, and to buy a snack or a meal. You could consult a *shawwafa*, if you wanted to know what the future held in store, and watch skillful acrobats or Gnawi dancers perform. Whatever you wanted, it was to be found at Bab Jdid, so being there was always exciting.

Once in a while, I lingered there after school to listen to one of my favorite storytellers. He told tales from *One Thousand and One Nights;* he recounted the life story of the valiant pre-Islamic Arab warrior-poet 'Antar, his beloved 'Abla, and his faithful horse al-Abjar. He talked about the successes of the Arab-Islamic empire under the great Caliph Haroun Al Rashid. He kept the audience enthralled. We laughed and cried with the characters, applauded the heroes, and sat or stood glued to the same spot until it was time for him to collect donations or leave for the day. My aunt and grandmother would often notice that I was late coming back from school, and they would tell Father. Father's main concern, he said, was that I would start associating with the wrong lot. Where there are large crowds, he said, there is also room for mischief for petty crimes. There was also cannabis, gambling, and no doubt other illicit activities. I would then plead that I was only there for the entertainment, to listen to stories and gaze at people and animals. Snakes, pigeons, and monkeys were always part of the big show. The monkey man had his little creatures from the Atlas mountains well-trained. People laughed at the way the monkeys responded to their master's commands. There were Berber musicians and a man from the Sahara who sold snacks of grilled locusts. I tasted the critters once or twice and did not care for them much. There was always something happening for everyone at Bab Jdid, until things got out of hand, and then the guards policing the area would make people disperse. The government of newly independent Morocco made a concerted effort to rid the population of what was seen by the colonial and new authorities as signs of underdevelopment. Loitering in public squares like Bab Jdid brought to a focus problems of unemployment, hashish peddling, and crime. All were anathema to the presumed progress of a modernizing society and a new nation that was reconstructing after many years of foreign domination. Some of the Bab Jdid practices were perceived as rooted in pagan rituals and associated with illiteracy and backwardness. As such, they needed to be stamped out. But often these solutions amplified the problems rather than solved them. People could not spend their entire lives in mosques, and there were not enough schools for everyone who needed education. Bab Jdid provided a place where they could work or pass away the hours until better days. But the inevitable came and Bab Jdid square was shut down. I was sad to see the storyteller go. He apparently moved to Marrakech, where he was still allowed to practice his craft.

Our house on Zenqat Zawiya Touhamiyya was a rental property with two main rooms around a small, open courtyard and a kitchen and lavatory. Upstairs were two more odd-shaped rooms that we used for company as well as for storing grain and old furniture. Our main living area was downstairs, where the family living room doubled as the children's bedroom at night, and the second room was father's. It was a modest home, but we were lucky we did not have to share it with other families as was the case for many of our neighbors. Two or three families were often crammed into a house the size of ours. Our courtyard had a well in one corner. The well had many legends attached to it, many relating to the jinn or spirits who supposedly inhabited it. We used water from the well for drinking, cooking, and other household necessities. The plaster walls were whitewashed and the ceilings made of ornate Atlas mountain cedar and pine. Most of our furniture was banquettes, narrow mattresses supported by wooden benches raised some twenty inches off the floor. The banquettes were filled with either straw or raw sheep's wool which provided winter hibernating grounds for the cursed bed bugs. When they came to feast on my blood during the sizzling summer nights of July and August, they left their mark, and the giant red welts would itch for days. My parents tried every available pesticide, but our relief only came when small fumigating canister bombs appeared on the market. They became the most efficient weapon in our war against the pesky bed bugs.

Our street was unpaved for a long time, so it was dusty in summer and muddy during the rainy winter months. But the sanitation services were reasonably consistent, as the streets in the medina were swept regularly. Every day, a garbage collector stopped at each house and blew a small brass horn. His two mules carried large woven baskets which collected the garbage and transported it to the dump outside the medina walls. In those days, mules, donkeys, and man-drawn carts were the only way to transport goods in and around the narrow street of the medina. "*Raa!*" and *Shaa!*" were one-syllable words to which the animals would respond. They moved at the utterance of one and stopped upon hearing the other. As children we got to ride some of these animals. The flour mill, especially, let us use their donkey to transport and deliver sacks of wheat whenever we needed to grind any of our grain into flour.

Occasionally, a mischievous boy or two would follow the slow-moving donkey, poke him in the rear, and the ensuing chaos would disrupt the busy but otherwise orderly street. For the donkey would gallop, kick its hind legs in the air, throw off rider and merchandise, and run away. The burlap sacks of grain sometimes would break and spill all over the street. Passersby would then cooperate in the virtuous act of collecting the grain before pedestrians could ruin it. We all knew and believed that symbols of Allah's bounty, such as grain, together with His written word, were not to be trampled upon. Thus, if we were walking on the streets of the medina and saw grains, a piece of bread, or a paper with Arabic written on it lying on the ground, we would pick the articles up, kiss them, and put them away in some place where they were not likely to be stepped upon by people's dirty shoes. The habit has stayed with me, and I still feel a little guilt when I put Arabic printed materials or old stale bread into the trash.

Although sophisticated zoning laws appeared to be totally absent, and residential parts of the medina were much quieter than the hubbub of the suqs, there was some order in the chaos. A major selling point for homes was proximity to a public oven (*ferran*), a public bath (*hammam*), or a mosque (*jaame'*). And some residential areas were deliberately set far from the suqs and thus were much quieter.

The life of the medina began at dawn and continued well into the night. Nearby small shops tended to every need of their clientele. My father was respected as a *faqih* or learned person and also as a clerk in the civil court, so his name usually meant we could get credit in most neighborhood shops: Ahmed the Berber grocer from the Souss region; Si Tahar the olive oil dealer; Ali the milkman; Benaissa the butcher; Thami the barber. They all had a page for us in their ledgers. At the end of every month, accounts were settled and a new page in the ledger was started. Since he only had his salary as income, Father kept tight control on the spending. He made all the major purchases and set limits on what we were allowed to buy on credit in his absence. He usually did the grocery shopping for the day before he went to work.

Father's role of *faqih* or learned person won him respect in the community but also responsibility. The status somehow extended to us, his progeny, who were known as the *faqih's* children. For him, the title meant he could recite from memory any verse from any chapter of the Quran. He could also recall dozens of sayings from the *hadith*, the *al-Alfiyya* of Ibn Malik (a rhymed treatise of Arabic grammar), as well as innumerable verses of poetry that he spent years memorizing in study circles. He was also called upon to settle disputes before they went into the Qadi's or magistrate's court. He had attended a *medersa* or religious school that offered a regimen of rigorous courses taught largely by rote. The medieval, austere setting of the medersa was always a mosque or a mosque-like edifice not unlike the monasteries in the Christian world. Students lived in poorly lit, unheated "dorm" rooms that were hardly larger than prison cells.

The closest I came to attending a medersa was my tenure at the Quranic school "jaame'," known as *kuttab* in the rest of the Arab world. The jaame' was an integral part of the education of most children of my generation. At the tender age of four, I was sent along with my two brothers, Abdallatif and Aziz, to the local jaame', Derb Le'babsa, which stood around the corner from our house. The teacher, Faqih Basri, was an emaciated, pale-looking man who wielded incredible power over the sixty or seventy of us who packed the large upstairs room. The power lay not in his charisma but in our fear of his long and hard-hitting olive sticks that he used mercilessly to achieve an incredible amount of memorization from his pupils. His own memory was particularly sharp in remembering who did and who did not pay the modest weekly tuition. He relied for his living on this small fee plus other gifts such as clothing, sugar, and prepared meals brought by pupils' parents. Even the sticks with which he hit us were supplied by a father who tended olive and other fruit trees on the outskirts of the medina. Olive sticks were favored because they lasted longer and stung the worst. Thus I now find ironic the symbolism of the olive branch as a sign of peace, because my Quranic school fellows and I dreaded it so much.

We began with the Arabic alphabet chant, following letters traced on the large wooden slate and chanting them over and over. Then we began memorizing the *Fatiha* and later other shorter *suras* of the Quran. The jaame' also used the apprenticeship system, as advanced students helped the faqih keep track of novices and helped them with their daily lessons. They would use lead pencil or simply the thicker end of a bamboo reed pen to write out whatever verses we were supposed to write and memorize that day. The test came when we had to parade in front of the faqih and recite what we had committed to memory. If it was not done to perfection, the olive stick was bound to strike and we could not leave school on time. When the day's memorization was satisfactorily completed, students would be ordered to the sink, where we would erase the lesson and prepare for the next day's lesson by washing and drying the slate and spraying it with a light coat of grayish clay we called *salsal.* Often our next day's verses were drawn in light pencil, and we would trace over them before we were let go for the day. That jaame' scene was apparent chaos. Loud noises filled the room. Many choral repetitions from different groups at different levels of learning could be heard from a distance in the street, as we went over verse after verse after verse. To keep awake and maintain a sense of rhythm, we swayed back and forth and used the bottom ends of our reed pens to pound on the thick oak slates that we held as we sat cross-legged on the floor's straw mat.

This memorization went on day in and day out except Thursday afternoons and Fridays, the Muslim holidays. We were filled with feelings of joy those days, for we did not have to spend them in the suffocating atmosphere of the Quranic school. Holidays were fun and there were periodic "graduation parties" when a student completed fifteen or thirty or sixty chapters of the Quran. The lucky student was made to feel very special and was entitled to decorate his slate as he wished, often with a large and colorful arabesque design. He was then sent around town to show it off to people who would often give him money, some for himself and some for the school. He also had the prerogative on his graduation day to give the whole school a day off. On such occasions, mint tea, cookies, and gifts of money went to the faqih and to the rest of us.

Fridays, the bread oven was closed, and it usually meant couscous that day for lunch. Si Alami Soussi frequently came to our house those days. He was a bachelor friend of father's and a regular visitor at our house when there was no other more exciting party for him to attend. He would show up after the Friday prayer and was known for his great appetite. Sometimes he brought other friends along to eat the giant dish of couscous, but there was always plenty to eat for everyone. That was a time when women ate separately in the kitchen and did not join us for the meal. They brewed pots of famed Meknes mint tea and guests drank it to the sound of Andalusian music. We all napped and then took one of Father's long walks.

After the jaame' came primary school, an adventure that began well enough. I was lucky that Father had a very kind French man, Mr. Bournine, as his colleague, who lent a helping hand in getting me registered at the Bab

Siba school, supposedly one of the best. Mr. Bournine was the head interpreter in the civil court, where my father worked as the court clerk, and was one of the nicest of the *pieds noirs* (as the North African French came to be called by the great folks of the metropolis). Mr. Bournine came along with Father and me for the long carriage ride, and he pleaded for my admission with the French principal, Monsieur Voilard, who looked to me like a giant. He must have been a man in his fifties, for his hair was graying and there were wrinkles on his suntanned, leathery face. He *was* big, perhaps six feet two, and had deep blue eyes and a raucous voice.

Mr. Bournine explained that I had attended Quranic school for three years and could read and write Arabic without difficulty. Monsieur Voilard responded that my Arabic language skills were not going to help me with arithmetic and French, but he would admit me anyway. My initial apprehension about Monsieur Voilard, however, was justified. He walked around the school with Si Khammar, his Moroccan aide and interpreter. The latter's main function was to be the groundskeeper and school janitor. To me then and now, Monsieur Voilard seemed to be a living example of the French colonial stereotype. He had little doubt that he had a civilizing mission, a mission far greater than himself. He was, it seemed, living the challenge of overseeing the proper education of some three or four hundred young Meknassi Moroccan minds. He was temperamental, chain-smoked his *Gauloises Bleues,* lived in the new city rather than the medina, had nothing to do with us or the few Moroccans on his teaching staff after hours, commuted to the school in the heart of the medina in his immaculate black Peugeot 203, and ran a tight ship. I was terrorized by even the sight of him and as a result managed to avoid ever being sent to his office.

The all-boy school was old. The building backed into the massive old city walls, which were built in the 1600s by Sultan Moulay Ismail, a contemporary of Louis XIV; they stretched right through our playground. Erected to protect the city from outside invaders and to keep things under control, the walls were dotted with large holes that served as the home of all sorts of animal life. Storks came from Alsace to spend the winters in the warmth of Morocco and settled there on their way further south. Hundreds of swallows and other migratory birds nested there. But the excitement was particularly high when sometimes during recess we would catch a glimpse of a snake peering out of one of the holes. One of the French teachers, Monsieur Moulin, who was a resident snake expert, would coax out the big reptiles with a special stick and catch them to the cheering of the crowd of schoolboys and teachers.

Classrooms were crowded, and throughout the primary grades, the ages of children ranged between six and sixteen. Many of my fellow students had been admitted at various ages, because they had no records of their birth, or their parents had neglected or were unable to have them registered in school at the right time. In many cases, there were simply no schools for them to attend. The fact that a class included children and teenagers at various stages of development made for an atmosphere in which only the most resourceful and fittest survived. The older boys bullied the younger ones and took away their snacks and school supplies. Rules were hard to enforce despite Monsieur Voilard's iron fist. I remember having to negotiate deals where I would help older boys with their language arts homework if they would leave me and my mid-afternoon snack alone.

I vividly recall two of my teachers in the primary grades, Si Ahmed Chentoufi, who taught Arabic, and Madame Hebreard, who taught French and arithmetic. I was always much more fond of the latter. She was a stunningly beautiful and always sharply dressed Frenchwoman, which made remembering her very easy. Madame Hebreard seemed to me like a movie actress. During recess, she smoked cigarettes with a long holder, and she wore long, tight skirts. I always wondered about the life to which she disappeared after school, what her house looked like, what she ate and drank and what she did for fun. Si Chentoufi, on the other hand, was a stern mustachioed man who took his work all too seriously. He was strict, had no sense of humor, and wanted us to take his teaching as seriously as he did. He did not hesitate to use physical punishment with a vengeance when one of us got out of line. To avoid his wrath, I made sure my grammar rules and my poems were duly memorized and my notebooks were kept neat, because he despised sloppiness. I was glad of my initial severe Quranic school training, for it helped me do well in his classes. I had already been primed in Arabic reading, writing, and good penmanship, which he enjoyed. I had two or three friends with whom I sometimes studied since they lived nearby. Mohammed Ben Rouijel Layachi was a friend throughout secondary school and later in college in Rabat. He was intelligent, kind, well-mannered, and came from a modest family. His father had a small tailor shop strategically located outside the *qissariyya*, the cloth and fabric store complex. Like me, he was a no-nonsense boy who was in school to learn and later, if he could, help his family get ahead in life. We both ended up choosing careers in teaching.

Friday afternoons the whole family often went on outings. A favorite spot was to the shrine of Sidi Sharif Al-Wafi, which had one of the nicest panoramic views in Meknes. "Sidi Sharif sure has the view up here!" Father would say. It was near the Hotel Transatlantique, initially built for French VIPs during the Protectorate. From the hill all of the medina could be seen stretching far into the distance. We would eat our picnic of bread and olives, cookies and oranges before we headed back home. Sometimes we went as a family to Lahboul gardens, a beautiful park on the edge of town, and yet close to the heart of the medina. It was planted with exotic flowers and trees, and had several fish ponds and a small zoo where my brothers and I would spend hours. Not far away was the municipal swimming pool, our refuge and playground during the hot summer months. Once in every great while the family would pile into a taxi and go to an even more exotic park on the outskirts of the city. Known as "*La Vallée Heureuse*," the happy valley was a living fantasy of a French landowner, Monsieur Pagnon, who had built it as a private retreat and installed a series of ornate gardens of flowers, rocks, and water falls, where all kinds of singing birds and butterflies gathered. More rarely, we were treated to longer outings to the nearby Shrine of Moulay Idriss, to the town of Ifrane, or even to Fes if Father was able to round up a friend with a large car or a pickup truck.

The games we played were simple but fun. Many were seasonal, and some were old standbys like "*Haba*," our version of hide-and-seek. We also had our own cops-and-robbers kind of games. Some of these had probably come to us from the French, but when the names for them were adopted, their pronunciation was distorted so they sounded like indigenous games. Marbles had a particular appeal to me and I became good at it. It required special skill. As in other parts of the world, marbles came in a variety of sizes and colors, and the game had a life, a culture, and a language of its own. This was true across cultures, as I was able to confirm many years later in discussions with a Mexican-American fellow graduate student who wrote an elaborate scholarly paper on the sociolinguistics of marbles in his community.

I was also fond of playing with a conical top, a "*trembu*" or "*tronbiyya*," as we called it. We would tightly wrap a string around it and propel it in the air but still holding the string. And we ran around the streets of the medina with old bicycle wheels, "*janta*," with the spokes removed. The skill of the game consisted in maneuvering and guiding the wheel without allowing it to fall in the midst of streets crowded with people, donkeys, mules, and bicyclists. On special days like Ashoura, we had Nwa'er, ferris wheel–like rides, some of which were scary. When the circus came to town, we had to beg Father to take us all to see it. Memorable also were the regional fairs that gave the artisans, the farmers, and the business owners an opportunity to show off their products. My brothers and I loved collecting the little trinkets the more advertising-conscious businesses gave away: key chains, pencils and rulers, or balloons.

In our seemingly placid lives as children, we were not generally bothered by the adult world around us. But at the same time, our attitudes to that world were being shaped, sometimes in the image of our parents but also by other adults who were in a position to influence our lives. Above all, we could not be altogether oblivious to what was going on in town and in the rest of the country and the world. France had its grip on much of North Africa, and there was a great deal of local resistance to the occupation. Often I would come home from Quranic school and hear of the arrest of someone's father or uncle by the occupation forces because he was *watani*, a "nationalist." On my street I would see French army regulars and police on their patrols. In 1953, arrests were intensified when King Mohammed Ben Youssef (Mohammed V) was exiled by the French to Madagascar and Corsica. Senegalese soldiers who were French army regulars roamed our streets, watching for any sign of the beginning of organized demonstrations. Occasionally, we would feel a little defiant and tease the soldiers by calling them names we knew they did not understand.

Demonstrations were often peaceful and awe-inspiring, but they sometimes ended in senseless violence and arrests and occasionally death on both sides. Tensions often rose very high, such as when Monsieur Manuel, the owner of the nearby brick factory, and his family members were assassinated by disgruntled thugs among his workers. This was one of the ugliest episodes in Meknes then and for many years to come. It was certainly the worst incident I remember in the period of resistance to French colonization.

When King Mohammed V eventually returned from exile, and later when France decided to grant Morocco her independence, the people's euphoria overflowed. Families crammed into flag-draped cars, taxis, buses, and trucks to go to Rabat and welcome the king home. For days, the country was transformed into one giant party. Strangers offered tea and *ghuriyyba*, and people took their living room furniture out on the streets, which were decorated with red and green Moroccan flags and with portraits of the king. Singing, dancing, and the blare of loudspeakers filled the air. As youngsters, we imitated the adults and had our own celebrations. We formed little orchestras with improvised instruments and made a great deal of noise. Independence was truly a happy time in our lives as children, in the life of our streets and neighborhoods, and in the life of the country.

KUWAIT *Saif Abbas Abdulla Dehrab*

*Saif Abbas Abdulla Dehrab was born in Kuwait in 1940.
He had his early education in Kuwait and Damascus.
In 1962 he went to college in the United States, and he
received his B.A. in 1966. He then joined the Kuwait
diplomatic mission in Paris and finished graduate school
in 1968. In 1976, he became the first dean of students at
Kuwait University. In 1980, he first assumed a diplomatic
post in Washington, DC. Then he returned to Kuwait to
resume teaching and chairmanship of the political science
department. During the Iraqi invasion of Kuwait, he
worked with Citizens for a Free Kuwait and was active
in the media and academic circles. He has several joint
and individual publications in Arabic and English. His
recent publications concern youth movements and attitudes
in the Gulf.*

SAIF DEHRAB, LEFT

CHILDHOOD IN THE SAND

Saif Abbas Abdulla Dehrab

I was born on the sand dunes near the shores of the Gulf. I was born into a humble family, but at that time my country Kuwait was also poor and humble. Everything outside the city walls was literally desert. I was born in a mud house, in a room we call *'Arish*, a kind of arbor made of interwoven twigs. The living standards in that house, at that time, probably were no better than that of rural India. Today I live in the United States with a good income. My life, like that of the people of Kuwait, is a story of change and transformation: from poverty to wealth, from ignorance to knowledge, from illness to health, from horse buggy to jet plane, and from the desert to New York and Paris. For all this, Kuwaitis may take some credit, but it could not have happened if we had not been lucky. We were lucky because we were there when a miracle took place: the discovery of black gold—oil. As for me, I attribute my luck and any success in my life to three things: to being born at that time, to my country, and to my mother.

I confuse my American friends with the fact that I have more than three birth dates! When I was born, my father was a sailor aboard a dhow travelling between India, the East African coast, and the Gulf shores. I was left to the mercy of my mother, who named me twice, only to have my father reject these two names and give me another when he returned from the sea. So my name is *Saif,* which in Arabic means sword. Never mind that Texans murder my name when they pronounce it, the nagging question is who on earth would name a child "sword" in the twentieth century? My father did.

The reason I have more than three birth dates is simple.

There were no birth registrations in Kuwait until the mid-fifties. By then, the school physician had checked my teeth, just like a horse, and registered a date for me in the school book. Years later, when I was seeking a scholarship to come to the United States, the official in the Ministry of Education pointed out that I could not go to America without an official birth date. "Why not choose a good month the Americans like?" the official said. "Like what?" I asked. "March, it is spring time and the Americans love it," he replied. So it was March that we chose. My friend chose March 18, and I chose March 21. I missed the Iranian/Indian holiday of "Nairoz" by one day. However, that date did not stick and was not accepted by local government bureaucrats when, four years later, I sought a job in the foreign service of Kuwait. The bureaucrats sent me to another physician who specified my birth as June 26. Years later, the passport authorities gave me yet another birth date: September 19. To this day, I have to stick with September 19, because all my official papers use that date. Further, the passport authorities in Kuwait gave the same birth date to my wife! But whatever the birth date, my story covers a period of over fifty years of opportunities and turbulence for myself and my country.

Next to oil, probably the best thing God gave Kuwait was its women. When Kuwaiti men were out at sea, it was the women who had to manage the family affairs, make sure that intruders would not come to the neighborhood, and even keep up the house renovations. My own mother was really a woman for all seasons. She was a wife, a mother, and a hardworking person. I can judge she was a fine woman and a hard worker, but I am not sure how good a wife she was, if judged by the fact that my father had a second, a third, and a fourth wife immediately after he got a relatively good savings account! Of course, having a second wife, in our culture, is not necessarily an admission of the first one's shortcomings. Men brag about it as a way of showing off their manhood or masculinity. It is amazing how a man believes he is virile and full of stamina by marrying a younger wife even if he spends night after night next to her without a creditable erection!

In the days of austerity, before the oil economy, my father was content with my mother as a wife. She had more than seven children for him, a vivid testimony of some sexual activity and satisfaction. Only when my father became better off did he start to act cranky and announce that he wanted a second wife. My mother agreed and helped him find a young, flexible, and juicy young lady. This new wife was almost my age at the time of my boyhood. It was hard for me to think of her as a stepmother.

My mother would always get up very early to do her morning prayers and present her *dua'a*, asking favors from Allah, which to me sounded like a shopping list that she presented to Him every day. Now, I believe Allah is generous, but I am not sure how much or how many of her requests were answered. I am sure her request that my father keep her as the only wife did not work. I confess I never heard her request this from God, but given my father's humble economic position, she must have taken this for granted, thinking that even if God did not forbid my father from doing so, his pocketbook would.

When the economy began to take a new turn, my mother, after praying, would milk the cows and goats we kept in our home. She made butter, yogurt, and also buttermilk that we sold to our neighbors. Also, she baked fresh bread every day. She sold that bread, along with whatever eggs were available, to a few lazy women in the neighborhood. The cash went to my father, who used to kiss the money (the bank notes, not the coins) while raising his hand toward the skies with his eyeballs rolled up as if he were looking to Allah and saying *alhamdo lilah* (thanks to God). Although my father was a religious man all his life, I noticed in his later years that he was never grateful and appreciative like he was in the old days of simplicity and austerity. Scarcity has its religious function.

I still do not know how my mother managed everything she did with such limited means. My father was a sailor for many years; he would travel to India, Iraq, Iran, and Africa for several months at a time, only to come home with limited earnings. Often the sailors came home with nothing, only to find themselves in debt and at the mercy of the seafaring oligarchy who owned the boats. When my father came back from a voyage, occasionally we would enjoy the mangos and coconuts he brought from India. Otherwise, I saw little or no change in our lives as a result of his work.

The first school I attended, probably beginning at the age of eight, was taught by a mullah, a man knowledgeable in religious affairs who teaches children to read the Quran, to write basic Arabic, and at times some simple arithmetic. My mullah was a *sayid*, that is, one who claims descent from the Prophet Muhammad. This sayid was a Shiite and more tolerant of coeducation than those from the other local school, which was run by a Hanbali sheikh. So my first school was mixed: boys and girls sitting side by side on a mattress woven out of palm leaves.

The girls, then as now, were far better than the boys in reciting and memorizing the Quran. Once they finished doing their lessons, the girls used to tutor the boys while the mullah sat watching. If one of us misbehaved, suddenly a nice thick stick would whack us. The mullah was not selective in choosing a spot of our bodies on which to land his stick. Our heads were easy targets. I do not recall that any one of us had brain damage, though none of us became nuclear physicists either. Beating children at school was normal practice. As a matter of fact, parents often said to the mullah the first day they brought their children to school: *"lek al-laham wa lena al-adhom."* Literally translated, this means, "The meat is for you mullah, but the bones are for us." In other words, the mullah could beat the kid as much as he wanted as long as he did not break any bones. The bones were the prerogative of parents to break!

I believe my generation was raised in an irrational age. We were not allowed to think in a way counter to our teachers and elders. I recall that on Thursdays, the mullah used to bring a colored pencil and a dye to mark our bodies before we left school. The objective was that if one of us had gone swimming in the Gulf during the weekend, the dye would wash away and the mullah would know. Now, in retrospect, what was wrong with going swimming? What else could we kids do at that time but go swimming? The God-given playground in Kuwait was, and still is, the sea. Had I asked this question then, probably I would have many scars attesting to my bravery and critical thinking.

The boys, when they finished their lessons, always had work to do at the mullah's house, which was separated from the school by a low mud wall. During shrimp season, the boys had to boil, dry, and peel the shrimp for storage. Some of us were fond of shrimp, so the vigilant mullah had to divide his attention between his shrimps and his teaching. Nevertheless, it was better for the mullah to seek our help, for otherwise the shrimp were vulnerable to the neighborhood cats circling around waiting for a chance to grab a delicious bite.

We went through the same ritual during the season of grasshoppers and dates. In cooking grasshoppers, we had to be careful not to let any grasshopper escape from the burlap sacks before they got to the boiling water. I learned how to make sure all the live grasshoppers dropped into the boiling water; I simply lowered the opening of the sack into the water first, thus cutting off the grasshoppers' escape route. Once in the boiling water, the grasshoppers could not jump away. For that talent, I was the mullah's favorite grasshopper chef!

In the date season, we used to clean and sort the dates and then place them in metal containers. Afterward we would wash our feet and press the dates by foot so that no pockets of air would let the dates spoil. When the mulla was satisfied that we'd done enough pressing, he would cover the container with lead and seal the edges with a hammer. It took more than one of us to carry those containers to the storage room in the mullah's house. And these were not the only tasks we had to perform; any household activity was fair game. We did this work in addition to paying the mullah our very meager tuition. He did give us, however, one Indian rupee, the equivalent to a quarter of a dollar, for our work each month.

So in those early days of my childhood, school was not all education and play. Consequently, we often did not attend. All it took was an excuse from a parent. Any excuse was acceptable, because morally and legally no family was under the obligation to send their children to school. But at the same time, if no written or oral excuse was presented, the absent pupil would receive a good beating. We were never considered innocent until found guilty. I was lucky, later on, to find a kind man working as a chief guard in the market who wrote me all the excuses I needed. I do not know how many times I had my grandmother and grandfather die, even though both had died years before I was born.

I continued going to the mullah until I lost interest, and my mother moved me to another school that was more advanced. There we were taught Arabic language and literature, English, geography, and arithmetic. We also had one period for physical education, chanting, and the recitation of poetry. I loved reciting poetry about the glory of Islam and the Arabs in the early mornings in front of the whole school. I had a strong voice (there were no microphones) and the ability to move my hands and body with every sentence; this movement was to make the boys believe these historic glories, inflame their emotion, and make them give me a big hand at the end.

In the new school, we did not sit on a mattress but in regular classrooms behind modest desks facing the teacher. Still, the headmaster did have a big stick. This school was far away and I had to walk several miles twice a day. On the way to school I had to pass through the old suq. By this time, I had learned both the Arabic and English alphabets, and I enjoyed reading the signs on the newly established businesses. There was a sign for Singer sewing machines. The next sign was for a pharmacy. But the sign that intrigued me most was that of a Christian missionary. "Al-kitab al-moqaddas" (The Holy Book) read the sign. I stopped once to gaze into the shop. I saw many books in Arabic and English. But I did not know for whom they were intended, since I saw very few people go in the shop. When I stopped once for too long watching, the man inside asked me to move along, since I was young and could not read any of the books. I arrived late to school that day but never forgot the sense of intrigue I felt about that missionary shop. Later on I realized how tolerant Kuwait was at that time.

Once when my father was away, I quit going to school. I told my mother that I had no books. But my mother grabbed my right ear, jerked it, and said, "Tomorrow you will have books." I thought she was just bluffing, but she took me to a modest bookstore in the suq to buy my books. "You *hmar* (donkey), go to school," she said. "I don't want you to become a *hammali*, a porter. Or a sailor. Look how your father is suffering in the bad weather and the rough seas. God knows he might not come back." In these cases, her predictions were wrong. My father came home safely. Her fear of my becoming a porter did not happen either. This was because, only a little later on, the newly-rich government employed all semi-educated and uneducated citizens in government posts as bureaucrats and administrators. One's birth as a Kuwaiti citizen was the only criterion for getting a job.

A new government school opened about this time, one that provided students with food, sports, shoes, and clothing. My friends described the Palestinian and Egyptian teachers that told them interesting stories about Egypt, Palestine, the Jews, animals, and wildlife. They also said that the school had a place where they kept live animals and that I could become a Cub Scout with neat clothes and badges. I told my mother I wanted to go to the new government school.

And before I knew it, there I was. The government school issued me my first pair of pants ever, two shirts, a pair of shoes, and uniforms for physical education classes. My books were new and full of pictures. The books were printed in Egypt with the pictures of King Faruq of Egypt on the first page of every book, even though King Faruq was already deposed and living in exile. The Kuwaitis were in a hurry. They did not have time to print books and put in the picture of the amir of Kuwait. We did not care. We felt lucky in those days to have all these new opportunities available to us.

At the expense of my government, I went through all stages of my regular education: grade school, college, and finally graduate school. But everyone in my generation in Kuwait was similarly lucky. For me, being lucky started with the time I used to sit in the street at night with my friends listening to an Omani worker tell stories about life in Oman and how the Arab folk hero Antar Bin Shaddad still existed and roamed the mountains of Oman. He used to tell us about the witches that move around from one town to another within seconds. "Wow, that fast?" one of us would ask. "What is *daqiqa*, a second?" I would ask. "When you grow up and buy a watch, then you will know what a second is," he answered. He himself did not know. This hard up Omani worker did not have a watch. I was determined to get one.

I was also lucky to survive, because my health was left to fate and chance. I was ill so many times that my family placed me on a mattress in a corner waiting to pronounce me dead. Until the age of 9, I had never seen a doctor except once in the American missionary hospital. That doctor felt I was a hopeless case. Had I been born three years earlier, I might not have gone to school at all, like my older brothers and sisters. Had I been a bit older, I might have been riding the seas just like my other two brothers. One of them lost one eye and was seriously maimed while at sea with my father.

I did lose many friends to accidents and illness. I lost one, at least, to the sexual desires of a man who used to pounce on children. For days we missed our friend from the storytelling sessions. His family kept looking everywhere for him. We, his friends, volunteered to see if he had fallen in the well. With a lantern in hand, one by one we were sent dangling to the base of the well only to find nothing. Some of the children said the wolf must have taken our friend. Some of us, in our fantasies, imagined that the witches from the mountains of Oman must have taken him. To our surprise, we found out that a human wolf had taken his life.

The killer, having raped the poor kid, killed him and buried his body right in the bedroom under his own bed. The cruel customs of our times made us, his friends, in the presence of the killer and male grown-ups, help dig up his decomposed body. That day we were sad but also knew we were lucky. The victim could have been any one of us. As children, we could not imagine what could have happened; years later, we learned that sex had driven the poor man. I hated the causes of my friend's death: sex, rape, and desire. I was so angry that I was hoping to see the man who killed my friend dead. I had no one to turn to who could alleviate my anger and explain to me what happened. One day coming from school, I saw the body of the killer suspended from a high post after he had been sentenced to die. I was told the uncle of the victim executed him, not the government. People said this was the best way to settle a revenge cycle. At first I felt good, but then tears came into my eyes; I remembered that man. I remembered that sometimes he was kind to us, the kids. For the first time in my life, I felt that even a wicked human being could be a victim.

As children in Arab society, we did not know the complex and natural mechanisms of sex that we would teach our children in a modern society. But, while talking about sex is taboo, seeing sex is not. Given the limited space that our families lived in, sex differentiation and identification started early. As a child, it was one of my favorite pastimes to go outside our neighborhood and watch men visiting prostitutes. I recall that the majority of the men were migrant laborers from all around the Gulf and the Middle East. The girls, who were always covered and veiled, at least to us the boys, came from the desert and from outside Kuwait. Concealing their identities was very important. I still remember the rituals taking place while we watched. A man would stand at an open door and ask the girl, "How much?" A price would be quoted. As with every transaction in the Middle East, bargaining would take place. After some negotiations, if agreement was reached, the man would enter the house and the door would be locked behind him. Immediately, we kids would hear some music from an old gramophone. Who said we were not romantic! This was how we listened to many songs in our childhood. Most of the songs were Iraqi and Egyptian.

Those images, however, made me morally confused. I was infuriated to see the girls selling their bodies. "*Haram*, sinful," I said to myself. But I kept going back to watch. I admit that even now I have not resolved this moral dilemma.

When I was about twelve, the government decided to send a group of Boy Scouts from Kuwait to Egypt for a camping assemblage in Alexandria. Committees met to interview and select the "good ones" to represent Kuwait. I was selected. The government gave us all the things we needed for that trip except watches. I remembered the Omani storyteller. "When you grow up and buy a watch, you will know what a second is." How could I go to Egypt without a watch? A watch suddenly became a status symbol that I had to have. My older brother, being proud of me for being chosen to go to Egypt, took me and my younger brother to the old city and bought two reasonably cheap watches. I immediately put on my watch. Suddenly, I felt I was two feet taller. But still I felt I was missing something. Ah, I said to myself: to look completely modern, elegant, and à la mode, I need a pair of eyeglasses. I did not wear glasses because my eyesight was good, so I borrowed the glasses of my younger brother, who was semi-blind without them. With the glasses on, I resembled Gandhi. I was thin, dark, and also hairless, for it was the custom to shave boys' heads. At that moment, I remember, with the watch on my wrist and the glasses over my eyes, my brother and I held on to each other and bounced through the market, knocking into people: I, because the eyeglasses did not fit me, and my brother, because he could hardly see. People kept asking, "Are you guys blind?" Indeed, at that moment, we were.

But I did not wear the eyeglasses to Egypt and Lebanon. For days I kept packing and unpacking my humble belongings in my Boy Scout bag and my one small suitcase. I packed my Boy Scout issues and did not forget a pair of orange swimming trunks that I was planning to wear to impress all the girls on the Alexandria beaches. That was about the time Egyptian movies were beginning to arrive in Kuwait, and we used to watch them in private homes. The children would move from one home to another. By word of mouth, we would hear where the next movie would be and before dark we would be sitting on the ground waiting for the images to appear on the screen.

The trip to Egypt and Lebanon was an eye-opener, for until then, all I knew about the world was Kuwait. We took Egypt Air to Beirut. It was July. It was hot. We consumed all the water onboard.

In Beirut we were supposed to have a short stop. It became a long delay for technical reasons. To me it made no difference as long as they fed us well. Indeed they did. It was my first experience with Lebanese cuisine: kibbe, hummus, shish kebab, and bottled water! Fabulous. After eating, through force of habit, I wanted to do my noon prayer. I asked one of the waiters to point out the direction to Mecca. He took me out to the balcony and showed me that from Beirut I could not see Mecca. He told me that the mountains hid Mecca. So, he said, if I insisted on praying, I could choose any direction I wanted. I knew he was teasing me. So I said, "I've never seen Mecca, but I know that Allah is everywhere." Then on the balcony of the airport I performed my prayer in total defiance of that waiter. This was in the mid-fifties. I should have realized then that the people of the Gulf were already becoming the envy of their fellow Arabs. I should have known that our new wealth was not justified and sanctioned by others. Ridicule and sarcasm was one way the other Arabs were settling their accounts with the people of the Gulf.

Our Boy Scout troop arrived in Cairo after midnight, but there was no time to rest. All our stuff was packed into buses, and we hit the road to Alexandria, where we set up our tents and slept till late afternoon. When our Egyptian hosts came knocking on our tents, our leaders were embarrassed that the "vigilant" Boy Scouts of Kuwait were sleeping late. The first order was to tidy our camp.

"Remember," said our leader, "the eyes of the Egyptians are upon you."

Nobody at that moment was prepared to start tidying our camp. If Egypt's eyes were upon us, our eyes were upon breakfast. Only after eating did we become cooperative enough to check our baggage. Alas for me, my suitcase with the orange swimming trunks was missing. It took Egypt Air a week to locate my bag. By then, the Egyptian girls on the beach were all gone!

In Alexandria I saw Gamal Abdul Nasser in person, for our visit to Egypt coincided with the nationalization of the Suez Canal. Nasser came and gave the Arab Boy Scouts and their teachers a roaring speech. What a charismatic leader! Tall, dark, and handsome, he was created and designed for politics. When he spoke, I do not believe people were listening to what he said but just observing in awe how he spoke. The Canal is Egyptian, he said. With blood and tears we dug the canal. It is Egypt's and only to Egypt does it belong. This was the gist of what he said and nobody disagreed. A few days later, after we left, Egypt was attacked by Israel, Britain, and France to punish her for nationalizing the Suez Canal. How unjust it was to do that to Egypt, I thought, and I realized then that politics could be unfair and immoral.

Besides attending the opening parade, going to museums, and visiting the palaces of the deposed King Faruq, we did very little in Alexandria. I was so moved by our pleasant visit that I kept reciting a Boy Scout cry in Arabic: "*akel, wa shurb, wa naum,*" which meant "eating, drinking, and sleeping." In Arabic it rhymes well.

Back in Kuwait, our Egyptian teachers, who were devoted Nasserites, presented the Suez crisis and the Israeli attack as a victory that Egypt single-handedly scored against Britain, France, and Israel. For several days during the attack on Egypt, we stood in the school yard and shouted, "Death to Britain, France, and Israel." Toward the end, we were encouraged to go out on strike. There were many demonstrations in the suq led by Kuwaitis, Egyptians, and Palestinians. I was persuaded to join. I did. But one day policemen suddenly appeared, and our leaders disappeared. We took a good beating. It was not a beating to kill, but it surely hurt. We all ran away. I learned later on that some boys not too knowledgeable in the art of riots and demonstrations ran away and tried to hide in the British Embassy, the place which was most protected that day. There they were beaten again, and they all promised the authorities they would not demonstrate again. I assume they did not. Kuwait was then a British protectorate and that meant that Kuwait officially behaved in a different fashion from what people desired.

The years that followed gave all Kuwaitis an opportunity to get an education and make money. Our Palestinian teachers did a good job in presenting the cause of Palestine as Jews against Arabs. I never learned that our enemies were the Zionists. I used to go home to preach to my family about the Jews and how they caused the disaster for the poor Palestinians. Only years later I learned that both the Arabs and the Jews were victims of their circumstances and that as the Palestinians suffered so did Jews suffer in the Arab world and in Europe.

At the same time, the Palestinians in Kuwait represented a healthy challenge to my generation. In school they were good students who valued education more than the secure Kuwaitis. I had tough competition from one Palestinian kid with whom I struggled to become the head of our class. Thanks to the grades in physical education, I used to beat him by a few points. The Palestinians were so good in school that whenever we found a conscientious Kuwaiti student, we would nickname him "the Palestinian." Of course, this was at the time of security and abundance in Kuwait. Later on, the second generation of Palestinians became as good or as bad as the rest of the Kuwaitis.

As my own limited world was changing and enlarging, I began to notice how traditional people around me were changing their ways and accommodating themselves to new situations. My father was busy making money through several easy jobs. While he was taking pleasure in his new wife, my mother discovered comfort in her independence due to her savings and the meager allowances that were reaching her from her older children. She traveled and visited the shrines of the Prophet Muhammad and the imams in Medina, Iraq, Syria, and Iran. She visited all of them. Then she added a new list of imams and Sufi saints that I had never heard of like Hamza, *Abu hiz-*

main, the one with two belts! I did not want to make her feel ridiculous, so I never asked her why this saint had two belts. Other than the Kurdish rebels, I had never seen anyone in Iraq wearing two belts.

My mother's own opinion of Iraqis was more complicated. She always wondered why the imams ended up in Iraq. She never thought, and I never told her, that the saints and imams went to Iraq but often could not leave because they were murdered at the hands of assassins or villains. She even thought, much earlier than I, a political scientist later on, that the Iraqi revolutionary government was corrupt and bad. Then, I did not believe her. Like so many Kuwaitis at that time, I was young, an Arab nationalist, and naive. We thought that all earlier Arab governments were traitors and stooges of imperialism. We believed that only revolution was the answer. We never realized that the revolutionaries could be as bad as those rulers and that real tyranny and regression could also be possible with them. My mother never used those words about the revolutionaries, but she used to say, "*khalhom ye-waloon*" ("Let them get lost"). She was right.

My childhood was not unique. Like the people of my generation, I am part of the events I have seen and experienced. My childhood, my country, my family, my mother, and my friends are always with me. I am a child from the desert dunes, from the beaches and the sands of the Gulf. I am the child of Arab nationalism, socialism, the age of revolution, wars, peace, invasions, and liberations. My story reflects fifty years of change and transformation in the nation that is Kuwait and in the Kuwaiti people who have benefited from the luck of wealth. I was lucky to have a mother who gave me an example of dignity and grace, virtues that are not always with a person during a period of such great change.

Hamza al-Din

EGYPT *Hamza al-Din, a noted performer and composer of Middle Eastern music, was born in 1929 in southern Egyptian Nubia, near the Sudanese border. He was educated in Egypt and received further musical training at the Academy of St. Cecelia in Rome. His many recordings and CDs include* **Eskalay** *(The Water Wheel). He has played in concerts all over the world, made his debut at Carnegie Hall in 1966, and has been a featured soloist at the Woodstock Festival, with the Grateful Dead in Cairo and in Japan, with Peter Sellars at the Edinburgh Festival, and, most recently, in the United States with the Kronos Quartet.*

FIRST VOYAGE

Hamza al-Din

 On a hot July morning in 1929, in a village of 3500 souls living along the Nile valley of Nubia, I was born to a tribal family composed of my paternal grandfather, grandmother, teenage aunt, a cow, a donkey, a modest flock of goats and sheep, plus pigeons, ducks, and rabbits. Of course, I also had a mother close by, but my father, another uncle, and an older aunt were living more than six hundred kilometers north in Cairo. My mother was the youngest in a family of eleven sisters and one brother. When her parents died, her uncle adopted her, and when the time came, he married her to his oldest son and she gave birth to me. That is why I was surrounded by my paternal relatives in a home shaded by a huge acacia tree on the banks of the river Nile.

I left that home for the first time around my fifth birthday. I was helping my mother pack for our trip to Cairo to be with my father. Because our village was flooded part of the year by the rising of the waters behind the first Aswan Dam, we couldn't raise enough food to feed us all. So my father and most of the young men were forced to migrate to find work in order to support the old men, women, and children remaining in the village.

Every detail of that trip to the city is still clear in my mind. Young men loaded our belongings onto the backs of donkeys to be carried to the dock and packed into the sailboat which would ferry us to the opposite shore of the river. There we were to board the steamboat to Aswan and then take the train to Cairo. We bade farewell to the older people and the young children and went out the main door of our house to head for the river. My grandmother hastened to gather a bit of dust from underneath my mother's feet as she took the first seven steps of her journey; my young aunt hurried to do the same for me. But she had a hard time doing that because I was so excited that I wasn't walking straight. In our culture, they save this dust until the family members return, and then they spread it out once more in front of the house.

Down by the shore, we climbed on the sailboat to travel to the place where the *posta*, which was the river steamboat that would carry us to Aswan, would stop. The sailboat slipped through the water and we fell silent, listening to the lapping of the water against the hull and the snap of the sail in the wind. We talked to bolster our spirits and then again became silent with the burning pain of the coming separation. We landed on the opposite shore and piled up our belongings with those of another family that was traveling; the man of that household became our guide for the rest of the trip to Cairo. In the evening, the steamboat appeared, big as a huge house with light spilling out of its many windows onto the face of the Nile. Before it landed, it cried out in a huge bass voice like the bellow of many cows together: "WOOOOOOOOO!" As the boat came closer to shore, a disturbing second voice came clattering from it, "KAR-KAR-KAR!"

The posta boat trip was a thrilling experience. I heard so many different noises and voices for the first time, including the high-pitched trilling whistle of the captain, each whistle echoed by a big bass bellow, "WOOOOOOOOO." Then a new repetitive sound, over and over, "KARATIKI-KRATIKA KASHSH!" That was the paddle wheel. The men talked in loud voices, the women were silent, because, I imagine, they were sad to leave their relatives and loved ones. But soon their thoughts must have turned to stories they had heard about the great city of Cairo. The posta stopped at every village on its way down the river to Aswan, making the same series of bellows and swishes over and over again. And more and more travelers boarded at every stop until the boat was fairly bursting.

At Aswan we left the steamboat and headed for the railway station. To me, then, the train looked like a string of long houses with lots of windows. We climbed up into one of those "long houses," stored our belongings, and sat facing one another on the hard wooden seats. The train started to move. New sounds. "KAR-TAKAKA, KAR-TAKAKA," sang the wheels of the train, first slowly, then faster and faster until the next station stop. A high-pitched, long whistle sounded before and after the stop.

The train became more crowded at every station. New people came on board; they looked different from us and spoke a language I didn't understand. And many vendors moved through the train, calling out, "Lemons! Fresh ripe oranges! Pomegranates! Dates!" Some men carried folded papers under their arms; my mother told me they were newspapers. That was her first lesson during the journey. Still more people came aboard, all during one whole night and the long day afterward before we arrived in Cairo.

The noise inside the Cairo station was unlike anything I had ever heard. And the station was so big! A huge covered space, large enough so that three villages the size of mine could fit in it, along with their palm trees and riversides! Other trains were arriving at the same time as we were but on different platforms. People were pouring out from all the trains, carrying belongings, and running in all different directions as though they were fleeing from danger. My father had come to meet us, and he carried me along, squeezing me happily from time to time, me, the firstborn son he had never met, showing me his love and tenderness. Some other men were with him that I didn't know and they carried our things. We left the noisy station and went out into the open air.

But outside it was a crazy place, too. Countless cars, smoke coming out from behind them, making many different sounds, "TEET-TEET! TOOT TOOT! AWOO-AH!" People riding on bicycles, their feet seeming to swim in the air, ringing little silver bells, "KIRALING! KIRALING!" Other men on smoking two-wheelers that sounded, "FRRRRRT! FRRRRRT!"

We climbed into a horse carriage which moved into the traffic, and the noise and smoke were so intense that I began to choke and cough. Finally we reached a street so narrow that the uppermost windows on each side almost touched each other. Then the carriage lurched into a large open plaza filled with people. On our left was a big water spigot, where people stood with all manner of pots and dishes to fill with water; several children ran happily around, getting soaked and dirty in the mud.

We came to a stop. We left my father with the carriage and our things, and my mother and I climbed the stairs of one of the tall houses around the square. There, at the open door of an apartment, stood my maternal aunt and her daughter Nema. I was a week older than my cousin Nema; we had been raised in the village as brother and sister until she went to Cairo with her mother to join her father. Just like I was doing now. God had reunited us. We all started talking, recounting the strange experiences of the journey. We had reached our new home in the famous area of Bulaq.

Bulaq is an ancient port of Cairo on the Nile, and one of the oldest quarters in the city. Around the plaza outside our apartment house were many small shops; early morning until after the evening prayer, the plaza was filled with a constant babble of grown-ups and children. On the street level of our building was a tiny coffee shop, its floor blackened with dirt and its rickety chairs and tables placed here and there. What amazed me most was the brown box that sat on a shelf just outside the entrance to the coffee shop. It seemed to talk and buzz. Sometimes I could hear male voices, sometimes female voices, moaning. At other times those voices just talked. My family told me that the brown box was the radio—the buzzing sounds were music, the moaning sounds singing, the talk was the newscast. And the moaning sound without music was the reading of the Quran.

Street processions often passed by with live music. Our balcony, high above the plaza, was my "preferred" vantage place, because my folks didn't want me to go down in the street and get lost. There were the vendors who hawked their wares in beautiful singing voices. I memorized some of those cries in my broken Arabic. Groups of men would sing ballads about the area's gang leaders, describing their bravery and their chivalry or insulting them rudely if they were from the next neighborhood. Once in a while, they would forget exactly what part of town they were in and would end up singing insults about the local gang boss. Then they were in real trouble!

Sometimes a wedding procession came through the plaza, led by two lines of men in military uniforms who carried instruments that looked to me then like huge, gaping copper mouths on their shoulders or strange metal windings around their necks. One man would bang together two cooking pot covers; others carried drums on strings around their necks. Those sounds! "FFOOOOKI! FFOOOKI!" and "TEEE, TEEEE" and "Kirra rrirra rirra rirra rum, boom, KSHSHSHSH!" The band was followed by men who had been hired to carry the bride and groom's dowry: a mirror, a small table, linens, and rush mats. The big pieces of furniture, including the bed, dresser, and big table, were on a flat, open cart pulled by a donkey or a horse. After that came the couple's family—a throng of brothers, sisters, cousins, uncles, aunts, parents, and grandparents. A lot of noise, but I didn't like it.

The Saeedi wedding processions were different. The neighborhood was filled with our Saeedi countrymen from Upper Egypt, and they had their own customs. Two or three of their musicians would carry *mizmar baladi-s*, country-style flutes, and some would bang away on the drums. They would walk along in a ragged line. Now and then a man carrying a long stick would approach them, stop the music, and call out names; one of the musicians would repeat the names, and these calls and responses would always end with, "Me and you," a kind of greeting. The man with the stick would give the musicians some money and they would start to play. "PEEP! pi-pi-pee-peep-PEEP!" A circle would open and another man would come with a stick and the two would dance in the open space, clashing their sticks together. Somehow I found I liked their kind of music.

The tomb of Sheikh Abu'l-Aila, the patron saint of Bulaq, was nearby, and there many circumcision ceremonies were performed that were important events in boys' lives. After each circumcision took place, a procession would come out of the tomb. Those processions seemed more religious, somehow. They were led by two long lines of men, wearing white cotton gullabiyahs and carrying big flat skin drums (*tars*). Those drums sounded together, "Dum-BAK boom, dum-BAK boom. . . ." In-between the two long lines, a man walked, tapping out on a smaller drum intricate rhythms against the rhythms of the tars. His hair was long and free like a woman's, and he rolled his head round and round as he played. Behind came men striking small cymbals, "Kiriring, kiriring." And after the cymbal players came a carriage pulled by two horses: the circumcised boy sat in front with the driver, wearing white, and surrounded by flowers. Children of the same age sat with him in the carriage wearing bright-colored clothes. All around and behind the carriage were mothers and sisters who clustered about, singing and calling in trilling, high-pitched voices. A few men of the family also joined the parade; I liked this kind of group very much. The one called Abu al-Ghait consisted of dervishes. Whenever I could get away, I would follow those dervishes and sometimes get lost. My parents found me only by the grace of God, and I was always severely punished and banished to the balcony once more.

Then something changed in our family. My father would go off to work as usual, but he would stay away overnight every other day. My mother's soft smile was seen less and less and her face became serious and sad. My aunt said she was disgusted with what was going on and started talking seriously to her husband. The atmosphere in the house became a storm of pain and sorrow. My father had married a second wife, and according to the rules, he had to spend one night with each wife. I heard people saying things like, "One wife makes your hair gray. What do you think two will do for you?" But my father had done it, anyway, and my love for him began to fade.

Now it was not just Bulaq but all of Cairo that was becoming too difficult for us. Within a month, I found myself, my mother, my aunt, and my cousin Nema getting ready to go back to Nubia. For there was no longer a reason for my father to keep the apartment we shared. My uncle could not afford to keep the place himself, so he had decided to send his family home with us and to lead the life of a single man.

That time we took our journey in reverse. We left the apartment and hired a horse carriage to take us through the plaza and the noises of the cars, the motorcycles, and the bicycles to the railway station. It was full of people like us who were returning to their villages. This time the train was crowded from the start with all kinds of people, vendors again buying and selling oranges, lemons, dates, and pomegranates, men covering their faces with newspapers as they sat on the hard wooden seats. But by the time we got to Aswan, only we, the Nubian passengers, were left. We carried our belongings to the dock, where we boarded the Posta steamboat again, and each traveling group made a place for themselves on deck for the two-and-a-half day journey south along the Nile, with all those noises of engine, whistle, horn, and paddle wheel. When we arrived on the east bank across from our village, we took a sailboat heading west and listened once more to the lapping of the water against the hull and the snap of the sail in the wind. On the western shore, we were greeted by all our relatives—my grandmother, my teenage aunt, and many others. We climbed the sandy hills toward home, and the donkeys carried our belongings. After a welcoming party and a freshly cooked dinner, I hugged my grandfather and went off to bed with him. At last I felt my ears begin to relax from the noises of those long trips back and forth, the constant clamor of Bulaq. I listened to the sighing sounds of the silence of the desert night and quickly fell asleep.

From that first journey, I began to understand how to make departures and returns to and from the same point in the musical compositions I was to create later. But in those early days my life flowed smoothly in the village, where I was close to my grandfather and close to home, learning from my relatives the customs of my people, my tribe, and my religion.

Akile Gürsoy

TURKEY *Akile Gürsoy is presently head of the anthropology department at Yeditepe University in Istanbul. She was born in
Istanbul, took a B.A. Honors degree in anthropology from
Durham University, England, and finished her Ph.D.
at Hacettepe University in Ankara. She has worked with
UNICEF on projects relating to child health and mortality
in southeastern Turkey and has taught at Marmara University. She publishes on migration, child health, and theory
in social science, as well as on medical anthropology.*

AKILE
GÜRSOY,
CENTER

THE COUP OF MAY 27, 1960

Akile Gürsoy

 Early morning, May 27th, 1960. A date which is to change the course of not only my childhood, but my entire life, as well as Turkey's political history. I wake up at dawn. There are unfamiliar, unusual footsteps and voices outside in the corridor. Doors open and close. Only later can I offer any meaning for the strange, insistent, and sinister sounds that prevail for hours in the darkness: the sound of tanks surrounding the presidential residence. When I get up and go out, I see that everyone else is already awake and dressed. I look outside to find unusually alert, armed, and stiff-looking soldiers everywhere. The tanks' gun turrets are directed at us. Someone enters our room and tells us not to go near the windows. We have been surrounded by some members of the army. It is a coup d'etat.

In my grandmother's room, everyone's face has a distraught look. Nanny Atike is crying. Everyone is anxious. I understand that early in the morning some soldiers forced their way in and took my grandfather away. There were twenty of them; they pulled my mother by the arm and pushed her aside while they forced him to leave with them. They tell me he has been taken to Harbiye, the army headquarters in Ankara. My mother is irate and indignant. I hear her say to the officers at the door, "They cannot do this. We are a democratic country. Who is responsible for this? Who will be accountable for all this? Are we going to be like Iraq? This will only be one coup followed by a chain of others." My aunt and others restrain my mother and make her return to our residential quarters.

Everyone around me is talking of treason. High treason.

Osman Koksal, the recently appointed head of the Presidential Guard, did nothing to stop the coup. Not one shot was fired back at the invaders. Only one soldier of the lowest rank tried to use his gun to stop the soldiers who were taking my grandfather away. "My commander, they are threatening to shoot our president!" Osman Koksal then had him quickly removed from the scene. He was the only soldier, a naive villager, they had been unable or had forgotten to replace the night before.

In the early hours of that morning, we have a visitor. The prime minister Adnan Menderes' wife, Berrin Hanim, comes with her youngest son, Aydin. They live nearby in the same compound garden. Aydin comes into our room with us, while the grown-ups gather in the sitting room of our quarters.

Outside, the soldiers who planned the coup have long since taken over the radio station, and since the early hours of the morning, have been broadcasting that there has been an army takeover. Military music and the national anthem are played at frequent intervals. They broadcast that the prime minister has also been captured in the province of Eskisehir. As far as they are concerned, the coup has been successful. All the leading Democrats (that is, all the MPs and governors) and the strategic parts of the country are in their hands. Within hours, our telephones are completely cut off.

I do not remember how or what we ate during the first couple of days following the coup. I don't remember being put to bed either. But I distinctly remember the third day of the coup, early in the morning, when I hear a loud and prolonged cry: "They killed him. They killed him." I rush out and see for the first (and last) time in my life my grandmother crying in long sobs. "They say he threw himself out of the window. But he was not one to commit suicide. They killed him." Everyone is crying, and I soon understand that they are referring to the minister of interior affairs, Mr. Namik Gedik. The officers at the door look slightly disturbed and guilty, but nevertheless superior, and nervously enjoy their newly acquired status.

All our forced optimism, indignation, and attempts to think of this reality as a temporary state collapsed with the news of this first death.

I learn that my father, who was away on a trip in Germany, is now on the way back to Turkey. Hearing about the coup and all that is happening here, he decided to come back early. Later that day, my mother and grandmother call Emine and me to the sitting room. They tell us that my father was arrested at the airport in Istanbul and taken away.

We have to pack and leave the presidential residence very soon. We are now all engaged in the process of picking out some essential things to take with us. The rest of our belongings will be sent after us.

At one point, we are told to leave all our jewelry behind. The only piece of jewelry we take with us is my mother's wedding ring, which she wears on her finger.

This is a very different kind of packing from what we are used to doing each spring. We just throw into suitcases what we think are essentials. We know we will never come back here again. We do not know where we are going, and we do not know what awaits us. We do not know when we will see my grandfather and father again. There is so much uncertainty now. I have to leave my school and all my friends.

I remember having to leave behind among packed boxes a doll dressed in Yugoslavian folk costume and a furry turkey that was my favorite animal toy. All the maids and most of the waiters are crying. In the main entrance hall, our bags are thoroughly searched. Now I can discern scornful grins on the soldiers' faces as they look into our bags and watch us go out.

This is how I left the residence where I had spent my early childhood, the first nine years of my life. My grandmother; my mother; Nanny Atike; my sisters, Emine and Bilge, and I all get into a car which takes us to the airport to get the plane to Izmir from where we will drive to Ilica. This is a long journey, and we arrive at our summer house there in the dark of night.

SUMMER OF 1960   If one were to imagine a prelude to heaven, most people who have been there would agree that Ilica provides the best scenery on earth with its unmatched coast along a clear turquoise and navy blue sea and the mixed scents of lavender and thyme that descend with every breeze that blows from the gently sloping surrounding hills. Our house here is situated among shade-giving aromatic pine and tangerine trees and is surrounded by olive groves and palm trees. If you descend down the narrow, white, high-walled stairs that take you to the seashore, immediately you encounter the salty sea sand and weed and fish smells of the Aegean Sea. This is the house where my grandfather hosted the late King of Iraq, the young King Faisal, in 1955, and this is the place where, after the coup, we have been allowed to come and stay.

I wake to the sound of cicadas singing relentlessly. As the grown-ups open and air and clean the rooms of the summer house, I go out to meet Akgul, the daughter of the fisherman whose family lives in a building in the garden and guards the house during the winter. In no time, we are out in the cracked, dry, sun-parched fields. I follow her and admire her agility as she confidently jumps with bare feet from wall to wall and rock to rock. In no time, we have gone beyond the lighthouse at the edge of the peninsula and reach the rocks from where you can descend and jump into the pool of hot springwater in the sea. As we dive into the sea we find ourselves immersed in currents of varying shades of hot water. Schools of silver- and gold-colored fish swarm around the rocks. I swim out into the cold, open green sea, where I let myself float on the water, closing my eyes from the blinding, powerful sun above. On the way back, we are accompanied by a local boy who tells us stories of giant octopuses and starfish and fishing boats which leave the shore early before dawn.

The following day, we are surrounded by a troop of soldiers headed by a lieutenant. We are told that we cannot leave the house anymore, nor is anyone allowed to visit. The lieutenant explains that this is what the military junta saw fit for us "for our protection." Nanny Atike can leave now if she wants to, but we have no choice but to stay under house imprisonment: we cannot go out shopping, visiting, or swimming. We are not supposed to lean over the walls and be visible to passersby either. Like Nanny Atike, Akgul and her family also chose to stay imprisoned with us. Her father, Kemal Abi, however, decides to live and work outside, so that he can help with the shopping and keep an eye on what is going on outside.

The soldiers will not look us in the eye. They become alert and touch their rifles upon seeing us approach. "We are not an enemy," says my mother. "I have orders to shoot anyone who walks out through the garden door," says one, looking earnest.

We are anxious. For weeks we receive no letters, no news from my father or grandfather. Our telephone is cut off. We have no visitors. Kemal Abi brings the papers, in which we read that we, the Bayar family, are having a wonderful (meaning decadent) time in our summer resort on the Aegean riviera, a house full of maids and servants. The headlines are full of news and details about the corruption of the Democrats and the heroism of the Turkish army, which has put an end to this state of affairs.

One day we see a group of young men noisily swimming right in front of our house. When they see us looking, they wave and laugh and pull their hands across their throats, shouting, "We will cut you to pieces." My mother hurries us into the house and shuts the doors.

I almost wish we would not receive any more newspapers. Every morning, reading the news, we sink into a deeper trap. We read that all the Democrats arrested in the first days of the coup are now in prison in Yassiada, one of the small islands in the Sea of Marmara. One day the headlines proclaim the words of General Gursel, now the head of the army and junta, to the effect that if there is any trouble, we will find a heap of skeletons on Yassiada. I cannot bear the fury and the subsequent silence the papers initiate in our house. The troops are changed every fifteen days, just when we get adjusted to the soldiers' various idiosyncratic ways.

Early one morning, I run out to the sound of a commotion and laughter outdoors. I cannot believe what I see. My cousins Kesibe, Simin, and Selmin have come with their mother, Aunt Selcuk, and their grandmother, Aunt Cemile, to stay in their house next door. Aunt Cemile is my grandmother's youngest sister.

In seconds we are rejoicing and embracing each other. We begin to dance up and down amidst their still unopened suitcases. Aunt Cemile tells how she managed to break through the circle of soldiers simply and effectively by saying, "You cannot stop me entering my own house."

The news of their arrival reaches the lieutenant in no time. He comes and Aunt Cemile is told that if she and her family stay, they too will be kept under house imprisonment. The choice is theirs. "Of course we will stay," says Aunt Cemile. "We came here to stay and to be near my sister."

Our rejoicing continues as they unpack and we all exchange news. They settle in as if there was nothing unusual in our situation. They too open their summer kitchen, which is outdoors in the backyard, just like ours.

"You should not have come, Cemile," says my grandmother. "You've put yourself and the children in danger together with us."

"Nonsense, my dear sister. What danger? we are all together now."

The troops now include Aunt Cemile's house and garden in the circle of "protection." My aunts and cousins too are not allowed to go out of the garden, nor onto their front patio where they can be seen. The small, fragile wooden gate separating the two summer houses, however, is kept open and unguarded. We are free to visit each other.

There is no doubt that our increased number has given all in our household new confidence and strength. The arrival of Kesibe and Simin, especially, has added meaning for Emine and me, bringing new vitality to our games. In a couple of days we form a gang which we call *Besler Cetesi* (Gang of Five). Our gang includes, in order of age, Simin (12), Emine (11), Kesibe (10), me (9), and Akgul (8). Akgul's sister and my sister Bilge (3) are too young to participate. My eldest cousin Selmin is too old. She is already fifteen and quite plainly looks down on the idea of running around the garden in a "gang" with us.

The five of us, however, begin to spend exciting hours outdoors climbing trees, which was forbidden by both the soldiers and our parents, and making houses for ourselves on treetops. We construct bowers in different places in the garden, each bigger and more developed than the previous one; we make mud ovens and cook little meat balls (*koftes*, which are in fact made of ground bread and which we manage to take from Nanny Atike). We use oleander leaves as plates. We invite each other for house-visits on different trees or inside different bowers.

The implicit objectives of our gang are to have fun, to increase our freedom, to fight injustice, and to support each other. Our gang has a treasure of collected items which include dead insects and shells hidden in a spot in the garden.

As the hot July sun relentlessly occupies the sky, our most immediate problem is that we are not allowed to go swimming. Our resentment increases as, day by day, we see in the distance dozens of children and grown-ups swimming leisurely by the beach across the bay. We put pressure on our mothers. "Why can't we swim? What harm would it do to anybody? Why don't you want to ask the lieutenant to let us go swimming?"

Eventually the lieutenant gives in. He consents to approach the higher authorities, and one day the written reply comes. We are allowed to swim, supervised by the lieutenant, and guarded by the troops.

Thus, Selmin, Simin, Emine, Akgul, and I go swimming whenever the lieutenant is willing to take us. We are accompanied by three soldiers, who oddly enough have their machine guns pointed not at anything else but at us. We are only allowed to swim for half an hour. We are forbidden to dive in or to swim too far. If we do anything wrong, or if the time is over, the lieutenant is quick to let us know by blowing his military whistle. Our gang soon finds ways of prolonging our half hour. When we feel that our half hour is coming to an end, we slowly try to distance ourselves from the shore, and then take a long time swimming back.

For us, this bizarre way of going swimming is definitely better than not swimming at all. Our mothers and grandmothers, however, have mixed feelings about us swimming, since we are directed by military whistles and supervised by machine guns that are pointed at us.

In the meantime, we have not failed to invent a secret language. It becomes very effective in allowing us to communicate and also in annoying the lieutenant (something we enjoy tremendously). This is the "PAR" language. It is a mutant form of Turkish 'bird language,' *kusdili.* The lieutenants never fathomed this secret language. Once one said, "Do you think I don't understand what you're saying? You are practicing French tenses." But my mother always said, "Don't annoy the lieutenant. Keep out of the soldiers' way."

Weeks after our arrival, we begin to receive letters (or rather brief notes) from my father and grandfather. These are outdated ones they have written from Ankara before being taken to the island of Yassiada. These letters, which the lieutenant brings, initiate unsurpassed emotion from all of us. The paper is touched and examined by all of us. He writes, "I still haven't heard from any of you. I understand you haven't received my last note. I would appreciate it if you would write news of your good health."

From the newspapers, we gather that the junta is setting up a high court, where all the Democrats will be put on trial. They are being accused of treason and corruption. Also, all the families of the Democrats have to declare their wealth in detail. The latter proves difficult because we are not allowed to communicate with anyone, including banks. Any mistake over a detail would be interpreted as our hiding or giving wrong information.

On some afternoons, patient and youthful Aunt Selcuk sits inside and draws and cuts paper dolls for all of us. She is very beautiful with her blue eyes and thick brown hair falling over her shoulders. She doesn't tire of drawing doll after doll separately for each of us.

One afternoon a noisy helicopter flies low over our houses, dropping colorful pieces of small paper. We run and pick up these pieces of paper scattered in all corners of the garden. The message written on them is most strange: "Dear Citizen, don't believe the bad news which you hear or learn. Make up your mind based on what you hear on the radio and read in the papers that come to your village. The Governor of Izmir." Of course, our interpretation is that there is some ominous news which is being kept hidden from public knowledge. This adds to our anxiety. Emine snaps at me when I want to use some of the pink pieces of paper to make a dress for my paper doll.

Some nights, we all gather and sleep in our house. These nights are full of endless hours of games, storytelling, and fun for us, the children. However, these are in fact the nights when our mothers and grandmothers have gathered in our house for fear that the soldiers will barricade the gate between the two houses and stop us from seeing each other.

The household is dependent on the lieutenant who comes in the early afternoon. He brings letters, if there are any. Without his presence and consent, we children cannot go swimming. Our mothers have different reasons for their dependency. The soldiers will not allow the daily shopping to be taken indoors before it is all checked in the presence of the lieutenant. This always takes a long time since every packet, including things like sugar and rice, is first emptied and examined.

Emine has to prepare for her primary school graduation exams, a requirement by state law, which she missed due to our departure from Ankara. Emine and my cousin Simin frequently retire to a room and try to work together. Simin also daily writes in her diary. We love to go and call them out from their industrious solitude. Through the window, we throw oleander flowers to distract them. The day eventually comes for Emine to take the exam, and on a hot morning in June, she leaves, accompanied by my mother and, of course, the lieutenant.

Despite our solitary confinement, two journalists are one day allowed to come in and interview my grandmother. I remember our excitement as we watch the journalists keenly asking question after question. My grandmother tells them that she is pained to read all the lies in the papers and that my grandfather's entire life had been spent honorably fighting for his country; that we have not a single penny which was dishonorably acquired; and that after reading the newspapers, she doesn't believe that the trials will be fair. She concludes by saying that Allah's will shall be done and that she believes in the justice of Allah.

When these statements appear on the front page of the newspaper the following day, life takes a further turn for the worse. The troops are changed, and the succeeding lieutenant is nastier and meaner than the previous ones. He will not allow street vendors to approach.

Our swimming episodes come to a halt. Our gang has begun to issue a newspaper of our own which we title *Voice of the Camp—Daily Wall Paper.* We protest our inability to swim by drawing cartoons of the lieutenant. We attach these cartoons to the tree by the entrance. The lieutenant, of course, sees the cartoons and shows his anger by tearing the paper down and saying, "No swimming today."

The following day, Emine engages in another verbal fight with the lieutenant. Emine says, "Is this the freedom you promised the country? Why didn't you wait for the elections?" We are once again forbidden to go swimming. A fight then breaks out between us when Selmin comes and says, "Why can't we leave this stupid man alone and just enjoy the sea, which is our only outlet? What have we gained by talking to him? It's just become a convenient excuse for him to go to the beach earlier to meet his girlfriend. I'm fed up with being stuck here!" she shouts.

Our mothers then intervene. They've had enough noise and shouting from us. If we can't get along with each other, they will close the gate separating the two houses. We will each have to stay in our house until we learn to get along.

One day, my mother and Aunt Selcuk are taken to the police station and interrogated about the arrival of the journalists. They are asked to verify that my grandmother did actually say the things that appeared in the newspapers. We are unaware that a law has been passed forbidding any praise or defense of the Democrats. I sit anxiously on the steps of our house, waiting for my mother to come back, while Nanny Atike cries in the kitchen.

Maybe it is true that necessity is the mother of invention. In July we find an innovative way of refreshing ourselves. Our gardens have small pools which can be filled by pumping well water. These tiny pools are designed for storing water for the garden. We begin working the pumps. After hours of labor, the pools are full. Not forgetting to add some salt to give a sea-taste, we throw ourselves into the icy cold water, emerging with shivering purple blue lips. It is a great joy, however, to push each other and jump in. We no longer have to wait for the lieutenant's approval!

Soon after, in the heat of summer, those of us who had played in the well water break out in an agonizing red rash. My mother tries to find some mulberries to treat our rash, and one of the local shopkeepers brings a basketful to our house. But my mother is caught by the lieutenant while she is hanging out a rope to pull up the basket. She is scolded and made to give back the berries. Time eventually healed our rash.

One day, the lieutenant comes into our house to talk over something. He comes in with his cigarette and sits down without being asked to sit. He stretches out his legs leisurely and scolds us. We are told that we can write no more than 50 words in each letter to our father and grandfather in Yassiada, because none of the officers checking the letters has the time to read stories, which meant petty trivialities. Anyway, the message is not the issue. By the time he leaves, we all have an uneasy sense of a vulgar, intrusive encounter.

The next time he comes, my grandmother places an armchair by the narrow back door and sits on this chair, blocking the entrance. She manages to mention in her first sentence that the lieutenant is the age of her own son. While they talk, the lieutenant is left standing. As I stand behind my grandmother and watch him sweat under the hot early afternoon sun, I experience a sense of victory, one of the very few brief moments of indignant triumph I ever felt after the coup. "Well done. Well done, my dear sister," Aunt Cemile exclaims. "You gave him a good lesson."

Despite our encouragement of each other, the nights always weigh heavily. My grandmother and Emine sleep in one room. I stay in the room opposite with my mother and Bilge. Nanny Atike is in a separate room at the other end of the hall. I am the only child sleeping in a separate bed. My bed is by the window. It is terrible to wake up in the middle of the night when everyone is asleep and all the house is dark and silent. Then I hear clearly the soldiers' footsteps just outside. Sometimes I hear the soldiers talk in a murmur or hear one quietly begin to sing a nostalgic folk song that expresses yearning for all he left behind in his village. Then I recall this conversation between my grandmother and my aunt:

"What would we do if one day they decide to kill us? What can we do with the children? Nothing. Nothing."

"Nothing. But I don't think they can do such a thing."

"It's been done before. If we think of Iraq . . ."

Will they kill us? Will they come in while we are all asleep? Can't we hide anywhere? Who would they kill first and last? I lie there and try to stay awake. Some nights the terror of these thoughts is too much and I get up and creep into my mother's bed.

One of our communal occupations in the house is letter writing. We each withdraw to our corner to write letters to my grandfather and father. This is no simple affair. We do not and will not write to them that we are kept in confinement. We do not want them to worry about us. We want our letters to give support and news of our well-being. Furthermore, we know they will be read at our end as well as the destination before being sent. Nothing should be written which will annoy the soldiers and hence cause the letter to be confiscated. I spend hours devising the best verbal arrangement for unproblematic content. In the end my letters inevitably end up sounding like this:

> *Dear Father,*
>
> *How are you? My grandmother, my mother, Emine, Bilge, and I are all well. So is Nanny Atike. Yesterday we went swimming. I hope you are well too. I miss you very much. I don't want to pass the 50 words limit. I kiss your cheeks. Write to me soon.*
>
> *Your daughter,*
> *Akile*

After this self-censorship, our letters are read aloud in the sitting room for a final check. Then I draw pictures on the letter, make post cards, and even add paper dolls. We put these in an envelope, which we hand unsealed to the lieutenant. No one reading these formal, canned letters could ever guess how meaningful and emotion-laden each single, clichéd word actually is.

We apply and make constant official attempts to leave Ilica but in vain. Finally, one day, the lieutenant says we can go to Istanbul. We must pack and leave in three days. So, after weeks of waiting, we are finally allowed to go. There is excitement, but also something ominous about our departure. They want us to leave the house at 2:00 A.M. in the dark, and they want us to split up and go in two cars to the airport.

"Why do we have to leave that early?" my mother asks. "It's only an hour to the airport, and the plane doesn't leave till 7:45. Also, we came here in one car and we will be happy taking one car."

"These are the orders. You will leave at 2:00 A.M. in two separate cars."

Our uneasiness reaches its peak two nights before we are due to leave. Aunt Cemile comes to our house. She says that a stranger, a woman, came up to her by the wall near the fig trees and quickly whispered while walking by that they are planning to split us up and arrest my grandmother on our way to Istanbul. What will become of us? My mother thinks of a way out. After Aunt Cemile came to Ilica, they had decided never to use her phone out of fear that this telephone too would be cut off. They wanted to keep that line for an emergency.

Now, the day before our departure, they decide to use it. My mother calls Mr. Selim Sarper, the minister of foreign affairs appointed by the junta but a more sympathetic member of the new government in Ankara. She does not find him, but she manages to talk to his daughter. She asks for help, telling her that we are being forced to leave Ilica in a strange way and that we fear a sinister intention. When my mother next tries to use the phone, the line has been cut off.

The device, however, seems to have worked, for just before we are due to leave, the lieutenant comes to say that our trip has been postponed. We are to remain here till further orders. The next morning we read in the newspaper headlines that we, the Bayar family, did not turn up to board our plane, and that my grandmother's arrest and removal to the island of Yassiada has been postponed. Once again, we experience relief and anxiety all mixed together.

The grown-ups are depressed. The atmosphere of doom is thinly disguised in their trying-to-be-cheerful voices as they call us for tea or meals. Our gang of five therefore decides to put on a play to amuse them. Immediately, we become engaged in writing a script. There will be good and evil spirits in our play. There is also dancing and singing and poem recitals. We collect money "for a surprise" and ask Kemal Abi to buy us small colorful fireworks. We prepare our front patio with seats for everyone. The stage is an elevated platform between two large oleander trees, in front of which we light our fireworks. We don't even need curtains, because the night is dark enough for us to disappear after our part on stage is done on the patio stage. We get lots of clapping from the elders, who for our sake laugh and appear genuinely amused. The play becomes an excuse for us all to enjoy being outdoors; the sea, the scents, and the starry sky overlooking the calm night of the bay.

The obvious sometimes comes as a surprise. The following day we were all surprised to be interrogated by the lieutenant about the "mysterious activities and lights" coming from our house. They think we were sending messages to the other side of the bay. "What were you doing with those fireworks?" the lieutenant asks me.

"We had a play."

"What did the lights mean?"

"We used them in our play for special effects."

"What were you saying?"

"I didn't say very much. I was mostly dancing. I was a good spirit. They didn't give me the part I wanted."

"What were the others saying?"

I feel cornered, and run away, saying, "Why don't you ask them?"

Kemal Abi brings news that there are rumors that we will be kidnapped and taken to the Greek island of Sakiz, which is only a few minutes distant from our shore. All the boats coming in and out of Ilica are being stopped and searched. The security forces have been doubled. Who would want to kidnap us? Our friends or our enemies?

Later in July, we celebrate Selmin's birthday. On her invitation card to my grandmother, she has written, "I invite you to my modest birthday party." This was an ingenious response to the news we had read in one of the national papers that "a modest cocktail party was held at the presidential residence yesterday." This implied that previous cocktails during our stay there had been extravagant.

"Have some of my modest lemonade, it's homemade," Selmin says. "Have some of my modest birthday cake. Take this modest plate and that modest fork and sit on this modest chair." For days, we used and laughed over the word *modest.*

August proceeds. This is a time to begin thinking of autumn and of school. My cousins make preparations to leave Ilica. Their father will come and take them. (My cousins' father is divorced from my aunt). However, just as arrangements are completed, their suitcases all prepared, the lieutenant brings word that their departure is delayed. They are not allowed to leave the house. We are more pleased than they are. A few weeks later, after petitions from their father, again they prepare, only to be told at the last minute that they cannot leave.

This process is repeated so many times that on the day they actually set off and leave, we can't believe they are going. Aunt Selcuk also leaves some time later, but Aunt Cemile stays with us throughout our confinement in Ilica.

The minute my cousins leave, it feels as though the troops have tripled in number, and we have become more vulnerable than before. The grip of the military junta does indeed become tighter. A couple of days later, we are struck with bad news: my grandfather has tried to commit suicide in Yassiada. Why has he done that? What are they doing to them on that island? My grandmother prays, looking out over the sea.

Again, we gather to write letters. "Dear Grandfather, I miss you very much. Take care of yourself. I hope you are in good health. I think of you a lot. I hope I can see you soon. We are all well. I kiss your hands and cheeks. Your granddaughter, Akile."

A few days later, we read in the papers that the Democratic Party has been abolished. The elections have been postponed. "Are we no longer a democratic country?" I ask. I try to amuse myself in the garden. There are dozens of stray cats everywhere. We love to find the kittens, which the mother cats carry from place to place and try to hide from us. I often go to Nanny Atike and show her a bleeding finger: "You see my finger, Nanny Atike? That yellow cat bit me again. What will happen if I catch rabies here? No doctor will come to save me. I will go mad biting all of you."

"Of course that cat will bite you. You're always after her litter. Keep away from them," she answers. But that summer, I can neither give up playing with the cats nor feeling the terror of catching rabies: a death full of shame, insanity, and despair.

Autumn progresses. The infamous winds of Ilica reign on the rising sea and keep all the sailors indoors. The weather gets colder each day. Nanny Atike is miserable because she hasn't heard from her only son, Nurettin. Emine has become ill-tempered. Bilge is unmanageable. I'm depressed and often cry as I spend hours learning to embroider.

As all the neighbors leave for their winter houses, the cats become more dependent on us for food. Emine takes up drawing. The days feel very long. Aunt Cemile makes jam from the oleander fruits ripening in her garden. We store this for its healing quality for coughs and colds. We try to keep warm in the stone summer house which is not designed for cold autumn days. Schools open. From our patio we watch the children of Ilica going to school in their white-collared black uniforms.

One morning, the lieutenant brings the mail, which includes Emine's primary school diploma. However, the diploma with her picture on it is torn to bits. We are all upset for days over this assault.

We are cut off from the world except for our censored letters, the daily papers, and the radio which we had borrowed from Kemal Abi. Every day we listen to the Turkish broadcast of the Russian radio. We all gather and listen to the accented and intermittent voice of the Russian station, which praises the army and the military junta. They obviously approve of the fall of the Democrat government. Also, there are subtle giveaways in their use of language. For example, they refer to the army takeover as an *ihtilal*, a "revolution." In our eyes, however, this is an *askeri darbe*, a "military coup d'etat," literally an army takeover, a treacherous deed. On occasions, my mother asks for *Paris Match* and *Time* magazines to be bought. These give us different, compact information from a distant perspective as compared to the more detailed and sensational Turkish press. My mother translates for my grandmother and aunt the news and articles relating to Turkey.

Apart from closely following the media to predict our fate, we also have access to a very individual source of collective information. These are our interpretations of natural phenomena. In Aunt Cemile's garden, there is an enormous *innap* tree which has been split into two by lightning. A freshly sprouting shoot, however, was making its way up to the sky. "This is like the fate of the Democratic Party," Aunt Cemile says. "It has had a blow, but there will be a rejuvenation."

Our private dreams are also a daily preoccupation as we make interpretations and projections. However, we censor our dreams the way we censor our letters. The worst nightmares are untold until bad enough news is already out in the open to justify having seen them. Then, somebody says, "I didn't want to tell you at the time, but two days ago in my dream. . . ."

I also recount my dreams. "In my dream last night we were all floating out in the open sea. The water is deep and dark. And we are far away from land and from each other. We know that when the sun sets, we will lose each other forever. The sun descends and descends; it is only a thin line on the horizon. We are about to be devoured by the sea and the huge waves. Suddenly, I feel my feet are touching the ground, and I find myself on an island, together with my mother. This means that all of you, all of us, also, are saved. This is how my dream ends."

"Good, good," says Aunt Cemile. "Tell me, Akile, is that what you really saw? That's marvelous. A good omen. This means that one by one all our enormous troubles will end. We will get rid of all the chains of pain one after another. Like a miracle."

And like everyone else who has had their dream interpreted positively, I feel a sense of achievement, of having contributed to our release. A good messenger bringing good news from the other side. Our day begins with an irrefutable feeling of well-being.

Still, I am haunted by what I have overheard about the Tsar's family. They were kept in Menfa and after months were all shot to death. The bamboo armchairs in the hall also seem ominous. I vaguely but disturbingly remember a picture of King Faisal sitting smiling on these chairs, facing my grandfather. Like the Tsar's family, he too died, together with all his family, killed the very first day of the coup in their palace. When filled with such fears, I remind myself and take courage from the fact that we are not royal and we live in a country with a history of democracy. I drown the worst of my fears by thinking, "It cannot happen here. It will not happen to us."

Of course, there was so much we never knew that summer. "Protected" and isolated as we were in our house, we had far less exposure to the humiliation and intimidation that the families of the other Democrats suffered daily in schools, at work, and in public. We were unaware of the extent of public slandering that was going on at the eve of the trials. These were to end in 1961 with a death sentence for fourteen leading Democrats, including my grandfather, and the actual hanging of Prime Minister Menderes, Minister of Foreign Affairs Zorlu, and Minister of Interior Affairs Polatkan, despite much effort on the part of national and international figures, including President John F. Kennedy.

Our immediate reality also included secrets which I learned years later. Neither we nor the soldiers knew that in the boathouse under our patio that summer lay tons of illegal explosives. The local villagers used them for fishing. They had hidden them in our garden thinking that the president's lodgings would be the safest place. When we unexpectedly turned up several days after the coup and the house became encircled by troops, they didn't want to tell us their secret, but they didn't dare leave the explosives there either. So, night after night, they sneaked in and gradually removed all the explosives.

One of the soothing events that summer was the arrival of a new lieutenant to head the troops surrounding our house. Lieutenant Asim Bey was the unexpected exception at a time when we were losing hope, and reality behind the garden walls was getting blurred. He was kind and considerate and was even embarrassed to see our solitary state. "What can I do for the children?" he asked my mother. My mother had replied that we were weary of being confined. So several times he took me and Emine for walks. We would always bring some wildflowers home, proof of the living world outside, for those left behind in the house.

Lieutenant Asim Bey also gave advice to my mother on how we could leave Ilica. He said that most of the wives of the Democrats had applied to observe the Yassiada trials that would begin on October 14. My mother took this advice and sent an official application. Thus, on the first day of the Yassiada trials, which were open to the press and to a selected public audience (and, in fact, to international eyes), we were allowed to leave Ilica, where we had stayed in confinement from June 3 to October 14, 1960: four months and ten days.

Rafiq Abdul Rahman

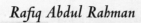

PALESTINE *Rafiq Abdul Rahman is the pseudonym of an engineer
who was born to a Palestinian family after the establish-
LEBANON ment of the state of Israel in 1948. He grew up in the
refugee camps of Nabatiyah and Ain Hilweh in Lebanon,
where he attended UNRWA schools before enrolling at the
American University of Beirut. He is currently employed
in the United States.*

A REFUGEE CHILDHOOD

Rafiq Abdul Rahman

 We grew up both as refugees and as poor people. At first, my family did not live in the refugee camps but in a Lebanese town. We were aware of our poverty but believed it was temporary. After all, we had lots of land in Palestine. Maybe we exaggerated our seemingly comfortable lives in Palestine, but we assumed we had everything that we wanted there and we were going to go back to that situation. And it did not matter much that we were poor because we were living among people that were not much better off than we were.

What mattered most for our family, I think, was not our poverty but that we were perceived as different, as refugees, among people who were living in their own town. It wasn't that bad, compared to the stories of other refugees. But our difference and our status as refugees would be expressed every now and then when tensions would arise between a member of my family and others.

Although we lived in the Lebanese town, I went to school in the Nabatiyeh refugee camp. We had a forty-minute walk to school, so we had to wake up early. Our house was open. It was almost like sleeping outside in the cold because the doors and windows were not completely closed. We didn't have any glass on the windows; they were just wood and full of cracks. Even when you closed the doors and windows, you could hear the wind whistle through them. We had a kerosene stove in the middle of the room where we would sit together. But it was only warm if you sat right in front of it. In the room where we slept, the only way we got warm was by burying ourselves under layers of heavy quilts and blankets. Of course it helped that we all slept together—we generated warmth from one another! The idea of getting out of that warm bed on a cold morning was the most dreadful thing.

To make matters worse, we had to wash with freezing water. We had an oil barrel that was transformed into a water tank with a spout. It was painful—I still feel the pain of that cold water on my cheeks and my fingers. That's the first thing that comes to mind—cold winter, early mornings, and getting up and having to go to school. My eldest sister was in charge of getting me and my younger brothers ready. She had to make sure we put on our clothes, combed our hair properly, and washed our faces. In addition, she would help my mother fix the breakfast. Mainly, we ate bread with *za'ter* (thyme) and tea. Sometimes we would eat *labneh* (strained yogurt) or *manoosheh* (bread with thyme and olive oil). And that's it. We ate breakfast very quickly and were off to school. My sister would wait until we were all ready and then she would get herself ready for school.

It was a long walk. I vividly remember the days when it was raining or cold. We used to wear plastic covers with hoods. You had to be at school on time. And rain was not an excuse. There were no cars then. We didn't have an option, since we had to walk, and it did not matter if our clothes or hair were wet. The important thing was keeping the books from getting wet. You could dry your clothes and dry your hair, but books would be ruined, especially notebooks.

Every day we followed the same routine when the bell rang. Each class would form a column on the playground. Each homeroom teacher would inspect his column, just as though we were in the army. They inspected our hair to make sure it was combed and our clothes to make sure they were tidy, not dirty—not too dirty, at least, because we used to wear our clothes for many, many days before we washed them. After they looked quickly at our heads and our clothes, we had to put out our hands. The teacher carried a wooden stick; if he noticed any dirt in the fingernails, or if they were too long, he would beat us. So of course it reminded us to cut our fingernails or at least clean them. We went to the class and sat down, the homeroom teacher would walk in, and we stood up and said, "Good morning, sir." And they would say, "Sit down," and then class started.

All our teachers in the UNWRA schools were Palestinians. Most were very nice and very dedicated. Some were more strict than others, but we felt they cared about us. Somehow, you could tell that they were tough on you because they cared about you. There was a sense of not only giving you an education but giving you a sense of mission, that part of one's duty as a refugee Palestinian was to make your life worth something. And one way of doing that was to get a very good education. Dedication to teaching became a part of those teachers; they saw teaching as a national duty. In retrospect, I think about the different ways they educated us. In the curriculum there was no political education and yet the teachers managed to slip in all sorts of information about our cause, what had happened, how it happened, what the Israelis did, and what the Arab governments did. There was continuous talk about the "situation," as if it were a class that wasn't in the curriculum but you were getting an education about it. On national occasions, like the partition of Palestine and the Balfour Declaration day, the teachers were not supposed to do anything special; otherwise, they would be expelled or suspended. Yet they managed to make sure we were aware of the coming of that special day so that we on our own could do something to commemorate the occasion.

My parents befriended some of the teachers, who almost always were from different towns. My father felt it was his duty to invite these people to a home-cooked meal occasionally, because they were living on their own. It created some very good, close relationships that have lasted a lifetime.

Aside from returning to Palestine, the only thing in my father's mind was that we should all be studying hard. Although he had never been to school, his dedication to education was unbelievable; he was willing to go to any lengths to make sure that his children stayed at school and achieved their full potential. We were a very big family (seven boys, three girls), and in some of the large, poor Palestinian families, there was a tendency to take at least a couple of the kids out of school and have them work in order to generate some kind of income for the rest of the family. For my father that was out of the question.

He made sure that everybody did their homework, the older brothers and sisters helping the younger ones. He was in control, watching everybody do their homework. Even with my eldest brother, who was not much interested in school, he kept after him. But when it was time for my brother to go to another town, for the higher classes, my father realized that it was not going to work. My brother tried for a few weeks and then insisted that he did not want to go to school. So my father gave up.

UNRWA rations were distributed in the camps but had to be transported home. Cars were too expensive, so we hired a mule. Women usually went to get the rations, but in our family the men did it. My father did it for a long time, but as his children grew up, he began to depend on us.

Before a school was built inside the camp, UNRWA had a school in Nabatiyeh, which I attended for one year. One of the first services for refugees was milk for the children. My first memory of milk is this UNWRA milk, served to us every morning in a tin cup, like army cups. The milk was distributed next to the restrooms. Why? Because of the water supply. Why? Because the milk was powder. They would dump the powder in these big barrels, pour the water from the hose, and stir it. I remember that milk as horrible! We would all try to get rid of the milk, but the teachers wanted to make sure we drank it because it was good for our health. We used all kinds of tricks to avoid drinking that milk, but most of the time, guess what, we had to drink it.

We knew about other milk, the real milk from neighborhood cows. To us this was a delicacy. Fresh milk from the neighborhood cow owner, that was something everyone liked. But there was not much of it. The one or two cows in the neighborhood did not produce as much milk as American cows.

In the second year of my schooling, we moved to the camp itself. In the cafeteria, UNRWA provided lunch for the children, and also distributed free milk according to the size of the families. All you needed was to take a bucket or a container and get your allotted amount of milk. For us, it was a long way back to the camp, so we'd take an empty bucket from home in the morning, go to the milk center, fill up the bucket, leave our milk at a nearby house, and pick it up at the end of the school day. We used all kinds of buckets for the milk and I remember some of them looked like paint buckets, metal buckets without covers. We'd make holes in them and attach a wire handle. We had to be to be very careful carrying that milk home, because the bucket bumped up against our legs and the milk splashed up from the bucket and spilled on our clothes. That was something we all dreaded, so we kids took turns and abided very strictly by those terms, because nobody wanted to do it.

With ten children in our family, the range of ages was quite wide, so relationships varied. I was in the middle—the fifth child—so my relationship with the eldest children was distant yet filial. They had a lot of authority, so you did exactly what they told you to do. Luckily, my older brothers were nice; they didn't abuse their authority.

I remember helping take care of the younger kids. My mother counted on me because she didn't have enough girls. She had three girls and seven boys. One girl was number three, and the other two girls came toward the end. The ones at the end really didn't count in terms of household labor, so my mother effectively had only one girl to help her with six boys. Sometimes I played a role close to that of a girl: babysitting, ironing clothes, and so on. My mother would say, "I wish you were born a girl." But she'd say that very, very quickly, because you're not supposed to wish that your son is a daughter. Yet she had enough boys, I think, so she could afford the luxury of that kind of thinking.

The interesting family relationships are those between you and the siblings closest to you in age. In our culture we have an assumption that between two siblings that come after one another, there is always conflict. Why? Because of jealousy. The older one is suddenly deprived of his mother's milk, and you can no longer sleep with the parents. He or she has to join the raucous group of kids all sleeping in one room. The new baby takes your place between mother and father.

If you are in the middle, who do you have conflict with, the one who is older or the one who is younger? It depends on the characters of the kids—who is the antagonist and who the defender. In my case, my antagonistic relationship was with my older brother, not the younger one. We fought all the time. Not ugly fights, just the usual sibling quarrels. And teasing, too.

We didn't have toys. We played games outside the house. Sports, like soccer and volleyball. And we played catch a thief or hide-and-seek. We played a lot of marbles outside in the neighborhoods. And we played other games, also. In one of them you draw a circle in the dirt, wet dirt—it has to be wet dirt. And you find metal objects like skewers to throw into the dirt. If you throw a straight line, you divide the circle. That part of the circle becomes a piece of land and then as you throw more metal into the circle, you add to your ownership of the circle until your opponent has almost no land left, and he loses the game. You own the circle. We often played that staking game.

My relationship with my grandfather was very close. I was his favorite grandson. When I fought with my siblings, everyone knew I was his favorite and no one could touch me or treat me badly.

I think my sisters and brothers came to accept the situation grudgingly. They would complain every now and then about the fact that my grandfather was unfair, but that didn't stop him because he had patriarchal authority over everybody. And that influenced the way my own parents treated me. They knew the old man was my ally, so my own parents favored me also.

My grandfather lived in a state of waiting. He was almost certain that the day when he would go home to Palestine would come soon. He believed one hundred percent in Nasser's ability to liberate Palestine. In his mind there was no other course. And he was one hundred percent sure that on that day he would go back to reclaim his land in Palestine.

He was always listening to the Egyptian radio station. He believed in Nasser so much. I remember him telling me that he dreamed he saw the face of Nasser in the face of the moon, meaning that Nasser was a saint and was going to accomplish all that he had promised.

With my grandmother—well, no one had a relationship with that woman, including my grandfather. Although my grandparents were living with us in the same house, they were not on direct speaking terms. Most of the time they would talk indirectly, through my mother. My grandfather would ask my mother to ask my grandmother something. Even if he was present, my grandmother would always talk about my grandfather in the third person. "He is doing this and that," she would say, as if she were telling that to somebody else. They didn't talk to each other. I don't know why; I just accepted the fact.

My grandmother was difficult to like. She was a very tough woman. Even in her village in Palestine, she was known as one of the few women who were tough and independent and did things their own way, even though their husbands were around. My grandfather was also known to be a very tough, independent man. So there were these two strong people living together and they had totally different ways of dealing with the world.

I was twelve years old when my grandfather died in 1961. He didn't live to see the disappointment that came with the 1967 war and the collapse of Nasser. He died still thinking that Nasser was going to do the trick. I was psychologically prepared for his death because he had been sick for many years. We shared the same room. My grandfather and all the kids slept in one room. My mother, father, grandmother, and my aunt stayed in the other room. The littlest babies, who might need care during the night, slept with my mother. The rest of us kids would put our mattresses in one big row and sleep together. I slept next to my grandfather, and used to wake up in the middle of the night and hear his moans years before he died. I must have been seven or eight years old when that bad period started. He seemed like an extremely old man even though he was only in his late 60s. When he fell ill the last time, it was a week or ten days before he died. During those ten days, I seemed to develop an acceptance that it was going to happen. I began to prepare for his death.

My grandfather loved my mother. He had a lot of respect for her and was always kind to her. He never actually said so, but I think he appreciated how my mother dealt with our large family and also with her mother-in-law and sister-in-law. Those two women were not very kind to her; indeed, they were extremely cruel, always combative, always trying to pick a fight. At least that's the story from my mother's side, and naturally as a kid, I always took my mother's side. Most of the time my mother tried to avoid fights by withdrawing or backing away from the argument. I think my grandfather appreciated how my mother dealt with a very difficult situation, trying her best to keep the family intact, in our refugee situation. In turn, my mother deeply respected my grandfather, appreciated his being with us, and never complained about anything he did.

As far as I can recall, my parents never had a real fight. It is astonishing to think about it now because the tension between my mother, my grandmother, and my aunt was so great that you would think it would rub off on her relationship with my father, that she might blame him for the fact that these two women were living with us all the time. I think my father and mother forged some kind of secret alliance against his mother and sister. They were a very close couple, as close as you can get in that environment where you aren't supposed to show any kind of intimacy. Husbands and wives did not show affection in public, not in front of their children, and especially not in front of the husband's mother. But my father did like to tease my mother, commenting about her family and aggravating her. And that was fun, because we used to sit there and watch. She'd play along with him to the point of actually getting a little bit angry. But I don't remember them having any real fights.

My mother and father had an arranged marriage. He didn't see her before the wedding night, but it ended up as a very good, loving marriage. My father was completely dependent on my mother. If he came home and my mother was not there, he would say, "Where is your mother?" He always tried to avoid making it seem as if he needed her. He would say she should be at home for everything to run smoothly.

My grandfather, my father, and my mother were always telling us stories about Palestine—what they owned, how they were going to claim it, how they were going to return.

At school, we learned about Palestine informally from the teachers and from the other kids. The kids would tell stories about Palestine. Sometimes it became a competition over whose land was more fertile and whose produced better crops. We also learned a lot from the radio, especially the Egyptian radio during the era of Nasser. The idea was that Egypt's duty was to liberate Palestine from the Zionists. So my father and my grandfather always listened to the news from Cairo and we listened too.

Most of the time I played with Lebanese kids in the grassy square. The Palestinian men from the camp would pass by on their way home from work. The Nabatiyeh kids were very cruel to these Palestinian outsiders. They would chase them and make fun of them because they were darker-skinned and poor. That was hard for me because I identified with the Palestinians as our people and yet we were kids playing in downtown Nabatiyeh, a Lebanese town, and we were part of that group as well. I didn't have the courage to speak up. They would think I was siding with the refugees and would make fun of me. Although I didn't participate in the teasing, I would watch what was happening with kind of a split personality.

          When I was twelve or thirteen, I had to move alone to Ain al-Helwah camp, which is near Sidon, to finish middle school and high school. By that time, my grandmother and my aunt had moved out of our house, after a big fight with my mother, and settled in Ain al-Helwah camp. When I went, my older brother had already graduated, and I lived alone with my grandmother. In reality, I was alone because of my detachment from her. Two of my aunts lived in the camp and I visited them frequently, but still it was tough because it was the first time away from my family. I ended up enjoying that time much, much more than I expected, because I found that I was living among my own people, the Palestinians. I knew where I belonged and I was more comfortable. These were people like me. We had all had the same experiences, we were all refugees.

    The years in Ain al-Helwah were some of the best years of my life, even though I was living in abject poverty. I was doing very well in school, and I was alone, so I gradually came out of my shell and met people. And I did naughty things I had never done before because I had been the perfect child. In Ain al-Helwah I did what the other kids did, climbed on people's fences and stole fruit from their trees, went to the movies at night, and on the way home sang in the alleyways. I studied, did good work, and finally had some fun.

          My memory of the political resistance movement in the camp is of its early days, when it was extremely secretive. Young men disappeared from the camp and nobody knew where they went. Rumors circulated that so-and-so had joined the resistance, which meant he had gone to Jordan because the training bases were there. In Lebanon the camps were still under the strict control of the Lebanese intelligence. Nobody dared to make a political move, let alone do any military action, and of course there were no weapons. Then we began to hear these fantastic stories about guerrillas; they were the first men to disappear and in the camps there was a kind of agreement to keep their departure secret.

    The resistance takeover of the camps was followed by a rush of enthusiasm. What changed most was the shift from the belief that the Arab armies were going to liberate Palestine to the belief that a people's war, guerrilla fighting, would do it. Although Nasser was still respected and revered by the Palestinians, there was a sense of disillusionment after the 1967 war. The gap was filled by the new resistance movement very quickly and very effectively.

In the camp, the idea that we were freed from the supervision of the Lebanese intelligence and the Lebanese police was overwhelming because we had been living in terror of them. Our first sense of empowerment was very localized, and then came the larger, more important sense that we could do something in order to change the long-term prospect for our future. Not only on the camp level anymore, but on the more general level, the idea took root that it was possible for Palestinians themselves, rather than the Arab governments, to inflict damage on Israel. There was the romantic hope that you were the small flame that was going to light the fires of all the others.

In the fall of 1968, I left Ain al-Helwah camp and went to the American University in Beirut. That was the beginning of a new life, but the end of my childhood.

Abdelaziz Abbassi

MOROCCO *Abdul Aziz Abbassi was born in Sefrou, Morocco. He was educated in Morocco, taught secondary school in England, and received a Ph.D. in linguistics from The University of Texas at Austin. He is an independent translator, writer, and teacher. His most recent translation into English is* **Arab-Islamic Philosophy: A Contemporary Critique** *by Mohammed ʿAbed al-Jabri.*

ABDUL
AZIZ
ABBASSI,
LEFT

THEFT IN BROAD DAYLIGHT

Abdelaziz Abbassi

 You sat down in a slightly reclining position on the smooth, straw-matted floor of the *hammam* changing room, surrounded by the small piles of clothing that belonged to other bath-goers. Though your heart was still beating like a drum from the Royal Guard Orchestra because of the hell-like heat inside, you felt rather relieved that the unpleasant ordeal of cleansing was over. Your mother had just finished giving you a post-circumcision bath, an event worse than the weekly one, which, in itself, should have been called "the skinning."

You were never fond of the weekly visits to the *hammam*. There were, perhaps, a few pleasant aspects involving typical childhood games with much fun and loud laughter, like when you and your siblings would surreptitiously pour cold water into the buckets of scalding water meant for your final rinsing; or when, single file, you would slide with the flow of soapy waters coming from nearby bathers. Other aspects, however, were downright painful. First, they would make you sit or stand in the Third Room, whose temperature was comparable only to that of the Day of Reckoning, until your skin was tender and ready to fall off your bones, or until you succeeded in feigning fainting or in fact did faint. Then, you were called over to the Middle Room for the grueling scrubbing phase. With the help of a burlap-knit scrubber, your mother or your nanny Rqiyah would work on your entire body until enough vermicelli-like dirt and dead skin had come off. At that time, you were soaped and washed; the coup-de-grace was the final rinse, when a whole bucket of hot water was poured over your head. Only then, were you declared clean and allowed to move to the First Room to rest awhile, have a bowl of cold water, eat an orange, and cool off before you were taken out to the changing area.

There, wrapped in an oversized towel, you were left waiting in the care of the Sitter. She was a woman of great stature and presence, at least according to this little boy who had not yet been "weaned" from bathing with the women. She sat on a makeshift pedestal in a prominent spot of the large sitting-room, observing all the goings-on, a bit like a Quranic school master but without the long stick. Her duties were to collect money, supervise the masseuses and hot-water-helpers, sell bowls of buttermilk to thirsty bathers, and, most importantly, entertain the women.

That day, a crowd of them sat around, or hovered over you, bare-breasted as usual and wearing only a *mizzar*, which hung from the waist down; they began to chatter. The hovering ones, who were trying to locate their piles of clothing on the floor, managed to join in. You just put your head over one of the mounds nearby and, half-dozing, you listened to the most recent gossip in town.

Who was marrying, who'd lost children to the measles. And another woman, who had just come out of the Hot Room and who seated her steaming back by your face, said, "You all have seen nothing yet. They say the Senegalese soldiers who came with the Christians are descending on the city every night bothering the daughters of decent folks . . . even married ladies."

"*Willi willi,*" hissed and whispered the women in chorus. The sound of the women's voices turned into a gentle lullaby that slowly sang you to sleep.

It was just another morning at the Ben Seddiq household on Garden Street. Your mother, along with Rqiyah, your favorite in a succession of nanny-maids, because of the special piggyback rides she gave you, was already on the roof washing clothes after thoroughly cleaning and mopping the downstairs. Cleaning and creating order in the house was no casual affair for your mother. It was an obsession. In fact, the idea of clean and cleansing seemed to affect everything she did, making play and fun a risky endeavor for the children.

Your maternal grandmother, Khitti, the only grandparent you actually ever knew, sat on her knees in the middle of the house, a quadrangular open-air patio that separated the four rooms downstairs, kneading the round loaves of dough which would later bake into crunchy *khubzat*. Your father had gone to the market with your older brother, whose chore that day was to help carry the groceries. You were chasing your younger sister and brother up the stairs, in-and-out of the guest living room, where the thick wool mattresses along the four walls made soft landings for each fall you took as you jumped on them, trampoline-style. There was no regular school for your older brother that day, no Quranic school for you and the younger siblings. It may have been a Friday or a day following some major holiday. It was some time after the year of the Big Flood, maybe before, maybe around the year King Mohamed V was sent to exile. But it was definitely before the French vacated Morocco.

You were the fifth born. In a land where superstition reigned and where five was considered an unlucky and unspoken number, you succeeded in deflecting the ominous strikes of the evil eye and survived. Perhaps it was thanks to all that counter-evil-eye paraphernalia you wore around your neck and your right ankle all those years. Several folded talismans, a silver Hand of Fatima, and an assortment of shells and beads were placed there to cast away Satan and his cohorts and the evil gazes of strangers. Or, perhaps it was better medicine, better hygiene, and better-prepared parents that interceded on your behalf. After all, the first three children to whom your mother gave birth eventually died in their childhood; a set of twins from the measles and one child from some unknown disease. Like all your siblings, you were born at home, delivered by Mama Zgania, the skillful midwife with the golden hands, whose reputation was unsurpassed in Sefrou, a small town nestled at the foot of the Middle Atlas Mountains, famous for its annual Cherry Festival and for being the Jewish capital of the land.

Khitti, with her silver bangs sticking out from underneath the Mecca-imported scarf she usually wore, had already finished preparing the daily bread. She left it to rise in a warm corner of the kitchen and decided to join the laundry party up on the roof. Shortly after that, the front-door brass knocker was pounded loudly. Your sister rushed toward the entry hall and expertly shouted, "Who is it?" "Someone close," answered a familiar voice from the other side. It was Khadija, your friend Hassan's older sister. Hassan, the son of Moulay Driss, the carpenter, lived a few houses away. Although he was several years your senior, you always liked to play with him and emulate his deeds and his tricks. Khadija had come to deliver a message ostensibly from him to you. "My brother, Hassan, would really like you to come to our house and play together with the large rooster we got him," she said in an eager voice. "Let me ask my mother's permission first," you replied, jumping with excitement. You ran up those stairs, two at a time, and asked your mother, who, too preoccupied to shower you with the usual one thousand and one pieces of advice on what to do and not to do in another household, simply acquiesced. To show your understanding of proper behavior in the company of an older person, you walked slightly behind Khadija all the way to their front door.

Hassan's parents' house was much bigger than yours. It had more rooms to explore, more nooks in which to hide during play, and, more importantly, a large garden in the middle of the house, whose lemon and fig trees had often been abused by children's feet like yours. But that day's visit was going to destroy all those pleasant memories.

As soon as you entered their house, Khadija slammed the front door shut. Normally it would be kept ajar or half-open. Instead, she locked the upper bolt which children your size could not reach. She then ushered you up the stairs to the second level.

"Why the extra precaution in the middle of the day?" was the question that flashed through your now-curious mind. As soon as you walked into the patio overlooking the garden, you knew there was something strange afoot. Hassan was nowhere to be seen; instead his father and several men in white were standing in a half-circle with somewhat mischievous looks on their faces. It did not take you very long to recognize two of them. There was Moulay Omar, the barber, who regularly cut your hair and that of your male siblings and shaved your father's head and beard. Next to him stood his assistant Larbi, the Bloodletter, who was always leaning over the backs of older people's necks sucking some superfluous blood through these strange *Kif* pipe-like utensils. "Why are they here while undoubtedly so many heads and necks must be awaiting their attention back at the shop?" was the next question buzzing through your head.

"How are you, son-of-Ben Seddiq?" said one of them. "Before any rooster games, we would like you to take your shoes off." Though totally unconvinced, you somehow complied. "Now, take off your trousers," they continued. You began to seriously question their intentions. You had no time to think clearly. Your mind started to race a hundred fields a second trying to figure out what lay behind Khadija's precautions and her blushing, behind all the confusion and the scheming.

These barbers, you were once told by your older friends and by your grandmother, performed other functions than just cutting hair and shaving heads and beards. They worked as caterers and waiters at social functions such as betrothals, weddings, and naming ceremonies; they also performed circumcisions, or Cleansing. You had perhaps heard of these words before, but what did they have to do with weddings, with cutting, or with blood? And why were the barbers there? Was it to cleanse or purify you before you were allowed to play with Hassan's rooster? Or, was it to cleanse and purify you after the incident, a few weeks back, when a female cousin on the verge of womanhood tricked you into playing body-intertwine with her? Were these people going to let the rooster's blood or yours? You had to assume the worst, so you desperately pleaded, "Can I go home to take my trousers off and come right back?" There was no choice, however, and they took them off for you as they laughed at your clever attempt to run away. You began to scream and call out for your mother as everything seemed to move in slow motion. Moulay Driss and Larbi grabbed your half-naked body, each from one leg, and forced you into a squatting position. Moulay Omar started towards you with a shiny pair of scissors in hand. Then one of them yelled at you, "Look at the little bird up on the tree." All efforts to struggle out of their tight grip proved futile. The last thing you remembered before fainting was biting desperately at someone's arm. Later, you found out that poetic justice had prevailed. It was rumored that it took Hassan's father months of doctor's visits, frequent dressings, and medication before the bite healed.

You woke up to the sound of some loud ululations. You were lying, barely regaining consciousness, on a corner bed of the spacious guest living room in your parents' house. You wondered what had happened to you. The answer soon became obvious when you tried to sit up. An excruciating pain brought you straight back to the horizontal position. It was coming from your *soul*, the beautiful term your grandmother imaginatively used to refer to the genitalia. You remembered in a flash the last scene at Hassan's house and realized what had indeed happened; what the scissors in Moulay Omar's hand were used for; whose blood was let after all and what purification and cleansing actually meant. A circle of women with smiling faces, vibrating tongues, and gawking eyes hovered over you. They took turns to ululate or praise the names of Allah in a chant-like manner. Those exclusively feminine, high-pitched, and joyful howls of theirs could not be more inappropriate under the circumstances, you thought. The only two persons who demonstrated normal behavior, you concluded, were your mother and your grandmother. They were crying and seemed sympathetic to your plight. The visiting women then left your bedside and went over to the middle of the room to console your relatives.

"Well, thanks to Allah for your son's safety, and congratulations to you. May we still be around for the next one, Inshaallah!" said a chorus of visitors. Your mother, who was trying to wipe the tears off her cheeks with the lower end of her caftan, turned pointedly to Hassan's mother, who sat at the other end of the room, and said in a bitter tone:

"No, no, Lalla Saadiya, you shouldn't have done this to us; we were not ready for this at all; besides the boy is still too young for circumcision."

"It was the right time and we all know that. If we had left it up to you, you would have delayed this obligation towards Allah and his Prophet indefinitely," replied Lalla Saadiya. The argument went on and on, interspersed occasionally by a burst of laughter among the women, a laugh mixed with tears by your mother, or the crow of some rooster from the rooftop. Then a heavy silence fell as you finally dozed off.

You were very lucky to have a grandmother like Khitti. She was good to you and the other siblings, always asking Allah to protect and preserve all of you from the perils of life, and always there to hear your truths as well as your fables. She would entertain you with her stories and tales, and, when your father was not around, would tell real-life jokes about people you knew, complete with impressions and at times graphic references. You had always hoped that if humor were an inherited trait, you could get hers. She had a keen sense of humor with a unique and colorful vocabulary even a child could appreciate. You still remember one of her best instances of cutting sarcasms. She made the following remark about one of your playmates whom she found either unpleasant or disrespectful: "Go away and behave yourself. You see, most kids are born to their mothers, but you must have been defecated by yours."

Khitti was skillful at conveying to you a more earthly and more human image of your parents; you tended to see them as super-humans because of their constant teachings to follow the right path and to do the right things. But, on the other hand, she was fair to them and very firm with you when it came to laying down the rules of the house or to communicating to you children's duties and parental prerogatives. She was especially good at explaining and simplifying problems and topics in which your mother and father would never willingly venture. And on this particular occasion, she made no exception. The second day of this ordeal had been reserved for visiting men who came to present their congratulations to the parents and to slip you a few coins or a large banknote, depending on their relationship or their generosity. But since their arrival was discreet and their departure more prompt than the women's had been the day before, Khitti sat next to you in between visitors and spent a long time telling you about what had happened and what it all meant. She explained to you that circumcision was an important religious rite in Islam; that all boys at some age, usually determined by the size of their bodies, or their *souls*, had to go through it in order to attain purity.

"But why didn't my own parents plan this ritual?" you asked. "Why did Hassan's family do it after misleading and deceiving me? Why the lies and deception?"

"You see," Khitti continued, "we have a custom in this part of the land whereby families 'steal' each other's male children for circumcision. Unbeknownst to the concerned parents, the plotting families prepare their plan in advance and make all the logistical arrangements with the barbers, the drummers and pipers, the gift-carriers, and what have you. . . . Then, after the ceremony is performed, they take the kids back to their homes. The practice, you see, is intended to spare hesitant or squeamish parents the difficult decision of performing the circumcision ceremony themselves. In the future your parents should do it for someone from Hassan's immediate family, Inshallah."

"But I don't think it's fair to the little boys at all, Khitti," you said in a tone of frustration and poorly disguised anger.

"Well, that's the way of the land, dearest little one, and there's nothing we can do to change it, it's just like that," your grandmother replied, as if to close the subject.

Your grandmother's explanations put a label or a name to the ordeal you had just undergone but did not quite alleviate the physical discomfort you experienced for almost a week. You alone knew how it felt to limp and waddle around circles of human beings as you tried to reach the water closet, afraid that a child might literally run into you or, worse, fall on you. You alone could describe how painful it was to accidentally peel off a piece of scab as you unfolded the bandage before urinating. And once ready and in position, you just stood there, perhaps waiting for a woman you did not know to finish washing parts of her body or her *soul* or for someone to turn the water-faucet on. You alone could fathom the helplessness you faced when an itch devoured you, yet you were not allowed to touch yourself.

You just lay there, day after day, in the midst of all those strange well-wishers, some of whom you were told had come from far away. You were expected to smile, be polite, and kiss visitors' hands. That was another thing you had to do to all incoming and outgoing adults: hand kissing. You did not mind kissing your parents' and relatives' hands as a traditional sign of respect and deference, but you most definitely disliked the practice of indiscriminately placing your lips on every right—or wrong—hand which happened to belong to your father's or mother's acquaintances. Admittedly, you sometimes did it with selfish designs and ulterior motives; the kissed hand, in some cases, would slip under the owner's djellabah, grope inside a large coin purse or a deep pocket, produce a coin, and tender it to you. You would first decline, wait for a sign of insistence to be uttered, then would take it without further ado, uttering back as a thank you, "May God replace it."

For a week, with your predicament having turned into a happy event, your house became a place of festive celebration. Your mother and grandmother, who had by now gotten over the initial shock, turned their attention to preparing elaborate feasts for all the guests who kept coming to present their congratulations. What was ironic and certainly cruel to you at this point of the whole circumvention was the fact that the same barbers responsible for your aches and pains had been hired again, this time to serve lunches and dinners and prepare mint tea for the hundreds of well-wishers. They were marching around like they were the rightful owners of the house, putting on haughty airs and ordering all your friends and younger relatives to go and play outside in the street.

Deception notwithstanding, everything and everybody was eventually transformed on this occasion: the house, your parents, your siblings, and your neighbors. You too were transformed. You did not believe in any more rooster games and you mistrusted barbers. After your suddenly shrunken *soul*, which had been treated with no more than mercurochrome and *daginau*, a talcum-like powder, began to heal and you were declared fully mobile again, you set out to resume your daily activities. You knew the special treatment was ending when your father, realizing you were back to your usual explosive energy, told you to go and play with the other children in the street. Child games were seldom an in-house affair, especially for boys. Playing at home, they argued, would clearly disturb the "order" of things and would somehow soil the cleanliness of the place.

But, now that you were circumcised, were you cleansed and purified like Khitti said? Were you absolved from all your previous dirt and misdeeds? You were told you had to go to the bath, the hammam, as a last ritual to heal the wounds, cleanse the body, and purify the soul. Hammams were used both by men and women. Men bathed from sunrise to noon; after they left, women came and stayed until or past the Dinner Prayer; then men would come in again until around midnight. Beyond personal hygiene, Muslim men and women would use these public baths to perform their required ritual body-ablutions after sexual intercourse and, for women, after menstruation. Children your age always wondered why their parents would patronize the hammams as frequently as they did. How could they enjoy it so much while you and most of your peers despised it? You thought it was perhaps to cleanse their bodies and to purify their souls of the frequent wounds they must have caused.

"May the wonders of Allah be with you, my son, wake up!" said your mother as you opened your eyes after a most restful nap. Your mother always implored Allah and his multitude of names and attributes to protect you and your siblings from the evil eye and from any spirits you might encounter. "We must all get dressed quickly and leave; they say the men have been waiting outside and are getting impatient," she said while motioning to Rqiyah and the others to hurry.

The muezzin of the Great Mosque was calling the Dinner Prayer as you, along with the remaining bathers, finally walked out the door. The women looked quite different with their djellabahs and veils on. You could not tell one from the other. As these ghost-looking shapes filed by in the poorly lit corridor, one of the men murmured, "How much dirt can a Child of Adam leave behind at the bath after half-a-day of tongue-loosening?" Like every other time when older people seemed to speak in riddles, you did not fully understand what the man meant. You did not even bother to ask Khitti for an explanation. She had already told you enough; besides, you still would not understand. At least, not until the next cleansing.

Fedwa Malti-Douglas

LEBANON *Fedwa Malti-Douglas is the Martha C. Kraft Professor of Humanities in the College of Arts and Sciences and adjunct professor of law in the Indiana University School of Law, where she teaches gender studies and cultural legal studies. The winner of the 1997 Kuwait Prize for Arts and Letters, she is the author of ten books, including a novel,* **Hisland,** *and coauthor of three more. Her latest book,* **American Fantasies: How We Imagine Law, Sex, and Politics,** *will be appearing from The New Press in fall 2002.*

FEDWA
MALTI-
DOUGLAS,
LOWER
RIGHT

AUNT NAJLA

Fedwa Malti-Douglas

 For as long as I can remember, Aunt Najla looked the same. Gray, thinning hair wrapped in a bun behind her head. A round face that seemed at times angelic. An overweight body with sagging breasts. Her whole body covered in a dress that memory has played with over the years: a dark brown (or is it beige?) top with a flowered bottom whose background color was the same as that of the top. Or is it the reverse? Flowered top with dark bottom? One thing is certain, Aunt Najla's wardrobe was limited. Was it because she made her own clothing, right down to the undergarments?

Aunt Najla's world in Deir el-Amar, Lebanon, unlike that dress sewn by my memory, was unchanged. She had been a stunning, well-educated young woman, who decided to dedicate herself to the greater glory of her brother, my father. Hers was a family story that smacked of the fairy tale: my grandfather was the pharmacist to the Emir in Beit el-Din, and she and her siblings were born in a room in that legendary palace that is a landmark of Lebanese history. I grew up with an almost innate knowledge of that room's location. It is not easy to forget: up a curved flight of stairs, behind those famed arches, overlooking a marble fountain. The room inhabited my imagination long before it did my reality. Numerous visits to the shrine as a child permit me even now to recreate it in my mind. This room was destined to coexist with me in America, where a watercolor painting of it with the arches permanently graced my uncle's living room wall. Aunt Najla's verbal reality had become mixed with a visual one.

For some health reason that was never explained to me, Aunt Najla did not leave the house. I remember thinking as a child how short her legs seemed to be for her body. The skin around her knees always struck my innocent eyes as a bit flabby. Unable to move easily, she did not take advantage of the three floors of the house inhabited by my father, the village physician. The top level contained a master bedroom with an adjoining kitchen and bathroom, three smaller bedrooms, and an enormous veranda or *balcon*, as we called it. The bottom floor held the formal salon with an adjoining room and my father's clinic, where he saw patients. Aunt Najla's presence on either of these two levels signaled an important occasion. Otherwise, her kingdom was the middle section of this large house.

And what a kingdom it was! It expanded from the enormous entranceway and held two large connecting rooms that in turn led to a yard with a giant fig tree and an adjoining chicken coop. It was flanked by an open veranda that was the primary location for social activities. From this veranda, Aunt Najla supervised many of the household activities. Upstairs. Downstairs. Nothing escaped her from this vantage point. Her eyes could easily reach the third-floor *balcon* and the upstairs bedrooms and even beyond them into the hills of Deir el-Amar. She could watch as my father, standing on the *balcon*, shot little birds flying over the house. She could usher in to the clinic my father's patients, whose lives seemed to merge with ours on a daily basis. Even the perfume of the lemon tree, whose roots were embedded in the bottom floor and whose leaves and fruit extended to the top of the stairway on the third floor, reached Aunt Najla when she sat on the veranda. She could watch, as I did, the soap being made. Deep cauldrons that were stirred with a long wooden spoon. Cutting the soap was a special event that produced uneven white squares with just as many soap shreds as squares lying about. Her feet, like mine, would get wet at cleaning time when water rushed through the veranda and carried away the day's dirt and dust.

The front room functioned as Aunt Najla's bedroom at night and a general family room the remainder of the time. When she did not eat or drink outside, she ate and drank there. She performed her bodily functions there— a portable metal receptacle on which she sat was an essential part of her room. She slept there. There was a big bed on one side and a smaller bed facing it. More mattresses were rolled out when needed and then put away behind a curtain. Although I could sleep either downstairs or upstairs when I was home from boarding school, I always liked sleeping in Aunt Najla's room. Was it that the room was infused for me with family history? Was it that the room was where I had cried over the loss of my father? Was it that she would tell me *Thousand-and-One-Nights*-like stories there at night? Or was it simply the small jar with burning oil that stood high on a stand on the wall and whose wick I could watch as it flickered into the night? I would lie

in the small bed, the one in which my great-aunt had died, listening to Aunt
Najla snoring, and watching shadows on the wall. The characters from
Aunt Najla's tales all came alive then. I could close my eyes and replay these
tales. I would reset them in the Malti house. How lucky for me that her stories were so flexible. Princes and princesses ran up and down the stairs in their
fancy costumes. The doors on the third floor of the house were transformed
into magical doors behind which hid great treasures. There was a story in
which the prince would open the doors to all the rooms but one. That forbidden door is still there for me, on the third floor of our house. These transformations were my own well-kept secret. I never shared them, not even
with Aunt Najla.

The front room always managed to look neat despite its multiple functions. My father cooked in it. The chickens met their deaths just outside it,
on the veranda, at the hand of his kitchen knife. What little blood spurted
on the stone was quickly washed away, never leaving its trace on Aunt
Najla's world. My father collected the blood and cooked it. Fried in a pan.
He firmly believed in its beneficial qualities. Aunt Najla never ate it. Cakes.
Spaghetti. Kufta. Smells wafted from Aunt Najla's kingdom and permeated
the rest of the world.

A metallic round tub would at times surface inside Aunt Najla's room.
This was the sign of an impending bath. I would stand in it as water was
poured over my body. What a long, complicated process. Water has to be
heated. Multiple hands scrub me. Mine. Aunt Najla's. With soap made in
the Malti house. Those uneven soap bars. Odorless but effective. And what
a great sensation from the towel wrapped around my body! The perfect co-
coon in which to hide after a not-too-comfortable bath.

When family friends arrived, they were received in Aunt Najla's space.
More official guests were invited to wind their way down the stairs to the
more formal salon, where Persian rugs lit up the room.

When the family got a radio, it went on a shelf in Aunt Najla's front
room. Everyone huddled around it. Neighbors dropped by to listen. Mysterious voices without bodies became part of the family. From the confinement of this room, one could reach an entire universe.

But it was the inner room, the space that led to the fig tree and the
chicken coop, that held all the wonder for me. Only one thing in that space
ever drew my eyes: a tall gray metallic structure with doors that opened outward. Aunt Najla was the only person who had the key to that house of
mystery. The rare times she would open it in my presence, I would strain to
consume it all with my eyes, the crowded shelves of hidden treasures. But
Aunt Najla would close the closet as quickly as she had opened it. It was
only years later when I was on my way to America that I would begin to

share in the secret contents of that hidden space. Aunt Najla opened it and pulled out some trinkets she had saved for me for years. One of them is my constant companion: a little perfume bottle in the shape of a bull dog. What did that bottle represent for Aunt Najla? Did someone give it to her as a present? The answers remain an enigma, forever buried with her in Deir el-Amar. Other objects which had spent their lives aging in the mysterious closet lost their reason for existence when Aunt Najla died. It was only her being alive that permitted their secret survival in the closet.

The fig tree dominated the yard. It had been grafted long before I was born. Different types of figs grew on it: pear-shaped ones, round ones—all equally sweet. The chicken coop was across the yard from the fig tree. Mornings away from boarding school always meant an adventure in the chicken coop collecting eggs. Still warm, some would be surrounded with straw. The chickens would have to be seduced into abandoning their comfortable resting places before the eggs could be removed. A few feathers would fly. There was only one rooster and I do not know how many chickens. Their number must have varied because once in a while one would end up the victim of my father's kitchen knife.

The yard was also the place where bread was baked on a round-top oven, which was carefully placed under the shade of the fig tree, away from the chicken coop. No one in the family made the bread. We brought in one of the village women for that purpose. She squatted in front of the stove with her dress tied around her knees, her hands with lives of their own like a working magician's. One would rise as the other fell; then, crossing each other, the hands held the dough and flipped it. Timing was crucial. The resulting bread? I would not dare to describe its delicious taste.

These pleasures were only to be had when I came home from boarding school. Listening. Watching. Joining in. One could look down on the yard and the veranda from the roof of Aunt Najla's front room. Climbing up there was a challenge for me, one that invariably earned Aunt Najla's fury. I never did this activity alone; my brother somehow always cooperated. When we reached the forbidden space of that roof, we could observe the cleaning, the cooking, the washing. More than that, we could see more clearly across the white stone houses of Deir el-Amar, across the terraced hillsides overgrown with olive trees, all the way to Beit el-Din.

Would it be fair to say that Aunt Najla was my surrogate mother when I was a child? She had given up a teaching career to live with my father after my parents' divorce. I was four at the time. She prided herself on her knowledge of Arabic, French, and English. The brother-sister bond would make that knowledge useless. But not her love of it. And some of her passion for reading percolated down to me. One of the books I carried with me to America and that still inhabits my living room was one Aunt Najla had won as a child in a school competition. Her name was inscribed in it. Now, the binding is loose, and her name faded. But the object as testimonial existence remains. In her youth, Aunt Najla had also learned to play the piano. And, there in the formal salon downstairs, was the proof: an upright instrument which sat by itself, lonely from nonuse, the symbol of a bygone period in Aunt Najla's life.

Decades later, I came to learn that Aunt Najla had always hated my father's wives—not only my mother but the woman he remarried long after his divorce from my mother. Two marriages had meant two sets of scenes between wife and sister. The broom seems to have been a favored weapon. My biological mother kindly revealed to me, as we both sat sipping a cup of coffee years later in America, that to her, Aunt Najla was always the villain, swinging the broom and trying to hit her with it. I wonder what Aunt Najla would say? Would she reverse the roles? I do remember the tall broom. I also remember the screaming. The battles always seemed to be centered at the bottom of the stairs leading to the third floor of the house, not far below the master bedroom. Strategically placed between the sister's kingdom and that of the wife. But my own visual memory is not clear. At times the broom is attached to my father's wives, at other times, to his sister. These physical battles turned into verbal written ones long after my father's death. His presence was not necessary to keep the conflict raging between sister and wife. Letters from both sides followed me to America, as if arbitration could be won from faraway relatives. What were Aunt Najla's feelings towards my father? Was she in love with him? Questions with no simple answers. But there are yet more riddles, ones that will also remain—and fortunately so—eternally buried. One thing needs no clarification: she was very protective of my father. His death from a heart attack did not come as a surprise to her. She had known all along the secret of his previous heart problems. Together, they shared this fatal knowledge.

Aunt Najla held other, more important secrets: family secrets. She was the oldest of five children and it was as though the mantle of transmission of the family history had been placed on her shoulders. She could revive for me family members, long dead, only to bury them once more. She told me how my grandfather, the pharmacist to the Emir of Beit el-Din, had died during the First World War by ministering to soldiers on rat-infested wagons. She told me how my uncle, the dentist, passed away at a young age. He was an artist of sorts; his calligraphic painting of a bird hung permanently in the salon downstairs. I would ask her over and over again to tell me about her sister, the one who held the most fascination for me: an aunt of mine whom I would never meet and who also died young. I never tired of hearing of her tragic death from a great fall off the high wall beside the fig tree. A wall that extended from the veranda and then dropped down sharply when the veranda stopped. Sadness would fill Aunt Najla's voice as the story unfolded. My grandmother was heartbroken. I wanted to know how and why. Her answers never satisfied me. The legendary aunt disappeared, but the wall remained. I would stare at it and wish that it could tell me the story. I would visualize the young woman gaily strutting on the wall, only to fall and die. She was the youngest of the siblings. When Aunt Najla got angry at me and my brother's climbing on the roof, was she thinking of this lost sister? Did she think one of us might suffer the same fate? She never expressed this fear to me.

There was a way for me to share in the collective Malti female tradition. Aunt Najla presented me with a doll made by one of the great-aunts or maybe even a great-grandmother in my family history. Its dark-painted face had grown old and wrinkled. Its black hair had become shredded by decades of hugging. Its body had become limp with the years. But this was a special doll, I understood, one which had shared the life of many a young girl of the Malti household. Did I cherish it? I am not sure. I think I was too naive. I was much more taken then with the white-skinned, blonde-haired specimen imported to the village and presented to me by my uncle's American family when they passed through the Lebanese ancestral home on their way to India. The American product could open and close her blue eyes, unlike my homemade, brown-eyed doll. But the Malti doll was quite a survivor and it took its place beside the American factory-produced model when I left for the United States. Both remained behind with Aunt Najla and my step-sister.

Why does mystery surround Aunt Najla? Even her body held secrets, secrets that she alone knew. Family rumor had it that she was perhaps a diabetic. For years, she had had a vaginal discharge. At first, it was barely visible. She did not disclose it to anyone. But, later, she would confess (yes, that is the right word) that the discharge had grown heavier and become more serious. This had gone on for years. Yet, she had told no one. Yes, my father was a physician. True, there was a brother-sister bond. But neither fact could wipe out the shame of the body. It was years after I left Lebanon that Aunt Najla was diagnosed with cervical cancer. How ironic it should be that she would leave Deir el-Amar for Beirut to have the operation.

Though she kept the vaginal secret to herself, there were areas of mystery that Aunt Najla shared with me. Mysteries that tied her body to the word. Aunt Najla would sit, I by her side. A spoon, a newspaper, and a blank, white sheet of paper were our companions. The newspaper would be placed on the white sheet. Then magic! Aunt Najla would take the spoon, rub it on the back of her head, and then rub the newspaper with the back of the spoon. Presto! Lifting the newspaper, she would reveal the printed word on the white sheet. A transfer. I never ceased to be captivated by this operation. I would sit transfixed, my hand resting in Aunt Najla's lap. She must have perceived my fascination. She never explained the process to me, perhaps knowing that once understood, it would lose its excitement.

Though she never revealed this secret to me, Aunt Najla did try to inculcate some of her philosophy into my young head before I left the village for America. Whatever happens is for the best, I can still hear her saying. Is this the way she would describe her life, I wonder? If I could revive her as she revived others in her stories, I would ask her to explain this more clearly. As a child, I thought I understood. Now, I am not sure I do.

When I returned to Lebanon years later, Aunt Najla was no longer of this world. She had disappeared, but the house had not. The fig tree still stood and there was the roof from which I would mischievously observe the activities around Aunt Najla's world. I made it a point to visit the family tomb, a large structure with a metal gate and a set of stairs. It had always held a fascination for me and how often did I wish I could enter it and see if anything remained of those long lost family dead. But I was never allowed more than a peek through the bars, having to leave the rest to my imagination. Aunt Najla had now joined the other members of the family. Her words would no longer revive them for me.

This piece was completed at the Bellagio Study and Conference Center, Lake Como, Italy. I am grateful to the Rockefeller Foundation and to the Center and its director, Dr. Pasquale Pesce, for the opportunity to participate in the at once contemplative and stimulating intellectual life there.

Awad Abdelrahim Abdelgadir

SUDAN *Awad Abdelrahim Abdelgadir is the owner of Nile Valley Herbs, a small, private company, based in Austin, Texas, which imports and distributes products from the Nile Valley. He was born in a village in Dongola province in northern Sudan, was educated in the Sudan, and taught for many years in Yemen.*

MEMORIES OF A NUBIAN BOYHOOD: GROWING UP IN A SUDANESE NILE VILLAGE

Awad Abdelrahim Abdelgadir with Linda Boxberger

 The lion is known as the king of the jungle, but the king of the Nile is the crocodile. Since our village is located right on the bank of the Nile, it is not surprising that there are many stories about crocodiles. Some of the stories are legends and some are rumors, but others are true. In my boyhood, I not only saw some scarred survivors of encounters with crocodiles but also witnessed a crocodile attack on two of my friends.

Our saintly ancestor, Sheikh Abdullah Tor Kulum-Mesid (God's Mercy Be Upon Him), is believed to have performed many miracles in his lifetime. One of the greatest miracles he performed was when he turned a crocodile into stone. This miracle cannot be disputed, as the proof still exists today. The stone crocodile lies on the floodplain below the mosque of Kulum-Mesid. The massive flood of October 1988 covered the stone crocodile with silt, but a future flood will surely uncover it again.

Sheikh Abdullah Tor Kulum-Mesid (God's Mercy Be Upon Him) was at that time the imam of the mosque and the teacher of the Quranic school. One day, it is said, he sent one of his students from the mosque down to the Nile with a pitcher (*ibrig*) to fetch water for washing in preparation for prayers. When the boy didn't return, the imam and the students went down to the river to search for him. To their dismay, they found only the pitcher lying on the bank and they realized that he had been taken by a crocodile.

The imam washed himself and sat and prayed on the bank of the river. He prayed and prayed until all of the crocodiles came out of the Nile and approached him. He asked for the crocodile that had eaten his student. The biggest of the crocodiles stepped forward and the imam told the others to return to the water. The big crocodile then vomited up the boy's body. The sheikh took his pitcher and mounted the crocodile. He sat on the crocodile's back and washed himself and prayed. After praying, he hit the crocodile on the head with his prayer beads and the crocodile turned into stone.

After that, Imam Abdullah had a sword brought from the village and he had some verses from the Quran written on the blade. He placed the sword on the water of the river and it floated, carried north by the current. It floated several miles past the village and then sank. From that time on, it was believed that for a hundred years no crocodile would attack along the stretch of the river where the imam's sword had floated.

But during my childhood, the imam's protection ran out. A crocodile attacked two of my friends within the stretch where the sword had floated. The attack took place on a Sunday; it was the market day in Suq as-Sair, a town across the Nile from our village. On that morning, along with other villagers, I put my donkey on the wooden sailboat that ferried us across the Nile. I was going to the market to sell some lemons from our lemon tree and buy some meat and vegetables for my family, as I usually did on Sundays during my summer vacation from school.

After returning to my village, I went with my friends for a swim in the large pool by the Nile. The pool was like a crater in the riverbank filled with water and connected to the river by a small channel. Although this pool was considered to be a safe place, parents would punish their children anytime they swam. Whenever they punished their children, the parents reminded them that the one hundred years of protection had expired, so that anyone in the water was in danger of being taken by a crocodile. After we swam, we would hide in the bean fields and rub dirt on our arms and legs to cover our disobedience.

While we were swimming in the pool, a group of boys on donkeys coming from the market passed by on the way to their village to the north. These boys were older than me and my friends and they teased us for swimming in the protected pool, calling us babies. They invited us to come swimming with them in the open Nile and then laughed and hurried away on their donkeys, leaving us in a cloud of dust.

We finished swimming and prepared to head home. But we heard the sound of the older boys laughing and splashing in the Nile, and we couldn't resist the temptation to join them. We went to the river bank and watched, hesitating to enter the water of the big river. There were at least fifteen boys swimming near the anchored sailing ferry. I wanted to get in the water with them, but I was afraid of being punished. While we were standing by a pile

of clothes and shoes guarded by the smallest boys, a boy named Mohammed took off his clothes and entered the water. I saw him greeting his friend
Mustafa; they were standing in the shallow water.

Suddenly, chaos erupted. The open jaws of a crocodile followed by half
of its huge body rose from the water between the two boys. With a twist
of his body, he grasped them both in his jaws and forelegs and he dragged
them under the water. I don't know if he was able to hold onto both of
them, or if he held onto Mustafa, who clung to Mohammed. All we could
see was the splashing and stirring of the water, which became increasingly
muddy. I stood staring at the water, frozen in shock as in those bad dreams
where you need to run but can't move. Naked boys erupted from the water
and ran in every direction. Mohammed and Mustafa were still under the
water. The crocodile was sitting on them, waiting for them to suffocate, in
its usual way of killing its prey. After two or three minutes, Mohammed
burst from the water, gasping for air and grabbing at the waves, struggling
to reach the bank. Wounded and bleeding, he fell by the pile of clothes and
vomited river water.

At the same time, the commotion of the screaming naked boys running
into the village had roused the ladies from their housework. A group of
women, including Mustafa's mother and sister, ran to the riverbank. When
they arrived, the crocodile rose out of the water in front of them, lifting and
shaking Mustafa's body in the air. In order to restrain Mustafa's mother and
sister from leaping into the water in a mad attempt at rescue, the other
women had to push them to the ground and sit on them. Soon the screaming and wailing of the women brought almost everybody in the village to
the riverbank.

A group of men led by Sheikh Abdelmajid, owner of the only shotgun
in the area, piled into the sailboat in an attempt to recover the body. Somehow, I was able to get into the boat along with the men. They set off after
the crocodile, heading in his direction, when they saw him surface for air, carrying the body. Imagine trying to chase a crocodile in a sailboat! The crocodile couldn't swim fast with his burden, but he could out-maneuver the large
wooden boat. At one point, the tired crocodile climbed out onto the bank,
dragging the body. He came out near where the women were wailing and
picking up dirt, throwing it into the air and rubbing it onto their heads in
grief. Mustafa's sister threw a stone at him in rage. He retreated to the water, and the chase continued. Eventually, the crocodile disappeared with the
body, and the men finally had to give up the chase.

The crowd returned to the village; they all went to Mustafa's house to
grieve and offer condolences. The search for his body continued for several
days, but it was never found. Mohammed was taken to the clinic, where his

wounds were treated. His face is still scarred from the attack, and he bears the nickname "Crocodile" (*Timsah*). The village recalls the incident with sadness but also with humor. One of my friends who was swimming that day was later found huddled naked in the palm trees by a group of ladies, and some people tease him about that to this day.

Not all victims of crocodile attacks were as unfortunate as poor Mustafa; the village contains several scarred survivors in addition to Mohammed (*"Timsah"*). One hot summer day, a boy named at-Toum went swimming in the Nile. After he had gotten away from the bank, he was attacked by a crocodile. Some friends who were with him tried to save at-Toum. When the friends pulled him from the jaws of the crocodile and tried to drag him towards the riverbank, the crocodile managed to pull at-Toum along with his friends back into the deeper water.

At that time, a group of men came down to the river to wash themselves after the hot and dusty work of threshing sorghum. Fortunately, they were carrying with them the long and heavy sticks which they used to beat the grain from the stalks. When they saw the struggle, they rushed into the water with their sticks to join the battle for at-Toum. The crocodile's behavior proved true the old Nubian belief that once the crocodile has gotten a taste of a victim, he will keep returning for that individual. Amidst the struggle, the crocodile returned to grab at-Toum, rather than trying to take any of his rescuers.

In the water, the group would manage to free at-Toum and carry him to the bank. When they would reach the bank, the crocodile would charge out of the water, grab at-Toum from the middle of the group and pull him back to the deeper water, still with his friends hanging onto him. Finally, the rescuers won; the crocodile gave up and disappeared into the depths. At-Toum was badly injured by the crocodile's jaws and claws during the extended struggle. He spent a long time in the hospital in Dongola and when he returned to the village he bore terrible scars, which he still has.

Crocodiles not only victimize people; they attack animals as well. One crocodile picked a victim that was too much for him when he attacked a camel. During the winter, male camels get very wild and aggressive. It is common for people to tether camels in this state to a tree near the river. The owner occasionally tosses food to the camel, and the camel can get to the water to drink when necessary.

One winter day, a camel that was tied to a tree on the bank of the river went for a drink. While he was drinking, a crocodile rose from the water and clamped his jaws on the camel's lips. The camel, irritated and wild, reared back and pulled the clinging crocodile out of the water. The crocodile planted his hind legs in the mud of the bank and pulled the camel back into the water. The struggle went back and forth. In the deeper water, the camel had the advantage, while near the bank, the crocodile had the advantage.

The camel in his wild winter state was not an easy victim, but the crocodile persisted. The Nubians say that after a crocodile has attacked, he will not give up. They say that the crocodile is such a coward that he pees on himself three times before he attacks his victim. Then, once he has overcome his shyness, he will not let go.

Unfortunately for the camel, the bank collapsed into the water, causing him to lose his foothold. Then, to add to his dilemma, a number of additional crocodiles appeared, as if they had been waiting for the moment. Soon, there were crocodiles all over the camel. By this time, some of the villagers had gathered on the bank. The Arab who owned the camel (in my area, the camel-owning tribes are called Arab) drew his knife and jumped into the water to try to save his animal. To everyone's surprise, he was successful in driving away all of the crocodiles and rescued his camel. Unfortunately, the poor beast was too badly wounded and died within a week.

After Sheikh Abdullah Tor Kolum Mesid's protection from crocodile attacks ran out, many parents punished their children severely for swimming in the Nile. I remember being beaten with the spine of a palm frond as punishment for swimming there. At the same time, other parents did not try to prevent their children from swimming. These parents did not care less about their children but believed that every person's fate is written by God and that there is no point in trying to affect that fate.

If you tell these parents that they should stop their children from swimming, they will support their fatalistic argument with the following story. Once there was a man who was so afraid that his children would get eaten by a crocodile that he moved from his home by the beautiful Nile into the desert. One day his son asked him what a crocodile looked like, so he used a stick to trace a picture of a crocodile in the desert sand. To his surprise and dismay, the drawing turned into a real crocodile, which then swallowed the boy whole. The moral of the story, which is believed to be true, is that you cannot interfere with God's will.

IRAN *Ali Eftekhary*

*Ali Eftekhary, born in a village near Qom, Iran, and edu-
cated both in Iran and the United States. He was one of
the first members of the late Shah's "reverse Peace Corps"
and came to the United States to teach first in the Amish
country of Pennsylvania and then in Watts, Los Angeles.
He now works in the Ministry of Education in Teheran,
where he supervises English language teaching in Iranian
schools.*

A MUSLIM CHILDHOOD

Ali Eftekhary

 My father was a liberal person for his time. My grandfather always wanted me to enter the Muslim clergy, but a friend of my father said, "Let the boy get his high school diploma first. Then he can decide. And just because he's the oldest son, don't put pressure on him." When I finished high school, my father gave me a key to the house and a key to my room and said, "Do what you like, as long as you don't go into the police or the army or security, because then you're not your own man." So I became a teacher.

If I had joined the clergy, I would have been following in a long line of seven generations in our family. My great-grandfather held the title *Eftekhar al-Islam,* or Honorer of Islam, and that is the name I bear to this day.

I was born in March 1937 in a small village near Golpayegan in Central Iran. My parents married young. My father was twenty and my mother was fifteen, a Sayid who traced her ancestry to the seventh Imam. I was their third child. Two siblings had died before me at an early age, two died after I was born, but then six more children came, so we are seven. We lived on the upper level of the family house, in a small room my grandfather had given my father upon his marriage. I was born in that room.

When my uncles were married, my grandfather built a bigger house of four large rooms, one for each married couple, with storage areas and fireplaces. There was also a larger storage room and an open oven, where we baked our bread once a week. The courtyard was covered with grape vines and surrounded by high walls. And we had an orchard where there were apple trees, plums, pears, and apricots.

We slept on pads on the floor. In the winter we all gathered around the charcoal brazier and drank tea. There was always tea, fresh tea. And I remember that when I was small, I would open the window of the big room to watch the fall of the snow.

My grandmother would cook meals in a huge clay pot: stews with meat, spices, broth, sometimes garbanzos, and sometimes white beans. We would eat that stew together and we would mash it up and put it on bread for breakfast. Sometimes we had *ishta,* or cream from the top of the milk, on our bread.

My grandfather was the religious leader of the village. He was also the surveyor, judge, and arbitrator of disputes both in our village and in surrounding areas. Still, even with all his responsibilities, he was a great farmer. Most of the lands we owned had been given to him in exchange for his arbitration and his surveying services. This land provided the food we needed, and we were self-sufficient. This self-sufficiency gave our family a great respect in the community. Most of the local religious leaders were like my grandfather. They had owned land for generations and were good farmers. Some of them also supervised the *wakf* endowments in their communities, distributing the income from the endowments as the donors had stipulated: supporting the poor, providing a huge meal for the poor on the holy days of Ashura, or maintaining the mosque. My uncle still administers the wakfs in our village.

Since they were self-sufficient, these religious leaders were able to send their children to *maktabs* (Islamic elementary schools) and later to *madrasas* (Islamic colleges) in Qom in central Iran or to Najaf in Iraq. Most of the Mujteheds and grand Ayatollahs in Iran were the sons of these local village clergy, just like the grand Ayatollah Golpayegany, who was born in my home town of Golpayegan.

In the center of the village lay the mosque, the public bath, and the cemetery. To the north was a water mill to grind the grain into flour. A spring under the mill ran into a canal which divided the village in half. Though every house had a deep well for drinking water, we enjoyed bringing water from the spring, because it was a meeting ground for all the boys and girls of the village.

When I was three, we moved to the holy city of Qom, where my father studied and taught Arabic, theology, and Islamic jurisprudence. We shared a four-room house with another theology student and his family from a village near ours in the Golpayegan area.

Living in Qom was very exciting, because a labyrinth of alleys and covered bazaars led to the great shrine. But children could not move around as easily as in the village, so I had to stay home.

To keep me busy, every day before leaving the house, my father used to give me a large sheet of paper with a Persian letter written in the top right corner. I had to fill the paper by copying that letter and show it to him either at lunch time or in the evening. Every time I completed the page he gave me a couple of small coins. When I finished learning all the Persian alphabet, he sent me to a maktab, a Quranic school, nearby. The teacher was a lady whom everybody called "Khonombaji" or "Khambaji." The twenty boys and girls in this maktab came from different backgrounds and were aged from four to about eight years old.

At the age of five and a half, I started elementary school. A few public schools for boys existed in Qom, but they offered courses such as music, painting, and sports, which were banned by religious leaders. So I had to go to one of the Islamic schools, which were private. The curriculum consisted of all the core courses taught in public schools, plus courses in Islamic studies.

Public school classes started on the 21st of September, and continued to the 21st of June. But in the Islamic school, it was longer. We had only a one-month holiday, and the other two months we had to go to school in the mornings from 8:30 A.M. to 12:00 P.M. We mostly worked on the Quran and Islamic studies.

Every summer my father sent me back to my grandparents in our village in Golpayegan. There I was free to do whatever I wanted, but I played so many tricks on my beloved grandmother that my grandfather sent me to the local Quranic school just to keep me busy. The village teacher had turned one of his rooms into a classroom for twenty boys and girls. The teacher sat near the door, for the room had no windows and the only light was from the entrance door. The teacher held a stick that was long enough to reach every child. Anyone who made a mistake in reciting the Quran or the Persian textbook would find that stick crashing down on shoulder or head. That man was stern, harsh but dedicated, and he really wanted to teach us something. He tried hard to achieve this goal, because he truly believed if we could read the Quran, we might some day say a prayer for him so he would be rewarded in the next world. But we were only children and did not think about such matters.

As children, we looked forward to our annual visits to the houses of the leading *mujtaheds* of the time, especially the late Ayatollah Borujerdi, the world Shiite leader. On the Prophet Muhammad's birthday, we would line up in school in our best clothes and march toward the Ayatollah's house. He would be sitting on the veranda. As we approached, he stretched out his right hand. One by one, we kissed it and then we left.

Ayatollah Borujerdi was a great man. I will never forget the day I watched him teaching. I was only ten years old and did not understand what he was talking about. All I could see was that he was talking and the students were talking back. It seemed to me that it was a very heated debate. Later I asked my father how the students dared to talk back to the great Ayatollah.

He answered, "This is the way it is in the madrasa. The Ayatollah is only a teacher and the students are the future mujtaheds. The Ayatollah has to be convinced or he has to convince the students. After the class is over, he is the exalted Ayatollah again." When I finished fifth grade in 1948, Ayatollah Borujerdi sent my father as his representative to one of the towns in the southern province of Fars; we spent four years there. I finished elementary school and the first cycle of high school, grades 7 through 9.

My high school years were the most turbulent time in Iranian history. After a fairly free election, several nationalists, including Dr. Muhammad Mossadeq, were elected to Parliament. At the time a big debate was in progress about the nationalization of the Anglo-Iranian Oil Company. General Razmara, the prime minister, did not agree with the nationalists, and he was assassinated. After his assassination, the Shah had no choice but to appoint Dr. Mossadeq, who was next in line, as prime minister. Mossadeq was a nationalist and a democrat. There was then relative freedom in the political arena, so the Tudeh Party of Iran (the Communist Party) was flourishing in the high schools and universities across the country. Those of us who were not only nationalists but also devout Muslims did not agree with their pro-Soviet philosophy and opposed them to the bitter end.

To be able to discuss the current issues, we all were devouring books, magazines, and daily papers. During the Mossadeq premiership, which lasted less than three years, a real democracy was at work. Nobody was afraid of self-expression. Religious leaders such as Ayatollah Kashani and many political leaders were working side by side for the first time in post–World War II Iran.

The nationalization of the Anglo-Iranian Oil Company brought national jubilation. At last we were free of the British domination! One of the greatest joys of my life as a teenager was when I stood on the shoulder of one of my friends and hung the Iranian Oil Company sign over the Anglo-Iranian one.

I moved back to Qom in 1952 and started tenth grade there while staying with relatives. All my expenses were paid by the late grand Ayatollah Golpayegany, who had known my father from the day he started his Islamic studies in Golpayegan.

The city of Qom has always been and still is the seat of the Shiite Ulama and of all the leading Mujtaheds. Thus it was difficult for the city's religious establishment to tolerate Communist Tudeh activity in this holy place. There were continual clashes between Muslim students and Tudeh party members. I remember well when the late Ayatollah Beheshti, one of the leading members of the 1979 Islamic Revolution, walked into our English class carrying an English-Persian dictionary and a book of essential English, the assigned tenth-grade English textbook. The Tudeh party members sitting in the back row did not notice the books; they only saw a tall clergyman walking into the classroom.

They shouted sarcastically, "This is an English class, sir, not one in religious studies."

Ayatollah Beheshti, a tall, well-dressed clergyman, looked at them and, in a very solemn but forceful voice, said, "I am your English teacher and your text is *Essential English, Book 4.* We are going to finish it this year; the final exam will consist of the units taught in all the tenth grades of this school. Now please open your book."

It was unheard of in those days that any member of the clergy could teach English. So some students waited to make fun of the Ayatollah for the mistakes they thought he would make. But when Dr. Beheshti began to read the first unit, the class became so quiet one could hear the flies. His mastery of English pronunciation and translation shut us all up.

He was the best English teacher I have ever had, the one who led me to choose English as my major. He used to say that no matter what one does in one's life in the future, one should know a foreign language. In the 1950s, such advice was prophetic. Years later, we both were working in the Ministry of Education. After the Islamic Revolution in 1979, when I heard that he had been killed in a bomb blast, it took me several weeks to overcome the shock of losing such a wonderful teacher. His fatherly advice during the turbulent days of the 1952–1953 school year still echoes in my ears. He was not only a teacher but a counselor. He never humiliated us students in class like some of the other teachers who thought they were God and we were idiots. Dr. Beheshti's morals, ethics, and respect for his students have had a great influence on me throughout my entire life and especially my own teaching career.

In the summer of 1953, we moved to Teheran. That was the most turbulent summer in Iranian history. Every day there was some kind of pro-Mossadeq demonstration. I watched the Shah's statues coming down. I saw the growing power of the Tudeh Party. On the day Stalin died, I saw the Party members demonstrating, wearing black bands of mourning on their sleeves. There were rumors of a Communist takeover or a Soviet invasion. I could not believe that Iran, a Muslim nation, could tolerate a Communist government, for religious leaders wielded a great influence on our people and they could change the course of history.

In early August of 1953, there were rumors of a CIA plot to topple Mossadeq. The American administration was afraid that Iran might become a Soviet satellite and they would have to face the Soviets on the shores of the Persian Gulf.

Unfortunately, to this day American policy makers underestimate the Iranians, who have three thousand years of history behind them. They have never been colonized, though Western colonial powers have interfered in their internal affairs for years. Iranians turned to America after World War II for help, looking for a supporter who had fought a revolutionary war against British colonists. Those same Iranians became disillusioned when the American administration sided with the British to topple Mossadeq. To this day, the Iranians have not forgotten the coup of 1953.

During July and August of 1953, there were pro-Mossadeq demonstrations every day. The morning of August 18, 1953, a friend asked me to go with him to downtown Teheran to the headquarters of the Iran Party, a pro-Mossadeq party. There were not very many people in the street, for the Tudeh Party had decided not to participate in the demonstrations. Years later, after the Islamic Revolution, the Iranians found out that the Tudeh Party had stabbed Mossadeq in the back, hoping that Mossadeq would fall and they would take over. By the time we reached the Iranian Parliament on Baharestan Square, we ran into other people heading to Sepah Square in the center of Teheran. They said that the Shah had appointed General Zahedi as prime minister before leaving Iran. On the way to Bahrestan Square, we ran into Daryush Foruhar, the Pan-Iranist Party leader, who was talking to Karimpoor Shirazi, the owner and editor of *Shuresh*, the pro-Mossadeq newspaper which had recently attacked the Shah and his family in fiery editorials. I overheard Karimpoor apologizing for not staying longer because he wanted his newspaper to hit the newsstand earlier that day. When we reached Sepah Square, we heard pro-Shah demonstrators from South Teheran. Someone said that the demonstrators had taken over the *Shuresh* newspaper. Worrying about Mr. Karimpoor's safety, we ran toward his office, but by the time we had reached the place, it was in flames. Then to our relief, we saw his green Chevrolet make a U-turn and speed away. Several months later he was arrested by Savak and tortured to death.

We came back to Sepah Square, and to our surprise we saw the South Teheran crowd led by a man waving the Shah's picture and shouting "Long Live the Shah." The rumors had become a reality; we had lost our national prime minister together with our dream for a democratic Iran. Knowing that the military would follow the protesters in full force, we ran for home. Soldiers were arriving in army trucks and were shooting live bullets at random. We could hear the bullets passing over our heads, and we dodged as best we could. The only escape was through the back alleys, which we knew well. By the time we got home it was noon. August 18, 1953. Radio Iran was silent. At two in the afternoon, the radio began again with military music, and the announcer reported the fall of Mossadeq. The rest is history.

The Post-Colonial Middle East (1971–)

 Events of the last fifty years have changed almost everything in the Middle East, as these chronicles of childhood
show. A thousand years ago, men and women had no doubts
about who they were and what was expected of them. Society was controlled from above, by kings and sultans; one's
place in the world was fixed at birth by gender, religious
affiliation (Muslim, Christian, Jew); occupation (teacher,
farmer, carpenter, merchant); and wealth (land, property).
One might rise in the system; men could move away to seek
their fortune elsewhere, like Suad Joseph's father. Women
could not do this so easily, though in the late twentieth
century many upper-middle-class girls like Nahid Rachlin
were sent abroad by their families for higher education.

Today nationalism, religious revival, women's movements,
technological revolutions, and global economic interdepen-
dence have splintered the systems that operated in the past.
As Abdelaziz Jadir writes, "He died, this me, a long time
ago." Today young people ask, "Who am I?"; "Where do
I belong?"; "What about the future?" The youngest of the
chroniclers here talk about their lives and their societies
in different ways: as a combination of east and west (Shafeeq Ghabra, Maysoon Pachachi, Esther Raizen); a renunci-
ation of violence (Lilia Labidi); a new appreciation of cultural heritage (Randa Abu Bakr).

But the past and its injustices continue to cast a shadow
over the present and the future, as attested to by Leila Abouzeid, remembering her father's fight against the French for
Moroccan independence, and Mustafa Mirzeler, who left

Turkey when the loss of possibilities for Kurdish peoples became apparent.

The signs of hope for peace in the area gained momentum in the 1990s, as Lebanon began to rebuild after the civil war, Algeria held new elections, and the Oslo accords of 1993 opened up the possibility of resolving the long conflict between Israelis and Palestinians. But as the century ended, those hopes were dashed, first by a new intifada or uprising in Palestine in response to Israel's failure to meet the terms of the peace accords, and then by the terrorist attacks in the United States in 2001 and the American response in Afghanistan.

What then remains of the past to inform the direction of the future? Family ties and religious affiliation, yes, but also the vivid memories of children who grew to adulthood during the tumultuous twentieth century, memories they share with us in these pages.

Shafeeq N. Ghabra

KUWAIT

*Shafeeq N. Ghabra was born in Kuwait and educated in Beirut, England, and the United States. He received his Ph.D. from the University of Texas at Austin and is a professor of political science at Kuwait University. He writes frequently in Arabic and English for journals and newspapers and is author of many books, including **Palestinians in Kuwait: The Family and the Politics of Survival**. He has also served as director of the Kuwait Information Office in Washington, D.C.*

MY CHILDHOOD: INNOCENCE, POLITICS, AND REBELLION

Shafeeq N. Ghabra

 Being a child was a mixture of being subjected to the will of adults and of not knowing what the future would bring. I experienced much love and care, being the oldest, but childhood was a concurrent mixture of happiness and burden. In many ways, being a child in the Middle East, at least for my generation, was quite confusing, particularly the period between adolescence and adulthood. I was one whose childhood was overburdened with the conflicts and sorrows of the Middle East, in particular the agonies of the Palestinian diaspora. I am now a citizen of a country, Kuwait, that has given me and my family political rights and a unique feeling of belonging. But this does not conflict with the fact that something Palestinian remains in me, something that is also rebellious. It is a part of me that I cannot deny and a part that somehow enriches my Kuwaiti identity. As a child, however, the story was somewhat different: being Palestinian meant dealing with all kinds of emotions and fears and created in my imagination the need to return to a home I had never seen, a place taken by "others." I belonged to a group that had somehow lost its country.

I was born to a Palestinian family in Kuwait City in 1953 during the hot month of August. The territory of Kuwait at the time was a British protectorate, and the city was a small one. My father, Nazem, an exceptionally skillful medical doctor from Haifa and a graduate of the American University of Beirut (Class of 1946), had accepted employment in Kuwait in 1952. Like many professional Palestinians, he went to Kuwait seeking temporary employment until he would be allowed back into Haifa. My father had worked in several Arab states after 1948—first as a doctor in the Palestinian refugee camps of south Lebanon, and then in Iraq and Saudi Arabia before settling in Kuwait.

My father's family, middle-class merchants whose origins go back to the well-known Ghabra Syrian family, suffered tremendously during the 1948 war. My grandfather lost his trade and all of his family sought refugee status in Egypt. My father had to shoulder the moral and financial responsibility of the entire family, which included his father, mother, and three unmarried young sisters. This is what led him to seek work wherever possible.

My mother, Nahla al-Tabari, came from Tiberias in Palestine and was the daughter of a leading notable in that city. She lived in Damascus with her family from 1948 until she married my father in 1952. My grandfather, Sudqi Abdul Salam al-Tabari, was working with the United Nations, making use of the bachelor's degree he had earned at the American University of Beirut in 1927. This, however, could not be compared to the life he had led in Tiberias. There, he had been a leader of his town, the owner of vast lands, a member of a large, influential, and wealthy family; in Damascus, he was living on memories of glories past while trying to take care of a family of eight children, in addition to his aunt, mother, and immediate unmarried female cousins.

I grew up in this family, burdened with the sad past of personal and national loss. The social network of Palestinian families around us was composed of relatives and friends who had suffered the same experiences in Lid and Ramlah, Tiberias and Acre, Jaffa, Jerusalem, and Haifa. Yet they all remained confident that in a few months or years they would return to Palestine as if nothing had ever happened. The olive groves, the orange trees, the shops, the Mediterranean around Haifa, Mount Carmel, and Lake Tiberias were all part of my upbringing in families that had lost their homes just five years before my birth. I heard all the stories about Palestine, both political and social. Even the bedtime stories my mother told me were somehow linked to Lake Tiberias or to the cave near the lake. Palestine was, to me, a living reality passed down to me through my family. It was a memory born in my consciousness that shaped my aspirations and being. During my childhood, I do not remember a week passing or a social occasion during which friends, relatives, or visitors did not speak of the tragedy of Palestine and the possibility of return.

Obviously, politics was an integral part of my childhood. Though I was only three, I remember the war of 1956: the news on the radio at home, the anxiety in the family because of my grandmother and aunts living in Cairo. I developed what I thought was a unique attachment to Gamal Abd al-Nasir, the hero of 1956. I also remember, as early as five or six years of age, dreaming of creating a *fidayeen* group and liberating Haifa. This was a recurring dream for years.

In the early 1950s, Kuwait had just begun its ambitious program of development. At the time, most of what is now built up areas of Kuwait City was open desert. To me, the areas outside of the city were wild and distant. In 1952 my parents were the first among the newly employed medical families to get air conditioning, due to the fact that pregnant women were given priority, and my mother was then pregnant with me. Electricity was slowly expanding to everyone, but drinking water was still brought via the sea from Basra.

In January 1958, when I was four and a half, my father received a scholarship from the government of Kuwait to specialize in cardiology and get his membership in the Royal Academy of Physicians (MRCP) in England. My brother Yousif, who was two and a half, was left at my grandmother's in Cairo while I accompanied my parents to Europe. In London, I learned English, and lost some of my Arabic despite my mother's constant attempts to keep the language alive in me. Meanwhile, a new world of children's entertainment in parks and playgrounds opened before me; my father bought me a scooter that I rode in the vicinity of our apartment. For two and a half years I enjoyed myself, playing and making new friends in the neighborhood. I also received a good deal of attention and love from my family and particularly my mother, who took me to parks and theaters.

It was in London that I became more aware of my feelings as an Arab. Being an Arab among non-Arabs in times of tension over Arab-British issues was not easy. I found myself getting into fights with other children. In Britain I was more "political" than my schoolmates and friends because of my interactions with my parents' friends and listening to their arguments about Palestine and the British. I talked a lot to other students about the British "handing" of Palestine to the Jews. Although my statements invited other children, particularly Jewish children, to exercise their muscles on me, I was not a fighter. I hated school for this reason and expected a fight everyday. I would curse Great Britain and London and Israel. I would accuse the British of being thieves. In order to tease the other children, I would tell them, "If I had an atomic bomb, I'd drop it on you first." As a result, my parents had to transfer me from more than one school.

During this period, my mother felt helpless; it was she who had to go to school every time the headmaster called regarding my behavior. Although my parents stopped talking politics in front of me and started passing on different messages to "de-politicize" me, it was too late; I continued to get into trouble. I enjoyed teasing the other kids and creating an uproar in school, although I continued to be beaten.

One day at the age of six, I came home with blood on my shirt. I had fought with three boys; they beat me badly. My father got angry, but then he came up with a simple solution: when he came home from medical school he would start boxing with me, punching me and teaching me to hit him back. I learned very well. Shortly thereafter, few children would pick a fight with me, but my newfound strength caused other problems. I became a bit over-aggressive, and other children complained about me.

My London years were special; being alone with my parents made a big difference. I interacted with both of them. My mother gave me a strong feeling of pride in my family, and she worked hard on my manners and behavior. I also saw how hard my father worked to pass the MRCP medical exams. For long hours during the night and through the weekends he would study; I was supposed to learn to be quiet. In some respects, he passed on to me this element of hard work and persistence; I would not, of course, realize this until later in life. Because of his long hours and absolute patience, he was able to pass his exams on his first attempt. He spent the rest of his time in Britain practicing and doing internships in British hospitals. This was a source of pride for my mother and for me.

After two and a half years in England, I returned to Kuwait with my father and mother. I was seven. It was the fall of 1960. On our way back we passed through Egypt to pick up my brother, whom I had not seen since we left him in Cairo on our way to London. We remembered each other from pictures, and we became fast friends. By then, he was five. Despite my weak Arabic and his nonexistent English, we were able to communicate.

In Cairo, I was encouraged to play with Yousif and the other children in front of the building where my grandmother and my single aunt lived. (My other two aunts had married.) There were dozens of children playing, and I spoke in Arabic to one of them. Suddenly, he shouted, "He's English!" I was astonished. I was speechless. Several other children came closer to me and asked, "Are you English?" Another shouted, "He's English. Don't play with him." The moment passed slowly. I said in a somewhat low voice, "I am an Arab. I am an Arab," but by then, the crowd was shouting, "English! English! English!" Yousif was shocked at what had happened, but he stood up for me. I heard him in his best Egyptian shout at our playmates, "He is my brother. He just came from England, and he is an Arab like me; he is not British. How dare you accuse him; he was with my parents in England and just came back." As he was giving his speech, I lost my courage, threw down the bike I was playing with, and ran upstairs to my grandmother's apartment.

This experience is ingrained in me. Even at such a young age, I was an Arab nationalist due to my upbringing. To be accused of not being an Arab was in insult. I decided never again to utter a word of English, and at the same time to master Arabic. After we arrived in Kuwait, my parents would beg me to speak English, particularly to impress friends and relatives, but I would stand silently. When I did speak, it would be in Arabic. I claimed I knew no English. But underneath the resistance, my early years in Britain did create something British in me: I liked the culture and had good memories of my years in London.

Once back in Kuwait, I was astonished to find how much it had changed during the few years we were away. New areas had been built, and much of the open desert close to our house had disappeared. Kuwait began establishing its own television station. Everything was in the process of changing; parks and clubs mushroomed, and in many ways I did not miss the magic of London. Some of that magic had already been planted in Kuwait.

During these years, Kuwait was starting the process of "Kuwaitization" of high and leading positions. While a new generation of Kuwaitis was being educated, highly visible non-Kuwaitis were to be naturalized as part of the process. In this context, in 1961, my father was granted Kuwaiti citizenship on the basis of a recommendation from Sheikh Sabah al-Salem. Kuwaiti law allows such a grant for those who have done enormous service to the country. My father was one of the country's leading medical doctors and had earned a good reputation and respect.

To me, this was at first quite confusing. Being a Palestinian until the age of eight and at the same time becoming a new citizen of the country I was born and raised in was perplexing. I would have to reconcile my "Palestinianness" with a Kuwaiti identity, and it would not be easy. While all Arabs identify as Arabs, each also has a certain political and subcultural aspect that determines how you look at yourself and how others look at you. One day as I accompanied my father on a visit to Crown Prince Sabah al-Salem, he told me that I was now a Kuwaiti; but, in front of the sheikh, I insisted that I was a Palestinian. Our discussion went on for several minutes, and the sheikh was impressed by my statements. He respected my choice, realizing that it would take a while for me to come to terms with this new identity, let alone lose my affinity for Palestine.

In Kuwait I attended al-Ma'mun School in the second and third grades (1960–1962). But my parents continued to be concerned about my English and sent me off at the age of nine to Brummana High School, in Brummana, Lebanon, a famous British-run Quaker boarding school. Its students came from all over the Arab world, the children of the best educated and professional elite of the Middle East; at the time, for those who could afford it, it was fashionable to send children and young adults to boarding schools. My flights to and from Kuwait during Christmas and Easter vacations were full of students studying at Brummana.

In Brummana, one learned lots of things, mostly independence and maturity. We took extensive field trips—swimming in the Mediterranean and visiting the historical sites of the Phoenicians and Crusaders. We also visited Bayt al-Din, where previous emirs of Lebanon had ruled, and the famous Jiita cave. We went north, we went south, we skied on Mount Lebanon; we saw the entire country. Our Sunday trips were wonderful, especially hiking in the woods near Brummana.

I established strong friendships with several boys from Lebanon, but continued to feel homesick. The boarding school experience did create an inner strength in me, making me more practical, stronger, and less emotional. However, as I look back on it, there was more pain than joy; too many familial opportunities are missed during such an experience. I would see my parents, my brother, and my newborn sister Sahar only on occasions.

I came home to Kuwait in 1965 and entered Shamiyyah Intermediary School, a public Kuwaiti school. As a result of the entrance exam, I was moved ahead to seventh grade. In Kuwait the kids thought of me as "soft." My Arabic was "Lebanized," which gave it a smoother tone compared to the more "tough" local Kuwaiti dialect; since I wasn't as soft as I spoke or looked, though, I ended up fighting with a lot of kids.

During these years, when I was twelve and thirteen, I established friendships with two Syrian boys, one a Christian Syrian who worked at night in his father's small shop, and the other who helped his father, who owned a plumbing shop. My parents were not happy to see me leaving their network to create friendships with boys they did not know. They wanted me to associate only with boys whose parents they knew well. Yet, these friendships meant a lot to me; these two boys were extremely honest, hardworking, and motivated. My parents would later come to appreciate them.

The incident that changed the course of my life, and the lives of many other Arabs, was the 1967 war. It was during my eighth-grade exams that the war broke out. During those days, I would go home and listen to the radio. The parents waiting for their children outside my school would always have their car radios on. At home, the radio was on all day long and into the night. I remember my father commenting, again and again, that based on radio reports there should be no more Israeli planes; he, however, was skeptical, while at the same time hoping that the broadcasters were not exaggerating as they had done in 1948. On June 10, my mother gave birth to a girl named Lubna. We debated the idea of naming her "defeat" or "war" or, sarcastically, "victory."

But suddenly, everything was over, and the truth came out—a total defeat for the Arab armies. It was a shock to everyone, including my father. He did not expect a decisive Arab victory, but neither did he expect a total, crushing defeat. With my family, I waited patiently to hear Nasir's speech of resignation after the defeat. I did not understand the whole speech, or what to believe, but I remember that my father felt that those who had made the mistakes should resign.

When I entered high school, ninth grade, in the fall of 1967, I devoted the entire year to being a teenager. I was fourteen by then, and I had learned to drive, to smoke occasionally, and to chase girls; during that year, I would leave school sometimes during the morning hours to meet a girlfriend. I went to parties and dances and learned to play guitar. My favorite bands were the Beatles and the Rolling Stones. During that year, two friends and I were known as the Gang of Three.

In tenth grade, I turned fifteen, and my life changed drastically. In Diyyah High School, where I was studying, I met a group of politically active Palestinian students. It was the fall of 1968. They kept talking about the fidayeen in Jordan and the Battle of Karamah in March of that year. They spoke of the duty of young Arabs and Palestinians to participate in the liberation of Palestine and to avenge the 1967 war. One of the boys had contacts with a teacher who had provided him with Fatah literature, which he passed on to me; it was a few pages explaining the principles of Fatah, which was the main group in the Palestinian Movement. At first I did not understand it, so I asked to meet with the teacher. He, however, refused to meet me on the basis that I was a spoiled teenager who could not be trusted. I had an urge to learn more and kept pressing my friend for information.

Finally, a meeting was arranged outside of school for three of us; our parents did not know about the meeting. I went to my friend's house and then walked to the nearby house of the teacher. There I participated in my first political meeting and heard my first lecture by a well-spoken leading Fatah member. The person who spoke was about 23. I recognized him from the Gazelle Country Club, where my family had membership. I had sometimes talked to him, but he never gave a hint of his political activities. He was sharp; well-read; and a former student of Abu Lyad, one of the principal leaders of Fatah, when Abu Lyad had taught in Kuwait at the same high school I was attending. During the meeting, we were sworn to secrecy and to serving the cause without hesitation. We felt a call to duty.

One part of the talk focused on self-education and personal conduct. The speaker argued that in order for us to be convincing to the masses we needed to educate ourselves about the history and politics of Palestine, of the "enemy," and of the Arab world. He declared that we would never be able to put forward a sound argument for our cause if we did not do so. He also insisted that we become models for others. No more fights with other youngsters, no more parties or dances, no more car racing, no more arrogance in dealing with others. As a national duty, the speaker said, our conduct had to change. He made a great impression on the three of us. The personal price he was asking us to accept was high, but we were willing to pay.

The meeting with Fatah activists turned my life upside down. My teenage friends did not inspire me anymore. I started reading, watching the news, and developing my writing skills. I was moved from a child's environment of comics, sports, and parties into an adult's environment of rebellion and revolution. In this new environment, the liberation of Palestine as the way to Arab unity was the guiding principle of thought. During that year, I focused on my school work so my grades would improve. The rest of my time involved political readings and discussions and fund-raising for the Palestinian movement. My first mission was to write a wall newspaper, which was a large board with news and articles hung on the main wall in the school, that would detail fidayeen activities in Jordan, the West Bank and Gaza, and Lebanon. I changed, and everybody noticed. I became consumed with the Arab future and increasingly informed about Arab and Palestinian history and politics. In some ways, my parents liked the change, but they also were worried that it was too much for a boy of fifteen.

These activities laid the ground for my first public speech. It was in spring of 1969, for an adult audience, during a fund-raising banquet for the Palestinian cause by the Kuwaiti Medical Society. The banquet's guest of honor was my father's friend Sheikh Saad al-Abdullah al-Sabah, defense and interior minister at the time and presently the crown prince and prime minister. It took me several days to prepare the four-page text. I consulted books and articles to be sure my facts were correct about the history of Palestine. Then I practiced until I had memorized the whole text. When I stood in front of the minister, the medical community, and my parents, among others, I felt a strange strength. I spoke normally and gave the whole speech in ten minutes. I even was relaxed enough to throw in a small joke about fund-raising. I discovered I could be a good speaker in the service of the cause.

One day during that spring of 1969, I was discreetly told that I was going to meet a principal Fatah leader during one of his visits to Kuwait. I couldn't believe it; I waited anxiously for the meeting. A lab technician in our school who had become our Fatah link wanted to reward me and my friends for our hard work. He picked us up in the afternoon at my house and took us to an apartment where we were welcomed by Abu Lyad (Salah Khalaf). At the time, he was a young man at the beginning of his revolutionary career.

During the meeting, we listened enthusiastically as Abu Lyad explained Fatah politics and goals. We were enthralled by the magic of sitting with a revolutionary Arab, a liberator, a man of courage. Abu Lyad explained to us what the struggle was all about and why Fatah refused to hijack airplanes, unlike other Palestinian groups. (Fatah remained opposed to this type of activity until Black September 1970.) Abu Lyad used terms such as "bourgeoisie," "proletariat," "middle class," "peasants," "imperialism," "Arab nationalism," and "noninterference in the affairs of Arab states." He used this language to explain how the nationalist Fatah differed from the Marxist Popular Front. I did not at the time understand all this terminology.

I went home, told my father what had happened, and asked him about Abu Lyad's use of words. He did not want me to get involved and told me to forget it. Involvement in politics in our region during those days meant facing the prospect of suffering, sacrifice, subversion, conspiracy, and persecution of family members. Additionally, those who were involved in politics rarely lived to see the fruit of their labors. My parents wanted me out, but they agreed to let me attend meetings and pursue political activities. At the same time, however, they demanded good grades in return.

In 1969 my parents enrolled me and my brother Yousif in the summer session of the Brummana National School in Lebanon. Lebanon in 1969 was the center of the Arab world. It was a place where intellectual life mixed with culture, politics, music, and art, where young people and students had a say over events and could leave a mark of their own. More than any other country in the region, Lebanon was influenced by the student rebellions in the West that symbolized change and confrontation for a whole generation. Lebanon produced books like no other country did, was the center of the Palestinian movements, and a place where students were rebelling against the system. I found myself in the midst of all this. Teachers at the school, as well as students, carried much of the debate and activity into daily interactions.

Our teachers helped us develop critical thought. We would discuss philosophical issues such as life, death, or violence. We held assemblies to discuss issues and events as they unfolded in Lebanon and the rest of the Arab world.

One day a few students from the senior class—two boys and two girls— had a run-in with the chef during dinner. The food was not well-cooked, so the four students cursed the chef in the cafeteria, threw dishes on the floor, and one of the boys almost hit the chef. The principal and owner of the school expelled the four, so in response we formed a committee to resolve the problem. I was nominated to head the committee, get the story from the students' perspective, and later meet with the principal.

During the meeting with the principal, which lasted for two hours, he defended his decision to expel the four kids, but I kept pointing out the alternatives for punishment short of expulsion. I explained what would happen to them if they had to leave school. They were all from Iraq, and some of them could not go back. I also questioned the educational benefit of such a decision and reminded the principal of his own statements on education during our assemblies. I used all of the skills I had learned from political meetings and debates. I told him that the four students would cause more harm to society out of school and that this was an opportunity to use the incident as an example to prevent such a thing from happening again. The four students were willing to abide by any punishment and to apologize to the chef and to the principal. After two hours of discussion, the principal said that he was convinced by my argument. He added that when I finished high school I should get myself a law degree!

Maroun Lutfi, a Lebanese from the southern city of Tyre, had a lasting impact on me. He was a senior who was one year ahead of me. Tyre was a center of Palestinian and Lebanese opposition as well as student rebellion. Maroun was a Maronite Christian but totally secular and leftist in his thinking. He was a member of a semi-secretive organization of Lebanese socialists, the New Left, headed by Muhsin Ibrahim and Fawaz Trabulsi. Maroun was in Brummana because his parents wanted to keep him out of trouble in Tyre. The secret police used to ask about him, and on more than one occasion, he was taken into custody for his activities. Maroun was impressive but also quiet and low key.

At one point, Maroun offered to take me to south Lebanon. It was a dream come true. For years I had discussed philosophies and collected contributions for the Palestinian movement and for Arab unity and other Arab causes. This was an opportunity to see things from the "inside." Thus one weekend during the fall of 1969 I traveled with Maroun to Tyre, where I met his friends. From Tyre we went to a Palestinian refugee camp, al-Burj al-Shamali, and met leaders and citizens of the camp. It was the first time in my life that I had seen how Palestinians lived. I felt an anger that stayed with me for years. This anger would cause me to almost lose my life on more than one occasion. The camps were run by the fidayeen, in particular by Fatah and the Palestine Liberation Army. When I visited the camps they had been autonomous, or "liberated," to use the Palestinian terminology of the time. After April 1969, following a bloody confrontation between the PLO and the Lebanese government, the camps were administered by the PLO.

In the camps I also had my first exposure to weapons. Carrying a weapon, or participating for a few hours in guarding an outpost on the outskirts of a camp, meant having control and immunity. Standing at night for a few hours guarding the post meant facing the Israelis, who were on the offensive, raiding camps in south Lebanon. At the time this activity meant self-liberation, self-actualization, manhood, a transformation of theory into practice, principle into deed. It meant a commitment to transform myself into a fighting Arab rather than a passive, defeated Arab like those I knew as a boy in 1967. This was a way of linking my political orientation with the Algerian liberation struggle I had read about, with Mao's revolution of the 1930s and 1940s, with Che Guevara's armed struggles. The camps looked like liberated areas in the Vietnamese or Chinese experience, and cooperation between people residing there made them seem like communes in Moscow during the revolution. Like many of my generation, I internalized the suffering of many Arabs by creating a revolutionary frame of thinking, believing that this would help bring an end to all suffering and occupation. We saw in the rebellion of the people of the camps the rebellion of all persecuted peoples, the road from oppression, and defeat.

In Tyre at night, there were always meetings and students planning something new in the form of a strike or demonstration. Some were expecting to suffer and others were preparing underground hideouts. The students were leftists, Ba'athists or former Arab nationalists, Communists, and Syrian nationalists. The New Left dominated among the young. They all supported the Palestinian movement and were willing to fight for it. To them the Palestinian cause represented a rallying point for challenging the Lebanese government and forging change in that country and the rest of the Arab world. Yet, what impressed me most was the effort the students put into reading and self-education and organization; they were exceptionally dedicated. They introduced me to Lebanese workers, peasants, and fishermen from Tyre who were acquainted with revolutionary theories.

For the next two years, almost every other weekend I would go to Tyre and the camps with my friend or visit Lebanese socialists in Beirut. We would stay with them, have long discussions, get new books, and go back to school. In the center of Beirut was a small library owned and operated by a veteran Communist; I read a lot of his Marxist literature, both philosophical and organizational. At the age of sixteen, I became a regular customer in all of the well-known bookstores of Beirut near the American University; I spent most of my pocket money on books—a habit that persists today. The market was flooded with books such as Sadiq Jalal al-Azem's *Critique of Religious Thought*, Nawal al-Sa'dawi's first book on women, and Paul Barran's book on socialist thinking. Books written by Marx and Engels and Lenin, among many, were in bookstores everywhere.

I joined a group of Lebanese socialists and started intense weekly study groups. Maroun introduced me to Nawwaf Slam, a friend who arranged for me to become involved in another reading group. The rebellion in the Omani province of Zufar and the constant clashes in Jordan between the army and Palestinians were galvanizing issues for us. I participated in more than one demonstration in support of student rights in Lebanon, the Zufar revolution, and the Palestinian Movement in Jordan. Participating in demonstrations was risky because the police tended to break them up with force; there were usually many arrests and injuries.

At school, we observed Palestine Day, and invited people from Beirut to speak. These activities put us in conflict with other students active in the right-wing Phalange Party of the Gemayals' and the Ahrar Party of Camille Chamoun. Some of the students from these groups had weapons, which were spreading among the right wing in Lebanon. We were in the center of heated activity as Lebanon was suffering increasingly from tensions both internal and external. Israeli attacks were constant in the south, and students in Beirut demonstrated on a daily basis to protest against these attacks and for their rights. The seeds of civil war were sprouting.

I often visited the campus of the American University of Beirut, where I had friends, many of them from Kuwait. I would accompany them to the university corner, where student activists and leaders gave speeches. The students discussed everything from the U.S. intervention in Vietnam to the Palestinian cause, student rights, Israeli attacks, and the activities of the right and of the Lebanese and other Arab governments. These students were usually harassed when they went back to their home countries, but what was most significant for all of us was the freedom of expression and the openness and courage to speak one's mind.

The political atmosphere in Lebanon from the fall of 1969 until the summer of 1971, when I graduated from high school, was unique. In Lebanon I saw a part of what I considered the real world, and also the intellectual world. I saw real poverty and tasted sectarianism and Arab and Palestinian nationalism, which derived from the Right and the Left, the government and the opposition, idealism and rebellion. Everything started and ended in Lebanon. Those who knew Lebanon in the late 1960s have a common bond and experience, for it was such a rich mixture of culture, politics, and humanism. Lebanon at the time was both a reality and a mirage, for with graduation I had to leave. In August of 1971, I went to Kuwait to see my family and then to the United States to continue my higher education in political science at Georgetown University.

In the years to come, my contacts with Lebanon and its revolutionary ideals continued. The magic of Lebanon and the causes linked to it had a continuing effect on me, and during vacations I traveled back and forth between Kuwait, Lebanon, and the United States. In that context, a more daring and adventurous chapter of my political life began, but my politics and later experiences have no place in a book dedicated to childhood experiences. My childhood, if I better understand it after writing about it, was a prelude to my riskier political and revolutionary commitments, in particular in regard to the Palestinian cause. The world of Lebanon and the struggle for Palestine from 1975 to 1981 tested much of my idealism and led to a maturing of my political understanding of the world.

Maysoon Pachachi

IRAQ *Maysoon Pachachi was born in 1947 in Washington, D.C., to Iraqi parents and spent her childhood between the United States and the Middle East. After completing high school in New York City and a freshman year at Bryn Mawr College, she moved to London, where she studied film under Thorold Dickinson at the Slade School of Art, received a B.A. Honours in philosophy from University College (London University), and a degree from the London International Film School. She now works as a film-maker and runs an independent production company in London, Oxymoron Films, for which she writes, directs, and produces.*

EAST WEST

Maysoon Pachachi

I spent the first year of my life in Washington D.C. in an apartment within earshot of the zoo. I used to drift off to sleep up on the tenth floor to the roar of lions and the calling of tropical birds. Maybe this experience gave me an early appreciation of incongruity and an understanding that the notion of "home" is not simple.

My parents were Iraqi diplomats like both of their fathers before them. We left Washington when I was one and a half, living first in Egypt and then returning to Baghdad, where I went to my first school. My sister Reema was born soon after and for my father's family this was a catastrophe. My grandfather, for all his intelligence and education, blamed my mother for not producing a son. She countered that it was not an occasion for blame, but in any case, it was the man's chromosomes that determine the sex of the child and not the woman's. As for me, I much preferred a sister anyway, and I remember teaching Reema to walk step-by-step down the corridor in our house through a patch of sun spilling in from the window.

In 1953 we returned to Washington, moving into a house in the Maryland suburbs; the four of us and our maid Hassouna, who'd accompanied us from Baghdad. Long before, she had worked for one of Iraq's "prominent" families. One of the sons had had an affair with her and she'd become pregnant—a disaster in the Baghdad of that time. Unusually, however, he "did the honorable thing" and married her, but this was only a formal arrangement so the child wouldn't carry the stigma of illegitimacy. By the time she came to work for my parents, Hassouna's son was already grown up. Hassouna was tight-lipped, square-set, and hardworking, and her hands always seemed to smell of onions and bleach.

My youngest sister, Leila, was born on a transcendent Easter afternoon with a cobalt blue sky and the yellow forsythia in full bloom. Reema and I were planting marigolds in the garden when Hassouna came out of the house shaking her head. "Your father's just called from the hospital—it's another girl. What a curse!" Reema and I joined hands and jumped up and down, shouting delightedly. We knew, somehow, that a brother might unseat us and we didn't want one. Hassouna clicked her teeth, disgusted, and stormed off to the kitchen.

I was the only non-American in my class and I tried hard to fit in. I won the spelling bees, played the scarecrow in *The Wizard of Oz* and a cowgirl in *Oklahoma,* and had a lot of friends. The only embarrassment was having to tell someone my "weird" name.

One day, in second grade, Miss Dawson pointed to an outline of the USA drawn in chalk on the blackboard. She said, "This is a map of the United Sates. I want you to draw it for me." I neither knew what "map" meant nor had I heard of the United States. To me it looked like a monster; New England was the head, the tips of Florida and Texas two feet, and up near Seattle was a tail. I decided it needed detail. I drew a big fiery eye and sharp teeth, claws on the feet, hair on the tail, and loops along the southern border like udders. Miss Dawson was furious; clearly I was being disrespectful. I was made to stand up at my desk for the rest of the class, and it was my mother who finally explained to me that a map wasn't a monster but a picture of a place from far away.

During the Suez War, I understood that I was not only foreign but also an Arab. My parents commandeered the TV and instead of watching the Westerns that I loved like *The Cisco Kid, Range Rider,* and *Annie Oakley,* I had to watch them watching the news. I sensed how disturbed and angry they were; "our country" had been attacked and this was part of an ongoing, unjust situation. I became conscious, really for the first time, of the Palestinian situation, and I began to understand that many Americans saw Arabs as criminals and Jew-haters. Janos, the Hungarian boy from across the street, asked which side I was on. I said Egypt. He said Israel, because they were Jewish like him and because Arabs hated Jews and wanted to put them in concentration camps. I couldn't make sense of it—I knew that my parents had Jewish friends they'd known since they were in school together—but what I did know was that I had to be quiet about being an Arab, because everyone would think I was bad.

In 1957, my parents decided to go back and settle in Baghdad.

We sailed out of New York on the *Cristoforo Colombo* and I had my tenth birthday on the ship somewhere in the middle of the Atlantic with no land anywhere in sight. I sat at the head table, center of attention in my new red and white dress, while 150 children I didn't know sang "Happy Birthday" to me.

When we crossed the straits of Gibraltar into the Mediterranean, I remember thinking that now we were in the "Old World" and everything would be different. Three days in Naples confirmed my feeling; there were grand, dilapidated buildings and shoeless kids begging and hustling on the streets. History and poverty.

In Naples we changed boats and traveled on to Beirut, where we met with my mother's parents. Since my school in Baghdad was about to start, I was sent ahead with my grandfather, Baba Chebir, as we called him. He was prime minister at the time, and when we arrived a guard of honour met him: two rows of men in army uniform, Bedouin *abayas* or Western suits, and a band playing the national anthem. Baba Chebir walked down the rows shaking hands and, not knowing what else to do, I followed suit. From being on the margins in America, here I was right at the center of things. "Home." Everyone would know who I was, but I, myself, was as unsure as ever of what I was supposed to do.

Suddenly, a very thin man ran across the runway and scooped me up— my uncle Nameer. He took me over to the perimeter fence behind which my four boy cousins and my aunt Ellen, American wife of my mother's other brother, Nizar, were waiting. I lived with them for a month until my parents came from Beirut with my sisters.

I loved the feeling of my uncle and aunt's house. They'd met when they were both studying architecture at Harvard and had come back to Baghdad in 1947, full of modernist enthusiasm. They loved art and their house was full of it—Calder mobiles given to my aunt by the artist, old pieces of brass and pottery picked up in the souk, and pictures by Jewad Selim, pioneer of Iraqi modern art and its best painter. I loved the way all these things, so full of aesthetic interest, somehow hung together in a kind of unfussy harmony.

My cousins and their friends were in the Arabic section at school, but I was put in the English section, since I couldn't even write my name in Arabic. Nevertheless, I felt I was in the wrong place, a foreigner again and, furthermore, I hated our Scottish teacher. He hit the boys if they acted up, had an unhealthy habit of putting us girls on his lap and fondling our knees and, worst of all, he was a racist. "Now, we don't want to go doing such and such like the Arab children, do we?" When my parents arrived from Beirut, I made a big fuss about being transferred to the Arabic section. I was absolutely adamant about it in a way that was very uncharacteristic of me, and they finally agreed.

In the Arabic section, I immediately became a kind of celebrity; I was "exotic" because I'd lived in America most of my life. I was deeply embarrassed, however, by my bad Arabic, and I didn't seem to know things even the stupidest person would know. One day our history teacher, Sitt Haddiya, stopped by my desk. She always dressed in mourning black and had a handkerchief crumpled in her fist in case she cried. "What is this?" she said, showing me a map of Iraq. "A map"; by this time I knew what a map was. "Yes. Of where?" "I don't know." She pointed to the word *Iraq*. "Well, what does this say?" "I don't know." "But it's your country."

I was tutored every day after school in Arabic, and my language improved steadily so that by the end of the academic year I'd passed all my fifth-grade exams and had done well. I'd learned fast—it was a matter of survival. Learning Arabic was easy compared to the many other things I had to try to understand. In the first week of school, during recess I was doing cartwheels and handstands with a newfound friend. She kept saying '*istakhfar Allah*' (God forgive me), and I began to wonder whether there was something inherently sinful about cartwheels. "You must say that whenever you turn the sole of your shoe to God, up there in the sky, so He knows you mean no disrespect." So God wasn't just in church as in Washington; He was right there above the playground.

I learned a lot that year in school—the facts of life, or a very vague approximation thereto, for a start. It was again in my first week and we were playing hide-and-seek. A pretty, much more "developed" girl than the rest of us took me under her wing. "I'll show you where to hide," she said. We crouched down behind a bush and waited to be found, passing the time with her telling me about where babies come from or, more precisely, about sex, because neither of us was really interested in the whole business of reproduction. She knew it was something about a man and a woman being naked and doing unspecified things to each other. We spent the rest of the year trying to investigate the matter but without much success. None of the grown-ups would answer our questions. Somehow between the ages of ten and sixteen, I pieced together the truth.

We had a hygiene class, which you might have expected to deal with the subject. Instead we were taught about TB, cholera, glaucoma, and bilharzia with graphic, terrifying descriptions of coughing up blood and pieces of lung and small bilharzia "worms" penetrating your skin and attacking your internal organs. Looking around the classroom, I thought it unlikely that any of us would get these diseases; we would never drink dirty water, eat food from street vendors, wade in the river, or live in a hovel without air or light.

It was the poor people on the streets that I worried about—beggars with missing limbs and clouded eyes, children in tattered clothes with runny noses, porters wearing shoes made of old tires and carrying impossibly heavy loads on their backs. In Baghdad I was made more aware of poverty and my privileged status than I had ever been in the sanitized suburbs of Washington.

While our new house was being finished, we moved in with my father's family. My grandfather had been almost entirely deaf for much of his life, and he was a difficult man with a volatile temper like my father's. A radical nationalist lawyer in his youth, my grandfather ran the first Arabic-language political newspaper. The Ottoman government closed it down and a warrant was issued for his arrest, but he managed to escape to Basra disguised as a bedouin. Highly educated—partly self-taught—he was a very religious young man, but, by the time he returned from law college in Istanbul, he was a wine-drinking, bacon-eating atheist.

My grandmother was his first cousin and his complete opposite. Deeply religious, constantly praying and fasting, she could barely read and always smelled of violets. Her life had been a difficult, tragic one. When she was nine months pregnant with my father, the horse pulling the carriage in which she was riding reared and she was thrown to the ground and fractured her hip badly. My father was delivered by Caesarian, the first in Baghdad, and my grandmother spent the next seven years in bed surrounded by lamenting women dressed in black. She was lame and in pain for the rest of her life, walking in her slow, step-drag-step-drag rhythm. I think she must have been very lonely with her only child away at boarding school in Alexandria and her husband living in Europe most of the time. I used to sit in the dark watching her saying her evening prayers; with a prayer rug at her feet, she rocked back and forth, lost in religious devotion. When she finished, she would smile, hand me a piece of candy, and ask me to go collect some fresh eggs from the chicken coop in the back garden.

We moved into our new house on the outskirts of Baghdad in January 1958. Designed by my Gropius-trained aunt Ellen, it was modern, single-story, with terraces at the front and back and surrounded by a walled garden seen through expanses of plate glass window. Two blue metal doors in the garden wall opened onto the street at the front and onto a palm tree grove belonging to my grandfather at the back; under the trees and between the crisscross of irrigation ditches my mother planted lettuce seeds she'd brought back from America; chicory, iceberg, and endive were things that didn't exist in Baghdad.

The garden was scrubby and dusty, but we had hope. There was an orchard of young fruit trees—peach, apricot, apple, orange, and lemon. Also, there was a fig tree for each of us three girls, six date-bearing palms, a vegetable garden, and a lawn of patchy grass fighting to survive in the dry earth.

One afternoon I was dancing "ballet" in the study and Reema was out in the garden with Hassouna. The light coming through the window began to get darker and darker and I glanced out to see why. Reema was looking up openmouthed at an enormous black cloud moving steadily towards her. Hassouna grabbed her and rushed inside. Reema came and stood beside me. We watched through the window; the cloud had shrouded the fruit trees like a thick black blanket. And it droned like a dozen airplane propellers. Locusts. Reema shouted and banged on the glass, then, in deperation, ran into the garden where she tried to kill the locusts by trapping them under an upturned flowerpot and beating them to death with a stick. She managed to kill five. When the locusts departed as suddenly as they had come, they left a devastated garden. Reema was inconsolable.

Besides Hassouna, the other important non-family member living with us was Butros, the Lebanese cook—an emotional man with an "artistic temperament" and a generous heart. One evening when my parents were out, we three girls and Hassouna sat in the kitchen eating. Karim, a handsome young Lebanese man who worked with Butros, was washing dishes. Suddenly, trumpeting a fanfare with his mouth, Butros appeared at the kitchen door. There he stood in an evening dress of my mother's—all swirls of chartreuse chiffon and a plunging neckline. He came gliding towards us while Karim sat down at the table, pushed the plates aside, and started to drum. Butros danced—moving his hips, shaking his shoulders, snaking his arms up and down his body. It was the first time I had ever seen belly dancing and I was mesmerized.

Butros had a wife and grown-up daughters in Lebanon, and Karim, whose room was next door, was his prospective son-in-law. My mother, however, suspected that the true nature of the relationship between Butros and Karim was different and this was tragically confirmed years later when Butros was back in Lebanon. His family had discovered that he and Karim were lovers and to cleanse the shame of it and restore the family's honour, one of Butros's brothers had killed Karim, cutting his throat. Maybe Butros came to Baghdad in the first place because there he was freer to love who he wanted, since no one knew who he was.

Every Thursday, we all gathered at my grandparents' house for lunch: my mother's parents, Baba Chebir and my grandmother Mama Nazik; my sisters and parents; my uncle Nizar and aunt Ellen; my cousins; my mother's younger bachelor brother, Nameer; my grandmother's forbidding mother, Unna; and me.

We often sat around a long wooden table under a huge, pink flowering judas tree in the garden eating kebab and *masgouf*, a Baghdad river fish. The real treat was to be taken out onto the Tigris in my uncle Nizar's silver motorboat. My grandparents' garden gave onto the river bank, with red and white jasmine twining around the barbed wire fence. We would drag the boat down to the river's edge where there was usually a group of young boys in *dishdashas* standing around in bare feet. Often they helped launch the boat and stood watching as we zoomed up and down the river. Sometimes we passed a *guffa*, or small dinghy, making its quiet circular way downstream. Much later, the remembered elation of those motorboat trips inspired me to spend all day riding back and forth on the Staten Island Ferry, the one time I ever played hooky from school. But my excitement during my spins in Uncle Nizar's boat was tempered by the sight of the boys standing on the bank watching silently with their feet in the water. Even then I was keenly aware of the unfairness of it all.

My grandparents' garden was the miracle—a reminder of the courtyard in my grandmother's childhood home in Aleppo, where she'd lived until she was married off and whisked away to this semi-barbaric country, as she considered it. Jassim, the gardener, an infinitely patient, humorous man, brown and wiry and always barefoot, taught us how to dig up carrots, pick sweet lemons, and cut roses. Together he and my grandmother created the garden on two levels with a walkway running down one side, shaded by tangerine and sweet lemon trees. There were two arbors covered in jasmine and grapevines, bed upon bed of roses, a huge ginko tree that dropped its sticky fruit on the grass, and, most unusually for Baghdad, a row of pine trees. As a child, my mother had collected the cones on holidays in Lebanon and planted them when she got back home. For thirty years the trees had been carefully tended and nurtured by Jassim and they now towered above the house. That kind of continuity seemed extraordinary to me. It still does.

My favorite spot was underneath my great-grandmother's bedroom window: a patch planted with cacti from Arizona with a huge, cascading bush of red roses to one side and a wisteria that climbed over the top of the terrace. The cactus grove was surrounded by a low fence and felt a very special place. I think it was where my grandmother kept her freedom.

She was forty when my grandfather took up his post as Iraqi ambassador in Washington and it was then that she escaped her mother, Unna, for the first time in her life. Unna had stayed in Baghdad. Having come to live with my grandparents at the beginning of their marriage, thirty-two years old and a widow for ten of them, she'd utterly dominated her sixteen-year-old daughter, allowing her little autonomy in the raising of her own children. So, for my grandmother, to be in America and without her mother was an exhilarating kind of freedom.

Sixteen millimeter home movies shot there express her palpable sense of release. On the balcony of a Tucson hotel, she brushes her long, honey-colored hair in the sun while she jokes with my grandfather behind the camera. In another shot, she sprawls on the grass in a pair of jeans and cowboy boots, laughing hysterically and trying to keep the fish she's just caught from jumping out of her hands. That was on a ranch in Colorado. The cacti brought back from Arizona and planted outside her bedroom window were part of that time in her life. Much later she did a painting of this corner of the garden and I now have it hanging on my wall.

Maybe because I was the oldest grandchild, I was very close to my grandmother. About four months before she died I stayed with her for three weeks in my parents' house in Abu Dhabi while they were away. During those weeks, she told me hundreds of stories about her life and secrets she didn't want anyone else to know, gave me recipes for quince jam and stuffed vegetables, and told surprisingly scandalous jokes. She said, "You know why I love you so much? Not just because you're my grandchild, but because you know who I really am. Other people don't understand."

In the late 1970s or early 1980s, the government purchased my grandparents' house by compulsory order; the site was needed as part of a huge new medical complex. The house was knocked down and the garden turned into a helicopter landing pad.

Sometimes my parents would leave me at my grandparents' for the afternoon and in the early evening, my uncle Nameer would drive me home in his sky blue MG. I felt very grown-up riding around in a sports car with my witty, knowledgeable uncle. I loved this time of day when there was still light in the sky but the shops were illuminated and the streets were full of people—idling under the colonnades of Rashid Street, eating kebab and drinking sherbet from the street vendors, sitting in the cafes smoking and playing backgammon. I wanted to be out there among them; that's where "real life" seemed to be. In the Washington suburbs, people were never on the streets like this, but either in their cars going someplace or sitting at home.

Compared to Washington, Baghdad also seemed very old and full of the past—like the *Mustansiriya,* where my aunt Ellen took me one day. The medieval school where Avicenna had taught and practiced medicine was now a museum. Inside, we studied the models of early operations—a woman lying in bed, a doctor bent over her and her clothes, including an anachronistic bra, neatly folded on a chair. Coming out into the huge graceful courtyard, I secretly decided I wanted to be an architect when I grew up.

The guard shuffled over and began talking to us. "This place contained the knowledge of the world, you know, but on that black day when the Mongols invaded, they sacked the library, set fire to the city, dragged people out of their beds and killed them, looted the shops—rice, grain, gold—everything. They threw all the books in the river and the river turned black with ink." I saw the whole horrible event through his eyes, the witness who'd seen it all. It was only later that I discovered this had happened some 700 years before in the thirteenth century. Iraqis seem to live with a very real and present sense of their bloody but often glorious history. Sometimes now, though, when I think about our most recent past, I wonder whether we will find ourselves opting for a kind of collective amnesia.

In the late 1950s, most older Baghdadi women and those from traditional families still wore abayas when they went out. I, myself, only ever wore one of these long black silk cloaks once, when my aunt took me to see *Al Kadhimain,* one of Iraq's biggest Shi'a mosques. Everytime I peered up at the mirrored dome, the abaya slipped off my head, no matter how tightly I held it. In the center of the mosque was the saint's tomb, surrounded by a sturdy iron grille festooned with hundreds of small green ribbons. Women were throwing themselves at the grille and pleading for divine intervention—to cure a sick child, to make them fertile, and, above all, to give them a son. They promised the saint devotion and good works if their prayers were answered, and they knotted green ribbons onto the grille to seal the bargain.

None of the women on either side of my family acted like this, but I knew that the frustrations expressed by the Kadhimain women were not unknown to them. It's true, Grandmama Nazik hadn't worn an abaya since she was twenty, but she'd been married off at sixteen to someone she'd never seen and the fact that it had turned out well was just a matter of luck. My grandfather was a kind, brave man, and in many ways ahead of his time. When Grandmama Nazik was twenty, the two of them traveled down to Basra. Before she went off to sit in the women's section of the train, she told my grandfather that when she stepped onto the platform in Basra she would remove the abaya and never wear it again. He didn't believe her, but that is indeed what she did. And when a few months later the king called my grandfather in and suggested that he tell my grandmother to start wearing an abaya again, my grandfather gently declined, saying that perhaps His Highness would tell her himself. And that was the end of the matter.

From my mother's side of the family, I learned that women had a right to education and didn't owe blind obedience to their fathers or husbands. I also understood, however, that when it came down to it, women didn't have much power outside the home. My role model, if I can be said to have had one, was my mother's great-aunt, Emet. She had gone off by herself to study at Columbia University at a time when such things were completely unheard of for women in the Middle East and then had come back to Baghdad and founded the first women's college there. As early as the late 1930s, Iraqi women started training as doctors and lawyers. Emet had a genuine interest in people, belief in their capabilities, and a rare talent of making anyone she was with feel important. She died of breast cancer just months before we got back to Baghdad and Grandmama Nazik told me that hundreds of people of all kinds had walked in her funeral. I regretted very much that I hadn't made it back in time to see her, and these days I sometimes feel guilty because I've made so many compromises in my life that I wonder if I've kept faith in any way with her example.

The women on my father's side were quite different. Largely uneducated, there were, nevertheless, formidably strong, intelligent characters among them who liked to argue heatedly about politics and tell wicked jokes. This was especially true of the older generation, my father's great-aunts who all wore the old-fashioned fringed *footas*, or scarves tied around their heads. My father's family, however, was very conservative, and early on I was aware of how circumscribed the lives of the women were. When we went to visit my father's aunt, I used to sit on an overstuffed chair in her airless parlor listening to the desultory gossip while watching my father's pale, obedient cousin out of the corner of my eye. She was also the oldest of three girls, and I used to wonder why she always looked as if she'd been crying and whether she ever went out into the sun and air. I realised that my life could easily have been like hers.

The year of 1957–1958 was remarkably eventful for us. Days after we moved into our new house, a lorry hit my father's car, and he was thrown out onto the road; he didn't break anything but was very badly bruised and had to spend a couple of weeks in bed. Then Reema broke her arm at school. After that we had two robberies.

One morning I woke to the sound of a crow cawing on my window sill, as usual. I opened my eyes to the familiar patch of dusty light on the floor, lifted my head off the pillow and looked in astonishment around the room. It was upside down; every bit of clothing was thrown on the floor, every book, every toy, every crayon. I sat there for a minute trying to find an explanation: "Maybe last night a wind blew into the room" or "Maybe Hassouna was looking for something and forgot to put everything away." I knew this was nonsense, but I also knew that you sometimes just had to accept the things that happened and eventually you might understand why. Reema's room was in the same state; we couldn't figure it out and no one would tell us anything.

It wasn't until we returned from school later that day that I pieced together the story by eavesdropping on Hassouna and Ali, the driver. Three men had broken into the house, wakened my parents, and held guns to their heads and knives to their throats. They'd called my parents "imperialists"; from the garden, they'd seen them and my uncle Nameer drink, talk English, and listen to Beethoven earlier that night. "On the contrary," my mother said, "We love our country and both of our fathers fought hard and sacrificed a lot for its independence." Unimpressed, the men demanded money and jewelry. My father only had a few pennies in his pocket, so one of the men tried to pull off my mother's wedding ring. She snatched her hand back, furious. "Don't you have anything better to do with your time, don't you have sisters and mothers, aren't you ashamed of yourselves?" Insulted, the man slapped her face, but she did not make a sound, afraid that my father would go berserk; he'd never been able to tolerate violence against women. In the end the robbers only took three carpets and a few silver table ornaments.

Years later my parents told me they always suspected that the robbery was not what it seemed. In 1957 when we were still in Washington, the much-hated uncle of the king, the Prince Regent, had come to the U.S. and was due to make a speech to the National Press Club; my father, then first secretary at the embassy, had been asked to write it. Still angry and upset about Suez, he'd written an impassioned anti-Western speech. The Prince Regent, close as he was to the British, said he thought someone else should give the speech. The ambassador had forgotten his glasses at home, so, my father ended up delivering that speech with the full force of his rhetoric, which was always his forte. The Prince Regent was furious and whispered, "You've had it." Because my father disagreed with the way the government was kow-towing to the Western powers, especially in its failure to support Egypt at the time of Suez, he decided to leave the foreign service and enter politics. The Prince Regent wasn't happy about this, and my parents thought that the robbery may have been a ham-fisted attempt at intimidation.

The truly important event that year, however, was the revolution. On July 13, the day before, my father had heard that he was not included on a list of the new Iraqi-Jordanian Federation's foreign service. The Prince Regent and the then Prime Minister (my grandfather had long since resigned) thought that his loyalty to the government was in doubt because of his alleged pro-Nasserite sympathies. That evening he returned home in a rage and decided to tender his resignation first thing the next day.

But by six o'clock in the morning everything had changed. I woke up to the sound of the radio blaring in the study—harsh, loud, declamatory. My parents were standing transfixed, listening. The monarchy had been overthrown by army officers and they'd taken over the radio and were issuing proclamations. I didn't have any idea what this could mean, but I studied my parents' faces carefully. They looked deeply worried. King Faisal and his whole family had been gunned down in cold blood inside the palace grounds, after they'd surrendered, and all members of the old regime who were in Baghdad had been arrested. My two grandfathers were out of the country for the summer, and I soon understood that as least for my mother's father this was a lucky thing.

We were very vulnerable there on the outskirts, miles from anybody. My parents decided we should join my father's mother in the center of town. Clearly, we couldn't travel in our huge white Plymouth with U.S. plates, so my grandparents' driver came to get us in their car. My mother worked quickly, bundling just the essentials in sheets instead of packing in suitcases, which would have called more attention to us. And she warned us to say nothing in English, absolutely nothing.

We sat silently as the car pulled into the road—children, mother, and Hassouna in the back and father and driver in the front. Across the street, the people from the encampment were watching. Migrants from the rural south, they'd built dung houses and pitched makeshift tents in a grove of palm trees opposite our house. The children used to stand in a row, barefoot in their dirty, ragged dishdashas, and watch me ride up and down on my new Raleigh bike. I never managed to talk to them, although they were just children like me. Even Reema hadn't been able to make contact when she'd gone over to retrieve her ginger kitten. Eventually, I would retreat into the garden, closing the blue metal doors behind me. My parents had always inculcated in me a notion of justice, and I knew the difference between my situation and that of the encampment children was profoundly unjust. I also sensed that it might have something to do with the revolution.

We made slow progress through the crowds; more people than I'd ever seen in my life—shouting, jostling, pushing, singing. At one point we stopped and people seethed around the car, peering in and rocking it dangerously. Earlier we'd seen someone pulled out of a car and beaten up. People had been dragged through these streets and killed, some had even been set on fire. Suddenly Hassouna rolled down the window and spat. Reema, who had measles and a temperature, was sitting next to her in pajamas. "Now you spit," said Hassouna. "This is where they dragged the Prince Regent. He was an awful man." But Reema refused.

We crammed into my grandmother's small annex. My father was drafted by the new government to act as liaison with the foreign press and to serve on a committee reviewing the cases of foreign office employees dismissed for disloyalty to the new republic. He did his best to protect those he thought were competent and would be of some use to the country. He would come home late at night and he and my mother would whisper in their corner of the roof where we were sleeping. She never knew when he left in the morning whether he'd return.

In that first month after the revolution, my mother lost thirty pounds. She was desperately worried about her family. The new government had already frozen the assets of all those connected with the old regime, and this meant my mother's father and her two brothers suddenly had nothing. She was particularly concerned about my uncle Nameer, who was still in Baghdad. He wasn't involved in politics, but he'd been a friend of the king's, his father had been prime minister, and worst of all, he collected guns. He'd had a consignment of hunting rifles delivered a short while before the revolution, and one day a couple of army officers turned up on the doorstep demanding to see them. Nameer explained that they were only guns for hunting and he had a permit anyway. Nevertheless, he was arrested. When my father heard, he didn't tell my mother but left the house saying he had something to do. He managed to get Nameer released the next day.

If my grandfathers had been in Baghdad, I don't know what their fate would have been. The prime minister had been killed two days after the revolution began, and the government was hunting down all the former members of the monarchist regime. We watched TV in amazement as a former high-ranking government official, disguised as a peasant woman, was chased across a field. When he was caught, his scarf was ripped off his head to reveal his true identity.

We lived under curfew for a month. For an hour here and there when it was lifted, my mother would go out, but she rarely took us with her. I spent my time up on the roof; one stifling morning as I stared out over the bleached dusty city, a low cloud of impenetrable black smoke suddenly rolled across the sky and blocked out the fierce Baghdad sun. An oil tank on the other side of town had exploded and for three days the sky remained black; it was like living inside an oven.

After lunch I'd lie down on my mattress and wait till everyone had gone to sleep, then I'd start to roam around. It was during one of these afternoon wanderings that I found a book on my grandfather's bookshelves about the French Revolution. It was a large red leather-bound volume, in French, with black and white engravings; there were pictures of rioting crowds and nobles being led to the guillotine that were just like what was happening in Baghdad. I noticed that the French Revolution had also started on July 14. I found an Agatha Christie mystery and read it and no one told me not to. I could do anything; no one was paying attention.

Immediately after the Iraqi revolution, American and British troops landed in Lebanon and Jordan, and my father was sent to New York as part of the delegation to the emergency meetings at the UN.

A week later, we left on the first regular flight out of Baghdad, taking with us the few things my mother had been able to pack on the day of the revolution.

We flew to Geneva and stayed with my father's father in his small flat opposite the railway station. The sky was grey and indefinite and it seemed to rain all the time. A couple of weeks later, my mother had some sort of argument with my grandfather, and one afternoon while he was out, she packed our things and we left without saying anything. I hauled one of the heavy suitcases and dragged my sisters behind me.

We took a train to Lausanne, where we met up with my other grandparents. An Egyptian student lent us his tiny flat. My mother and I pulled a mattress off the box spring and onto the floor; Reema and I slept on it while she and Leila shared the springs. Grandmama Nazik slept on the sofa and Baba Chebir slept on the floor beside her. They had started their life together at a time of enormous political change, at the end of the Ottoman Empire and the beginning of the Iraqi state, and they'd been involved at the very heart of it. They'd had to face danger and uncertainty, had had to improvise and make do. And here they were doing it again, this time in completely different circumstances.

Later on, in 1959, they settled in a small flat in Beirut near the Corniche, where Grandmama Nazik began to paint to assuage the pain of loss and conjure up images of things loved. Her first painting was of a family lunch under the flowering judas tree, the next a lantern-lit party in her garden at night. Later on, she told me she was quite happy in a way, despite all the loss. At last she could live a normal life with her husband; he wasn't a politician or an "important" man anymore. They weren't in the public gaze, and I think my grandfather accepted all this with good grace. Ironically, the revolution, while dispossessing her of everything, gave her a new kind of power.

From Lausanne we traveled to Rome to join my uncle Nizar, my aunt Ellen, and my cousins. We stayed at a cheap, once elegant *pensione* with peeling, somewhat risqué frescoes on the staircases. It was in Rome that I turned eleven. As a birthday treat my mother took me and my cousin Kumait, twelve days younger than I am, to St. Peter's. We looked at the Pietà and the ceiling of the Sistine Chapel and then went out on the roof, where someone took a photograph of us standing in front of the dome and looking out over the Eternal City.

By the end of the summer, my father was asked to stay for the General Assembly session and we went to join him. As the Pan Am flight to New York took off, a sharp, unexpected sadness came over me. I somehow knew I'd never live in the same place as the rest of my family again, nor anywhere where I had such deep roots. I was going back to the free West, but it was lonely.

It was a night flight. At one point I woke up and didn't know where I was.

Everyone else was asleep and the lights were off. I needed the toilet so I got up, stumbled toward the door, opened it, and found myself standing in the cockpit, looking past the pilot into an inky sky splattered with stars.

Over the next nine months, we moved another six times between New York and Washington, and I went to three different schools before we finally settled down in New York, where my father became Iraqi ambassador at the UN. America seemed to have changed entirely during the year I'd been away—and I was now almost a teenager. I wore big circular skirts and bobby sox, played spin-the-bottle, and had a crush on Frankie Avalon. One way or another, I almost managed to fit in.

Esther Raizen

ISRAEL *Esther Raizen teaches Hebrew language, literature, and culture courses at The University of Texas at Austin. A native of Israel, she came to the United States in 1982 and received her Ph.D. from The University of Texas at Austin in 1987. Her recent books are* **No Rattling of Sabers: An Anthology of Israeli War Poetry** *(1995),* **Biblical Hebrew: An Analytical Introduction** *(1999),*

Modern Hebrew for Beginners *(2000), and* **Intermediate Modern Hebrew** *(2001).*

THEY ALL BURNED IN OUR FIRES: LIFE IN TEL AVIV OF THE 1950S

Esther Raizen

 I often wonder why my childhood years seem to have been uneventful, when episodes of polio, diphtheria, an earthquake, and two wars passed by in succession. I guess that thousands of miles and a number of decades away, with the perspective of an adult accustomed to riding the fastest lanes of the information superhighway, it becomes hard to connect to that which was simple, almost always predictable, and infinitely rich.

My life was divided evenly between school and play during the day, with long evenings set aside for reading or for Paul Temple, the foxy radio sleuth. Saturdays were family days, with long morning strolls or a couple of hours at the beach. Chores were minimal, and friends were easy to find. Everything was within walking distance, and we were free of fear, as cars rarely crossed our street, and crime was not even a word in our lexicon. Seasons and holidays came and went. With our families always in the background, we grew up very slowly and gradually without really noticing it.

Tel Aviv in the 1950s was a wonderful place for a child. We lived in a small apartment—a bedroom, a living room, a kitchen, two balconies, and a bathroom, probably no larger than sixty square meters altogether. My older brother, younger sister, and I shared a bedroom which was large enough to hold a bed, a crib, and a two-door closet. Climbing from the crib to the top of the closet was a favored activity. My mother tells me that when I was about two and a half years old and first discovered the dusty top of the closet, I took an afternoon nap in that crawl-only space, while she, joined by distressed neighbors and friends, was searching the neighborhood for me.

Climbing often got me in trouble, but I think that my parents did not really mind it. I was born in 1951, which was just in time for the polio epidemic; coming down with polio when I was a couple of months old, I was not even supposed to walk like a normal child. I ended up running, climbing, and dancing, and the disease, which devastated so many of my peers, would catch up with me only in my late thirties, at which point it did not matter much.

Trees did not offer much of a climbing thrill—a cypress or two, a couple of small terebinths, and some acacias. There was no way you could climb a cypress, and acacias were just big bushes. But such bushes they were! They had the most delicate flowers, yellow fuzz balls with the sweetest of fragrances, one matched only by that of the humble daffodil, white with a golden crown and thus fondly referred to as "king of the swamp."

Our neighborhood was defined by small streets bearing historical names taken straight out of the dramatic conquest of Canaan: Gilead, Mount Nebo, Jericho, Bashan, En-Gedi. Reality was much less dramatic—twelve or so two- and three-story apartment buildings surrounding a large empty lot, a glorious eyesore which offered the best puddles in the winter and endless digging and dirt-throwing opportunities all year round. The back side of the lot was occupied by an enormous half-finished basement, perhaps a bomb shelter, which was dark and full of muck, household and construction garbage, and a sweet sense of forbidden pleasures. On a lucky day you could find there a bullet or two, which you would open. Collecting the gun powder, you would spill it on the sidewalk to spell out your initials. You would then ignite one end and jump back, admiring the fast moving, hissing flame and the permanent mark you had just made on history. If you were very lucky, you would find a small piece of roofing material, which, when thrown properly into a bonfire, would burst, producing considerable noise and sharp debris to the delight of all, parents not included. Creativity reigned, nature and trash were all we needed for our small pleasures; apricot pits and bottle caps or Admiral Nelson heads from cigarette boxes (rubbed into shape by a bottle cap) were the legal tender. Crushed leaves, limestone, or coals were the tools of sidewalk artistry, and soccer games were a routine. Being a girl, I could never advance beyond the goalpost, but I did quite well as a goalie and was happy with that.

School days were short—from eight o'clock to twelve o'clock, and, at times, when school was too crowded, a second shift of twelve o'clock to four o'clock. We went straight from elementary school to high school, where days became longer, ending at two. School was a few blocks away, books and notebooks were small, and work was never too hard. Our teachers were a little older than our parents, and we generally liked them. Many of them had been there to teach our older and younger siblings and knew our families well. An Iraqi woman joined the staff as an English teacher when I was in fifth grade. Named Victoria, she wore high heels and makeup and had the strangest accent that had guttural *chets* and *ayins* reserved only for radio anchors. Real people did not talk like that. I had no reason to know that she was an Iraqi. She never talked about that, and I was not particularly interested in her personal life. I wonder whether my mother was the one to have enlightened me; she was keenly aware of differences and may have had some misgivings about an Iraqi teacher. Victoria turned out to be a good one. She brought with her the state-of-the-art multi-media package of those days: a workbook with stick figures for illustrations and a hand-operated record player.

Classes were large, some forty-three students in each; teaching was frontal, unimaginative by today's standards. Paper was scarce, and there was no time to waste. One break during the day was snack time, which is when you would sit at your desk and eat what your mother had put in your lunch bag. Twice a week an upperclassman would come and check that your fingernails were properly clipped and that you had a lunch bag and a clean napkin. Those were usually embroidered, a traditional present from an older sibling. Art, music, and shop were an integral part of the curriculum, and Israeli folk-dance music was played over the speakers for whoever wanted to dance during the larger break of the day. We danced with fervor. Israeli folk dancing was one of the signatures of the socialist youth movements, distinguishing their members from those who danced to foreign tunes and could not wait to be poisoned by disco music. Our legs craved the vast distances of the Negev, the Galilee, and the Judean Desert. We were the blue-shirt elite—pioneers; lovers of nature; children of the outdoors; pure, real Sabras.

Roasting potatoes in a bonfire was a ritual for the fifteen or so neighborhood kids. These were casual bonfires, once or twice a week, almost always extinguished by Mr. Winter, a neighbor who abhorred the smoke and noise associated with the festivities. We reciprocated without fail every holiday of Lag Ba'omer—after weeks of collecting wood of all sorts, including lumber craftily stolen from construction sites, we would light a major bonfire, burning an unmistakable effigy of the plump man side by side with that of Gamal Abdel Nasser.

I do not associate Nasser with the Sinai War, but I remember very well the elated sensation of listening to the intercepted phone conversation between him and King Hussein during the Six-Day War and the joy of "Nasser is Awaiting Rabin," one of the spirit songs of 1967. I recall neither the Sinai War nor the Six-Day War as "wars," the way I remember 1973, during which I was enlisted and involved enough to understand what war really meant. In 1956 I was five years old and constantly scared. I dreaded the forced blackouts, the air-raid sirens, and, most of all, the frantic run downstairs with the rest of the neighbors, realizing that I was exposed to danger as there was no place to hide other than the lower floor of our apartment building, which provided no protection, fortified as it was with sandbags and brick walls. I did not know what we were supposed to be protected from, but I imagined it to be something very colorful falling out of the sky, like the fireworks on Independence Day that terrified me enough to crop up as a recurring theme in my nightmares way into my adult years. My sister must have been one month old when it all began, and my father was gone for many days. He came back one day, very tired, and I could not figure out why my mother burst into tears when we opened the door and saw him. He brought from the desert two shoe brushes with strange writing on them, and that was all. He never talked about the war. When the Six-Day War began, he was already too old to be drafted and served as an administrator in the civil defense system. My brother, a member of Kibbutz Nahshon, which was straight across from the infamous Latrun police station, was the one to be worried about in 1967. I did not worry for long, though, as the kibbutz was freed from Jordanian pressure on June 6. My father came from work straight into the bomb shelter with a bouquet of flowers and announced that the border was removed some forty-five kilometers to the east. For me, that was the end of the war. I was a teenager, the days were warm, we were free to do as we wished, everybody was happy, and life was good. Nasser and Hussein were on their knees, and we spent endless hours making fun of the Voice of Thunder from Cairo, whose anchor announced in dramatic Hebrew glorious victories, which, we all knew, were the figment of Arab imagination. It was fun, and war was nothing to be concerned about. At least not for a couple of more years.

Two cypress trees grew side by side at the corner of En Gedi and Jericho. By an accident of nature, one of them grew sideways and never developed much but was strong and flexible enough to carry your weight as you were pushing up and down. There, rocking up and down, we would take turns yelling our battle songs and other works of poetry dedicated to Mr. Winter or another favorite neighbor, Meyer, or Meye. The oldest child of the only Orthodox family in a neighborhood which was inhabited mostly by blue-collar workers, Meye always wore a dark tailcoat with black hat and shoes, complemented by long earlocks, a stubble of a beard, and screaming acne. He went to a special school, and, needless to say, never played with us. His mother, a very pious woman, older than most mothers in the neighborhood, always wore turban-style hats, which stuck out like the feathers of an exotic bird. She was a favorite target of our "water mine" games. Smoking hollow twigs under the family's back window on the Sabbath was another entertaining activity. We did not understand where these people came from, but we did understand very well that they were different, which was a good enough reason to dislike them. Our parents must have known that we were taunting these poor people but never intervened. They did not like them either, I suppose. Our favorite tree-song was dedicated to *Meye mit zein kratsene eye*, or, roughly, "Meyer with his itching balls." This brilliant slogan in juicy Yiddish must have been generated by one of the neighborhood adults; we understood Yiddish quite well but not with the degree of sophistication required for such a production.

My mother has always maintained that I spoke Yiddish fluently as a child. But she is also certain that I was potty-trained at the age of one and read daily newspapers and discussed politics at the age of four. No, I don't think I spoke Yiddish, although I understand it well enough. My parents spoke perfect Hebrew; used Yiddish sparsely, often in songs of great longing for something which we never knew or understood; and, on rare occasions, switched to Polish. They clearly disliked that language, using it only when they wanted the content of a conversation to be concealed. In retrospect, I have figured out that all our neighbors were of Polish or Russian descent, with an occasional Bulgarian and one Hungarian. Though I never knew her by name, I remember the Hungarian woman very well.

Part of the evening ritual was summoning the kids to supper. Each family had a typical call, which usually consisted of the children's names, yelled plainly or in a sing-song manner. The Hungarian lady's daughter, Edna, who was my sister's age, endured the daily misfortune of being summoned home in a thick Hungarian accent, with the first syllable heavily accentuated, and the *a* pronounced as *o*, which, I would learn many years later, is common in Ashkenazic Hebrew. To our ears, accustomed to the word-final accentuation of Sephardic Hebrew, this was ridiculous. The lady received the nickname *éemo édno*, "Edna's mother," which we would yell every evening in perfect imitation of broken Hungarian Hebrew. At supper time, we were also ready for a neighbor who would announce himself to his wife from over a block away—*Aviva, ochel!*, "Aviva, food!" Our happy choir did not seem to bother him; he must have been too hungry to notice us. The best was Mr. Lubimov, who would periodically groan loudly and call to his wife, *Salah, ani met!*, "Salah, I am dying!" We loved to reproduce that one under his window, especially since he never died. He was very old and a Communist. Not that we knew what being a Communist meant, but we kept our distance from him and his daughter, who was six years my senior and a member of the youth movement BANKI (The Alliance of Communist Youth).

Election days were always exciting, but, unlike other opportunities for mischief which I always welcomed, involved a very personal discomfort. Kids were happy to steal not only the *qof* ballots (for the Communist Party) but also the ones marked *mem* for MAPAM, the socialist United Workers Party. Here I found myself on shaky ground; both my parents were loyal members of that party. I was sure they were the only ones and did my best to hide it. Only later would I learn that quite a few families in the neighborhood voted for MAPAM. I did not know the details, but it was clear that the 1950s were politically difficult for my parents and also for family friends who were associated with the party. The name Moshe Sneh was often mentioned at our house, and I could sense that my parents felt the need to criticize him but never did it wholeheartedly. He was their compatriot and an admired doctor, but obviously he had done something wrong.

I also heard the name Mordechai Oren, who, I understood, was a victim of some sinister plot. Perhaps I was aware of politics at the age of four after all. In 1953, I would learn later, Moshe Sneh and his followers were kicked out of MAPAM because of their anti-Zionist stance and shortly thereafter joined MAKI, the Israeli Communist Party, mother of all evils. Mordechai Oren, a MAPAM representative, was falsely accused in Prague of espionage and sabotage, tried publicly, and sentenced to fifteen years in prison. At this very young age, I knew quite well that the Communists had betrayed us, Jews, that they were once the greatest hope for the world, and that my parents and their friends were desperately involved in a love-hate relationship with a great country called Russia.

I must have been seven or eight years old when I had a rare, eye-opening conversation with my father. We were standing on the balcony that faced the street on Yom Kippur and watching the neighbors on their way to synagogue. Standing there and not going to synagogue felt quite natural; I never set foot in a synagogue until I came to the United States in the early 1980s. What struck me as odd was the stark contrast between the dressy appearance of the neighbors and my father, who was standing there in his everyday pants and an undershirt. I must have asked him about it, for he never would have initiated a conversation on the issue. Instead of answering, he went inside, picked up a heavy brown folder, and dug out a piece of paper. I don't remember whether it was written in Yiddish or Hebrew. But I immediately recognized his perfect handwriting and was amazed to learn that he had written a poem as a youth back in Poland. He read it to me, and even though it was quite long, the main theme was simple: the red flag was destined to replace the praying shawl. The dramatic message weighed heavily on the moment, and he was uncomfortable, clearly ambivalent about it. The poem disappeared afterwards, never to be found or mentioned again. I walked next to him, under the red flag, on one or two more May First marches after that, and then we stopped going. We listened to the Red

Army Choir records less and less and eventually got rid of them. I can still sing *The Internacional* from beginning to end, though, and I miss the thrill of marching amidst a hostile crowd. Yom Kippur never meant much to me.

My father worked two jobs. During the day he was an administrator with *Kuppat Holim,* the Labor Sick Fund which developed into the national health system, and at night served as a language editor for *Al Hamishmar,* MAPAM's daily newspaper. My brother would later join the staff of *Al Hamishmar* as a reporter and editor and would stay with the paper until it closed down in the 1980s. My mother worked at home, sewing pajamas and night gowns for a lingerie firm. I did not know much about either of my parents, and I still know very little about their younger years. Both came from Poland in 1939 as illegal immigrants, my mother enduring the heroic journey of the Tiger Hill, the last ship to leave Europe before the war. Both left their families behind, never to see them again, and came to build a new society in the old Jewish homeland. After a few years on a kibbutz, they moved to Tel Aviv and started a family. They came with nothing, lost all that was in their past, worked desperately hard, were neither depressed nor frightened, and managed to build a solid future and raise children who knew how to live, nothing short of a miracle if I ever believe in one. I cannot imagine the horror of living with the knowledge of what happened in Europe. My brother and sister were named after my father's parents, and I was named after my mother's mother, but we never talked about our lost family members. We had no grandparents and aunts or uncles, but I don't recall experiencing a need to feel their absence. After all, none of my friends had them either. The Holocaust, I seem to remember, was an academic issue for us as children, something to commemorate once a year and then go about our business. An occasional neighbor had a number tattooed onto his or her arm, but we viewed it matter-of-factly as just another sign of someone who came from "there." *Éemo édno* had one—it made no difference, we still gave her a hard time. Our parents rarely talked about their past, and we knew not to ask. Only in the mid-1980s, when my brother's oldest son began working on his "roots" project in preparation for the class *Bar Mitzva* celebration, would names surface into the open. When my father passed away in 1998, we engraved them on his tombstone, together with his name. Strangely enough, I still find it hard to remember these names, as if the urge to not think about them is stronger than the need to know that they ever existed. Only one name is clear in my recollection—my father's brother Yoel. My parents must have talked about him, for I remember not only his name but also a special sense of tragedy associated with him. For many years, I thought he had been killed accidentally while cleaning a rifle. My sister, who went through a "roots" project with her own children, tells me that he perished in the Battle of Stalingrad. I tend to accept this version, which provides a perfect explanation to that special sense of tragedy. Yoel was not exterminated by the Nazis like the rest of the family members. He was a Communist and died in the service of the sun of all nations, great mother Russia. We all knew that Stalin was no better than Hitler. Both burnt in our fires.

I think that I was supposed to dislike Orthodox Jews and despise the Revisionists. I ended up hating Orthodox Jews and not minding the Revisionists. I feel uncomfortable using the word *hate*, but the statement is unpleasantly true, for this was hatred, mixed with scorn and a constant need to challenge. Such sentiments would push me and my friends to walk some two hours to old Jaffa in search of the warmest pita bread on Passover, when a crumb of bread could not be found in Tel Aviv, or to eat ham sandwiches in public. For many years, I lived with the knowledge that the empty lot by our house, which was the center of my childhood outdoor activities, was designated by the city as the site of a future synagogue. The lot was still empty when I moved out of the neighborhood at the age of twelve, but many years later, when I visited the place with my own children, the synagogue was there, bringing back old anger and resentment.

Where did these sentiments come from? After all, as a child I had absolutely no contact with orthodox Jews with the exception of Meye's family. My parents could not have hated Orthodox Jews—their own parents were devout *Hassidim*, followers of the renowned Radziner Rebbe. Did I learn it from my brother? From *Al Hamishmar*, which I read with zeal? I will never know. I did know, though, that my parents disliked the Revisionists, and that, as a young socialist, I was supposed to dislike them as well, for they were fascists and capitalists, and that was that. It was easy to despise Menachem Begin, who was pompous and ugly and spouted words of poison. But my parents had good friends who looked and talked exactly like them, who were poor like them, yet were sworn Revisionists. Capitalists were supposed to be rich, I thought. Besides, I was practically raised on Edmondo D'amicis' *Heart*, a most wonderful book with an obvious fascist tint. I had a good friend, Niva, whose parents were members of the LECHI group ("The Stern Gang"), which was supposed to be the worst of them all. Niva was a great girl, and her parents were simple, hardworking, sweet, and sincere people, just like mine. She died of leukemia at the age of seventeen, and we were all devastated. At her funeral, amidst the mourners and beggars, as her body was being lowered into the grave, someone began to sing. Shaky voices became stronger and stronger, and the words of *Chayalim Almonim*, "Anonymous Soldiers," the LECHI anthem, filled the air. Everybody was stunned, struck with awe, overcome by the cleansing power of grief and camaraderie. Everybody but the beggars, that is. They went about their business, pulling on our sleeves, pushing their collection boxes into our faces, and assuring us that charity would save us from death. When like them, one lives at a cemetery, life must become a collection box, a meaningless journey to the hereafter through empty walls and the jingle of an occasional coin. We knew better, for only a few years later we would come to that cemetery time and time again, bid good-bye to friends, and go back to the world of the living, which our parents had created for us. Our lives were simple and predictable, but we were very rich. Our parents were real people who taught us, without many words, how to live, love, let go, and make sense of the contradictions that life would throw at us.

Lilia Labidi

TUNISIA *Lilia Labidi is professor of anthropology and psychology at the University of Tunis, Tunisia. She was educated in Tunisia and in France, where she received a doctorate at the Sorbonne. She is currently coordinating research projects in social sciences in cooperation with local scholars in Egypt, Senegal, Tunisia, and South Africa. Her published works include "The Thirty-year-old Generation, Living Memory of History" (1985), and she has organized several photographic exhibits in Tunisia, such as "Women and Politics, 1930–1955" (1988) and "The Death of Love" (1994). The latter deals with the bitterness resulting from colonial repression.*

LILIA LABIDI, FRONT

THINKING OF VIOLENCE

Lilia Labidi

To write about my childhood, to objectify it, I need to identify events I believe shaped me. Some assumed significance many years after they took place, in the course of a psychoanalysis with Jacques Lacan. Here I want to pinpoint two events that seem to me to have been crucial in my personal development.

The first begins with my father, who, before I was born, wanted to immigrate to Brazil or Canada but was unable to do so, because he didn't want to back out on his engagement to my mother or perhaps because my mother's family was opposed to the idea. So he took a job as customs inspector on the Tunisian-Algerian border. Since my mother was against the move from the beginning, she did not handle the situation well within the family. I believe it was from this move that the term *border* took a particular significance for me. The Tunisian-Algerian border. The borders of language. The borders of culture.

The Roman ruins of Haydra, near the town where we lived, were the scene of our childhood play, my brothers and I. The whistle of the train that went between Tunisia and Algeria, and the ringing of the telephone—both signs of "modern" technological developments—were our only connection to the rest of the world. Holidays and weekends our family devoted to historic and cultural expeditions. We chugged along in our car, visiting tribes in surrounding areas, learning the histories of populations and of the conflicts that set one tribe against another. We discovered the richness of tribal life, and we learned about its values of honor, solidarity, hospitality. In earlier times, this area had been a place to search out ancient wonders, but in our time it had become the object of attack by colonial powers. The scarred walls of our house testified to the battles that had already taken place.

My parents wanted to give us a modern education but one which took place within tradition, so they wanted to use all the educational resources available. Thus my brothers and I were enrolled in two different school systems. In the mornings, we followed the curriculum of the local French school and in the afternoons we attended the *kuttab*, the Quranic school. Was I upset by those French studies in the mornings? I don't remember precisely; what stays in my memory from those times is an incident which may appear banal but assumed great importance in my child's eyes. One day the French teacher, to punish me, shut me up in a large armoire. There was a rabbit inside there with me! In the dimness I saw the poor rabbit, staring back at me with its shining eyes; I crouched in a corner, terrified, staring back at it. Did I cry? I don't know, but I do remember this incident as striking me at a time when I was just learning to distinguish between good and evil. This French teacher, merged with the colonizer, with colonial authority, how could he be the promoter of good, of what they then called modernity? It was probably about that time that two opposed, contradictory systems began to take root in me.

In contrast to the mornings at the French school, the afternoons in the kuttab became a kind of creative space. The bareness of the room where we sat on the floor was brightened by the sunlight streaming through the window. Such light! The ink we used to write on our Quranic slates, despite its strong odor, introduced us to the beauty of Arabic calligraphy. When the *meddab* or teacher, seated in the circle of students, initiated us into Quranic knowledge by occasionally rapping us on the fingers with a slender stick, I felt indulgent toward him, for I believed we deserved such treatment. What I reproached in the behavior of the French teacher I pardoned in the Tunisian teacher.

After some months, my mother persuaded my father to ask for a transfer. But there were no openings in Tunis, so Ghardamaou, another town close to the Algerian border, became my father's next post. Here the setting was completely different. Instead of the peace and quiet of the Haydra ruins, we had all the noises of a small city where cars, motorbikes, and bicycles were not unusual. Ghardamaou was a city cut in two. The Tunisians lived in one part and the French army was billeted in the other. Here was an additional opposition, one that soon gave rise to another.

The French soldiers often gave out candy and chocolate to the children in the streets, but I never took any, for my mother's voice rang in my ears, as she said, again and again, "Don't take anything from the French soldiers," reminding me in this way that we were under French occupation and that we were not to have any contact with the occupier.

But one day on my way to school, the *ftayri*, the local doughnut seller, called out to me. He wanted to give me some cakes, but I couldn't accept. Why refuse him, when he had nothing in common with the French colonial soldier? Why refuse, when he enjoyed offering children the cakes he hadn't been able to sell the night before? My simple response to him, "I'm fasting," seemed to please him and in his pleasure he said, "I'll keep some cakes for you and give them to you on your way home." And he did. And I got back to the house with a whole box of sweets, my reward for what I now think was his recognition of the ethical nature of my answer. Perhaps my larger reward was that ethics and culture became associated in my mind with resistance to the oppressor.

Some time later, my parents were able to return to Tunis. I was placed in a new school, where I enjoyed the classes in art, civics, and Islamic civilization and history but turned away from all the subjects given in French. Tunisia had by now gained its independence, but I was still waging a battle against the colonial language, without perhaps being truly aware of what I was doing. How could I be expected to learn the language of those who had been our oppressors, when every day in family conversations we heard stories of the evils of colonialism? Did I have any idea of the price I might have to pay if I clung to the ethical views of this child who was just seven or eight years old? Was I jeopardizing my promotion to a higher grade? The school administration summoned my father. My teachers told him that my grades were fine in all subjects except . . . French. I wondered why failing to learn the colonial language should be such a serious problem! But this was all it took for a family meeting to be called, and I learned the outcome quickly enough: I was to be enrolled in a boarding school outside of Tunis where only French was spoken.

In this new environment, I spent my first days trying to understand my confinement to a place where 95 percent of the children were of French origin. The school was run with an iron hand by a French couple, and the majority of the staff were European. Most of the pupils were daughters of French settler-farmers in Cap Bon, the northwest, the south, or from the area of Bizerte. I understood very quickly that I had to make a decision because there was no way out. Should I continue my stubborn refusal, or should I just adapt? I decided to throw myself into the French language. With some pupils I exchanged my chocolate snacks for help in French; with others, I copied and recopied the assignments they had been given as punishment, in return for help with my own homework. I no longer had any courses

in Arabic. A few months later, my teachers judged that I had made significant progress and my parents were reassured.

But the same opposition was quickly reconstituted, even in this French
environment. For among the monitors and supervisors in the school there
was one young Tunisian woman, a student at the teachers college. Amina,
in order to earn money, worked in our boarding school several evenings a
week. Very rapidly, the Tunisian girls gathered round her. There were maybe
five of us. When all the French girls were sound asleep, our days began. We
shared the food that Amina's mother had cooked. We listened as she told us
stories of our heritage. She taught us how to pray.

And so the years passed until it was time to go to secondary school. I was
fortunate enough to succeed in the Tunisian and French tests and when the
moment came to choose my secondary school, I said to my father, "I will go
to the French school," where Arabic was taught as a second language. The
violence I had known, I was later able to express in words, with memories
of the Quranic teacher, the sweets seller, and the Tunisian monitor guiding
me and helping me preserve the kingdom of my childhood.

The second experience took place when I was about ten. In many ways,
it helped to direct me to the kind of life I have led since, and to encourage
the particular theoretical orientation I have given to my work. One day,
while my grandfather and I were walking in the center of Tunis, a man came
up to us, bent over, and kissed my grandfather's hand. This happened very
quickly and I found myself overcome by emotion and very upset. Why was
I so shocked by this behavior?

The custom of having one's hand kissed by a man of lower status, as an
act of respect, had always been a common practice, but in 1860, Muhammad al-Sadeq Bey, Tunisia's sovereign ruler, had revised the Tunisian law so
that this gesture was made into an act of submission due only the Bey and
his chief representatives. I could not understand why my grandfather, who
was an *amin*, an expert in agricultural matters recognized for his probity and
high morals, would accept what to me seemed an act of submission. True,
he was also an advisor in the Bey's court, but in my young eyes, he was the
essence of right and justice, and I was convinced that this gesture was wrong.
I was certainly too young at the time to make a very reasoned judgment, but
I was sure that our new, free Tunisia needed new values.

This was a period when public discussion of societal questions was
everywhere, when critical views and new ideas about the future were widely
voiced, particularly on the radio, which had become, for a population still
largely illiterate, the main space for public debate and for the formulation
of a new civic morality. In the new Tunisia—independent, autonomous,

and free to construct itself as its people wanted—the gesture of one person kissing the hand of another in obeisance seemed anachronistic to me. Anachronistic with regard to that moment in Tunisian history, and anachronistic with regard to the history of the nation. But also anachronistic with regard to the history of my own family, a family of maraboutic origins, one of whose leaders had risked his own life by strongly protesting the exorbitant demands made by the *mehalla*, the tax collectors, on the population during the 1860s.

To understand what the institution of the mehalla meant to the people, one must know a little about its activities. The mehalla visited the countryside twice a year, once in the summer in the northwest at the time of the harvest, and once in the winter in the Sahel and the south, when dates and olives are gathered. In the beginning, centuries earlier, such visits were occasions for kings to visit their subjects, consolidate allegiances, collect taxes, and bring recalcitrant tribes back into the fold.

These taxes became increasingly onerous and in 1863 they were extended to include towns and cities that had previously been exempted. So unpopular was this move that it led to an insurrection in 1864 after the *mehalla* chief Zerrouk, whom my family's memory enshrines as the incarnation of evil, demanded immediate payment and tortured or put in irons those who refused to obey. The tax collectors broke into private homes, confiscated family belongings, beat people, and raped girls while their parents were forced to watch. Even today, tax collectors are unpopular figures in part because the memory of Zerrouk and his methods remains strong.

My father had told me something of our family's experience with the mehalla. The mehalla had come to his great-grandfather, who was a sheikh, the people's representative vis-à-vis the central authority, and the sheikh paid what was asked of him. But he hadn't counted on the greed of the zealous agents. A few days later, he received a second visit; the agent demanded further payments. By that time, the sheikh had no more liquid assets, so he was forced to sell most of his land in order to pay the sum demanded. Other family heads, too, hoping to get rid of the agents, had chosen to sell property or turn over the titles to moneylenders—often foreign creditors or others supported by the colonial authorities. In this way, entire families eventually lost all their property. Now, the agents returned for a third time. This time my great-great-grandfather strongly slapped the mehalla agent. He chose to rebel; he refused to be humiliated further.

Eugene Delacroix's painting, *La Perception de l'impôt Arabe* (*The Collection of Arab Taxes*), dates from this very period, for it was completed in 1863. The work was inspired by a conversation the artist had with the Moroccan Ministry of Foreign Affairs, in which they discussed recent tax increases and the arrest, on the grounds of sedition, of those who did not pay. The painting appears divided into two triangles by an imaginary line from the upper right to the lower left. In the upper triangle, at the top left, a *ksar*, or local palace, stands on a hill. At the foot of the hill, groups of men are fighting in a clump of trees. Behind them, another group, guns in hand, is advancing through swirling dust. In the lowest triangle, across the bottom of the painting, the dead of both sides are thrown together on the ground. The painting is a clear statement that the collection of taxes was an act of great violence. Delacroix illustrated well the tension over the collection of taxes and the extraction of goods which existed at the time between the central power in Tunisia and the tribes of the countryside.

For me, Delacroix's painting clarified the sudden emotion I felt that day, long ago, when I witnessed a person lowering himself to kiss my grandfather's hand. I realized that, even as a child, I had experienced a kind of violence within myself. As an adult, I would write about this violence, believing that the enemy was not only in others, that it was not a question of "us" and "them," but that there was an enemy within ourselves, too, and we needed always to be aware of it. The struggle against colonialism liberated us from a certain kind of domination, but we also had to understand our own internal violence—something that perhaps South Africans are coming to understand through their efforts in the Truth and Reconciliation Commission, to find truths that will allow for reconciliation within oneself and with others.

My childhood was marked by the two experiences I have described. In objectifying these memories, I have seen them in terms of political emancipation and individual emancipation, as acts of violence leading to a kind of freedom. The political struggles of Tunisian reformists and those of women like Jamila Boupacha and Jamila Bouhaired, heroines of the Algerian revolution, whose stories I heard as an adolescent listening to Tunisian radio in the evenings, were acts of freedom that took place in the context of such violence. These acts, together with works of art and imagination—be they ancient ones like the ruins of Haydra, more recent like the painting of Delacroix, or those being created today, are what allowed me to think beyond violence in order to not be beaten down by it, and to put words in the spaces that violence had filled.

Translated from the French by Elizabeth Fernea

Suad Joseph

LEBANON *Suad Joseph is professor of anthropology and women's*
UNITED
STATES *studies at the University of California, Davis. Her research*
on her native Lebanon has focused on ethnic / religious con-
flicts, women's networks, family systems, and the social-
ization of children in notions of rights, citizenship, and
nationhood. Her books include **Muslim Christian**
Conflicts: Economic, Political and Social Origins
(coedited with Barbara Pillsbury). She is convenor of a
faculty seminar at the University of California Humani-
ties Research Institute on Gender and Citizenship in Mus-
lim Communities.

EYES OF INDIRECTION

Suad Joseph

As far back as I can remember, I had big eyes—big brown eyes that saw everything. Before I learned to speak, before I learned to listen, before I learned to walk, before I learned to reach out, my eyes could talk, hear, gesture, and touch. "Eyes like those take a lifetime to make," my friend Dipok said.

In rural Lebanon in the mid-1940s, elders often taught children that they could speak, listen, move, and feel through the language of eyes. Children learned to observe others closely and were continually reminded that they were being observed by others. Persons often spoke to each other through glimmers of the eyes, nuances of speech, intonation of the voice, and shifts of the body. Recipients of such indirect communication focused on interpreting the meaning of what they had observed and attributed intentionality to their conclusions. In this face-to-face society in which persons expected and hoped that most of their lives would be spent with familial and known others, meaning was always complexly woven into multiple modes of communication. It was assumed that meanings, and the vehicles through which meanings were communicated, were shared and decipherable to familiar others, making it possible to observe, recognize, understand, and respond appropriately.

Perhaps because I was the youngest in my family, perhaps because I was a female, I spent a lot of time watching Mama, Baba (my father), my older sisters, and brothers. I learned indirection at the side of Mama and my oldest sister, Linda, who was like a second mother to me. I watched them talk through indirection to others, listen to the indirection of others, decipher their intentions, and respond.

Mama spoke with her eyes. She had big brown eyes. She saw everything, heard everything, felt everything with her eyes. I was sure of it. Mama was an expert at indirection. She was particularly acute in interpreting the meanings of interactions. Relatives and friends frequently came to her to discuss their encounters and indirectly ask for her views. She always offered a confident view. To my child's eye, Mama was always right. It seemed that few others won arguments with her about interpreting indirect communication.

I watched Mama's eyes. Her eyes always told me what to do. A glance from my Mama was all it took. Her eyes told me when to say no, when to say yes, when to be silent, when to speak up, when to fear, when to hope. She taught me to look at other people's eyes. To listen to what their eyes said to me. To watch their bodies, their gestures, their movements, and to see the words behind the words. I was to give more weight to the readings of indirect than direct communications. I developed a sense of certainty that Mama was talking to me with her eyes and I had to listen.

Eyes were always watching me, Mama said. So we had to be diligent in our behavior and our own observations. She took great pride in immaculately dressing us in clothes daily washed and ironed despite our meager means. Baba came home one day and told her she was right about people watching us. He said he was doing business with a rather well-to-do man at the man's home. It was early morning and Baba said the man told him he wanted to go to the balcony because he and his wife liked to watch some brothers and sisters walking together to school. He said the children were so well-groomed and so well-behaved that he and his wife enjoyed the sight of them. Baba walked to the balcony. As many school children paraded past the house, the man pointed out the children he admired. Baba's eyes opened wide, he reported, as he turned to the man and said, "These are my children!"

Mama liked to tell that story. Each time I heard it, the thought of unknown watching eyes loomed large from invisible balconies. The thought of known eyes loomed larger. Baba had seen. Mama would find out. That God, in my Maronite Catholic upbringing, was omnipresent and omnipotent was not difficult for me to understand. Wasn't God more powerful than Mama and Baba?

Learning indirection meant learning to watch, to observe. The more I understood indirect modes of communication, the larger my eyes became, or so it felt. My most important recollection of early childhood in Lebanon was that of silently watching. I conjure up a picture of a small child in a short plaid dress, one black braid quietly lying behind each ear, and eyes covering the rest of my face, big round brown eyes, watching.

Many family stories conform to my memory of a child schooled in the language of indirection. I loved guavas as a child. Baba never planted guavas in our garden, but our neighbor, Assad Elias, had a big guava tree. Mama taught me never to ask for gifts from others. She seemed to make a special case about the guava tree. I was not to ask Assad Elias or the wife of Assad Elias for guavas. It was never acceptable for me to stray from home, but Assad Elias lived right next door. When he stood on his balcony, I could see him from our house. I made a point of standing at the door looking for him on his balcony when the guavas were in season. When I saw him, I would saunter in front of his house and stand silently next to the guava tree. He would laugh the wonderful laugh which I loved and Mama loved mimicking, "Ah, ah, ah." Greeting me, he would ask me how I was doing and how Mama and Baba were. After the round of pleasantries, he would pause and then ask me if I wanted an orange. Looking at the ground, with my hands locked behind my back, I would shake my head and say we had oranges at home. He would ask if I wanted an apple or grapes. Still staring at the ground, I would shake my head and say we had apples and grapes at home. He would scratch his head and say do you want some guavas? Not moving my eyes, I would silently shrug my shoulders. "Ah, ah, ah," he would laugh, coming down to give me guavas. But I had learned I was not to take something offered to me. Assad Elias would offer the guavas repeatedly and insist that I take them. There was a delicate point beyond which saying no was no longer acceptable. At that point, which I learned judiciously to assess, to reject the guavas would have been to insult our neighbor. Surely, I could not insult a respected elder. I had learned that, too.

I had already learned many lessons about the culture of indirection. I was to learn more. Mama may not have meant for me to use her lessons in this way. She thought me incorrigible. But Assad Elias shared the culture of indirection. He knew the meaning of my silent guard at the foot of his guava tree. That he took pleasure in pretending ignorance at my expense, no doubt, also taught me that indirection was fraught with uncertainties. There were the possibilities of misinterpretation. There was the necessity of patience, waiting for others to understand. There were the occasions of frustrated ambitions because of the willful or benign ignorance of others.

Mama's story of her marriage to Baba added uncertainty to my mind. While she told me the story years later, it slipped easily among the anxieties indirection at times stirred in my child's mind. Orphaned at a young age, Mama had been raised strictly by her older brothers. How strict, I was to learn only years later from my aunt Mariam, Mama's sister. In Mama's stories, her brothers were always heroes. When Baba came with his mother to call on Mama's brothers, her oldest brother asked her if Baba was acceptable to her. She answered that she would do whatever he wished. Three days later Mama and Baba were married. Mama was fond of another man, but her brothers did not ask her about him. That's just the way it was then, Mama would explain.

I often tried to imagine what Mama's life would have been like had her brothers asked or had she told them whom she wanted—until I realized that I would not have been born had Mama and Baba not married. That short-circuited those thoughts. But from that story, thoughts of Mama's obedience, and the power of brothers to shape the lives of sisters lingered with me.

When my sister Linda became of age, suitors lined up at our doors. They called on Mama and Baba as friendly visitors. They came sometimes with their parents, sometimes with siblings, sometimes with cousins, uncles, or aunts. Almost always they came with someone who already knew our family. The visits over coffee and sweets were packed with meaning. Mama, Baba, my brothers and sisters, and I all watched where they sat, how they looked, how they moved; we listened with our eyes to their eyes. Afterwards, Mama, Baba, and Linda spent hours excavating their memories of the visits and comparing interpretations. Even forty years later, Mama would recount almost word for word, gesture for gesture, glance for glance, what was said and meant.

I watched. My sister Violet watched. The younger brothers watched. The oldest brothers got involved in interpreting positions and taking positions. Somehow Linda found herself engaged but not to the man she wanted. But Mama asked Linda whom she wanted and Linda told her. Without Baba initially knowing, Mama agreed to let Linda elope with the man she loved. The dramatic story of the last-minute elopement filled many hours of storytelling in our family.

I learned many things about indirection. Particularly I learned that fulfillment of my desires usually required the active involvement and compliance of others. Desire was not to be satisfied through my autonomous actions. I could hint, imply, and create situations for others to read, interpret, and act upon, but others needed to act for my wishes to be realized.

When I visited family or friends with Mama, I was to always say, "No, thank you," when offered goodies to eat. Mama's piercing gaze reminded me if I forgot. The hostess, however, would always repeat the offer. "No, thank you," was the refrain, but my surreptitious glance at the goody must have told my hostess something else. She would insist I take the sweet or fruit. Mama would glance at me, her eyes giving the slightest nod. Not because she wanted me to have the goody, I thought, but because she did not want to offend the hostess whose insistence made my acceptance necessary.

My desires would be fulfilled not only because I sought to fulfill them but also because others recognized them and acted. I got the guavas and the sweets not only because I wanted them but also because Assad Elias and our hostess saw that I wanted them, offered them to me, and insisted I take them. At that delicate point at which continued refusal would have become an insult, there was a crucial shift of responsibility for the fulfillment of my desires. At that point, it was their insistence, their dignity, their hospitality that was at stake. Fulfilling my needs was done, partly, to fulfill the needs of others. The culture of indirection offered me avenues for asking without singularly taking the responsibility for asking or getting.

It also taught me that action on my part was a necessary condition for the fulfillment of the desires of significant others. It was an act of love and caring for me to read, interpret, and act upon the desires of intimate others. The older I grew, the more I saw that it was my duty to figure out what dear ones needed and to do it for them before they asked for it, perhaps before they recognized that they wanted or needed it. I saw my brother Edward take the meatless back of the chicken that Mama had served herself and replace it with a meaty piece. I saw my sister Linda acting out humorous antics if Mama was sad.

Reading indirection was not all focused on Mama. We read what Baba needed, we read what each of the siblings needed, we read what others close to us needed. I came to think that it was rude to ask directly for most things. I learned to ask indirectly and to identify intimacy and friendship in terms of significant others' capacity and willingness to understand and respond to those communications. Mama frequently told the story of my first silver dollar that a relative gave me in Lebanon shortly before our early fall departure for the United States. I had heard Mama saying we would need new winter coats when we arrived in the States. "What will you do with the dollar?" he asked. "Buy Mama a fur coat," I reported.

My memories of my early childhood in Lebanon and the family stories about me don't always line up, though. Mama, Baba, and my siblings always told stories of an active, strong-willed, confident, bold, brave rascal—me—who nevertheless managed to win the affection of the sternest of my uncles, 'Ammi Yusif. Mama's eyes would twinkle mischievously when she told the story of my peeing on 'Ammi Yusif when he held me over his head and the way he still held me there because he did not want to startle me.

But Mama thought maybe I redeemed myself with 'Ammi Yusif later. 'Ammi Yusif at times sold oranges directly from his gardens. I was visiting when a man came to buy some oranges. The man picked the oranges he wanted and put them on the scale. A burly man with stubble on his face, he wore the baggy peasant costume common to the area. While 'Ammi was not looking, I saw the man putting several more oranges in his baggy shirt. When he came to pay, the oranges remained in his shirt. I looked at 'Ammi and asked, "And those in his shirt?" 'Ammi Yusif looked at me, then at the man.

The man paid for the oranges, then looked at me. I didn't want to see those eyes again.

To my family, this was a story of my bravery. They have many stories of my boldness, so many that my third brother, Edward, used to talk about me as "Suad the hero." I insisted I was strong enough to do anything, Mama said. I wanted to help pack and move our household goods when we were preparing to leave Lebanon. My siblings laughed. "How will you carry it?" Mama queried. "I'll pull it behind me," Mama proudly reported my answer.

Stories of this heroic child were repeated so often when I was growing up that they are engraved like legend in a memory to which I have access but don't remember creating. To me, the story about the oranges was a story of my eyes, watching. It was a story of learning to observe the behavior of others, identify intentionality, and respond. It was a story of a secondary skill of observation I had developed while learning the primary lesson of translating indirection. To me, the story of pulling the baggage was one of my seeing and reading and acting on what I understood as Mama's indirect request for help with moving the household goods.

Sometimes there were things I could not see, did not know. Those were often the most dangerous. I learned that if my eyes did not see, the eyes of others did. Mama and Linda spent most of their time in the downstairs room of our house preparing meals, making coffee, cleaning, and doing daily chores, only a step from the patio where I played. Mama and Linda thought they could see everything. But even their eyes missed some things. Once I was playing quietly by myself when a stone swooshed hard through the air past my head, just barely missing me. The shouts, triumphant and terrified, bewildered me as I saw Raymond, my second oldest brother, running toward me. Confused and frightened, I froze at his charge. It was only when he pulled me away that I saw, inches from where I had been sitting, a rattlesnake, dead at my brother's feet. My brother had seen the snake poised. His village reputation as a marksman was earned only in part by this shot. Thus I learned that the watching eye of others was often for my benefit.

When I was six, my family moved to the United States. My parents continued to raise their children, particularly the daughters, as if we were still in our village in Lebanon. The small Lebanese community in our upstate New York town supported and reproduced those village norms with and for each other. As I grew older, I often found communication with my "American" friends would flounder around misinterpretations of meanings. I learned that "Americans" use the language of eyes very differently and gradually desensitized myself to the older vehicles of meanings I had known.

Returning to Lebanon again in 1993 after a twelve-and-one-half-year absence (I had visited before in 1980), I was amazed to find how quickly I began again looking at eyes, averting eyes, watching gestures and movements, and seeing the words behind the words. Seventeen years of civil war had changed Lebanon in many ways. It certainly was no longer the place my parents had frozen in time at their departure in the late 1940s. Yet the tools of indirection and the skills of observation Mama had taught me were still vital in my relationships with my friends and family.

Acknowledgments: I dedicate this paper to Mama Rose, who taught me how to use my eyes. I wish to express deep gratitude to Paul Aikin for many insights over the years.

Abdelaziz Jadir

MOROCCO

*Abdelaziz Jadir grew up
in the northern Moroccan
countryside, which he has
described in the short stories
he has published in Arabic.
He was educated in Morocco
and some years ago launched
a regular literary radio
program in Tangier, for which he serves as host and
interviewer of literary figures throughout the Arab world.
Recently, he was selected as the literary critic/correspondent
for **Al-Hayat,** the well-known Arabic newspaper
published in London. He lives and works in Tangier.*

CHILDHOOD MEMORIES

Abdelaziz Jadir

 My mother said, "You told me one morning, son, 'Mother, don't come to school with me, I'll go by myself, stay home and make lunch.' I was devastated with acceptance as much as I was devastated with fear; I said to myself, it's good for you to walk to school by yourself, you'll feel that you've grown and become a man. But the devil whispered to me that if I let you go to school alone I would never see you again, for you could be killed by a reckless car or kidnapped by thieves and that would be the end of me because I'd either be murdered by your father or, should he fear God, be divorced. I overcame my fears and opened the door for you after breakfast and you left. I shut the door and prayed, thanking God and praising Him, and asking Him to watch over you with his gentleness.

"You weren't late coming home in spite of the five kilometers between our house and the school. But you didn't have your bag. I asked about it and you said you had no idea where it went! I said to myself, thank God you returned safely, and to hell with the bag even though we were very poor in those days."

My own son said, after he'd silently listened to his grandmother, "Poor dad used to lose his bag and all his stuff and Grandma didn't get mad, but when I lose something you punish me! Grandma has exposed you!"

And everyone laughed.

BURNING   My mother said, "What can I say to you, my son, if what they say is written on the forehead and cannot be erased by the water of truth.

"You used to accompany me wherever I went. And one morning, I remember it like this very morning, we went to the bakery; it was a building with no other buildings around it. I went to give the bread order with the baker and you stayed outside as usual. But when I came back, I found no trace of you even though I'd been inside such a short time. I ran in all directions and I imagined your father coming home from work and you're still lost and he would either murder me or remember God and divorce me. And suddenly my eye fell on the wood barrel which sat on the right-hand side of the baker, and in which he would throw the ashes, what was left of the wood that was used to cook the bread. I came closer to the barrel and lifted its cover and I saw you standing inside, over the embers and ashes, and the smell of grilled flesh was seeping from you. I snatched you out of the barrel and ran home. I opened the door, I don't know how I did it while I was carrying you. I put you on my bed and screamed for Haddad's wife—Rahma. She registered the fear in my voice and ran down and when she saw your condition she called her husband and he came and saw your condition and his wife ordered him to go quickly to the closest pharmacist and buy the necessary medicine.

"And when I checked up on what had happened to you, my eyes were full of tears. The fire had eaten up a side of your right leg, the skin on your thigh was loose on one side and burned on the other, while the heat had dug air pockets and filled them. I could not bear the sight of this red thigh without skin.

"Haddad came back with a plastic bag full of medicines and the pharmacist with him. He took the bag and set it on the table and told us, his wife and I, to leave. Your screams were escalating, the pharmacist took off your clothes, or whatever remained of them; the fire had eaten parts of your shirt and pants. Haddad ordered us to leave the room, and we heard the sound of a key turning in the door when we did. After a while, we heard your voice get louder as though it wanted to go through the roof and into the sky. Haddad's wife kept holding onto my arm, 'Don't worry, Fatima, this was something that was written by God on us, and what has been written cannot be escaped. Patience, Fatima, patience. How did the Prophet succeed in conquering the nonbelievers? With patience.'

"When your father returned from work, I told him what happened and he didn't believe me. He went to the baker and was told it was true. And in spite of all that, he kept feeding me guilt: 'You considered him a man, right? Otherwise you would have never let go of his hand!'

"Those were black days. . . . You spent almost eight months in bed; during the first three Haddad used ointments but the burns would not dry up, and so Haddad found another medicine, and it was whale tusks. Do you remember those teeth you used to play with as children and their size varied from small to medium to large? Haddad brought hundreds of them and I would grind them to a powder and shake it on the burns. And in a very short period of time, your thigh's skin returned and your leg improved, and the burns disappeared; all but a piece of skin which has never sprouted any hair."

My son turned to me and said, "Dad, take off your pants so we can see if the burn scar has disappeared."

Everybody laughed and I quickly said, "Okay, not now . . . when we go to the beach."

The trace of that burn remains on my thigh; its length is six inches and its width resembles the width of a sheep's tongue. This evidence, which is a reminder of an escape and a witness of a moment of childhood's strength—or its desire to exercise mischief—is also a witness of the stubbornness of reality and its cruelty. And is life anything but a collection of time's evidences, a collection that we call our bodies, our souls, and our minds?

GRAND-   My mother's brother tells me: "I came with your grandfather
FATHER   Muhammad al Arabi that morning you were born, I remem-
           ber it like it was today, and we brought butter and lard and milk and bread. Everyone present ate. Your grandfather was very pleased with you, he held your little hand and said, while admiring your fingers, 'This hand won't feed its owner or fill him up.' He meant that a fellah's hand must be big so it can be filled with seeds when it is time to plant them. 'This hand is the hand of the pen,' he continued. 'It won't win without the pen, but its owner will read and be successful in his reading, God willing.'

"On the seventh day after your birth, your grandfather ordered the slaughter of the biggest sheep and all the people came and ate and drank and prayed for your happiness and health, for all eternity. I am reminding you because it was your grandfather who named you."

In the mid-seventies, I bought a tape recorder with the intention of recording some of my grandfather's stories. In those days he had very few teeth, and he said he was fifteen years above a hundred. He used to make my aunt help him leave his room so he could sit all day under an umbrella in the sun. Other days he would ask her to bring his horse and tie it close to him so he could admire it. And he would also do this with the cow or the sheep. Other times, he would mount his horse and go around to see how nature and his property were doing. He'd tell you how he bought this piece during the days of occupation or this land during the days of Moulay Abdel Aziz, or Abdel Hafiz, or Muhammed the Fifth, or to tell you some details about this battle or that. Or he would repeat some popular folk song that was directed toward who was then the king.

I remember he would go to market every Tuesday morning, riding his white horse and dressed in a white shirt and djellaba with a white headdress; he had a white beard and even white eyebrows. He was like a good *wali* or a king walking in the markets. I was fascinated with him. It was impossible for a child or adolescent who'd once heard or was fed his heroic tales not to be.

With my grandfather's death, my mother lost her greatest support, after God—as she would like to repeat.

Knocks on the door in the early morning, resisted by the dream which makes the knocking a part of itself, just like the ear which resists them, so it could remain in the world of sleep. My mother woke up; she stood in the doorway of my room where the light was on and I was reading a novel, as usual; I remember that it was Caldwell. She told me, "Your grandfather died, poor man, God bless him," and the tears ran down her cheeks. Knocks on a door in the early morning or a night meant a relaying of someone's death.

I hugged her to express my sadness and my deep love for her and said, "Don't cry, say God bless and that's enough." But she answered, "I can't lock up my tears or my heart will give out. His presence was my only support. When your father comes home, tell him your grandfather died and that I went there. You go to school. I'll send your cousin to fix your food."

Three days later mother returned, her face filled with scratches; some were very deep, dug in with her nails. I heard father scolding her, then cursing her, but she just went on saying, "I've lost my greatest support after God."

Two days later the rift between my parents grew deeper, and she left our house and went to stay with her brother. Her absence stretched out to a month. Since we were not allowed to see her, we would sneak away from our father and go visit her in her exile; we would visit her and cry at our bad luck.

THE ZAWIYA   It was probably the love of knowledge which led me to the mosque/school. It was at the bottom of a house which had been given to the faqih. The mosque was called a zawiya because it had a space for students, and a large space for prayer, and the people who prayed would read the Quran between the evening and night prayers, and sometimes they read for hours after the night prayer.

The zawiya was in an angle or corner of the street and had two fronts, so did it get its name from its purpose or its location? The faqih had a white beard which moved whenever he spoke and moved more when he spoke with anger or passion. He had a helper named Ahmed who was like a faqih-in-waiting until life could give him a better role. One of his duties was to tell us one day, "Look, tomorrow you have to be bald. This is the beginning of summer and whoever is not bald tomorrow will have wronged himself." He brought out a handkerchief full of coins and distributed them among the students, saying, "This is so none of you will use poverty as an excuse."

The students returned the next day with shaved shiny heads. I was the only one who had refused the coin and still had hair. Ahmed ordered the others not to speak to me. So I sat alone for three weeks admiring the cosmos until the hair sprouted on the others' heads and they resumed talking to me.

We would, sometimes, before memorizing prayers, split up into two groups, and play semi-innocent games in the zawiya. One of these games was the Yankees and Indians.

MISCHIEF   I visited the city immediately after I had received my primary school certificate. That visit was a gift from my father for my success. My father bought me a pair of jeans and two shirts and gave me an allowance. I went to the station and my soul was about to pop out of my body with excitement. I waited for a long time and then got on the car.

The train took off, eating the earth as it went. At Abi al Ja'd station, many people got off and so did I; we went into a modern café, the only one in the city which had a jukebox in it. We danced to the tune of the famous 'get ready' LP until someone warned that the train was about to leave again. I ran with explosive speed, my breath ran out and fear shook me, and when I reached the train people made room for me and I jumped on board.

I spent two weeks in Beni Mellal with my father's uncle and his cousin Rahma. And my young cousin Ahmed did not leave my side. The first thing I wanted was to visit the nearby mountain, and climb it.

One night we did. Ahmed and his friends took me to the Asmid mountain because I wanted to see the monkey who lived there. We suddenly heard a sound and everyone looked at each other. Ahmed said, "In a little while we'll throw rocks. I hope none of the monkeys are ferocious or else we'll get hurt." At a distance, and on a different hill, a monkey appeared. One of us threw a stone, and then we all threw rocks at it. It let out a long shriek and disappeared. We came closer to the edge of the mountain and saw a large group of monkeys, so we went on throwing rocks at them; they attacked us with rocks and were clearly angry. One of us said, "You know why they're angry, don't you? Because you threw a stone at the grandfather monkey and probably hurt him." Someone suggested that we leave quickly before we saw our end at the hands of monkeys and their uncivilized grandfathers, which would be the first black page in our histories.

DESIRE   When I visited Beni Mellal a second time, I went out with my cousin, and he told me that he had to meet with a few friends first. We met up with them and they spoke with each other about this or that, and after an hour we began to walk until we found a street with signs that read "knocking forbidden" on most of the doors of its houses. Suddenly, one of those doors on which we were not allowed to knock swung open, and a woman peered out of it, wearing a nightgown with her chest barely covered and her thighs showing. One of my cousin's friends said, "God, look at the meat," and it seems she heard him because she answered him, "Looking alone won't cool off the body." And then the door on the right swung open and a young woman shot her head out from behind it; she wasn't bad looking. As soon as the shortest of my cousin's friends saw her, he screamed, "My girl!" and she ran toward him and hugged him and kissed him, finally pulling him to the door. Before crossing the house's threshold, she turned to the remainder of his friends, winked at them, and said, "If you are men like him then come in and test your manhood. And those of you who aren't can leave." My cousin said to me, "Go in and get a taste of some good meat." I rejected this idea, but his friends praised his suggestion. And when they saw that I was definitely against it, they left me and walked up to the house. At that moment, a man left the house next door while buttoning up his pants. He looked at us three boys and spat, saying, "So even you have discovered where you came from? Damn your sugar-seeking generation." I waited for the daring boys for twenty minutes, until each and every one of them came out spitting and buttoning up his pants.

I visited the countryside once with my family, and for this occasion my father went to buy vegetables and fruits and oil and sugar, as we were to celebrate spring with my uncle's family. Another time I went bathing in the well and we ate fruit. During one of those visits, when I was about eight, my cousin said to a friend, "Let's go visit our girlfriends."

My cousin grabbed a cow and stood up on a rock, then wiped his hands on its back. He unbuttoned his pants and put himself into her. He kept rubbing her with his hand and bringing her toward him. After a short while, he screamed, "Ah God, ah God, God, my God."

And his friend stood on top of the same rock and made the same movements and said the same things. They asked me whether or not I wanted to, also, and I remembered the man coming out of the door at Beni Mallal, saying, "Damn your sugar-seeking generation." Then I said to myself, "Let's see this sugar," and answered yes to my cousin, except I asked for a clean cow that no one had put that liquid in. They laughed and brought me another one. I climbed the rock. But her behind was too far away. I tried to ride her but I couldn't because I was too short. So I got tired and the cow brought down her tail and left without looking back at me.

An entire season after the failed experiment, we were in the country once again, and I went with my cousin and his friend to the well. We repeated the experiment but with a goat this time, and it was successful.

This kid thinks he was ten when he went with his father one spring to visit his aunt in the Zum valley. She lived in a large house and kept horses outside.

The shorty loved to look at horses, but, when he was coming near to one, he heard a sound like crying. He heard someone repeating, "Ah ah ah." He walked toward the source of the sound and saw that it was his aunt's son, another cousin, stuck to Mustapha. Their pants were down. The cousin was grabbing onto Mustapha and kissing him every once in a while. He saw his cousin biting Mustapha's ear and the other asking for mercy, "You're going to kill me," and his cousin saying, "Ah Ah Ah Aaah," and pushing Mustapha hard, onto the floor. Then he went to the sink and washed up, looking at the kid, me, and saying, "secret." So I understood that it was a secret between them. The cousin asked him, "Are you a man?" The kid hesitated, so the cousin said, "Try and you'll understand." He was still hesitant and when the cousin asked why, the kid asked Mustapha to wash up first. He did.

So Mustapha bent over. The kid approached him and imitated all of his cousin's movements, and realized in the end that he was a man. He was happy with utmost excitement when he felt that warm liquid; he smiled and recorded this strange event.

This was a period of free time and idleness.

BEST OF COMPAN- IONS He remembers that the book was a permanent presence in his parent's home, and that the French book came in before the Arabic one. Madame K, the French woman, kept his father busy with books. The kid remembers *Spirou, Les Pieds Nickeles, Asterix.* . . . That lady taught the kid the French alphabet and he spoke to her in her mother tongue. He remembers that he liked *Tin Tin* comics and also *Double John, Blake,* and *Zembla.* Once he walked to Madame K's house, and she gave him a book he still remembers; he liked it a lot and looked for more by the same author, and thus found an entire series called "espionage." Before the kid finished that academic year, he'd devoured tens of books in this series.

For after discovering James Hadley Chase, he went on to read Dashiell Hammett, with whom he was also enamored, and he read *The Maltese Falcon,*

The Big Knock-Over, and *The Dain Curse.* . . . The kid soon discovered a spy series about Ian Fleming, a part of the 007 series that Sean Connery embodied on screen. And the kid remembers that once an older friend told him that the 007 series had ended and that there was to be a new one and it was 008. The friend's brother, who lived in France at that time, would be the actor in it. So we kept waiting for the film to come out and to see his brother on the screen and he kept giving excuses from his imagination or from his memory. Every once in a while, he would show us a picture of his brother standing next to the Eiffel Tower, or hugging a French blonde, or smoking a pipe, or standing next to some gypsies whom our friend tried to pass off as his brother's fellow actors. And after a few years the town's cinema presented a film that had the partial title of 008. On a pilgrimage to the cinema went all the kids, waiting to see an actor whose brother and parent lived in their own neighborhood. Even though the actor was not in any of the commercials or movie posters pasted on the walls, the kids still went into the theater in great excitement. One said, "Abdu will probably play a sheikh who kills all the Christians." Another said, "You blind idiot, don't you see that it's a cop film! He's going to play a thief!" The lights went off, and the kids strained to find Abdu's name among the credits. Then Abdu's brother yelled out that he would have a stage name. But the film was a satire on the 007 films and its main character was a woman, so the comments began anew: "Your brother's a woman! God damned him!"

"No, they gave him a fake face!"

Some of the people at the cinema began to tell us to keep quiet. After a while the hands, arms, and fists began to make their way to our friend's skull.

In my heart there stayed a love for the police novel. When I met the American writer Paul Bowles he told me about a writer who wrote in this genre, his American friend Patricia Highsmith, so I read her *Deep Waters* and *Strangers on a Train.* When I met her, I asked if I could kiss her forehead and she agreed.

Maybe the best moment of my life was when I discovered Dostoevsky. I had a friend in a religion class, and one day we spoke about what we were reading. He gave me a book, and I read in it so deeply that I was startled when the bell rang. I told him that in exchange for the Dosteovsky book I would give him a very important book by a modern philosopher, Sartre, *Le Diable et le bon Dieu.* "Fine," he said, as long as you return the Dostoevsky to me. But my friend, I think, knew the fate of his book.

Dostoevsky was the first tree I found in the forest of Russian literature and then in the Soviet one later. Once, I found Erskine Caldwell's *God's Little Acre* and was surprised to find the unity of villages and towns all over the world. I knew a thousand Tyty Waldens and tens of thousands of Darling

Jills and I felt the same way when I read *Le Pillier* by the Turkish novelist Yashar Kemal. I read the same curses from Turkey that travel around Morocco and that old women spill on their sons.

The book remained the one true love in the life of the kid.

And he always remembered his grandfather who saw his little hand that would never be good for planting seeds or feeding its owner but only for the pen.

Many times he thought of Larousse's slogan: A human being sends knowledge on all the winds, winds that blow in every direction. And he liked to think of himself as always sprouting knowledge.

When I showed the kid what I'd written about him based on memoirs he'd written at various times of his life he wrote under it:

He died, this me, a long time ago.

IRAN *Nahid Rachlin*

Nahid Rachlin was born in Iran, came to the United States to go to college, married an American, and stayed on. She has been writing and publishing short stories and novels in English since 1978, when **Foreigner,** *her first novel, was published by W. W. Norton. Her stories have been reprinted in many recent anthologies such as* **Arrivals, Cross-Cultural Experiences in Literature,** *and* **Stones from the American Mosaic.** *Awards include the Bennet Cerf Award, PEN Syndicated Fiction Project Award, and a grant from the National Endowment for the Arts.*

WOULD I HAVE BECOME A
WRITER WITHOUT MY SISTER?

Nahid Rachlin

As I sit in a room in my apartment in Manhattan I clearly see myself coming back from high school in Ahvaz, a town in southern Iran. I am looking for my older sister, Pari. "I wrote a story today," I would say as soon as I found her in one of the many rooms in our large, outlandish house. I would sit next to her on the rug and read to her or tell her about the rigidities at school or some shocking scene I had encountered on the street. (Walking by the lettuce fields early one morning, I saw a half-naked woman lying among the bushes, her blouse torn and blood flowing out of her face, which was so badly beaten that it was barely recognizable; then police appeared on the scene.)

Pari always responded not to the story itself but to the anguish that the story expressed. She listened not so much to my story as to me. I remember the intensity of my desire to express my feelings and reactions to what went on around me, and my equal eagerness to hear her reassuring voice. I was also an avid reader and searched for whatever I could find in the town's single bookstore: novels and short story collections, mostly translations into Persian of American and European writers such as Hemingway, Dostoyevsky, and Balzac. I would read some of the passages to her, and she would say, "You could do that."

She loved movies and the two of us would go to see whatever was shown in the two movie houses in town, again mostly American and European movies dubbed in Persian. She had vague aspirations to one day become an actress. If I close my eyes, I can still vividly see her standing on the stage of the auditorium at our high school, which was for girls only; a similar high school for boys was in another part of town.

Wearing striped pajamas and a mustache, she danced and sang with similarly dressed girls in an imitation of an American musical. I would watch her and dream about writing something that one day would be put on a stage, with her acting in it.

I can hear my father's voice saying to her scornfully, "Don't you have any sense? An actress is just a whore." About my writing, he would say, more respectfully, "You're just a dreamer." In those days, I wrote about my immediate experiences; now, as an adult, I find myself mostly writing obsessively about the faraway past, people and cities I knew growing up. It is as if that period of struggle has much more meaning for me than what is occurring in the present. How could my stable, predictable married life compete with the turmoil of those days? (I have been married to the same man for twenty-six years, and we have one daughter who attends law school and has a clear vision of her own goals.) Though I have written various versions of the same events so many times, I still haven't managed to diminish the feelings raging behind them. . . .

When I was six months old, my grandmother took me from my mother, who already had four children, to be raised by my aunt, my mother's older sister. My aunt had been unable to have children herself even though she had been trying for years. My mother had promised her, even before I was born, that the next child would be hers. This was in response to my aunt's repeatedly begging my mother to let her raise one of her children. "God has enabled you to have so many of them, so easily," she kept saying to my mother. So early one morning, my grandmother bundled me up and, carrying a bottle of my mother's milk with us, she took the ferry from Abadan, where my father was a judge, and then the old, sooty train to my aunt's house in Teheran. At the time, my aunt was living with a husband more than twice her age who died not long after I was taken to them.

One day, when I was around ten years old, I was playing with a friend in the yard of our elementary school when I saw a man standing on the steps of a hallway looking for someone. I immediately recognized my own father, a thin, short man with a pockmarked face and a brush mustache but giving the impression somehow of being strong and powerful. My heart lurched. What was he doing there? I had come to view my parents as distant relatives whom I saw occasionally on holidays when they came to Teheran. I knew they were my real parents, but because my aunt's attention to me was so thorough and she expressed her need of me so openly, I had no yearning to live with them or any sense of having been abandoned.

"Let's go home," my father said as he approached me.

I looked at him for an explanation.

He picked me up and held me against him. "I'll tell you on the way." He kissed me and then put me down.

I said goodbye to my friend and followed my father outside.

"I have already spoken to your teachers, you aren't coming back here any more."

"What?"

He held my hand in his and said, "I'm taking you back to live with us. You're reaching the age when you need a father to look after you."

I didn't reply. A knot had formed in my throat. I was on the verge of crying. But it was not until I saw my aunt, her *chador* wrapped around her and her face wet with tears as she handed me a suitcase she had packed, that the reality of what was happening hit me full-force. I clung to my aunt. "I don't want to go," I said.

"I don't want you to go," she whispered to me, "but what can I do if your father insists on taking you back?"

What she was telling me was true; she had no legal right to keep me. But I have often wondered whether, if she had not been so afraid of men or so passive, being a woman in a vulnerable position, she would have been able to persuade my father to let me stay with her. From then on, I saw my aunt several months out of the year when she stayed with us in Ahvaz, where my parents had moved and where my father had established himself in private practice as a lawyer, or when I spent the summer with her in Teheran. After all these years, I'm still aware of my longing to be with her, of having been cruelly ripped away from her.

As we sat on the airplane, my father repeated again, "You need a father to look after you." I nodded shyly, trying to fight back my tears. I was in a daze as we got off the plane and went through the dusty streets that were lined with palm trees, the air smelling like the oil from the refineries. When we entered our house, my mother was sitting at the edge of the pool in the middle of the arid courtyard, talking to the old, live-in servant. My mother was wearing a jersey dress, her hair was set in a permanent, and her lips were red with lipstick. (I already missed my aunt's face, free from make-up, and her long, naturally wavy hair.)

"Oh, you're here," my mother said, getting up and coming over to me. She leaned over and embraced me—I was keenly aware of how tentative her touch was, compared to my aunt's firm, sturdy arms around me. My mother stepped back and, scrutinizing me, said, "That dress is loose on you."

I blushed. I was wearing a checked orange and yellow dress that my aunt and I had carefully picked out in a shop near her house. Then my mother quickly went back to talking to the servant in an agitated tone, instructing him about his chores for the day—how much fish to buy, which rooms to clean, and the need for new mosquito repellent.

I was grateful when my sister Pari came over and, taking my hand, led me into her room. We talked incessantly on that afternoon, and it seemed we never stopped. "Mother is too absorbed in too many things to pay much attention to any one of us," she said, attempting to comfort me against my mother's cool greeting. From her intense focus on me, it seemed she had been lonely in the middle of her own family.

So I had to adjust to a new set of parents with very different values from my aunt's. My parents, having lived in Ahvaz and Abadan, cities filled with foreigners employed by the oil refineries, were in some ways Westernized; they did not practice any religion, whereas my aunt was old-fashioned and staunchly religious. I had to learn to live with siblings—two older brothers, two older sisters, and one younger sister. I had to adjust to a new school in the middle of the year and had to try to make new friends.

Our house overlooked a busy square lined by food shops and teahouses. Horse carts were parked in one corner along with taxis. In the morning, Arab women would sit on the sidewalk to sell milk, butter, and cheese, which they kept in large pots set out in front of them. One of the two cinemas in town was on the square. The air was always filled with a variety of sounds— Arabic and Persian spoken by vendors advertising their merchandise, Western music from the cinema, and prayers from the nearby mosques.

Our house had more than a dozen rooms split between two floors. All the children had their rooms upstairs, but there was nothing about the rooms to indicate that they belonged to children. It was as if we were not allowed to be young or to indulge in whimsical or frivolous activities or tastes. My room was next to Pari's, but we often slept together in one of our rooms, talking and confiding in one another in bed. When my aunt visited, she would sleep in my room. In the same way I did as a child, I would keep her up asking her to tell me stories. Legends, fairytales, and the true stories of our neighbor's lives were all told to me by my aunt in the same slow, formal way with beginnings, climaxes, and morals at the end. And all of them were equally riveting, equally believable.

Though we had all that space in the house to move around in, I was always aware of the air somehow being choked—with my father's dominant personality, trying to impose his ideas and thoughts on us, and with my mother always complaining. Her complaints usually had to do with daily aggravations, but sometimes they had to do with my father. I overheard her say to my aunt, on one of her visits, "he's been staying out late at the nightclub with those belly dancers." She cried when my father left on business trips, saying, "I know what he's doing."

My father, though less mocking of my writing than he was of my sister's acting aspirations, was suspicious and afraid of what the written word could do. He occasionally would spy on me. He took away a novel by Maxim Gorky, entitled *The Mother*, that I was reading and tore it into pieces. "Where did you get that Communist filth? I could lose my license if my daughter was caught reading a book like that." In fact, I had bought it from a bookstore which occasionally would smuggle in a book that had been censored or banned. Communism was considered the enemy of the country at the time and was used as a catchall for anything even remotely progressive or liberal. One female teacher in my high school whom I had admired was arrested on charges that she was spreading "Communist" ideas in the school.

At school, I made one close friend. Wearing our gray uniforms, the two of us would walk around the schoolyard. Since obedience, even subservience, to the mostly male teachers was the mode, we were fearful of them. While walking, we would talk obsessively about our plans for escape from the narrow confinement of that town and the life prescribed for us: graduating from high school, marrying someone selected by our parents, and having many children.

"I want to become a writer," I said.

"I want to become a ballet dancer," she said.

Once, a famous Iranian writer whose fiction she and I had avidly read was coming to town. I found out, to my excited amazement, that he would be visiting my father one afternoon to discuss a legal matter. After looking through some of his books, my father promised to let me and my friend Nazan meet him. We started to plan for his visit by each buying a new dress and a copy of his latest novel in which we could ask him to write his autograph.

I read the book twice and some of the passages several times. How could he make these characters so real? When the afternoon finally arrived and we entered the room where the writer was sitting, I felt as if I were going into a magnetic field. Nazan and I sat across from him, and he asked us questions about ourselves, smiling at us in a patronizing way. Then we gave him the books to autograph. As soon as we left the room, Nazan and I opened the books to see what he had written for each of us. I have no memory of what he actually wrote, but recently I wove a story around the incident and how his two autographs, one more complimentary than the other, break up the friendship between the two girls. I titled it "A Poet's Visit," and it was the first story I published in a commercial magazine.

Not long after, I managed to convince my parents to let me go to the United States to study. They agreed, I think, partly because they were afraid that with the degree of restlessness I showed, I would get myself into trouble one way or another. Their decision was made easier since my brothers, in the United States themselves, managed to get a generous scholarship for me which paid for my room, board, and tuition at a small southern women's college. Nazan did a similar thing, following her brothers to England.

The closeness between Pari and me sustained itself throughout the years I was at my parents' house. I saw her graduate from high school, get married to a wealthy man in town, and have a son whom she later had to give up when she got divorced. The custody of the child automatically went to the husband even when, as in my sister's case, the grounds for divorce were his cruelty to her; he put a lit cigarette to her skin, she said.

Our closeness lasted during my early years in the United States. She got married a second time, she confided, mainly to get out of the grip of my parents, who never stopped blaming her for the divorce. Our closeness was ruptured by a tragedy that remains painfully in the background of my life: the beginning of her episodes of manic depression which made communication with her nearly impossible at times. The illness led to a second divorce and has landed her in a mental hospital in Teheran, where she will probably spend at least part of the year perhaps for the rest of her life. During our last conversation, long distance from New York to Teheran, when she was in a period of relative calm and lucidity, she asked me, "Are you still writing? Will you send me the last thing you wrote?"

In college, I withdrew every day for periods of time and wrote. Occasionally, I would mail a piece to Pari and wait eagerly for her response. But I did not think I would make writing my profession. I was eager to be independent and refused to plunge into an occupation that entailed no guarantees of publication or financial support, and so I studied psychology. I met my American husband right after college; now he teaches psychology at a university. Only when at home with a baby was I able to justify spending time daily writing fiction.

My first visit to Iran after twelve years of absence, the feelings that it aroused in me, and my psychological search for a mother was the inspiration for my first published novel, *Foreigner*. The crumbling marriage of my second sister, combined with my own adolescent dreams and desires to escape into a different culture, constituted the core of my second novel, *Married to a Stranger*.

Another reason I am drawn to writing about my past has to do with a desire to bring into the present a reality which is no longer represented in my life here in America. The differences between the Iranian and American cultures are vast; in order to adjust to the American way of life, I have had to suppress much of my own childhood and upbringing without always being conscious of it. Sometimes I wake in the middle of the night with a dis-

orienting feeling that my past has vanished altogether and I am floating un-
anchored. I get out of the bed and begin to write. Then I can see Pari with
her radiant face, wearing a tight red dress that draws the eyes of passersby
to both her, the pretty daughter of a well-known lawyer in town, and me,
intense, shy, wearing a white cotton dress with butterfly designs, and holding onto her arm as we walk across the square. I can see her following a man
into a room of a film studio and myself waiting for her in the reception area;
she comes out, her face all flushed, and tells me, as we get to the street, "He
wanted me to take my clothes off." I am sitting with her at the edge of the
pool in the middle of the courtyard of our house, frogs jumping in and out
of the water, bats darting back and forth under a canopy on the other side,
telling her about something that happened at school. I can see her in a
wedding gown, sitting next to her dark-suited husband among the guests in
the large, brightly decorated salon of our house, her face reflecting a vague
dreaminess and discontent.

I am lying next to my aunt and she is telling me stories. I keep demanding, as she is about to fall asleep, "Tell me another one."

I am coming home from school with other girls, all of us in uniforms,
passing through a bazaar full of food shops, clusters of smoked fish, fresh
dates, and bananas hanging on their doors; through a small park filled with
palm trees and a little cafe where we sat sometimes to have ice cream; then
through narrow, cobble-stoned streets, followed occasionally by boys from
the other high school who would come close and furtively brush their arms
against us or sneak a letter into our hands, expressing a desire to meet us secretly somewhere. When I come home, I am hit by loneliness if Pari is not
there. My mother, remote and agitated, goes from room to room, tries to
put everything in order, or sweats over her cooking in the kitchen, while my
father talks in mysterious tones with a client behind the shut doors of the
large upstairs room he uses as his office. Standing on the balcony with Pari,
we talk and laugh about the boys passing by, whom we know by sight and
have classified as "the handsome but conceited one," "the one who's trying to
imitate Alain Delon," "the one with the tiny eyes and funny-looking head."
Reaching over to the tall palm tree on the street and picking golden, fresh
dates to eat . . . all that becomes a part of me again, though the scene before
me is of Manhattan high-rises, some of their windows still lit at late hours
of the night.

Will I ever run out of steam writing about my past? It seems to me I could
write indefinitely about that period—about my mother, who married at
the age of nine and had ten children (three of them died), and whose oldest
son is only fifteen years younger than herself; about my aunt's suffering with
the two husbands and her yearnings for a child in a culture where a woman's

life is meaningless without children; about various aspects of my sisters' and brothers' lives; about all the girls I grew up with, some of them becoming trapped in bad arranged marriages and some with enough determination to get away to freer worlds. Then I could go back and expand some of those early brief sketches and short stories and bring to them new perspectives I have gained through writing and living longer myself.

There seems to be no end to the material I can draw from. But one question is always with me, haunts me. Would I have become a writer without Pari's encouragement? The question is always followed by painful regret that I have not been able to give her anything as sustaining in return. She, like myself, was always looking for escape from the circumscribed roles set for her as a woman in a culture that so dramatically discriminates against women. In what way do her flights into mental illness correspond to my flights into the fantasy world of fiction? For though I draw from experience, much of what I write still has to be imagined, fabricated, and distorted. When Pari looks at her hand and says, "It's turning black from the lotion you sent me," or when she burns any money she gets hold of, saying, "I can always make more of it," is she trying to say something else?

Mustafa Mirzeler

TURKEY   *Mustafa Mirzeler was born around 1960 in Kiremithane*
 *village on the outskirts of the Taurus mountains in Adana,*
KURDISTAN   *Turkey. He was an apprentice to his father, a well-known*
professional storyteller, who trained him in the Anatolian
oral tradition. After graduation from high school, he went
to Germany as a guest worker, where he worked in a steel
factory. In 1980, he came to the United States and received
a B.A. in sociology from California State University, San
Bernardino. During graduate studies at the University of
Wisconsin, he spent two years researching the African oral

tradition and became an
apprentice to African
storytellers in northern
Ugandan and Kenyan
villages. He received his
Ph.D. from Wisconsin in
anthropology and currently
is visiting assistant profes-
sor at Western Michigan
University.

MY CHILDHOOD MEMORIES AND
THE LEGENDS OF KURDISTAN

Mustafa Mirzeler

 My hometown, Kiremithane, lay at the edge of the cotton-laden plains of Chukurova, in southern Anatolia, Turkey. To the north of Kiremithane, the snowy peaks of the Taurus Mountains rose abruptly on the horizon with dark clouds hovering over them. The river Saricham (the word means yellow pine) descended from the Taurus Mountains flowing through the cotton fields and vineyards in Kiremithane. Although Saricham was called a stream, it was not really a stream, but rather a huge seasonal river. In the spring, it swelled to a muddy flood and flowed like a giant river, scattering foamy mud and caving in the banks along its course. The Saricham stream changed its course every few years, leaving deep gullies here and there that were filled with bramble thickets and thick tall reeds.

In the winter, when the stream swelled, children climbed up the high hills, to watch the frighteningly roaring muddy water, until their heads spun with dizziness. In the summer, Saricham flowed like a thin thread and formed bubbling ponds, which were covered by decomposing vegetation, which reeked. Tortoises stuck their heads from the shrinking muddy ponds and disappeared in the water when they saw children approaching. At the end of the summer, the stream dried up completely along with all the vegetation, except clumps of brambles and thistles. Children herded camels, cows, goats, and sheep in the cracked stream beds. The women gathered cow dung with their children as they sang sorrowful songs.

Kiremithane was a huge village, with a population of about 5,000 people by the late 1960s. More than half of the population were Kurds and the rest were Yoruks (nomadic Turks who lived at the outskirts of the Taurus Mountains), nomadic Arabs, and gypsies. In the summer months, the population of Kiremithane grew, as seasonal workers came from different parts of eastern Anatolia to work in the brick kilns or in the cotton fields. Most of these workers lived with their relatives in Kiremithane in order to save money for a much needed brideprice.

In those days, most men in Kiremithane worked in the brick kilns. Making brick was a traditional occupation of the Kiremithane natives. According to local legends, the art of making bricks was inherited from the people who lived in the area, long before the Ottoman Turks occupied the region. In fact, when the kiln workers dug out the soil to make bricks, they frequently uncovered ancient Roman villages beneath the earth, which had large brick and pottery kilns. In the Turkish language, Kiremithane means the place of brick.

Our home was at the edge of Kiremithane, on the banks of Saricham, next to a huge vineyard. At the edge of the vineyard, stood a lone, huge mulberry tree. In front of our home lay thistle fields, which stretched all the way to the deep gullies created by the shifting courses of Saricham. Amidst the thistle fields stood a ruin of an ancient Roman kiln. At sunset, an owl used to perch on the musty arches of the kiln and cry ominously. Whenever my father heard the sound of the crying owl he cursed it under his breath.

When the evening breeze blew, the thistles rustled, and the field resembled an undulating enormous cloth, decorated with purplish flowers. In the evening, when the darkness settled, the sounds of crickets and frogs coming from the dry stream bed thrummed like the wheels of a huge mill. In those days, my family used to gather, in the evenings, under the grape trellis in front of our home. In the light of the flickering lamp, we would sit around my father, listening to the stories of Kurdish legends. The ruin of the ancient Roman kiln would shine in the silvery moonlight. In the distance, the sounds of sad Kurdish songs could be heard, rising at intervals and mingling with the sounds of howling dogs and braying donkeys.

My father used to talk of old-time Kurdistan. In the days of my adolescent years, he claimed to be ninety years old, although he did not know his actual age, and people spoke of him as the storyteller of the seven villages. As a master storyteller, my father incorporated well-known Kurdish legends into the Anatolian historical tradition known as *destans*, working the images of both traditions of fantasy and reality together, artfully creating rich metaphors in his performances that often moved the members of the audience. During my childhood, it was a storyteller like my father who kept the Kurds and the Turks in the villages in harmony as they created a past that vaguely resembled the official history.

My father used to tell me that he had known the stories and legends for years. He had learned them informally, since the transmission of images of Kurdish oral tradition required no apprenticeship. He had learned his craft by observing the storytellers telling stories, and thus, my father's stories were the amalgam of the lore of all the storytellers he had met. His stories had their roots in the countless legends and local gossips he had heard and in his personal experiences as a child and as a mature man. He was a skillful storyteller with an extraordinary ability to project the images of tradition and the images of his memory, which he managed to suggest were reflections of people's thoughts, emotions, and their past all at once.

He would employ images from the Kurdish, Turkish, and many other Anatolian oral traditions, in order to create the picture of a well-balanced society. Like many other storytellers of his time, his basic aesthetic tools consisted of the ancient mythic images, his rich personal experiences, and his ability to weave these two together in each performance into new combinations. At each performance, he gave the images new interpretations.

As my father told stories, he artfully engaged members of the audience in dialogue and got them involved with the interpretation of the images. This way, the members of the audience became rhythmically and emotionally involved with his performances. The members of the audience were familiar with his stories since they had heard them many times, but they knew that he would develop the theme differently each time.

People used to call my father Blind Memed, since he had cross-eyes. Yet his cross-eyes were as sharp as a hawk's. He was brown with a thick white beard and a mustache, like most Kurds. His broad shoulders were weakened, and his back was slightly hunched. But in spite of his old age, he never gave up telling stories, singing sad Kurdish songs, or telling about sad love stories of the Kurdish legends, and the Kurdish tribal feuds, to the people in the villages on the banks of Saricham and on the slopes of the Taurus Mountains. At the end of each story and song, people were often in tears, and they would offer him flour, barley, wheat, or money for his performances.

My father disdained the sedentary life in the villages. He longed for the old Kurdish nomadic way of life: moving to the mountains during the summers and living in the villages during the winters. Perhaps for this reason, he often traveled to the distant Kurdish villages on the slopes of the Taurus Mountains, to tell stories. I often went along and helped him carry his bag. Sometimes on the road, he would remember his childhood, would talk of his own village at the foot of Mount Suphan in eastern Turkey, and would tell me how his own father used to gallop off to distant villages and bring back the scents of pine and thyme.

As we walked together on the dusty roads, my father would begin to narrate his childhood memories. "In Kurdistan," he would say, and once started, he would never stop talking. He would go on: "Eagles made their nests at the rocky peaks of Mount Suphan, and the brigands and the timid gazelles wondered on its slopes. When the spring came, the bare rocky slopes of Mount Suphan used to be covered with myrtle and hyacinth. The green headed cranes used to rise into the sky as we slowly climbed with our sheep and donkeys on the narrow paths towards the high peaks. It was wonderful when our tribe slowly migrated to the mountains. In summers, we used to pitch our tents on the rocky highlands, near the cliffs. I remember my mother had long black hair, and she wore yellow and green long silk garments with a red *kusshak* cloth tied around her waist. She used to churn milk in our tent, in a goatskin bag.

"At the beginning of autumn, we would return to the plains, to our villages. There the grass used to grow so thick that even a snake could not move through it. We used to cut the grass, dry it, and stack it to use as fodder when winter came. In the winter, it was so cold we used to stay in our adobe homes that were partially buried under the ground. Everywhere the ground was covered with knee-high snow. At night, the sounds of hungry wolves and bears would mingle with the sounds of howling blizzards."

"I remember," my father would continue. My father used to tell us about the great struggle against the Ottomans, when the Ottomans defeated Ubeyidullah, the great Kurdish sheik. Ubeyidellah used to go from village to village trying to mobilize the young Kurds to refuse to fight in Yemen. But after the defeat of Ubeyidellah my father was one of the young Kurds who ended up going to Yemen after all. My father stayed in Yemen for fourteen years and he married a Yemenite woman. This was long before he married my mother. My father had children in Yemen, but the Ottoman Pasha forced him and many other soldiers to abandon their wives and children and return to Kurdistan. My father kept a handful of soil which he brought from Yemen and he used to tell us that we should sprinkle that soil on his grave after he was dead. In Yemen he had learned to speak Arabic, and he used to sing Yemenite songs for us. He told us about our brothers and sisters in Yemen whom we had never met.

Often, as my father and I walked along, my father would shift from his memories of his father, to his memories of Sheikh Said, the well-known Kurdish sheik. "I was a young boy during the Sheikh Said rebellion," he would say, "and I remember Sheikh Said's resistance against the Turkish government. The Turkish government captured Sheikh Said, and carried him off. Then the Turkish soldiers scattered people in the Kurdish villages, burning their homes and raping women. The day they captured Sheikh Said, a dark cloud descended from Mount Suphan and moved toward Mush, the

Kurdish city in eastern Turkey. Kurdish women tore their clothes and pulled their hair, beating on their chests, ululating and crying at the same time. Many young men went to the mountains, became brigands, and fought the Turkish soldiers. During those upheavals, my father disappeared and we never saw him again."

At this point my father's cross-eyes would fill with tears, and, in his thick and powerful voice, he would launch into the famous sorrowful song, which Kurdish women sang for Sheikh Said at the time of his capture.

> *There is no cloud in the sky, what is this smoke?*
> *There is no death in the neighborhood, what is this lamentation?*
> *Here is Mush and its road ascends*
> *Why are those who are gone to Yemen not returning! What is the matter?*

My father would then tell me again about how he walked with his brothers and sisters all the way from Mount Suphan to Chukurova in southern Turkey and then settled down in the village of Kiremithane at the outskirts of the Taurus Mountains. "On our way," he would say, "the Kurds died like flies in the snow from the cold. Many of us were barefoot and we didn't have anything to eat. The Turkish soldiers roamed the roads, through the villages, slaughtering the Armenians like sheep, raping women, chasing the Kurds, burning their villages. We lost my mother and two of my older sisters on the road. We do not know what happened to them. My older brother Suleyman carried Dilshah, our younger sister, on his back. Dilshah was very young. She cried for my mother and my sisters until she died from crying. We had to abandon her dead body to the wolves and vultures on the snow-ridden road and resume our walk. The Turkish government had soldiers on the mountain roads to keep us from returning to Kurdistan. We had to move on toward Chukurova.

"Only I and my older brothers Suleyman and Ahmed reached Chukurovo, and we settled in the village of Kiremithane, on the banks of Saricham, working in the brick-kilns. There was nothing in Kiremithane then except thistle fields, thick reeds, and bulrush beds. A few vineyards stood near the banks of the stream. As the slopes of the Taurus mountains were slowly filled with people like us, dislocated Kurds, we could no longer live a nomadic life; we were bound to the soil. We clung to our newly found land, and slowly began to mix with the Turkish villagers. Our customs changed. We went to the same mosques and sat in the same coffee houses with the Turks."

Once my father had begun to talk about Kurdistan and the legends of the mountains, he would go on for hours. He would continue: "When I was a boy, I actually saw Sheikh Said, the great sheik of the Kurdish revolt against the Turks." He was very proud of Sheikh Said. Listening to my father's stories made the time go quickly, and we were able to travel many miles without getting tired.

   When we arrived in a village, young men would lead us to a village guest house, owned by the *aghas* (rich land owners).

These guest houses were usually of sun-dried brick and plastered with mud mixed with chaff and cut straw. They were painted with chalk, like all the other village houses. The roofs had layers of thick reeds resting on top of thick poles laid wall to wall. The reeds then were plastered with thick layers of mud mixed with chaff and straw. Sometimes birds built nests between the roof poles, near the entrance, and layers of bird droppings sometimes covered the thresholds of the guest house. A guest house usually also had a kitchen and a large living room cum bedroom, where guests could sleep.

The hearth lay at the end of the living room where the fire leaped and disappeared up the mud-plastered chimney. The white walls were often covered with sour-cherry color tapestries. Some depicted young maidens combing their long black hair under a tree near a flowing silvery spring. Others showed a group of women with long black hair and beautiful large black eyes, who sat on the divans by a fountain or sat in the middle of a garden filled with beautiful flowers, smoking a *narghile*, or water pipe.

Another favorite subject was that of a maiden who sat on a beautiful ebony horse, holding on to a handsome young man, who brandished a gun. In this particular tapestry, the background was a desert landscape in which the galloping horse cast a long dark shadow on the pebbly earth under the silvery light of the full moon.

In the guest house kitchen was a large fire place, the hearth stones blackened with smoke. Copper pots and pans polished with tin hung on the walls and a spoon-holder of white cloth embroidered with birds and flowers hung near the fire place. It was filled with wooden spoons. Large round copper trays polished with tin stood against the walls.

   The *ashik*, or minstrel, was usually a handsome young man who played the *saz*, an Anatolian string instrument played by plucking. The ashik sang in a beautiful vibrant voice. Ashiks usually traveled from distant villages, and they frequently visited the villages on the banks of Saricham, or the villages on the slopes of the Taurus Mountains. They also traveled as far as the villages on the shores of the Mediterranean sea, near the ancient city of Tarsus. Sometimes the ashiks formed groups and traveled together. They usually never held traditional jobs.

Whenever a well-known ashik came to the villages on the slopes of the Taurus Mountains, the villagers sent messages to a storyteller known as *destanci* (narrator of tribal histories and legends), such as my father, to join the ashik with his stories.

After my father had been introduced to the ashik in the village guest house, my father and the ashik talked about the traditional history of the villages and about the famous Kurdish and Turkish legends. The legends were usually about the local young men, who had armed themselves and had taken refuge in the mountains to fight against the Ottoman and Turkish government or against the exploitation of the aghas. Often times the brigands would die in the process of fighting, and they would become local legends, and their life stories would become a part of the local oral tradition. When my father and I were ushered into the guest house, we would meet the ashik who sang songs to accompany the storytellers.

When a storyteller and an ashik went to a village, the agha allocated one of his wives, some of his daughters, or a few village women to cook for the performers. An adolescent boy usually helped the women in the kitchen to cook, wash dishes, and serve the guests, and this job fell to me whenever I went to the villages with my father.

During performances, the guest house kitchen was always filled with women of all ages. The older Kurdish women sat at the threshold between the kitchen and the living room, eagerly waiting for my father to tell the legends of Kurdistan. But the maidens usually sat back near the fire place, waiting to catch a glimpse of the young minstrel to listen to his songs, and perhaps take a peek at young men of the village who sat in the living room with the minstrel and my father, the storyteller.

When the women had finished cooking, a few of the maidens and a few adolescent boys, including myself, would carry the food in on large round copper trays and place it at the center of the living room. The maidens and the young men in the guest house, including the ashik, would always exchange quick glances. Back in the kitchen, the maidens would discuss the ashik, and the other young men. If the descriptions interested certain maidens, these young women would volunteer to help pick up the empty trays (to get another look). But the maidens would always eat in the kitchen with the rest of the women, while the tea steeped in a large tea-pot on the three stones.

Tea was followed by general conversation. The villagers often asked the ashik and the storyteller personal questions, and asked about maidens in their villages. Then the ashik would begin, usually by recounting a dream about a beautiful maiden. Then came songs praising the dark locks and the full pink cheeks of the maiden in the dream.

The ashik's dreams always seemed to take place during the day, mostly while the ashik napped under the cool shade of a mulberry tree, near a clear spring. The maiden who appeared in the dream of the ashik was usually described as having bright large black eyes, and dark locks flowing out from her head scarf. In the dream, the maiden appeared on an errand to fetch water from a well or spring. In the background, gazelles and birds drank water too, but timidly.

The ashik would have dreamed different versions of the same dream, he said, until he fell in love with the girl in the dream. When this happened, the audience said that the fire of love had entered into the heart of the ashik. The ashik thus began to sing sorrowful songs about the maiden in the dream. A typical song might be as follows:

> *I passed by that abandoned vineyard at dusk*
> *My dark-locked beloved was fetching water from that silvery spring*
> *Red roses blossomed on her cheek.*
>
> *The gazelles gazed at her wide black eyes with envy*
> *She wore a yellow Kurdish garment with red silk around her*
> *narrow waist*
> *Oh my beloved, you moved like a poplar tree.*
>
> *Oh my beloved do not look at my smiling eyes*
> *Put your hands on my burning heart*
> *And pour your water on the embers in my heart.*

As the ashik continued to play his saz and sing this kind of song tears would begin to trickle down his face. The audience, too, would be so moved that they, too, would shed tears as they smoked their cigarettes. Soon the thick clouds of the cigarette smoke filled the room, and streaks of tears glistened on people's faces as the flames in the hearth leaped and disappeared in the chimney. About this time a maiden with a vibrant voice would begin to sing from the kitchen, constructing her song spontaneously by combining verses of well-known local songs, singing in response to the ashik.

> *Oh the beloved of the unknown maiden*
> *I wish I were the one you dreamed of*
>
> *May Allah soften the heart of my cruel father*
> *I wish I were the one you glimpsed*
>
> *I wish I could dive in the ponds of that spring like a green duck*
> *I will not forget you, my beloved poplar*
>
> *The water of Muhammad flows clear*
> *And I will glide on the gleaming spring in that dream*

When the maiden stopped singing, everyone in the room would fall silent, until the trembling voice of the ashik broke the silence, asking the people if they had seen the maiden which he had described in his songs. Older men sitting near the hearth usually responded to the minstrel emphatically, saying, "Truly, Allah has dropped the embers of love into your heart, lad. May Allah be with you. May that maiden appear on your way. Unfortunately, the maiden you described does not live in this village. If she did, by the love of Allah, we would take you to that maiden's home, and talk to her father on your behalf." The rest of the members of the audience would add, almost in chorus, "May Allah be our witness, the old man told you the truth. There is no such a maiden in this village. But you might want to go to Degirmenci village near the headwaters of Saricham stream on the upper slopes of the Taurus Mountain. People say that they have seen many young maidens in that village which fit your description."

After such exchanges between the ashik and the members of the audience, the ashik would go to the corner with the younger men of his age. I would help the maidens serve tea to the audience, and the performers. Another young man would replenish the fire in the hearth.

After the tea, my father would move toward the spot where the ashik had sat. He would praise the ashik's poetry and then clear his throat before beginning his own performance. His stories usually mirrored the ashik's lyric poetry and the songs of the maiden in the kitchen, and he would combine it all with images from old Kurdish legends. He often told a story about a Kurdish hero known as Ahmedo and his lover Khadija. The words flowed from his mouth, like wind blowing from Kurdistan.

He usually began with a description of Mount Suphan and the Kurdish nomadic tribes moving on its narrow paths toward the cool peaks where eagles built their nests. Then came a beautiful song which he sang with trembling lips as tears flowed down his cheeks toward his white beard:

> *Fly, green headed cranes, fly*—
> *Fly to your home on the headwaters of cool springs on Mount Suphan*
>
> *Fly, green headed cranes, fly*—
> *Fly to the cliffs of Mount Suphan and greet the wild hyacinths and narcissus*

The message of the story of Ahmedo was always complex, one generated by my father's words, by the tone of his voice, and by the artistic movements of his body. Even though the story would slightly change in front of different audiences, the plot of the story remained the same. The characters moved from conflict to resolution, following the familiar patterns established by the traditional and contemporary images.

When my father told this story, he managed to transport the members of the audience to that fabulous land, by combining the images of the ashik's song, the images on the tapestries in the room, the images of the landscape around the Taurus Mountains, and the ancient images of the Kurdish oral tradition. Through this artistic fusion of images, he linked the contemporary world in the southern Anatolian villages with the grandly mythicized past in Kurdistan, thus transforming the unknown images and patterns into familiar ones.

For instance, in his innovative performances, he would transform the image of Saricham into the image of a clear flowing spring on the slopes of Mount Suphan, or to the waters of the legendary Euphrates river. He would artfully transform the image of the ancient Roman ruin in front of our home into an old castle ruin. The owl that perched itself on the ruin became an eagle who aided Ahmedo on the peaks of Mount Suphan. Or he would transform the image of the thistle fields in front of our home into the undulating garment of Khadija, the lover of Ahmedo, when she rode on the ebony horse with Ahmedo under the silvery moonlight. This was like the picture on the tapestry in the guest house where we sat listening to the story. The physical attributes of Ahmedo would match those of the ashik in the room, and the image of Khadija, lover of Ahmedo, would mirror the maiden that the ashik had dreamed about. The mulberry tree which appeared in the story of Ahmedo would be like the mulberry tree in front of our home, which stretched like an umbrella near the banks of Saricham.

My father would continue the story of Ahmedo until morning. The flames in the hearth would die out except a few embers beneath the ashes. As morning approached, the cocks crowed, the dogs howled, and the donkeys brayed. The kerosene in the lamp ran out from burning all night, and the lamp flickered, casting a dimmer light. The pine trees rustled in the morning winds and the mulberry trees murmured in the darkness in front of the guest house. The members of the audience yawned and stretched themselves, and dispersed one by one, leaving me, my father, and the ashik alone. After everybody left, we fell asleep, covering ourselves with heavy quilted blankets.

Leila Abouzeid

MOROCCO *Leila Abouzeid was born in 1950 in El Ksiba in the Middle Atlas region of Morocco. She was educated first in Rabat and then in England and the United States. **Year of the Elephant,** the English translation of her first novel, **Am al-Fil,** was published in 1989 and has been translated into Hebrew and Urdu. **Return to Childhood,** her memoir, appeared in 1998, and her most recent novel, **Last Chapter,** was published in English in 2000.*

LEILA ABOUZEID, RIGHT

RETURN TO CHILDHOOD

Leila Abouzeid

 My earliest memory is of a bus trip. We were on our way from
Sefrou, my mother's home town, to El Ksiba, a Berber village
in the heart of the Middle Atlas where my father, Ahmed
Bouzid, worked as an interpreter for the French. It was on
that bus trip that I first began to understand that my father
was involved in political activities, activities that were dangerous for us, his family.

We had gotten off the intercity bus between Fez and
Marrakech and were waiting for the El Ksiba bus, at the corner of a smaller road that ascends the Middle Atlas mountains. The driver's assistant brought our luggage down from
the roof. The bus resumed its journey. My mother sat down
on the ground and put my sister Naima on her lap. My older
sister Fatiha sat next to her while my youngest uncle, Sidi
Mohammed, lifted the pieces of our luggage and placed them
in front of her.

As with all our trips to Sefrou, my mother was returning
loaded with brass cooking pots, wood washing basins, wood
trays, braziers, and short brooms. She would say, when she
was in a good mood, "I buy useful things to have near me
when I need them." She was convinced that in El Ksiba she
was living in the wilderness. But when she was upset, she
would criticize herself and say, "Smart women buy gold, but
I buy pots."

A truck appeared on the main road from the opposite direction and turned toward El Ksiba. My uncle waved and
walked over to it while my mother shouted, "Say, you are Si
Hmed Bouzid's brother-in-law."

The driver stopped and looked down. "I only have one place," he said. "The truck is full."

"Nobody else but me needs a lift," said my uncle. "I want to go to El Ksiba to tell my brother-in-law, Si Hmed Bouzid, that we've arrived."

"Get in, then," said the driver.

My uncle walked around the truck and climbed into the passenger's seat. The truck began to move. The sound of its engine changed, grew distant, and finally faded away. Silence prevailed, a mountain silence offset by the cry of a sheep and a distant voice answering a call in Berber. Refreshed by the mountain air, I left my mother and sisters by the El Ksiba sign and wandered along the side of the road beside the wild *boubal*, with its soft yellow corn wrapped in its leaves. I remember the peace of that place, for of course I did not know then what that day was to bring to my family.

We were three girls with our mother by that sign that day, and if Khadija had not been dead we would have been four. Khadija had died of measles in Rabat, where we had lived for eight months. During that time, the *Nasara*, the French Christians for whom my father worked, allowed him to enroll at the Institut des Hautes Etudes, which was located in the green-domed building that now harbors the Moroccan Faculté des Lettres et des Sciences Humaines.

We had lived in one of two apartments on the ground floor of a building across the road from Moulay Youssef Hospital. Our next-door neighbors were Jmia and her husband, a black Moroccan couple. They shared their apartment with a poor French family whose father was a caretaker in the nearby Christian graveyard. Every time my mother sent me on an errand to Jmia, I found the Frenchwoman sitting on a chair in the courtyard in front of her room mending socks with a sewing basket on a table in front of her. I cannot remember her in any other way. By contrast, my image of Jmia is that of a slim, tall, very black woman wearing a Moroccan dress with her head wrapped in a scarf.

That was the apartment where Khadija died and Naima was born. Khadija died before she could talk. She was probably no more than two years old. Once when she got lost a policeman had asked her, "Who are you?"

"Me," she had replied.

"And who is your father?"

"Ba," she had answered.

One day soon after Khadija died, my father came home and found my mother crying. "What's the matter?" he asked.

"It's Jmia," she answered. "Here I have lost my baby and that woman still puts rouge on her cheeks."

"Suppose she does, who's going to see it anyway?" he retorted.

My mother told that story with a smile every time she spoke of Jmia and always concluded it this way: "She was a great neighbor, may God bless her soul if she is dead and mention her with good words if she is alive. She stood by me at the time of Khadija's death, but I wish that she had not put rouge on her cheeks."

Did I think of Khadija that day, by that road sign? I am certain I did, because it had become my habit to say, "If Khadija had not died, she'd be with us now," or, "If Khadija had not died, she'd be three now." I had not forgotten her and still haven't. To this day, every time I drive by La'lou graveyard, where we buried her, I look at the gate and say, "May God bless your soul, Khadija."

Only a few days ago, I had Naima's two daughters with me, and I slowed the car down and told them, "See that gate there? To the right is the grave of a little sister we had. Her name was Khadija. She died the same year your mother was born. Ask God to bless her soul."

Sarrah asked, "Why?"

"Because He answers children's prayers."

"Why?"

"Because He loves them."

And if I still remember her now, I must have thought of her that day, by that road sign, less than a year after her death.

We heard a bus coming. It made a turn toward El Ksiba, reached the sign, and stopped. The driver's assistant jumped down and came over to my mother. He squatted beside her and told her something. She began slapping her thighs and rubbing her palms together and saying in a tragic tone, "O my empty house! O my mother!"

The man said, "Stay here until I return. I'm going with the mail to El Ksiba and I'll be right back." He got on the bus by the back door. It resumed its monotonous roar and disappeared up the road.

Then my mother told us, "The Nasara have put your father in prison. Not because he did anything bad, but because he is a nationalist. *Nationalist* means someone who wants the Nasara to get out of our country, and that's honorable." But her moaning disturbed me much more than the news. It was difficult not to think of prison as something bad, since it made her lament and moan.

In El Ksiba, where we lived after leaving Rabat, certain inmates of the local prison were assigned to us by the French administration to do errands in the village. Those prisoners had been arrested for minor infractions of the law; most had injured somebody or stolen something. One had been arrested because he did not salute the French Contrôleur Général when he passed him on the street. One day while still serving his sentence, he was taking the dough for our bread to the village bakery when he met the same Frenchman riding his horse. He put the breadboard on the ground and saluted him with both hands. The Frenchman asked, "Two salutes? Why?"

"One is for you and one is for the horse," answered the inmate.

Every time my mother heard that story, she would say, "The poor man must have told himself, 'If he could put me in jail because I did not salute him, he might increase my punishment if I don't salute his horse.'" Then she would add, in a sad tone, "It is the law of the powerful. The law of the jungle."

And now, I thought, she says that jail is honorable! When the bus returned, Belaid the assistant helped us get on and we went back in the direction from which we had just come. At Zaouit Cheikh, we got off and Belaid took us to his house, but we soon left it and took another bus to my father's hometown of Béni Mellal. There we found my paternal grandfather's house crowded with people. Some of them began to cry when they saw us, and my grandmother started beating her breast.

Then my uncle Sidi Mohammed entered carrying a brass candlestick, and my mother asked, "What's that?"

"That's all they left you. It was behind a door and they did not see it."

She said, "Who do you mean 'they'?"

"Your father-in-law and his son Ma'ti."

"Oh no!" she cried.

"Yes," he answered.

That day marked the beginning of our troubles, which my mother would describe in detail over and over again, to the end of her days. But her perceptions were different from mine, for I was a child.

In my paternal grandfather's house in Béni Mellal, there were Bedouin blankets, rugs and mats, earthen pots and jars, trunks, and looms set in the rooms. My grandfather was always sitting in the courtyard with a brass tea tray in front of him and a wooden sugar box next to him.

By contrast, in my maternal grandfather's house in Sefrou there were banquettes, cushions stuffed with wool, pillows in velvet cases bordered with silk trimming, fine curtains, beds, carved wooden cabinets, storage spaces and shelves displaying antique Fez bowls. At that fine house in the city they mocked my father's family. They said, "Meat is all they eat." "One cone of sugar a day." "All they care for is their stomachs and penises," implying that all the men of my father's family were interested only in eating and having sex.

But at my paternal grandfather's house, they mocked my mother's family for their excessive concern with material things. They said, "City dwellers live surrounded by tiles and marble, and they are avaricious and stingy. Their possessions are so dear to their hearts that there is not a thing that costs money for which they would not affectionately use the diminutive form— they even say, 'the little egg, the little bread.' And they are reluctant to part with anything." Then my grandfather would add, "As for me, sir, I will eat and drink whatever I like, no matter what the cost, for tomorrow I may die."

Every time my grandfather said that, he followed it with his story about the Fassi, the merchant from Fez, which he told while leaning on a large pillow in the courtyard. "My friends and I went to Fez and bought all our merchandise from that Fassi, and afterward he invited us to lunch. So we went. We got to his house and found that it had a really impressive door. Inside were tiles up to the ceiling and carvings and pillars. There were mattresses stuffed with wool so high that one needed help to climb up and sit on them, and also velvet and embroidered cushions. So, anyway, the Fassi clapped his hands and a black maid came with the hand-washing basin and kettle; then she placed the table in front of us and brought the food. It was only some salads and some bowls of ground meat and eggs. When we left we were still hungry. So I stopped, sir, by the butcher, bought a leg of lamb, took it to the caravansary and cut it up myself, and my friends made a charcoal fire and we grilled the meat and had lunch."

Another thing I remember from that day at my paternal grandfather's house in Béni Mellal, in addition to the crowd and the crying, was Kabboura, the sister of my paternal Uncle Said's wife. On that day Kabboura insulted my mother. I had heard that my paternal grandmother had wanted my father to marry Kabboura, but when he refused and married my mother instead, Kabboura married his best friend, a carpenter who played the lute. After Kabboura revealed her animosity toward my mother that day in my grandfather's house, my mother would often compliment herself with respect to Kabboura, saying, "She should be grateful to me! I'm the one who taught her how to conserve peppers and cook lemon chicken."

The next thing I remember from that visit is that my mother, my sisters, my maternal uncle Bouazza, and I were in a room locked from the inside and a huge woman, not Kabboura, was banging on the ironwork of the window. Still another strong image is my mother, my sisters, my uncle, and I sitting by a thorny hedge surrounding an orchard opposite my grandfather's house, and my cousin Aicha, who was my age, peeping at us with contempt from the doorway, eating a slice of melon, and then throwing the rind toward the hedge.

El Ksiba is the diminutive of Al Kasaba ("the citadel"), the Arab name for a Berber village in the heart of the Middle Atlas. One gets there from the Tadla Plain after a difficult ride past houses built of plastered earth, situated among oak trees and oleanders growing along the sides of a little river. After seven kilometers, the road splits in two. One fork goes to the village; the other has a low white wall along the road that in the years before Independence announced the administrative quarter where the French worked and lived in luxurious mansions. Moroccan soldiers' families also lived in that quarter, in more modest houses, all alike, inside the whitewashed walls of a fort. The walls also enclosed two larger, better houses for the two Moroccan civil servants employed by the French. We had lived in one of these houses.

Past the fort was the administration building, followed by the Frenchmen's houses, all in a row. Then the road went on up to the village of Imilchil, running parallel to the river and through what was then a summer resort reserved for the French. The village center lay two kilometers from the administrative quarter beyond a small pine forest, past the administration's vegetable and fruit garden, and past the school and the hospital.

It was to the administrative quarter that my uncle, Sidi Mohammed, had gone that day to inform my father of our arrival. I do not know how my father learned Berber, because he was from Béni Mellal, which is an Arab town. The name is a distortion of Béni Hilal, the name of the primitive Bedouin tribe that achieved fame by migrating from Arabia to North Africa in the twelfth century. The historian Ibn-Khaldun was referring to the Beni Hilal's anti-urban tendency when he wrote his well-known words: "Whenever something is arabicized, it is destroyed."

My father's family was notable for their social status, not their wealth. A Bedouin's social status, however, was traditionally determined by his ability to consume and offer food, not by his possessions, and those practices resulted in the dissipation of the family's financial resources. Besides, the necessity to be always on the move prevented the Bedouin from amassing many possessions and from leaving any permanent architectural heritage.

My paternal grandfather, Hammadi Bouzid, was a well-traveled tradesman, but he was not rich. Surprisingly, however, he owned his own house. He had two wives, the younger of whom was my father's mother, Khdija. She was a gorgeous, fair-skinned Berber. My grandfather had brought her home from one of his business trips. However, as soon as I became aware of things around me, it became clear to me that she spoke Arabic with a local accent, and nothing about her denoted her Berber origin except her fair skin and the tattoos on her cheeks. So she could not possibly have been the one who had taught Berber to my father.

My father had entered school by order of the central government and was the only educated member of his family. This is how my mother told the story: "The local district officer came and took him. He was the eldest of his mother's three boys, the one who looked most like her and the one whom she preferred. People said in those days, 'The Nasara are going to teach their language to our children and turn them to their religion.' Women advised her to give him an herb to make him have a fever when they came to take him."

"But what happened to those who refused to send their children to school?" I persisted.

"They went to prison."

So my grandmother had given my father that herb and carried him on her back, covering him so he would sweat, and his face would turn red. But they came and took him anyway.

My father was smart, but the French authorities allowed him to study only until he finished primary school. Then they appointed him as an interpreter in the town of Moulay Ali Shrif, far away. There he met Driss, the carpenter of the French administration. My father admired the life of city girls and asked Driss to find him a wife in his hometown, the city of Sefrou. The result of this search was Driss' sister-in-law Fatma— or Fettouma, as she was called, my mother. It is extraordinary that a family in Sefrou would even consider such a match, because that town had a refined Andalusian culture, and its people, like all people of Andalusian origin, were full of chauvinism. They hated outsiders and would never marry their daughters to them, especially if they were Berbers or country people. Yes, my father was educated and yes, he had a good position, but he was an outsider and a country man. The reason they agreed to permit their daughter to marry him was that she was already divorced and had a baby girl. Later, whenever my father brought her trouble and unhappiness she would say, "May God punish him who matched me with you." She meant Driss, of course, my Aunt Khnata's husband.

My father married my mother and took her to live in Moulay Ali Shrif, but he soon was transferred to El Ksiba and they moved there. As time went by she would often say, "He was a good man in Moulay Ali Shrif, the land of *baraka* and prayer, where women could not be seen anywhere and when you did see them they were covered from head to foot as in Hijaz. But he changed when he came here to this den of vice that does not know God."

And that was only the beginning of our troubles. During the next three years, we were forced to move several times because of my father's political activities, his nationalism. My mother struggled to support both him and us until 1956. That was the date for which my father fought hard, the date Morocco achieved its independence from France.

EGYPT *Randa Abou-Bakr*

Randa Abou-Bakr was born in Cairo in 1966. She received her Ph.D. in comparative literature from Cairo University in 1998 and currently is a lecturer at the Department of English, the School of Humanities, Cairo University. Her research interests include comparative literature, modern and contemporary Arabic, English, and African poetry and literary translation.

MUSIC AND I

Randa Abou-Bakr

 I have always secretly wondered at my intense passion for
music and have always believed that, somehow, there was an
unknown influence behind this overwhelming fascination
with melody. Since there were absolutely no musical talents
in my immediate family, it seemed that this must be some
sort of heredity, a thing inherited from one of my great-
grandfathers, which in me turned into a serious compulsion.
Yet, having given the matter serious thought, I have come
to realize that my passion for music could be the outcome
of a combination of very small and seemingly insignificant
factors.

For Arabs and Egyptians, music is an essential part of our
cultural and emotional makeup. Yet if you ask most people
in Egypt, I am sure they will appear to be only dimly aware
of the influence of music on them. They would probably
not want to admit that music has such a great place in their
consciousness, and even perhaps not see that it exists in their
psychological constitution as a people. The very fact that we
are only half-conscious of that in itself testifies to the extent
of the very powerful penetration of music into our sensibilities. It might also have to do with our conception of the
term "music," which differs in many respects from that in
the West. Our musical heritage mainly combines words to
melody so that it is not as common to speak of "music" as
such but of "songs" or "singing," which usually fall under
several classifications (short or long, using a local dialect or
classical Arabic, using purely Egyptian rhythms or combining Arab with Turkish ones, and so on). Thus, the word
combines two major branches of art in one: melody or pure

"music" and poetry, which are the lyrics, whether in classical Arabic or in a local dialect. The Western conception of music, mainly in Europe, seems to differ from ours in the Arab world. In addition to there being an independent concept of "pure" music, the Western appreciation of music has always seemed to me to be class-based. My European friends usually approach classical music in a radically different way from the way they deal with, or even talk about, other kinds of music. Even within the modern age, they view various kinds of music as belonging to different categories, with the audience playing an important part in their perception of each kind.

In the history of Arab music, no such thing exists. The heritage of our music springs from one source and is appreciated by all classes. In recent years other types of music have emerged, but all are still related to their original source; and because Arab music usually matches lyrics to tunes, this makes music a companion for people wherever they go and whatever they do. You do not need to go to a concert to listen to a symphony, nor take the music with you in the form of a record or a tape. Rather, you carry the music inside of you and become the performer whenever you please: you sing to yourself or to your friends while you are carrying on your daily activities and even while you work. People in the Arab world are all singers and performers of melody. You do not need any equipment to listen to your favorite piece of music; in a minute you can be the singer and entertain yourself or the people around you.

Perhaps this was overdone in our household. As early as I can remember, I used to hear my parents sing—to themselves most of the time. My father would also sing to us some songs from his hometown in southern Egypt. Though the dialect would often sound strange to me, I would be fascinated by the rhythm and the unmistakably sad melody, combining both melancholy and pride: a curious combination in most Egyptian folk songs. This was in addition to the rhyme, which under no circumstances should be broken, so that the listener is always challenged with anticipation of the next rhyming word that would complete the meaning of the line.

My mother, a great admirer of Om Kolthoum, the legend of Arab singing for almost a century, would always play her songs at home or sing them to us when we were very young. This opened up a world of splendor to me. As a four-year-old, I knew some of Om Kolthoum's long odes in classical Arabic by heart and would delight in singing them, not because anybody wanted me to but because they were familiar to me from hearing my mother sing them at home. The unfamiliar classical Arabic diction, and the often sophisticated sentiments, usually escaped me, but I remember finding a mysterious pleasure in learning those melodious words and pretending I understood.

Because I was extremely shy as a little girl, I never attempted to sing in public or even to a small audience and always thanked God that my parents never asked me to do so as some of my friends' parents did. While at school, I would feel miserably embarrassed during music classes, when the teacher asked us to sing—even in chorus. I would sing to myself, but not to anybody else. Yet it was at school, especially in primary school, that I got closer to musical instruments and soon became a principal member of the school's band, the accordion being my favorite instrument. This did not, however, stop me from trying my hand at other instruments like the drums and the piano.

This life of musical pleasure did not go on for long. In junior high school, my interest in music started to wane. This wane in interest was strengthened by or, rather, was partly the outcome of the fact that my new school did not have a large music room like the primary school, nor was it known for an interest in musical activities. The new school was more "academically inclined." This must have coincided with my own temperamental change as an adolescent. At that time I considered my interest in music as something belonging to "childhood" and thought it should be spurned by the more adult me! I was also getting a reputation for being a "nerd," which, in our part of the world, usually does not fit in with interest in "nonacademic" activities. Though my interest in playing music weakened in adolescence, I found myself more and more inclined towards listening to music. Om Kolthoum became an all-encompassing passion, as I was now able to appreciate more fully the depths of meaning in her songs. At the age of fourteen, I could have been safely termed an Om Kolthoum addict, much to the alarm of those around me, who thought I was still young for such a strong fascination.

My adoration for Om Kolthoum, who had some of the most difficult and also the most eloquent poems of the Arabic language put to music and then sang them, must have also been strengthened by my growing interest in classical Arabic poetry. During my early years in secondary school, I discovered I had fallen in love with the Arabic language—with Arabic poetry in particular. Since that time I have maintained a steady adoration for both. The rhythms of classical Arabic poetry fascinated me and I found in them an impressive kind of music equal to that which drew me to songs. At that time I knew almost nothing about English poetry, which was introduced to us in the final year of high school. That was to be a discovery of yet another kind of music which I was to like very much, yet not as passionately as the music of Arabic poetry.

At that time, in the late 1970s, I had also taken up the veil; this was an unsolicited decision, which I took in spite of the objection of my parents, who thought it was a dangerous step that could link me up with disreputable Islamic groups. The late 1970s in Egypt witnessed the birth of the so-called Islamic Movement and the resulting political violence that followed from its confrontations with the government. Though by that time the attitude of the government was not yet declared, ordinary people waited with vague apprehension for the outbreak of such a confrontation. Because the veil was not common at that time, it was easily linked with other manifestations of the emergent movement and was labeled "extremist." As the government started to lash out at members of the Islamic Movement, there was fear, which I saw at the time as totally unjustified, that veiled girls would be subject to persecution and even imprisonment. Though I took the veil as a purely religious gesture that had nothing to do with politics or the ideology of the Islamic Movement, my parents were concerned about the symbolic meaning of such a gesture. They were afraid I was stepping into dangerous ground and were, rightly this time, apprehensive about the development of the ideas of the so-called Islamists, and of the way it would lead into confrontation with the state.

My parents, however, need not have worried about *me* in all that. I was not involved with the so-called Islamic Movement, although its influence had penetrated youth circles. I saw it around me at school, with friends and teachers, but I had little sympathy for it. What I resented most was the high austerity with which they regarded the arts, especially music. I came across several books and conversed with people who equated music with the greatest of evils. Music, however, had become an integral part of my emotional makeup, and had come to acquire spiritual significance for me. I was aware that throughout the years it had made me a better person and there was no way I could believe otherwise.

Did music save me then? Perhaps. What I know is that it had provided me with a clear sense of what was beautiful and worth pursuing in life and what was not. I was in high school then and my love for Arabic poetry was also growing and was coupled with a newly born admiration, mixed with the awe of the unknown, for English poetry. Which I was studying in the last year of high school. I couldn't help comparing Al-Mutanabbi to Shakespeare and Aboulkasim Ashshabbi to Wilfred Owen, and was eager to learn more about that foreign genre that is almost as fascinating as Arabic poetry, yet has its own music and rhythms.

In college I chose to study English literature and was drawn by the language and the culture which is inseparable from it. The fascination with the unfamiliar led me to be interested in Western music, and I soon started to passionately explore its various styles. For a while my sensibilities were more susceptible to Western rather than Arab influences as my academic pursuits were more geared toward English rather that Arabic literature and culture.

These pursuits were not only about music, but, as I see it now, were a reflection of the general movement of society in the early-to-mid-80's. That was when the effects of "open-door" policies in economics had started to be felt in all areas of life, including culture and the arts. Along with American and European goods, American and European movies came to Egypt, together with other forms of cultural manifestations that were shown everywhere on TV and other mass media.

For a while I was so into Western music that I nearly completely abandoned my pursuit of pleasure in Arab music. However, my fascination with Western music proved to be short-lived. I was soon aware of the absence that was left inside me. I realized that with Arab music I could reach a level of gratification that I was never able to experience by listening to Western tunes. The rhythm of Arab music was like a drum beating in my inner ear and inner heart and it needed to re-emerge as a part of my emotional apparatus once more. That was not difficult to do. A three-hour evening with my favorite song by Om Kolthoum, whom I hadn't listened to for a long while, was enough to make me aware of what I was missing, and to rekindle the old passion.

After I had resurrected my old love for Arab music it was difficult to appreciate any other kind of music. The next step was to brush the dust off the volumes of Arabic poetry in our library and resume my reading of my favorite poets. I was surprised to see that it was still possible for me to find a place for English poetry in my heart, perhaps because the appreciation of poetry is partly intellectual, partly emotional. With music, it was more than the appreciation of an art form; it was a strong passion whose roots go deeper in my being than those of ordinary artistic sentiments.

I watched the old love being resurrected and my fascination growing more and more, but I stopped marvelling at its source. I now know that music (Arabic music in particular) is the simplest yet most sophisticated expression of culture and that because it addresses people's emotions as well as their intellect and is available to all, literate and illiterate, it is perhaps the most complete kind of cultural expression. I know that, personally, it gives me the most wholesome pleasure imaginable. I was not alarmed by the discovery that I had fallen captive to Arab tunes and was unable to fully appreciate any other kind of music. In my early thirties I now don't feel all that awkward holding my lute, a distinctively Middle Eastern instrument, and playing for my friends. In the midst of my gratification I hear them cheer and I say to myself: "Music *has* saved me! Maybe from a worse fate than my parents had ever imagined!"

POSTSCRIPT

 In the fourteen years since I began this book, the world has become more interrelated than ever. The political and economic situation has changed globally. Different challenges face not only Middle Easterners but also all the citizens of the world, including Americans. The thirty-six men and women who have written about their lives in this volume have also changed. Five have died. Many of the others have become parents and grandparents. Their descendants must deal with new realities. But history has not disappeared completely. Elements of the values, fears, and hopes recorded here remain. As always, the past will continue to inform and shape the future.